THE BIBLE AND POSTHUMANISM

Society of Biblical Literature

Semeia Studies

Number 74

THE BIBLE AND POSTHUMANISM

Edited by

Jennifer L. Koosed

Society of Biblical Literature
Atlanta

Library of Congress Cataloging-in-Publication Data

The Bible and posthumanism / edited by Jennifer Koosed.
p. cm. — (Society of Biblical Literature. Semeia studies ; Number 74)
Includes bibliographical references.
ISBN 978-1-58983-751-5 (paper binding : alk. paper) — ISBN 978-1-58983-752-2 (electronic format) — ISBN 978-1-58983-939-7 (hardcover binding : alk. paper)
1. Bible—Criticism, interpretation, etc. 2. Humanism. I. Koosed, Jennifer L. editor of compilation.
BS511.3.B485 2013
220.6—dc23 2013035221

Printed on acid-free, recycled paper conforming to
ANSI/NISO Z39.48-1992 (R1997) and ISO 9706:1994
standards for paper permanence.

for Avielle Rose Richman

forever chasing fireflies

www.aviellefoundation.org

Contents

Part 1
Beginnings

Humanity at Its Limits

Jennifer L. Koosed

What does it mean to be human? We are poised somewhere in between animals and divinities; aided, enhanced, and altered by technologies; changing and changed by our environments, both natural and cultural. Arguably, the Bible begins as a speciesist manifesto—only humanity is created in the image of the divine, only humanity is given dominion over the rest of creation. However, the Bible also contains multiple moments of disruption, boundary crossing, and category confusion: animals speak, God becomes man, spirits haunt the living, and monsters confound at the end. All of these stories explore the boundaries of the human in ways that destabilize the very category of the human. All of these stories engage thinking that broadly falls under the umbrella term *posthumanism*—a catchall of disputed definition that points beyond various human-centric ideologies.

As defined by Peter Singer, speciesism "is a prejudice or attitude of bias in favor of the interests of members of one's own species and against those of members of other species" (2009, 6).[1] In his groundbreaking book *Animal Liberation*, first published in 1975, Singer presents what he calls "a short history of speciesism" in Western culture, which begins at the beginning—the creation accounts in Genesis. Focusing on the passages where God gives man dominion over the earth (Gen 1:29; 9:2–3) as well as the parts of the story where animals are killed (God clothing Eve and Adam with animal skins, Abel's sacrifice of sheep, the "collateral damage" of the animals in humanity's punishment through flood), Singer roots the ideology of human exceptionalism in biblical mythology. Even though he acknowledges that there is an undercurrent of compassion in the Hebrew Scriptures better understood as stewardship rather than dominion, he

1. Although popularized by Singer, Singer himself attributes the term to Richard Ryder (2009, 257 n. 4).

does conclude that "there is no serious challenge to the overall view, laid down in Genesis, that the human species is the pinnacle of creation and has God's permission to kill and eat other animals" (188). In this, Singer is in agreement with Lynn White Jr.'s equally influential article on the environmental crisis that also points the finger unflinchingly at the biblical tradition with special attention to Genesis (1967).

Although Singer later acknowledges that the biblical Scripture and the traditions that grow out of it may be even more complex than he initially thought (2006, 616), most thinkers still begin with the biblical commands to be fruitful and multiply, to subdue the earth, and to have dominion over it, in addition to the ontological distinction that accompanies these commands—that only men and women are created in the image of the divine. Without excusing these verses and the ways in which their interpretations have certainly contributed to speciesist ideas and actions, other thinkers have complicated this story of origins as they have complicated the Genesis accounts themselves.

All of the essays in this volume underscore the complexity of biblical texts and traditions; many draw on Jacques Derrida's equally complex reading of Genesis's creation stories in *The Animal That Therefore I Am*. Derrida focuses his attention on the second creation story, specifically the scene where a naked Adam names the animals (2008, 15–18). The image of a man naked before the animals is a reflection of Derrida's own naked encounter. One day, stepping out of the shower, he is startled to find his cat looking at him. In his own shame, Derrida is taken back to a time before shame, even before time, when Adam stood naked before all other animals, under the watch of a God supervising but also surprised. Further, this particular encounter becomes the incident that initiates a meditation about the relationship between human and nonhuman animals with particular attention to the ways in which the history of philosophy has defined the nonhuman animal as other. All that humanity is—reasonable, intelligent, communicative—is all that the animal is not. Animals lack *logos*, the ability to respond, even the ability to die. Or, at least, so say the philosophers who Derrida interrogates, from Descartes to Kant, from Levinas to Heidegger. Throughout his critique of the philosophical tradition, Derrida returns again and again to his cat in order to highlight its particularity: "I must immediately make it clear, the cat I am talking about is a real cat, truly, believe me, *a little cat*" (6).

Not all of his readers have been so taken with Derrida's *petite chat*. Donna Haraway, while acknowledging her great debt to Derrida and his decisive critique of the Western philosophical tradition, finds his encounter with his cat quite disappointing. Despite the fact that he does repeat his desire to focus on the singularity of his cat and not transform her into a sign or figure or allegory, to take her point of view seriously without appropriating it, Haraway argues that he fails the simple test of curiosity (2008, 20). He wonders about his cat but never actually researches what her experience could be. Perhaps Derrida spent too much time thinking about Adam, naked before all of the animals, and not enough time considering the example of Eve, curious before the snake.

Haraway pursues her own biblical beginnings, not with Genesis but with one Christian appropriation of Genesis, the Gospel of John. For her, the *logos* becoming flesh is not the ultimate sign of the special status of the human being; rather, the *logos* became *flesh*, not just man:

> Sign and flesh; story and fact. In my natal house, the generative partners could not separate. They were, in down-and-dirty dog talk, tied. No wonder culture and nature imploded for me as an adult. And nowhere did that implosion have more force than in living the relationship and speaking the verb that passes as a noun: companion species. Is this what John meant when he said, "The Word was made flesh"? (2003, 18)

Rather than reifying our differences and distinctions, in this moment, all flesh is collapsed into divinity, all language (reason, logic) is collapsed into bodies, all nature is collapsed into culture. These are not mergings and meldings that obliterate difference; instead, they complicate our categories through border crossings and borrowings. She signals this collapse that does not negate difference in the use of the term *naturecultures*. Her manifesto ends, "The word is made flesh in mortal naturecultures" (100).[2]

Of the making of genealogies, there is no end. Animal studies represents only one strand of posthumanist thinking. Other possible points of origin include the various technological innovations (like cybernetics) and their associated theoretical models, which emerged in the late 1940s and early 1950s, "that removed the human and *Homo sapiens* from any particularly privileged position in relation to matters of meaning, information, and cognition" (Wolfe 2010, xii); or Michel Foucault's concluding paragraphs in *The Order of Things*, where he declares, "As the archaeol-

2. For various explorations of the boundary breakdown between nature and culture, see also Haraway 1991 and 2008.

ogy of our thought easily shows, man is an invention of recent date. And one perhaps nearing its end" (1971, 387; see Wolfe 2010, xii); or Derrida's deconstruction, notions of the trace and hauntology (more on this later idea will follow); or Slavoj Žižek's channeling of Lacan in his articulation of the relationship between the Symbolic and the Real; or … for readers who are not yet weary, I direct them to Cary Wolfe's work from the first time he used the term in the essay "In Search of Post-humanist Theory" (1995) to his latest post-hyphen, posthumanist exploration *What Is Posthumanism?* (2010).

Philosophers and ethicists have been addressing issues of animals and humans, specters and divinities, for decades. Peter Singer's work has been focused on the relationship between humans and animals since the 1970s; Donna Haraway first explored the intersections of human and machine in the 1980s and has recently turned her attention to the intersections of human and animal; much of Jacques Derrida's later work (some posthumously published) addresses specters, animals, and divinities. Many other theorists have built upon these foundational works and animal studies, posthumanism, and hauntology are widely explored in philosophy and literary theory. Various religious studies scholars (in ethics, theology, comparative religions, history of religions) have also engaged these ideas, especially incorporating animal studies into their own research.[3] However, these ideas have just now been filtering into biblical studies. Many of the essays in this volume first were presented over the course of a few years during annual meetings of the Society of Biblical Literature. These initial experimental forays into reading the Bible in light of posthumanism have developed into this volume. *The Bible and Posthumanism* addresses a variety of approaches and perspectives, serves as an introduction to the hermeneutical power of these theories, and thus acts as an invitation to further work.

Hannah M. Strømmen opens the volume with an essay that further explores some of the introductory issues I have raised here. She too notes that philosophers and ethicists often begin by blaming the Bible for the subjugation of animals. She too reflects upon Derrida's encounter with his cat and his meditations on the biblical creation stories. Strømmen makes no attempt to exonerate the biblical text, but through a reading of another biblical beginning—the renewal of the world in Gen 9—she seeks

3. The American Academy of Religion's Consultation on Animals and Religion began in 2003.

to complicate the question of biblical blame. Denise Kimber Buell's essay also offers an introduction to the issues. Whereas much of this volume addresses questions that arise when we look at the nonhuman animal, Buell's essay focuses on another aspect of posthumanism: immaterial entities and hauntology. As Buell explains, *hauntology* is a term coined by Derrida in *Specters of Marx* (1994) to account for the ways in which the past effects the present and opens up the future. The Bible, as a document that presupposes the reality of spiritual forces and human interaction with these forces, is primarily concerned with entities beyond the human (angels, demons, deities). The New Testament especially is full of "haunts." But Buell's use of hauntology also traces how certain ideas "haunt" New Testament studies, like nineteenth-century spiritualism. Buell deftly explores these multiple levels of haunting, in order to ultimately address issues of agency and responsibility. Strømmen and Buell work in tandem to introduce many of the major issues in posthumanism in general and this volume in particular.

From little cats to the king of cats, the volume's second part is about lions roaming through the wild, in the Bible, in ancient Near Eastern texts and contexts, and in philosophy. Hugh Pyper examines the lion as a metaphor for the biblical sovereign, both human and divine. Unlike most other ancient Near Eastern cultures, Israel rarely identified its kings with the lion, reserving such figuration for its God. In addition to engaging Derrida's *The Animal That Therefore I Am*, Pyper also uses *The Beast and the Sovereign* to explore the political and existential ramifications of a God, beast and Lord, who creates a humanity, caught in between both. Ken Stone is also concerned with philosophy as he brings Balaam's ass (Num 22) into conversation with Wittgenstein's lion. Beginning with Wittgenstein's quip in *Philosophical Investigations*, "If a lion could talk, we could not understand him," Stone explores a range of interspecies communication, not just communication between human and animal, but between God and all creatures. Conversation is not always a panacea, but refusing to engage in dialogue leads to violence, and is a form of violence itself.

The next section examines the human body in the places where it is invaded, possessed, goes mad. Each paper addresses the interrelatedness of the psychic and the somic—bodies in pain are minds in crises and vice versa. Each paper regards the body not as a stable, bounded entity but one that is in constant flux, penetrated and penetrating: opening up to God is opening up to love is opening up to madness. Heidi Epstein reads a musical rendition of the Song of Songs in a film about possession: Michal

Waszinski's 1937 movie adaptation of Ansky's play *The Dybbuk* (written between 1912 and 1917 and subtitled *Between Two Worlds*). She explores the meanings of bodies, masculine and feminine, natural and supernatural, divine and demonic, alluring and grotesque. Rhiannon Graybill continues the conversation about possession and madness as she discusses the book of Ezekiel and Daniel Paul Schreber's *Memoirs of My Nervous Illness* (1903). In Schreber's memoir, he describes God possessing his body, transforming it. Once again, we see somebody "between two worlds"—masculine and feminine, natural and supernatural, divine and demonic, alluring and grotesque. Schreber's prophetic experience lends insight into Ezekiel's. George Aichele's subject Lars is also poised between the two worlds of sanity and insanity. In the movie *Lars and the Real Girl* (2007), Lars buys a life-sized sex doll (Bianca) and believes that she is his girlfriend. Together, Bianca and Lars inhabit a contact zone (to borrow language from Haraway); they are not just human-technological comminglings, but they are also natural-supernatural transformations. As Graybill argues that Schreber's experiences should not just be understood psychoanalytically but also theologically, Aichele proposes that a purely psychological reading of the movie misses its theological dimensions, as Bianca is also Mark's Jesus, neither human nor nonhuman but somehow posthuman, and Lars, his family, and his entire community are transformed through her life, her love, and her death.

Consideration of human anthropology in Christian community brings us to the fourth part of this volume: Fathers. The two essays in this section explore early Christianity's engagement with biblical texts, both gnostic and orthodox, and the ways in which their understanding of the human is defined through interaction with both "spiritual" bodies in one essay and "animal" bodies in the other. Building on his previous work, Benjamin Dunning focuses on Valentinian interpretations of creation myths. He suggests that within their tripartite anthropologies, the concepts usually associated with immateriality (*pneuma* and *psychē*) also have material dimensions. Rather than neatly dividing into material and nonmaterial parts, Dunning demonstrates the internal fissures and ambiguous borders of these "heretical" definitions of the human. Eric Daryl Meyer reads Gregory of Nyssa reading the Song of Songs, and we return to Derrida's analysis of the human-animal distinction in philosophical discourse. As philosophers strive to transcend the animal and yet ultimately "fail" to do so, Gregory of Nyssa endeavors to distinguish between human and animal, spirit and matter, literal and analogical meanings in ways that ultimately collapse the categories.

In these two essays, we are poised between the angels and the animals, but also enmeshed in them in complex and constantly shifting ways.

The role of sacrifice in delineating the categories of animal, human, and divine is the subject of part 5. Robert Paul Seesengood opens this section by reflecting on the commonality established between human and nonhuman animals through the biblical understanding of blood, and the consequent ambiguity in some passages concerning the morality of animal killing. Meat, in at least some circumstances as understood by some Jews and even some early Christians, is murder. Seesengood explores this issue in order to open up an even broader conversation about humanity and animality, flesh and word, sacrifice and slaughter. Taking the knife from Seesengood, Yvonne Sherwood uses it to cut deeper into the history of sacrifice and into the scholarship on sacrifice. Ranging widely through the works of contemporary and classical philosophers, historians, Christian and Jewish theologians and biblical interpreters, anthropologists, colonial explorers, and science writers, Sherwood weaves a variegated essay that addresses the ways in which sacrifice (in practice and in text) establishes our most fundamental categories of identity and undermines them at the same time.

The last essay by Stephen Moore takes us to the end of the world where we find a God-Man in the form of a slaughtered (though still alive) Lamb: humanity, divinity, and animality again converge in ways both strange and familiar. Moore finds an apocalypse both full of animals (figuratively) and empty of animals (in reality), which leads to an analysis of the sacrificial logic of the book of Revelation.

These last three essays especially interrogate the ethics of the human use of animals and the biblical contributions to the question.

Cited specifically in Stone's essay, but also operating as an undercurrent in most of the other contributions, Wolfe suggests, "our stance toward the animal is an index for how we stand in a field of otherness and difference generally" (2003, 5). How we think about and how we act toward the animal (or better: the *animals* in all of their infinite variety and multiplicity)[4] brings us back to ourselves, but not in a way that once again obliterates the animal. Animals are at the core of who we are and how we think: they are in us, and they are us. And their plurality, our plurality, stuns. Our ability to confine and define falters. How do I even

4. Derrida uses the French portmanteau *l'animot* to disrupt the violence the singular "animal" does to the "heterogeneous multiplicity of the living" (2008, 31; cf. 41).

think about myself apart from the 90 percent of "me" composed of various microbes; how do I understand any fundamental notion of identity if I cannot even draw an unambiguous line between "me" and "not-me" within my very body (see Haraway 2008, 3–4)? Not only has "the boundary between human and animal [been] thoroughly breached," but also "machines have made thoroughly ambiguous the difference between natural and artificial" (Haraway 1991, 151–52). The categories of life are impossible to delineate with clarity and surety: human, animal, plant, organic, inorganic, living, dead. The difference between a rock and the boy who throws it may be so obvious as to vitiate the need for definition; the difference between a tree and the monkey who climbs it may be evident; but what about a sponge?

The sponge actually lives in the borderlands between single-celled organisms organized as a colony (like blue-green algae) and the most primitive of multicellular animals. It spends most of its life as a single organism, a division of labor distributed throughout its different cells: collar cells, skin cells, interior cells, skeletal cells. Yet if the sponge is disintegrated, even down to its single cells, it does not die:

> The single cells, now freed from their association, began to look and behave like amoebae. They extended little lobes and moved along the glass surface. But before long a remarkable process began to take place. Whenever two single cells approached each other they extended filaments and touched; then they promptly united into a single body. A third cell was quickly added, then another and another, making a small mass. Separate nearby masses united, producing large colonies and eventually one single assembly that formed a crust on the surface of the slide. In the space of a few hours or days the aggregate had regenerated itself, and then differentiation began, producing the four different varieties of sponge cell. The tubular structure was built, the skeleton, the middle body, and the skin. (Young 1986, 99–100)[5]

Each individual cell carries within it the organization of all the others, and it can change and morph depending upon its circumstances. How it does this is a great mystery. Rather than demonstrating difference and hierarchy, Aristotle's Great Chain of Being may instead indicate something else. The Great Chain of Being is more like a web, each species connected and interdependent, each more sophisticated than assumed, each a world of

---

5. Young is describing an experiment conducted by the biologist H. V. Wilson.

wonder. Instead of finding divinity at the apex of the chain, perhaps it is spread through and across the web. Perhaps God is a sponge. Perhaps her name is Amanda.

In James Morrow's novel *Only Begotten Daughter*, the messiah returns in the body of a girl, conceived in a test tube with sperm but no ovum, grown in a glass womb. As Julie Katz tries to make sense of her origins and abilities, she finds solace in only one place—at the bottom of the ocean, in the company of a sponge named Amanda. Later as a middle-aged woman, stripped of her divinity but still inspiring, Julie Katz is crucified. In the final act, a sponge is lifted to her lips. But instead of vinegar or water, the sponge has been soaked in hemlock. The sponge itself, then, transforms the poison into tetradotoxin, which produces the symptoms of death without death and consequently saves Julie's life. Julie awakens to find this very same sponge carefully cleaning out her wounds. She is confused:

> — Some would say the miracle was entirely my own doing, Amanda notes. You were always so kind to me, so I paid you back: Androcles and the Lion, right? But that strikes me as a hopelessly romantic and anthropomorphic view of a sponge's priorities. Others would call the whole thing a gigantic biochemical coincidence: under optimal conditions, sponges will metabolize hemlock into tetradotoxin. I am not persuaded. Still others would claim that God herself entered into me and performed the appropriate alchemy. A plausible argument, but rather boring. Then there is a final possibility, my favorite.
>
> — Yes?
>
> — The final possibility is that I'm God. (Morrow 1990, 309)

Amanda continues: "Years ago, I told you sponges cannot be fatally dismembered, for each part quickly becomes the whole. To wit, I am both immortal and infinite" (309).

Humanity has its limits. When we are dismembered, it is fatal. We are neither immortal nor infinite. When we touch another animal (my dog is asleep at my feet); when we incorporate technology into our bodies and into our identities (I extend outward, tapping on a keyboard to transform my thoughts into digital impulses that will later be stamped onto the fiber of trees so that you can hold this part of me now in your hands); when we move beyond our bodies to consider spirits demonic and divine (my bedroom dresser knocks loudly in the night, the transoms move without warning)—then we are at the end. A threshold has been reached, but that is where all thinking begins. This volume is an expedition to the multiple frontiers of the human, all of which should prompt us to ask not only, What does it mean to be human? but also, What should it mean?

Works Cited

Derrida, Jacques. 1994. *Specters of Marx: The State of the Debt, the Work of Mourning and the New International*. Translated by Peggy Kamuf. London: Routledge.

———. 2008. *The Animal That Therefore I Am*. Edited by Marie-Louise Mallet. Translated by David Wills. New York: Fordham University Press.

Foucault, Michel. 1971. *The Order of Things: An Archaeology of the Human Sciences*. New York: Pantheon.

Haraway, Donna J. 1991. *Simians, Cyborgs, and Women: The Reinvention of Nature*. New York: Routledge.

———. 2003. *The Companion Species Manifesto: Dogs, People, and Significant Otherness*. Chicago: Prickly Paradigm.

———. 2008. *When Species Meet*. Minneapolis: University of Minnesota Press.

Morrow, James. 1990. *Only Begotten Daughter*. San Diego: Harcourt Brace.

Singer, Peter. 2006. Animal Protection and the Problem of Religion: An Interview with Peter Singer. Pages 616–18 in *A Communion of Subjects: Animals in Religion, Science and Ethics*. Edited by Paul Waldau and Kimberly Patton. New York: Columbia University Press.

———. 2009. *Animal Liberation: The Definitive Classic of the Animal Movement*. Updated edition. New York: HarperCollins.

White, Lynn, Jr. 1967. The Roots of Our Ecological Crisis. *Science* 10:1203–7.

Wolfe, Cary. 1995. In Search of Post-humanist Theory: The Second Order Cybernetics of Maturana and Varela. *Cultural Critique* 30:33–70.

———. 2003. *Animal Rites: American Culture, the Discourse of Species, and Posthumanist Theory*. Chicago: University of Chicago Press.

———. 2010. *What Is Posthumanism?* Minneapolis: University of Minnesota Press.

Young, Louise B. 1986. *The Unfinished Universe*. New York: Simon & Schuster.

Beastly Questions and Biblical Blame

Hannah M. Strømmen

I begin with two questions: Can animals repent? And can God repent? The first question is yet another in a long line of questions asked of the animal and its ontological status (e.g., do animals think, are they machines, can they suffer, can they feign, can they feign a feint, do they die?). The second question emerges in reading Gen 9. We are faced with the God who promises never again to blot out his creation, who offers the rainbow as a divine sign of remembrance, inscribed in the sky, God's signature: never again such anger, never again such destruction. This is his promise, his covenant, with the remaining trace of human life: Noah, along with select followers, both familial and animal. Both these opening questions teeter at the edge of knowledge. Their very uttering is a spilling over at the limits of the human. The question of repentance and therefore accountability sets in motion reflection around human/animal/divine distinctions as these figures relate to law, response, and responsibility. Could we hold an animal accountable for its actions? To explain itself, or to ask for pardon? For most, the very idea is absurd, certainly within the remits of the law. Could it be "within" divine nature to repent? Thinking "the beast and repentance," or "God and repentance," the "and" sits uneasily, as if we are already participating in an anthropomorphizing movement that is somewhat improper to the subjects in question. We are already at the threshold of the human.

"How to begin?" Jacques Derrida asks in *The Beast and the Sovereign*, reflecting on the idea of the threshold, "a beginning, the beginning of the inside or the beginning of the outside" (2009, 312). Where do we stand in addressing the question of the animal today? And from *where* do we begin? Are we safely inside the rational bounds of knowledge, or do we risk madness in thinking the animal: a losing of the self, so carefully pieced into *human* shape and prodigiously patrolled through centuries of philosophical thought. Responding to one of Derrida's intentions to say "a word about the Bible," with which, he says, he "meant to start at the very beginning" (2009, 343), we follow (both temporally and with a sense of allegiance) Derrida's critical thinking on the animal figures in the Western cultural landscape. Biblical beginnings echo also in his opening words to *The Animal That Therefore I Am* (another significant work dedicated to the question of the animal): "In the beginning"—already, Genesis then, in the beginning, and a word on the Bible, so to speak. Evoking the naïve innocence of originary Genesis-nakedness, unself-conscious and unblushing, Derrida hopes for "words that are to begin with, naked, quite simply, words from the heart" (2008, 1). Following his intention to say a word about the Bible in regard to animality, our response comes from *outside* biblical studies, bare-faced but lingering on the threshold of the Bible, hoping for hospitality despite being something of a stranger to that foreign literary landscape in which we cannot hope to stand both feet "inside," and yet *do* hope to poke our noses into.

Echoing Jacques Lacan, Derrida argues that what "separates Man from Beast is the Law," what he calls the experience of the Law (2009, 102). These are matters of response and responsibility, or rather, the potential absence of them. "God, himself, like the beast, does not respond"; or at least "we cannot count on his response," Derrida writes, and therefore cannot be counted on or held accountable for upholding the law, constructed to preserve and protect the vulnerable, exposable, accountable human (57). This, Derrida argues, is by reason of *language*, that philosophically metonymic name for the "human proper" (55). The nonhuman has, by default, "the right to a certain irresponsibility" (57) in not being counted on to answer for its actions, or to repent, and consequently must be kept at bay as a destabilizing Other. In "'Eating Well' or the Calculation of the Subject," Derrida discusses the notion of "subject" in philosophical discourse, who or what answers to the "who" (1995, 258), and suggests we are not done with thinking through everything that "links the 'subject' to conscience, to humanity, to history … and above all to the law, as subject subjected to the law, subject to the law in its very autonomy, to ethical or juridical law, to political law or power, to order (symbolic or not)" (259). The animal that stands outside the law (like the sovereign or the divine) figures in Western philosophy and conceptual thought as an uneasy sub-subject, tantalizingly "outside," sometimes submerged in nature, sometimes the secondary subject prop to the human proper, not *enough* subject or not *properly* a subject of discussion. What is at stake in the question of the animal is facing up to "the gaze called 'animal,'" which as Derrida says offers to our sight "the abyssal limit of the human: the inhuman or the ahuman, the ends of man" (2008, 12).

Notions of biblical guilt and scriptural accountability loom large but spectral in orbiting these questions of divine/animal agency, accountability and law, response and responsibility. Perhaps the question, then, is rather: can we ask a book to repent? And not just any book, but perhaps the book of all books—the Bible. Addressing the question of the animal from within theology and religious studies, and more particularly from a biblical studies perspective, demands reflecting at some length on the blame accorded to the Bible for the thoroughly anthropocentric attitudes that have come to dominate (at least) Western intellectual thought in the arts and humanities. Peter Atterton and Matthew Calarco point out that the "'end of humanism,' the 'ends of man,' the 'end of philosophy,' the 'death of the author,' the 'death of God,' the 'death of man,'—these apocalyptic shibboleths are becoming self-defeating utterances amid a discourse that has said hardly anything about animals in comparison" (2004, xv). Holding these ideas of blame, the animal at the limits of the human and this need to say "more," we cannot, I argue, think about that obstinate human/animal binary without simultaneously addressing the problematic idea of the Bible as source and origin to humancentrism and consequently engage in critical readings of biblical texts with this theme in mind.

Pointing the Blame: Biblical Guilt and Philosophy on the Animal

Responding to the question of the animal today leads perhaps first of all to the increasing body of research taking place within the disciplinary pens of philosophy. Somewhat unexpectedly, this particular philosophical body of work frequently begins quite literally with a word on the Bible. The Bible is brought up *in the beginning*, in prefaces and introductions to rigorous discussions over the status of animal life, only to be named and shamed as "blamable" but not itself put under analytical investigation. Engaging with the ontological and moral status of the animal in the world, the Bible is held accountable (albeit mutely so) for our rigid, exclusive, and even idolatrous (to use a theological term) notion of the "human."

Anchoring popular and philosophical conceptions of the "animal" in the deeply entrenched humancentric structures of Western intellectual thought, the tendency is to mount the Bible as a an originary, stable point of blame, to be put on trial, hurriedly condemned, and thereby rushed to marginal spaces of muted censure. Of course, no philosopher says exactly this: I will take the Bible to court and put it on trial for the killing and eating of millions of animals, for intensive farming, hunting, fur production, pet keeping, and other similar practices so commonplace in the Western world. Nonetheless, there is an implicit assumption—for it is by no means an overtly developed argument or articulated accusation—that the Bible is guilty of animal abuse, or at the very least partly responsible for the current ideological underpinnings that justify animal abuse. While it is not afforded the privilege of closer examination—perhaps deemed somehow unquestionable or not of sufficient philosophical interest—the Bible nonetheless persistently stands accused of sacrificing the animal in favor of the human, thereby acting as scaffolding for the metaphysical assumptions that have traditionally held the human in place: central and aloft. The human is privileged by the divine, prime receiver of the Word, Logos—powerful gifts that have long equated humans to sovereign masters over the nonhuman in creation.

At this point it would seem only prudent and proper (and we will think more about prudence and propriety) to draw attention to some specific instances in which the Bible is referenced (or accused) in the current philosophical debate around the figure of the animal. Cary Wolfe writes in his introductory remarks that "the animal as the repressed Other of the subject, identity, logos" reaches "back in Western culture at least to the Old Testament" (2008, x); and yet none of the diverse contributors to this astute and exciting collection of articles, *Zoontologies*, follow up on this particular heritage. It is briefly and peremptorily brought to the fore only to be dropped again as a muted point. In Peter Singer's preface to *Animal Philosophy,* his second reference to the long history of animals having "no ethical significance," or at least "very minor significance," is the apostle Paul (after Aristotle), further mentioning two theologians, Augustine and Aquinas (2004, x). From this vantage point Singer opens up into "most Western philosophers" (x). In the introduction to the same book, Atterton and Calarco contend that the transition from Aristotle's man as "rational animal" to simply "rational being" (in which "man" is exclusively and exhaustedly subsumed) was made "all the easier by the biblical story of man being made in the image of god and having dominion over the animals" (xvii). A biblical story, then, is thought to have smoothed the passage from thinking of man as a certain *kind* or *type* of animal in creation to man as something else altogether in light of his ability to reason.

In *Zoographies: The Question of the Animal from Heidegger to Derrida*, Calarco discusses Emmanuel Levinas and the ethical relation to the "Other," who for Levinas is necessarily a *human* other. Calarco turns Levinas's position on its head, drawing his own "neoreligious" conclusion where the encounter with the animal is "transcendent," a "miracle," but is quick to avoid this turn to religious language by affirming his resolve for a "complete shift in the terms of the debate" (2008, 59), as if he were echoing Levinas's own words: "enough of this theology!" (2004, 47). He goes on to warn that we must adopt a hypercritical stance toward the "ontotheological tradition" we have inherited, "for it is this tradition that blocks the possibility of thinking about animals in a non- or other-than-anthropocentric manner" (Calarco 2008, 112). Theology is not merely to blame then, but it is also a stumbling block for contemporary attempts to think about the animal. In the introduction to *The Political Animal*, Stephen R. L. Clark references a number of specific biblical passages (Lev 19; 22; 23; 25; 26; Deut 22; 25; Ezek 34; also the book of Proverbs) to demonstrate "these commands, these tacit bargains," implicit in *owning* animals and yet not treating them as mere things (1999, 4–5). His is a more "positive" account of the biblical legacy, but remains nonetheless referential and elusive, never expanded upon in the main body of the argument.

In Paola Cavalieri's *Death of the Animal*, one of her "speakers" (in the first essay of the book, a dialogue-shaped discussion) suggests we need to instate "distance from the revered legacy of our history, what I am referring to in particular is the idea that some points, or perspectives, of the past should be rejected as archaic" (2009, 2). The same speaker warns that although narrative form is something humans have always "craved" and "cherished" as modes of understanding self and world, we must ensure that "such narratives are not translated into normatively hierarchical frameworks" as "they determine roles and questions of status" (5). This becomes more explicitly directed to the Bible and theology when she writes that according to "the most widespread" of these culturally and conceptually determining narratives, "human beings were made by God in his own image, while nonhuman beings are mere creations. The latter are only a preparatory work, while the former are the apex of creation, directly molded by God" (5–6). This reference is put forward with confidence, without recourse to specific biblical text, context, or sustained analysis. The assumption is that we, in the West, already know what she is talking about, the point speaks for itself, the biblical text is transparent and unequivocal. Cavalieri uses this point as a synecdoche for the history that has justified the systematic subjugation and suffering of animals: "such a story supports the normative implication that humans are superior beings, entitled to use nonhumans as they see fit" (5–6).

What Cavalieri seemingly calls for is violence toward the "sacred," a fundamental purge or erasure of the biblical trace. Our "revered" history—scriptural scrolls and biblical stories—has ensnared us in its mythical and powerful image of the human, favored by an imaginary divine Godhead forged from, and in order to serve, human conceit. Without further ado, she suggests, this particular conceptual corpse needs burying. A relic of the past, it still clutters our thinking of the animal, and thus demands immediate iconoclastic action. Invoking the ethical dimension inscribed in the question of the animal, issues of "right and wrong" as she puts it, this is a point of some urgency, lest we allow the biblical to run wild and cause all sorts of further havoc (Cavalieri 2009, 2). What we need, seemingly, is a taming of the biblical textual body and its legacy, for fear that we risk the Bible becoming something uncontrollably monstrous, a dangerous haunting.

Marc Fellenz picks up on the same point, and sums up the blame in the following statement: "The traditional ethical models found in Western philosophy and theology have been premised on human uniqueness: the belief that as rational (perhaps ensouled) beings, humans have a putative value and destiny that surpass that of any other animal" (2007, 31). He writes about "the religious concept of animals as part of the *human dominion*" (2) and points out the necessary "proximity" between human and animal within religious sacrifice, which proximity is also the prerequisite for scientific experiments on animals for human gain; it is a case of life and living in a way that *corresponds* (13). Whether this is a point that accords greater significance to animals in biblical accounts of sacrifice or not, the relation Fellenz sets up implicitly foregrounds biblical sacrifice of animal bodies as the origin to scientific experimentation on animals (another, modern "sacrifice" of animal life for potential human gain). This is an interesting point, but one that surely needs validating through specific reference to biblical sacrifice narratives, rather than ploughing forth under the assumption that we all know exactly what takes place in such sacrificial structures, as if these scenes are straightforwardly transparent and given.

Fellenz also refers to biblical stories and myths from Greek antiquity to convey the way in which the transformation of humans into animals is a frequent trope used to signify punishment (16). One of the foundations for assuming the ontological inferiority of animals is according to

Fellenz "theological in nature," embodied in the religious myth that "we humans are ensouled beings, created in the image of a God who made the world, including animals, for our use" (34). He does present some of the ways in which Christian theologians have worked against this trend, but stays clear of specific textual references to the Bible, and ultimately the theological arguments are swept under the carpet: "we need not rely on them, nor become entangled in other theological complexities" (36), a sweeping motion reminiscent of Cavalieri's proposed disentanglement from the biblical (2009, 4).

Of course, these are all *philosophical* texts on the moral and ontological status of animals. Why should they engage with biblical texts and scriptural exegesis? Further, this is not to say they are necessarily wrong. Rather, the point is that to respond to the question of the animal as it relates to our cultural inheritance and historical textual sources, it is problematic, reductive, and misguided to plot an uncritical notion of "the Bible" as origin point, or as stable homogenous meaning, knowable and unequivocal, especially without revisiting these textual sites. Moreover, for biblical studies itself, these biblical texts need to be revisited and responded to philosophically, with a conceptual deconstruction of human/animal/divine distinctions in mind.

Even if these contemporary philosophical references are merely the result of religion's "prolonged stammerings" (Bataille 1989, 96) in the world today, the Bible nonetheless plays the significant part of both fundamental beginning and ensnaring tangle. It represents a dangerous labyrinthine structure that serious philosophers would be better off avoiding. As if that messy business is a job for biblical scholars and theologians alone. If it were not for the fact that the above-mentioned philosophers are producing valuable and timely publications on the animal, *and* all point to the Bible as culpable, this troublesome biblical body of literature could perhaps feasibly be left for biblical scholars to dissect in the dark, or for theologians and religious people to peruse in peace. As this is clearly not the case, however, and, additionally, as the biblical corpus and its creatures arguably have much to offer in the posthumanist debate, it is of paramount importance that we turn to the Bible as a textual supplement to our thinking around and about the question of the animal. Instead of attempting to erase the biblical trace we would be better off turning toward that textual body, undress it of its outer layers, unravel its secrets, go through its pockets anew, and review the strange and fantastical, domestic and divine creatures that inhabit its spaces.

Genesis 9: The Accused, the Cursed, and the Naked

"Starting from Genesis" (Derrida 2008, 1), the point of beginning and blame, we start also with bare humanity, naked, and on the threshold of knowledge to this nakedness. In his book on Genesis, *Creation and Temptation*, Dietrich Bonhoeffer writes that "we cannot speak about the beginning; where the beginning begins our thinking stops, it comes to an end" (1966, 11). And yet, he says, asking about the beginning is an "innermost impulse of our thinking." It is both where we inevitably turn and attempt to return, and simultaneously where our thinking collapses (12). This seems to be one way of describing the urge to hark back to a biblical beginning for the story of humancentrism, plotting a pure origin but ultimately deflating this point into intangible vapour. Skipping *the* so-called biblical beginning, I would like to direct attention to another beginning: Gen 9. Risking the impropriety of such a move, I would like to argue that this other biblical Genesis scene resituates and reembodies the human in creation as it emerges out of an unveiling of nakedness on one hand, and of good and evil on the other, both signifying troubling *exposures* that erase and retrace the contours of the human/animal/divine, aligning creatures within a divine contract of autoresponsibility.

Self-conscious, self-referential thought begins with Genesis, with coming to know oneself as first and foremost naked. Derrida writes that "the property unique to animals, what in the last instance distinguishes them from man, is their being naked without knowing it" (2008, 4–5). They are consequently not properly "naked" as such. In short, Derrida says, obliquely referring again to Genesis, animals are "without consciousness of good and evil" (5), thereby linking the specifically *human* coming-to-awareness of nakedness in the biblical creation narrative—resulting in self-consciousness and shame—to notions of accountability and guilt, right and wrong; in other words, gaining the preconditions for ethics and law. To be conscious of good and evil is to be *like* God (Gen 3:4), according to the speaking serpent. Echoing this, the Lord says, "See, the man has become like one of us, knowing good and evil" (3:22). Through hungry curiosity and God's own creation the human is imparted elements of the divine via the animal. Gained proximity to the animal and the divine entails the curse, reconfiguring human/animal nature and inserting physical dissociation and detachment—a diversion of the divine from his reckless, free, curious creatures. The human's response to the coaxing creature is a devouring curiosity and desire for internalizing, taking in, *every* part of divine creation, a greedy urge to let no part of God's nature go unexplored, untasted. The original home of creation, for divine, human, and animal alike, is now split apart. As Walter Brueggemann comments, "creation is in contradiction," sovereignty is "assaulted" from the outset (2003, 33). This turning point is a wrenching apart of the divine-human at the same time as the human has become divine-like. Divine sovereignty is already "less" by virtue of human presence and agency. Creaturely freedom is excess, the incalculability of what is to come, embodied in a curious consuming appropriation of creation.

The uncanny encounter between curious, hungry human and cunning, word-uttering beast is the rupture that enables the human to *know* like God but also to become double, not merely or fully itself. This "more than" is signaled in self-consciousness, the recognition of its own human body as other. The first humans are *taken by surprise* at nakedness, and then by the necessity or desire to cover and conceal. The human now exists culpably, always potentially guilty and endlessly split, as if the self stands under constant risk of surprising itself and being held to account, exposed. In other words, the human—now endowed with self-consciousness and divine-like knowledge of right and wrong—can never know itself fully, exhaustively; it is never wholly or purely itself. Accountability is always to come.

The act of eating the fruit is where human freedom meets divine-like knowledge, where hunger for knowledge meets ongoing digestion in the shape of a chewing or mulling over of what has been said and done. If one calculates responsibility and accountability, a mediating propriety between divine and beast are now the proper marks of the human. But perhaps the garden of Eden itself stands impossibly and awkwardly as the pure origin of harmony and peace. As Brueggemann points out, the serpent is *part* of creation, and thus "the seductive voice of evil is intrinsic to the creation; that is, the creation in principle is under siege from evil that contradicts the intention of the Creator" (2003, 37). The serpent exposes a divine lie, uncovers the secret: the humans will *not* die if they eat the fruit; and so despite the consequences, the serpent has, perhaps, the last word (as well as *its* last word). The banishment and covering of human nakedness marks the beginning of technology, while the beast slips silently into the dominion of "nature." Clothing, as Derrida says in *The Animal That Therefore I Am*, has become one of the (necessarily endless) properties of man (2008, 5). Clothing derives from techniques; shame and technicity need to be thought together, he says, and in this same leap the animal is subsumed into that Other, Nature: naked, speechless and shameless, unaccountable, and what must be kept at bay and under human domination through laws and properly established order. Claus Westermann affirms the way in which the genealogies of Noah explain and reveal the emergence of culture and civilization in the ancient world, in light of Noah as the "foundation of viticulture" (1994, 10). In other words, these are lines of production, cultivation, and progress in the name of the human.

With the Godlike knowledge of good and evil comes the human condition of nakedness and shame. Turning to the world of Gen 9, after the flood, and Noah's fraught position as the second "first" man, the biblical text presents another traceable origin point in man. Much biblical scholarship sidesteps the Noah figure of Gen 9:20–27, unable to reconcile him with the righteous Noah under God's protection, noting the inexplicability of the passage, or sliding into the skin of the story and accepting the judgment of Canaan at face value. Another way this passage has been circumvented is through monolithic categorization into themes that preclude anything that falls outside this mapping. To take one example, Westermann molds Genesis into three shapes: creation, achievements, crime and punishment (1994, 18).[1] Although not universal, this particular and arguably representative thematic segmentation tends to divert attention from the anomalies that resist the categorization.[2]

This categorization frequently finds an ally in the methodologies that fixate on split authorship and fragmented textual strands. John Bergsma and Scott Hahn call Gen 9:20–27 a "compressed, elusive narrative" with "awkward features," which has been an exegetical puzzle since antiquity (2005, 25, 27). Another response in scholarship seems to have been to *add* to the story, to *give* it sense, to insist on *more* lurking in the text than is told. This "more" has mostly taken the shape of a dirty secret, sexual deviancy, something unspeakable; and, like road kill, it is both tormenting and

1. See also tools for interpretation and "proper" interpretive approach in Longman 2005 for methodological instructions.

2. Of course, some scholars make this point under the argument that Gen 9 is divided in terms of authorship. Both Cohn (1996, 14) and Skinner (1910, 147–87) solve the issue by arguing that there must be two Noahs, as the Noah of Gen 9:20–27 simply does not "fit" the body of the "righteous and blameless patriarch who is the hero of the flood" (Skinner 1910, 181). See also Carr 1996; Brett 2000; Humphreys 2001; Murphy 1873; and Longman 2005.

tempting to turn one's gaze in that direction.[3] Bergsma and Hahn contend that refusing this "more" to the story is succumbing to a conservatism in regard to anything not made entirely explicit and literal in the text, and go on to explain away the "awkwardness" of the narrative by inserting sexual transgression into the empty space left in the silence of the text itself (36).

I would like to stay with the awkwardness that this text—as it stands—embodies, in thinking about how it might explore human/animal/divine boundaries as unwieldy, drawn up, undone, retraced, and erased. Unlike Adam, Noah is marked from the beginning, as always already other to himself,[4] exceptional and yet part of a flawed humanity, aware of the nudity that man covers up beneath appropriate, apposite layers. Or perhaps wary of the exposure the human is liable to, of wrong footings. Noah's curse is a careful covering up and covering of tracks. Noah stands in relation to a past that has been obliterated, a lost origin that is erased in everything but memory. Moreover, Noah as the new first human is also the first carnivorous man, splitting creation further through distinguishing between the edible creatures and the inedible consumers and cultivators. A seemingly minor rewriting of God's first creation, folded between God's covenant to Noah and his emphatic invocation against murder or killing, the gift of a carnivorous diet is frequently bypassed, or merely mentioned as one slightly disharmonious effect of God's reconciliation with human life, between the great event of the flood and the great tower of Babel. Put starkly, God as giver of life, human as receiver of God's blessing, and animal as edible (and therefore perhaps the moment that is unwittingly referred to as blamable in the Bible) slyly inserts itself in what is perhaps the third beginning narrative of Genesis, namely in the re-creation after the great flood that wipes out all life. But already here absolutely knowable origin points and creaturely divisions are being sliced and displaced. Drawn up, sketched, erased, rebegun, these biblical narratives continuously interweave different clauses to readjust the complex, parasitical divine/human/animal relationship.

3. Bergsma and Hahn are one example of this, inserting "maternal incest" as what takes place to explain Noah's anger and curse of Canaan—the illicit offspring of incestuous sexual practice. The other three trends in scholarship that Bergsma and Hahn note regard voyeurism, castration, and paternal incest.

4. As already mentioned, Cohn (as does Skinner) argues that Noah is literally double, claiming that the drunken Noah who curses Canaan is a different Noah from the "hero of the Flood" (1996, 14).

In Gen 9 humans are given a new beginning, this time with the animal-as-edible: "into your hand they are delivered. Every moving thing that lives shall be food for you" (Gen 9:2–3). In Robert Alter's 1996 translation of Genesis, where he hopes to uphold the "profound and haunting enigmas" he believes Genesis itself cultivates, he laments that the bodily emphasis in ancient Hebrew is lost in many translations. He draws particular attention to the repeated reference to the "hand" as symbol of capacity for care and power, compassion and violence (1996, xiv). In other words, the hand is a site for good and evil, a space of decidability and responsibility. God faces the blank space left after the flood, in which he has poured his wrath and wiped out life to start creation anew, and imbues it this time with an offering to humans that is a new opening up—a devouring—of the animal other, but perhaps also arguably a *responsibility for the living*, to all that lives, given into human hands. This would constitute a mimicking of God's own promise in his covenant to *all life* at the start of Gen 9, a covenant that signals nondeath, nondestruction, a negation of divine domination, a repentance.

The "fear and dread" that accompanies the animal gift to humans is a giving over of the divine sovereignty that caused destruction, as a trembling aftereffect of excessive divine power. Standing in the aftermath, in Gen 9, this divine excess is subdued through divine dissemination to the human. Terror of the divine must be erased or at least transferred if the divine is to reestablish relations with creation at large. So "fear and dread" are put to human account. But it is not purely a mark of terror, but rather a sign of power that resonates with the responsibility gained in the moment both ethics and nudity are uncovered in Gen 3. This is the tension into which the human is given, and in which the human-animal relationship trembles. And yet in the covenant, the divine, human, and animal are thought as one. This is a moment in which divine calling and human and animal response and responsibility feature together, simultaneously; and *in response* Noah stands silently, like a speechless beast, facing an incalculable future of fruitfulness, an excess of being through divine blessing.

Revolving around acts of eating, the scene in which Eve takes and eats in disobedience is retraced in Gen 9 with God as the figure who (perhaps repentantly) holds out the "animal" to Noah and his human fellows. In a sense it is a reverse sacrifice, in which God offers a gift of life in turn for his excessive, sweeping erasure of all life in the great flood.[5] Recognizing this

5. Longman points out that the Hebrew word for "rainbow" is the same as that of

excess, the divine gift is another form of excess, animal flesh, not *needed* for human survival but a supplement, a gift. Knotted into the strings attached to this divine offering (between the so frequently quoted "humankind made in God's image" and covenant with *all life*), God requires a "reckoning" or "accounting": "from every animal I will require it and from human beings" (Gen 9:5), a matter of response and responsibility. The laws against murder that follow this (9:6) stand arguably in such tantalizing proximity to the gift of animal-as-edible as to evoke an uneasy relation to the proper terms of life-taking and spilling of blood.

The Noah of Gen 9 is the first carnivore, a mythical beginning, but Noah is also "a righteous man," "blameless," at least comparatively in his generation (Gen 6, 9). In other words, Noah has lived responsibly, properly, more or less guiltlessly. Feeling himself watched over by God, as the only man not blotted out, Noah lives uneasily in the new world, haunted, jumpy almost, and mute in response to God, as if his position as the new first man—carnivore and a father of fathers—is vulnerable, and if not guilty he is nonetheless blamable. Eager to uphold his blamelessness and haunted by this desire to remain proper and shameless, Noah thrusts blame outward at the other who has exposed him, lying flat out, naked, and drunk in his tent. Noah's shame at being caught in this state must be transferred to another's account. Ham, stepping inside the tent in which Noah lies, trespasses the threshold outside which his father's manhood is erected, proper and upright before God. Once conscious and upright again, Noah responds with a violent curse, as if he were covering the disgrace of improper, drunken nudity with divine-like retribution. Only what is God-like is "big" enough to cover his exposure and beast-like state as unconscious, naked, unknowing, and powerless before the other.

Writing about the "incomparable experience" that is called nudity (2008, 4), Derrida reflects over the "reflex of shame" that accompanies his experience of nakedness in the eyes of his pet cat, and declares himself ashamed of his shame. Surely this is Noah's experience too. Shame at his shame. But why? "Ashamed of what and before whom?" Derrida asks. "Ashamed of being as naked as a beast" (4). Robbed of his rational faculties in his drunken state and unconsciously naked like a beast, Noah is no longer *properly* man; he is suddenly closer to the serpent crawling on its

---

the bow as weapon. Taken in this sense, he argues, it could stand as a symbol of God hanging his bow up, pointing at God himself, thus acknowledging wrongdoing or repentance for destroying all life (2005, 119).

belly. There is something abyssal and secret about this textual moment, akin to Derrida's gaze of the animal other. Noah is exposed by his own son, the very person whose submission depends on paternal fidelity and filial piety.

When Noah discovers what has happened—that he in effect, has lost face or become animal—he curses Ham's son Canaan, transferring guilt from himself, across his son, effectively crossing Ham out, unable to face him directly in his embarrassment. Mimicking God's anger at humankind in Gen 8, Noah curses Canaan as if he himself were the divine father, the sovereign Godhead. Noah's curse reasserts his authority as head of the household; it gives him back his "face." Noah's anxiety at boundaries being overstepped by his son catching a glimpse of his nakedness is tantamount to setting in motion a destabilizing hierarchical topsy-turvy. But Noah, by invoking this curse, has himself turned the divine/human/animal structure on its head. From being caught in a beast-like state of unconscious nakedness, to a human response of shame and covering, Noah leaps into divine clothing and doubles this gesture by making of Canaan the lowest of the low: a slave, muted and tamed, beast-like before the Master. Cursing Canaan, the innocent son of Ham is a sign of sovereign, divine power; Noah need not be held accountable, he need be neither fair nor reasonable in his reign as the sovereign Father of humanity.

It seems that if we are to engage in a posthumanist project that aims to look beyond or across from the human as center, we must endeavor to look also beyond notions of purity, blame, and the Bible as the stable, unquestionable origin point in Western culture, through deconstructing, deranging, and displacing these biblical texts via the question of the human/animal/divine. But not with filiopietistic goggles; rather with a critical curiosity in reading animality as a parasitical network of living and being in the world. It cannot be a matter of hunting down, capturing, or taming biblical meaning and message, but rather an opening up to themes that deflect notions of the pure, self-contained, and self-possessing human. The question of the animal demands response and responsibility in one movement, in which our assumptions concerning the ontological status of the "animal" as first and foremost "eatable," made-producible, a *thing* of industry, are questioned in engaging with biblical ontologies, our scriptural history and its afterlives.

Works Cited

Alter, Robert. 1996. *Genesis: Translation and Commentary*. New York: Norton.

Atterton, Peter, and Matthew Calarco. 2004. Introduction. Pages xv–xx in *Animal Philosophy: Ethics and Identity*. Edited by Peter Atterton and Matthew Calarco. London: Continuum.

Bataille, Georges. 1989. *Theory of Religion*. New York: Zone.

Bergsma, John Sietze, and Scott Walker Hahn. 2005. Noah's Nakedness and the Curse on Canaan (Genesis 9:20–27). *Journal of Biblical Literature* 124:25–40.

Bonhoeffer, Dietrich. 1966. *Creation and Temptation*. London: SCM.

Brett, Mark G. 2000. *Genesis, Procreation and the Politics of Identity*. New York: Routledge.

Brueggemann, Walter. 2003. *An Introduction to the Old Testament: The Canon and Christian Imagination*. Louisville: Westminster John Knox.

Carr, David M. 1996. *Reading the Fractures of Genesis, Historical and Literary Approaches*. Louisville: Westminster John Knox.

Cavalieri, Paola. 2009. *The Death of the Animal: A Dialogue*. New York: Columbia University Press.

Clark, Stephen R. L. 1999. *The Political Animal: Biology, Ethics and Politics*. New York: Routledge.

Cohn, Norman. 1996. *Noah's Flood, the Genesis Story in Western Thought*. New Haven: Yale University Press.

Derrida, Jacques. 1995. "Eating Well" or the Calculation of the Subject. Pages 255–87 in *Points ... Interviews, 1974–1994*. Edited by Elisabeth Weber. Translated by Peter Connor and Avital Ronell. Stanford, Calif.: Stanford University Press.

———. 2008. *The Animal That Therefore I Am*. Edited by Marie-Louise Mallet. Translated by David Wills. New York: Fordham University Press.

———. 2009. *Beast and the Sovereign Volume 1*. Edited by Michel Lisse, Marie-Louise Mallet, and Ginette Michaud. Translated by Geoffrey Bennington. Chicago: University of Chicago Press.

Fellenz, Marc. 2007. *The Moral Menagerie: Philosophy and Animal Rights*. Urbana: University of Illinois Press.

Humphreys, W. Lee. 2001. *The Character of God in the Book of Genesis: A Narrative Appraisal*. Louisville: Westminster John Knox.

Levinas, Emmanuel. 2004. The Name of the Dog, or Natural Rights. Pages 47–50 in *Animal Philosophy: Ethics and Identity*. Edited by Peter Atterton and Matthew Calarco. London: Continuum.

Longman, Tremper, III. 2005. *How to Read Genesis*. New York: Routledge.

Murphy, James G. 1873. *A Critical and Exegetical Commentary on the Book of Genesis*. Edinburgh: T&T Clark.

Singer, Peter. 2004. Preface. Pages x–xii in *Animal Philosophy: Ethics and Identity*. Edited by Peter Atterton and Matthew Calarco. London: Continuum.

Skinner, John. 1910. *A Critical and Exegetical Commentary on the Book of Genesis*. International Critical Commentary. Edinburgh: T&T Clark.

Westermann, Claus. 1994. *Genesis 1–11*. Translated by John J. Scullion. Continental Commentary. Minneapolis: Fortress.

Wolfe, Cary. 2008. *Zoontologies*. New York: Columbia University Press.

Hauntology Meets Posthumanism: Some Payoffs for Biblical Studies*

Denise Kimber Buell

Haunting can quickly become a loose term for everything: what doesn't sound sexier when described as "haunting"? It may not be controversial to think of texts as spectral, neither alive nor dead (see, e.g., Wolfreys 2002, esp. ix–xiv); biblical texts haunt with their overflowing potential for being activated and materialized in different ways: Matthew as the quintessential Catholic Gospel, yet also a Jewish Gospel; the Fourth Gospel encrypts Sophia traditions under the sign of the Logos and is the Gospel that has become the poster child for Christian claims to exclusivity—no one comes to the father but through me—but haunted by its status as the apparent favorite of the elusive so-called gnostics; and of course there are Paul's writings, the radical Jew haunting the "second founder" of Christianity, but also the resource for recent Continental articulations of radical democracy haunted by Corinthian women's expression of the spirit in ways apparently too free for the great man.

But haunting is not merely a sexy term to apply to Paul or a synonym for memory. Rather, studies of haunting ask what kinds of memories are being excluded in specific contexts, what kinds of countermemories

* A version of this essay was originally presented at the 2009 SBL Annual Meeting in New Orleans but has been expanded and revised, drawing upon material from two additional talks, "Exorcisms and Possessions in the Gospels," Kraft-Hiatt Lecture, Brandeis University (March 2010); and "Cultural and Temporal Complexities of Remembering Jesus: Engaging the Submerged Legacies of Spiritualists, Occultists, and Theosophists," presented in "The Many Faces of Jesus: Memories and Identities—Challenges and Complexities," Concluding Seminar of "Jesus in Cultural Complexity" Project, University of Oslo (October 2011). Thanks to James Grzelak for his feedback on drafts of this article.

have been or may be forged to resist dominant practices and arrangements of power, what traces make themselves felt even when unspeakable, and what kinds of futures are being called into possible existence by the spectral. Such questions put our scholarly commitments, questions, even obsessions in New Testament and early Christian studies in a new light. As Avery Gordon puts it: "Ghostly things kept cropping up and messing up other tasks I was trying to accomplish. … The persistent and troubling ghosts in the house highlighted the limitations of many of our prevalent modes of inquiry and the assumptions they make about the social world, the people who inhabit these worlds, and what is required to study them" (1997, 8).

There are ghosts in the houses of biblical and early Christian studies. Some of these have been identified and questioned—specters of anti-Judaism, racism, heterosexism, colonialism, sexism, "secularized" Protestantism. Indeed, multiple *Semeia* volumes have featured essays limning methodologies and theoretical perspectives aimed at exposing these specters (even if not named as such) and providing alternatives modes of biblical interpretation. As decades of feminist, race-critical, postcolonial, and minoritized biblical scholarship and theologies have repeatedly insisted, we need approaches to biblical studies that enable us to tackle the very real concerns of the histories, afterlives, and persisting presences of slavery, colonialism, racism, sexism, heterosexism. And we need to do so in ways that continue to, on the one hand, critique and undo the modernist notion of the human subject as ideally autonomous, self-willing, and masterful (not to mention male, white, wellborn, well educated, straight, European or American, able-bodied, and so on), while, on the other hand, we rethink what it means to be human without further disappearing or disenfranchising those to whom being fully human in this modernist sense, with its corresponding notion of agency as the freedom to act without constraint, has been denied or limited. In this essay I suggest that recent scholarship on haunting and posthumanism can help advance efforts to live and work in terms of alternative understandings of how we are human and what agency means.

A brief sketch of one site for bringing hauntology and posthumanism together helps illustrate what I shall be advocating in this essay. I have found haunting especially valuable for working through how to speak about race and ethnicity in the study of early Christianity. Haunting redirects questions about the anachronism or historicity of these concepts; furthermore, an orientation to haunting helps articulate the necessity of wrestling with not simply the historical contexts and afterlives of our source materials but also the historical contexts and afterlives of our methods and interpretive frameworks (see esp. Buell 2009c, 2010).[1]

I have argued that race haunts early Christian ethnic reasoning in the futural sense of communism in Europe in Marx's writings. The language of *genos*, *ethnos*, and *laos* in texts remembered and interpreted as early Christian (such as the letters of Paul) and overall rhetoric of peoplehood (regardless of specific vocabulary) has been activated in ways that define Christianity paradoxically as a nonethnic and nonracial and yet the only authentic people of God or full expression of humanness. While not functioning as simply racist or protoracist, early Christian forms of universalism adapt ancient discriminatory logics and can sustain modern racist interpretations (Buell 2005, 2009b).

At the same time modern racisms also haunt our very ways of engaging biblical texts and writing early Christian history (Buell 2005, 2009b, 2009c). Shawn Kelley (2002) and Susannah Heschel (1998, 2008) have demonstrated different kinds of modern European racialized practices and legacies infusing biblical studies. Focusing on the North American context, Sylvester Johnson has compellingly argued that "to participate in divine identity [such as implied by the concept 'the people of God'] is to be haunted by the specter of illegitimate existence," a haunting he confronts by calling for a "Canaanite perspective" that values "the heathen" as "legitimate existents" (2004, 130, 132; see also 109–33).

To speak of race as conceptually spectral is to challenge the assumption that pinning its origins to a specific historical site might contain and neutralize racism; we cannot find its one origin and root it out (Stoler 1997). To speak of race as conceptually spectral is to insist that we must find a way to live so as to create a hospitable memory for all those who have died and been oppressed under the sign of racial difference, which is also to enable a future in which such racialized deaths and inflections of power will not occur. Doing so means we must change the story that Christianity came into being as a voluntary, universal religion out of and in distinction from an ethnically or nationally based Judaism.

I have recently come to see that the specter of racism in early Christian ethnic reasoning needs to be interpreted beyond the horizon of human

1. Without foregrounding haunting, I set out the bulk of these arguments about early Christian "ethnic reasoning" in Buell 2005.

relations. That is, to analyze the practices and rhetoric of peoplehood, it is insufficient to focus only on sociological/anthropological dimensions. In early Christian writings, intrahuman differences such as peoplehood and "race" or "ethnicity" are rhetorically and ritually inscribed as the result of transformations and interactions with nonhuman forces. The questions of what counts as human and what kinds of humans count get answered in part through defining the shifting boundaries of the human in relation to forces portrayed as not-human.

Collective belonging in earliest Christian discourses and rituals was forged through interactions with nonhuman agencies. The Acts of the Apostles uses the Holy Spirit's entering into both Jews and Gentiles to demonstrate not only the scope of God's power but also the means by which this new "way" indexes membership in Israel throughout the known world (see esp. Acts 10:34–48; 15:8). Paul and his audiences seem to agree that the collision of *pneuma* with *psychē* and *sarx* produces ontological shifts even when they disagree about what these were and their consequences (Stowers 1994, 279–84; Hodge 2007, 72–76). After all, folks like Paul, the author of the Fourth Gospel, Clement of Alexandria, and the author of the Gospel of Philip all presuppose that the kinds of difference produced by rituals such as baptism only make sense in the context of presuming divine agencies.

In the Fourth Gospel, the possibility that Jesus is possessed by a *daimōn* is raised three times to account for his speech or actions (John 7:20; 8:48, 52; 10:20–21). Hypothesizing that Jesus is being controlled by a demon expresses dissent from the idea that Jesus is not just sent by God but says and does God's will on earth. In turn, the Gospel portrays these dissenters as themselves aligned with demonic powers, which, notoriously, becomes also an assertion about intrahuman difference. In John 8, for example, Jesus' debate with "the Jews" concerns the basis for Jesus' authority to claim that he speaks God's words. His opponents are characterized as viewing him as having a demon, while Jesus in turns accuses *them* of being aligned with the devil (8:44) because "your will is to do your father's desires,"[2] implying that they are descendants of the devil, not of

2. The Fourth Gospel immediately proclaims Jesus' relationship to God as an instrumental one, as the Logos through whom God made the world. Jesus describes his relationship with God as one of instrumentality, repeatedly emphasizing that he does nothing on his own authority but only what God wills (John 5:30; 8:42; 12:49–50). Jesus also presents himself as the witness to God (John the Baptist witnesses to Jesus'

God or Abraham. Membership in God's people turns out to be measured, in a range of texts, by one's relationship with nonhuman agencies and by the rhetorical classification of these agencies and the effects that intra-actions produce.

Thus concern for the relationships and porousness between the human and nonhuman have come to demand my attention, drawing me to investigate further what posthumanism and transhumanism might have to offer biblical and early Christian studies from a perspective oriented to hauntings. In what follows, I bring hauntology together with posthumanism to tackle questions of agency in biblical texts as well as in a more recent chapter of religious history, the popular nineteenth-century movement of Spiritualism. Both biblical and Spiritualist accounts of agency pose a challenge to the understandings of agency that I long embraced as a feminist, especially in narratives about and practices of exorcism, possession, and mediumship.

A central goal of much feminist biblical criticism has been to recover suppressed evidence for ways in which women and subordinated men have always been contributors to religious formations. Uncovering glimpses of female leaders in the Jesus movement and early Christianity has been a crucial contribution of feminist scholarship. But if we assume, along with most Western Enlightenment thought, that agency is measured by evidence for an individual acting on and in the world seemingly out of her or her conscious intent, and that the ideal of feminist activism is to ensure that all individuals be able to live in the world as such self-constituting and autonomous agents, we encounter a number of problems, two of which I mention here. First, we may be hard-pressed to find examples of historically oppressed folks who conform to these ideals—does this mean that we must interpret them merely as victims or reject their own accounts of

---

identity as the one "on whom the Spirit descend[ed] and remain[ed]," 1:33; see also 5:31–39). In response to Jesus' teaching in the temple in Jerusalem, listeners question: "How is it that this man has learning when he has never studied?" So Jesus answered them, 'My teaching is not mine, but his who sent me'" (7:15–16); and "the one who believes in me, believes not in me but in the one who sent me" (12:44). See also: "I and the Father are one" (10:30)—which "the Jews" react to as blasphemy (10:33), but which is countered in terms of instrumentality: see 10:34–38; restated as that which the followers should believe (14:10): "Do you not believe that I am in the Father and the Father in me? The words that I say to you I do not speak on my own authority, but the Father who dwells in me does his works. Believe me that I am in the Father and the Father in me, or else believe me for the sake of the works themselves."

acting in the world through the agency of spiritual powers, including deities and ancestral spirits (see Keller 2002)? Second, feminists put ourselves in the tricky position of relying on notions of agency and subjectivity that we have also found very problematic. The ideal of an autonomous self is one presented as universal but clearly forged with a particular masculine, heteronormative, elite, imperialist self in mind and that only emerges as an ideal in modern European thought.

One response to these problems has been to focus on the level of the text to expose a gap between "rhetoric" and "reality" leading to the assessment that texts about women and other structurally subordinated folks, including enslaved persons or those marked by colonization, are rhetorical devices rather than historical actors. A posthumanist feminist orientation to haunting allies us with a different kind of intervention, one that is equally concerned with rhetoric but, in imagining alternative forms of agency, does not rule out the agency of those who get figured and materialized as enslaved, colonized, feminized, or otherwise structurally subordinated (e.g., Anzaldúa 1987; Sandoval 1995). To do this, we need to see how the rhetoric expands far beyond an anthropocentric field of relations.

Ancient texts, including Gospel narratives, presume that how we are human is conditioned by the spiritual powers that interact with and may even become part of us. Early Christians present conversion as a process by which ritualization, including the training of one's senses, produces the right kind of human, one developed to welcome what they classify as divine spiritual matter and to ward off, and expel if needed, spiritual matter classified as demonic (Buell 2009a). This process presumes hierarchical power relations, whereby the human body has meaning and personhood as the "instrumental agency" of the human mind and ruling soul, which are in turn instrumentalized in relationship to spiritual powers as well as usually other humans.[3] In what follows, I sketch a hauntological approach that can evaluate these different ways of being and becoming human (or something else) in ancient and modern contexts without privileging a bounded notion of agency or romanticizing an instrumentalized one.

3. Mary Keller coined this term "instrumental agency" in her important work on spirit possession (2002, esp. 73–100); I have developed this notion for early Christian accounts of conversion in Buell 2009a, 263–84.

Hauntology Meets Posthumanism

In this section I explain more fully how I am understanding and using *hauntology* and *posthumanism* before turning back to biblical texts. Joshua Gunn has helpfully noted that haunting is an "idiom" generated to offer a response to the death of the "humanist subject of modernity," and thus emerges together with and as a form of critique of humanism. He describes haunting as

> a theoretically informed orientation to criticism that mourns this death in a useful manner. (I use the conspicuous term "idiom" to denote that haunting is more than a vocabulary and cannot be understood in relation to a singular concept, e.g., the figure of the ghost; rather, as an idiom, haunting refers to the way in which a theoretical perspective is lived and "owned"…). As an orientation toward critical work, haunting attempts to preserve the central values informing rhetorical criticism while nevertheless embracing the notion of a subject that is constructed, decentered, fragmented, performed, and/or split. (2006, 78–79)

I agree with Gunn's characterization of the goals and values of haunting as an orientation that challenges a notion of the coherency, transparency, certainty, and autonomy of a human subject while still being an ethical orientation presuming that even contingent constructed subjects are accountable for our interpretive frameworks and actions. In what follows, I discuss in more detail how this perspective can be "lived and 'owned.'"

Approaching Hauntings

"Hauntology," coined by Jacques Derrida as a pun on "ontology" in his *Specters of Marx*, remains a key touchstone for scholarship on haunting (Derrida 1994). For Derrida, hauntology rejects the possibilities of epistemological certainty, specifically our ability to know "others" but also to know the present and, by relation, the past and the future. The "other" arrives as the specter whose death, temporality, and being must remain unknowable to us: "as a posture or orientation, hauntology attempts to resist ghost-busting [that is, forming dogmas and orthodoxies that falsely imply secure knowledge] by embracing the figure of the specter or *revenant* as a haunting reminder that we can never completely reckon with the past, nor secure the future. Specters urge us to remain open to both by abjuring the present" (Gunn 2006, 83). For Derrida, the openness that specters call us to is an ethical project, and one that he articulates in terms of the messianic, but a messianic moment that cannot be determined in time or content (Derrida 1994, 167–71).

This openness has its appeals but also its limits, especially for those seeking to enact and effect change in the world, including changes in encounters with biblical texts or, for example, early Christian history. It is indeed valuable to insist on the ongoing resistance of biblical texts to singular meaning, and to insist on the impossibility of any utopia to realize itself. These interventions help disrupt totalizing claims and their totalitarian risks. Nonetheless, we must not only also trace, diachronically and synchronically, pluriform and specific acts of meaning-making in conversation with biblical texts or acts of scripturalization more broadly speaking to expose their situated limits. Making a case for how the specificities of my own contextual contingency lead me to choose certain interpretive options over others seems to me a vitally important aspect of reading for and in light of haunting—to aim for a way of being and knowing and "other-worlding" (Haraway 2008, 3). In my case, being shaped in and through feminist interpretive frameworks, I find myself especially drawn to the way that Avery Gordon has articulated the project of haunting.

Gordon's work closely interfaces with feminist, antiracist, decolonizing, and queer critical perspectives already flourishing in biblical studies. Indeed, it is within these forms of biblical studies that Gordon's work has begun to receive some notice (Donaldson 2007; Liew 2008; Buell 2009a, 2010). In contrast to Derrida, Gordon insists strongly that there are "real alternatives" to present conditions that are "already here, embedded in the practices of subversion and not hiding in some elusive or fantasmic futurity" (2011, 5); we need to reckon with ghosts to identify these real alternatives and forge new futures, even if they will contain their own limits and flaws. She thus challenges the Derridean insistence against attempts to bring utopian/messianic hopes into reality, but she does not naively assume that any utopian vision lacks flaws or can be perfectly realized.

Gordon differentiates her approach to haunting from Derrida's specifically by questioning his insistence on epistemology—or, more precisely, the impossibility of knowing the other or the time of the arrival of the Messiah. She questions the "absolute necessity to affirm … otherness":

> Awareness of the limits of knowledge, awareness of the impossibility of knowing it all, and awareness of the dangers of being a know-it-all are

> certainly important conditions of a just praxis, but they are not sufficient in and of themselves. Ontology, by contrast, takes us onto the terrain of what Michel Foucault called subjugated knowledge and to the person and their being. Persons are not merely mortal (finite beings) but living breathing complex people who cannot be approached or treated justly if there is an absolute necessity to affirm their otherness. Quite the opposite is needed by them and by us. (2011, 7)

Gordon links attention to haunting to historically minoritized and structurally oppressed groups, precisely those whose agency has been structurally prevented from appearing freely in control, including of historical narratives: "Any people who are not graciously permitted to amend the past … is bound to develop a sophisticated consciousness of ghostly haunts and is bound to call for an 'official inquiry' into them" (1997, 151). That is, haunting as an orientation embodies an ethical stance that enacts an agency other than that of the self-willing modernist subject; rather, haunting is a mode of relation that already has been developed, a form of subjugated knowing and contingent being. For Gordon, haunting signals a "something that must be done" in the face of the limits of knowability. The goal of orienting oneself to haunting is "to link the politics of accounting, in all its intricate political-economic, institutional, and affective dimensions, to a potent imagination of what has been done and what is to be done otherwise" (18).

Gordon elegantly articulates a form of feminist intersectional perspective but seeks an approach that is more dynamic and affective than most; haunting is "a paradigmatic way in which life is more complicated than those of us who study it have usually granted" (7). She introduces the notion of "complex personhood" as a facet of the tenet that "life is complicated": "That life is complicated is a theoretical statement that guides efforts to treat race, class, and gender dynamics and consciousness as more dense and delicate than those categorical terms often imply" (5). Complex personhood, as a distillation of her intersectional approach means, among other things, that "even those who are called 'Other' are never never that. Complex personhood means that the stories people tell about themselves, about their troubles, about their social worlds, and about their society's problems are entangled and weave between what is immediately available as a story and what their imaginations are reaching toward" (4).

Complex personhood undergirds Gordon's approach to haunting as a way of articulating the imbrication of the social with the individual. Each individual's complex personhood is specific, yes, but more specifically the result of the entangled systems and relationships into which each of us comes into being and continues to be shaped. This view of personhood as highly contingent and relational, let alone the call to take ghosts seriously, might appear to render the individual, including the scholar, unduly passive. But *like* Derrida, Gordon asserts that we have a responsibility for discerning and responding to ghosts (e.g., Derrida 1994, 11). That is, even if ghosts/specters have a kind of being and agency (whether or not one acknowledges them), the responsibility for responding to haunting rests with the living, thus preserving ethical accountability without denying agency to the nonliving. Posthumanism helps further refine questions about the meanings and practices of agency to cultivate such ethical accountability.

Approaching Posthumanism

If posthumanism and hauntology already share common ground as perspectives forged in light of critiques of the modern humanist subject, there is nonetheless more to say about posthumanism and the benefits of conjoining its concerns with the idiom of haunting. Even with a nod to external agencies (of the ghostly matter), the work entailed in reckoning with ghosts may seem to be rather anthropocentric. Posthumanism can, ideally, help move an understanding of haunting away from a concern with agencies attributed to human causes, even if such agencies exceed individuals (i.e., capitalism, racism, fascism) to offer fresh ways to engage those agencies that permeate biblical texts such as deities, spirits, angels, as well as nonhuman animals.

The thinkers especially associated with posthumanism in the sense of responding "to the legacies of humanism by breaking up, fracturing, distributing, and decentralizing the self-willing person, questioning its subjectival unity and epistemological conceits" include Niklas Luhmann, Francisco Varela, and Gilles Deleuze, and Felix Guattari (1987), as well as Donna Haraway (1991, 1997, 2008), N. Katherine Hayles (1999), and Cary Wolfe (1995, 2003, 2009) (Weinstone 2004, 10).[4] One hallmark of work claiming to be or being tagged as posthumanist is a concern with a human-technology interface and with rethinking the human in terms of cybernetic, networked systems.[5] Haraway and Wolfe have been also at

4. See Weinstone 2004 and Wolfe 1995 and 2005 for discussion and bibliography for Luhmann and Varela among others. I do not engage their work directly myself.

5. Although this is not the aspect of posthumanist work I find most compelling

the vanguard of stressing also the importance of the human-nonhuman animal interface (Haraway 1991, 1997, 2008; Wolfe 2003).

Posthumanism (and transhumanism) denotes the variegated efforts to rethink the human or, at times, to think about transforming the human. It is a misunderstanding of posthumanism to see it as an abandonment of concern for the human; rather, posthumanism considers "how subjectivity, bodies, agency, and cognition are altered by engagements with" other animals, the "environment," and nonorganic matter and technologies (Weinstone 2004, 4). Donna Haraway's now decades-old argument is also relevant for early Christian history: boundaries humans might have claimed were stable between the human and nonhuman clearly are not, including the boundaries between "human" and other "animals," between organism and machine and between physical and nonphysical (Haraway 1991, 151–53).

I hold the term *posthumanism* rather loosely, employing it along with *haunting* to expand and rethink intersectional analyses. Intersectionality has generally considered those axes of power and identification that produce intrahuman difference in particular contexts (be that status, gender, race, age, ability, etc.), and I have proposed that "we should stretch intersectionality to include relations that exceed the human plane and 'make connections between entities that do not appear proximate in time and space'" (Buell 2010, 315),[6] using Haraway's figure of the cyborg and haunting to accomplish this expansion. Bringing an orientation to haunting together with posthumanism enables us to resituate even apparently intrahuman concerns, such as racism, showing them to be legible and thinkable only also in relationship to nonhuman agencies. Furthermore, haunting offers an excellent orientation for discerning alternative understandings of agency that have a mixed legacy for current posthumanist concerns.[7]

---

for biblical studies, it does provide provocative analogies with ancient discourse about idolatry as well as about how humans relate to *technē*. It helps us to ask questions such as: (How) Are humans made things? If so, how is being human different from being something made by humans? How is a statue animated by a deity different from a human animated by a deity?

6. The embedded citation is from Barad 2007, 74.

7. By "mixed legacy" I mean that part of what haunts posthumanist writing, including that of Deleuze and Guattari, is the temptation to reinstall the heroic humanist agent. As Weinstone astutely notes, "despite posthumanism's interest in undermining the humanist subject. … a singular, salvific, and renegade figure, that of a Prometheus, still serves as an index of contemporary posthumanism's reliance on

In recent years a groundswell of feminist scholars, including Haraway as well as Karen Barad, Nancy Tuana, and Stacy Alaimo, have contributed to posthumanist thought by rethinking the human in terms of dynamic matter (where "matter" includes both organic and inorganic; see essays in Alaimo and Hekman 2008). They reject the idea that human, thing, animal, space come together and may mix—as preexisting entities. Instead, they suggest that we should imagine dynamic intra-actions that *produce* such differences, contextually and contingently (Barad 2007; Tuana 2008; Alaimo 2010). As Alaimo puts it, "understanding the substance of one's self as interconnected with the wider environment marks a profound shift in subjectivity. … the existence of anything—any creature, ecosystem, climatological pattern, ocean current—cannot be taken for granted as simply existing out there" (2010, 20–21). This feminist materialist approach to complex personhood complements but also challenges Gordon's concern for the interaction between the individual and the social in a wavering temporal field. The challenge is to account for more than the human "others" of concern in Gordon's writings; for Tuana, Alaimo, Haraway, and Barad, that which we take to be not-human, from the microbe, the solvents used in making plastics, the silicon naturally occurring in some geological formations, our pets, also must be included among "those who are called 'Other' [but] are never never that" (Gordon 1997, 4). These seeming others not only interact with us but at times become us, through what Alaimo calls "trans-corporeal" exchanges.

The ancient texts with which we work also tend to take for granted the existence of nonhuman agencies and to presume that human personhood is characterized by contingency; our very being is relational—we exist by our relations not simply as and with other separable beings but as localized, embodied manifestations of substances that exceed these local forms, whether those substances be conceived as elements, environment, humors,

---

solo figures of creative and often heroic autonomy" (2004, 10). In other words, even when conceived as assemblages of the human and nonhuman, a humanist notion of agency (freedom from constraint and oppression, freedom to create) tends to prevail in some of these works: the human part of the (individual) posthuman assemblage is usually foregrounded as the controlling element, who is free to transform that self into a new kind of being (10–11). These forms of posthumanism can certainly offer resources for rethinking both anthropology and Christology, but not so much for radically rethinking agency or for decentering the singular heroic figures in biblical narratives, including Jesus and Paul, or the heroic scholarly interpreter.

or spirit forces, deities, and the like. David Frankfurter notes that this is a world "in which local forms of great gods spoke as oracles, seers transmitted the words of spirits, and local cultures lived in familiarity with a great range of ancestral and landscape spirits" (2010, 28). Human-human relationships of power and collective identity get crafted in part by attempts to classify spiritual powers as either divine or demonic or to define some humans as properly or improperly receptive to spiritual powers, the right or wrong kinds of agents. Posthumanist questions can help to address concerns central to ancient texts, especially the agency of nonhuman forces, and the question of how we are human (see Buell 2014).

It may seem ridiculous to some to propose that we take nonhuman agencies seriously. Within the academy, this response may arise because interpretive approaches and methodologies take for granted that nonhuman agencies are illusory (a "strong" version of secular disenchantment). But methods that reductively explain away nonhuman agencies have increasingly come under criticism for structural hostility to theological positions as well as for colonialist and racist epistemologies and ontologies (e.g., Chakrabarty 2000, 97–113).[8] We need robust ways of assessing and engaging theological frameworks without merely dismissing them as quaint or primitive ghost stories of Other peoples from Other, less reasonable times, a move that may slide into a patronizing condescension of those for whom nonhuman agencies are alive and forceful in the present.

What I am proposing is more allied with those whose vantage points already presume that is it not ridiculous to take nonhuman agencies seriously (e.g., many religiously committed communities or, alternatively, from environmental materialism, science studies, animal activism, and the like). Posthumanist writings allow advocates of nonhuman agencies who are not religiously affiliated to engage nonhuman agencies without assenting to the rhetorical terms of the ancient texts and their ethical implications and without assenting to Christian theological frameworks. Using posthumanist resources, we can ask new questions about incarnation, transformative flesh eating and blood drinking, and bodies that may become stones, sticks, beasts, divine, or human—and various kinds of human to boot. (At the same time, it is worthwhile to explore how theological heritages haunt posthumanism in generally disavowed ways, but that is for another essay.)

8. For an especially effective articulation of this, see Keller 2002, 1–101.

Posthumanist feminist work has helped me to rethink the textual and social worlds of Roman-period texts with their presumptions of nonhuman agencies and intra-actions that produce and transform bodies in socially significant patterns, including relations among humans. Our ancient sources as well as our current world can imagine selves as produced in and through complex relations, relations that themselves differentiate matter into bodies we mark with power-saturated categories such as human, divine, machine, beast, and so on. Although many of the ancient texts do assert at least one ultimate preexisting entity (God, the One, etc.), processes such as speech, thought, and emanation are the means by which this one becomes increasingly differentiated and by which the ensuing beings also intra-act dynamically, such that what becomes "human" is also imagined as capable of becoming something else, again, by way of intra-action with other beings.

Accounts of spirit possession and exorcism constitute one site for this intra-action in ancient texts that I find especially challenging to understand, so it is to these I shall turn my attention in the next section. In the final section, I turn to a path-not-taken in religious studies from the nineteenth and early twentieth centuries to highlight an alternative approach to agency in the history of New Testament and early Christian studies. Spiritualist biblical interpreters, in part because of the high value placed on "mediums" for spirit communication, offer quite a different way of interpreting spirit possession and exorcism than became standard in historical criticism.

Reconsidering Possession and Exorcism

What I am suggesting we can accomplish by attention to what haunts closely complements the approaches advanced by feminist and other liberationist theologians and biblical scholars whose

> visions for the future may be linked with re-visions of suppressed, marginalized perspectives and agents based on our readings of ancient sources. These submerged perspectives are made visible precisely because of contemporary reflections and future visions. But the interpreter may also understand these traces, these "seething absences and muted presences" as, in a crucial sense, evidence for paths-not-taken which may bear an imperfect, wavering resemblance to those being charted for the future. The element of the labor that modulates between envisioning a more just

> future and the re-visioning needed to see these traces can be imagined as a willingness to acknowledge and engage haunting presences. (Buell 2009c, 169)[9]

Laura Donaldson offers a terrific example of how haunting as a theoretical position may begin this process of interrupting and transforming such dominant narratives by enabling one to identify and engage the counter-memories that the Gospel texts, and most biblical interpreters, render unspeakable. Donaldson centers the silent and often uninterpreted character of the daughter of the Syrophoenician woman of Mark 7:24–30. She suggests: "Rather than evoking the illness pejoratively identified in the Christian text as 'demon-possession,' the daughter might instead signify a trace of the indigenous; and rather than manifesting a deviance subject to the regimes of coercive (Christian) curing, she might also be experiencing the initial stages of a vocation known to indigenous peoples for millennia as shamanism" (2007, 104–5). Donaldson's emphasis rests on disrupting the blind spot not only in postcolonial analysis to gender but also in biblical studies to Christian interpretation that (even unwittingly) reinscribes colonialism by rendering indigenous religious traditions other and inferior, unable to speak.

Although considerable attention has been paid to the persistence and eloquence of the Syrophoenician woman's exchange with Jesus on behalf of her daughter (e.g., Schüssler Fiorenza 1992, 96–100, 103, 160–63), most scholars have not questioned the Gospel's characterization of the daughter's condition as an illness, a case of problematic spirit possession, in need of a cure. Donaldson enables us to identify as a haunting the indigenous traditions whose practitioners and modes of being, including ways of relating human with nonhuman agencies, have been redefined within dominant Christian tradition as illegitimate. As David Frankfurter puts it, "Christianization itself involved the reorganization of traditional and institutional pantheons to bring Christianity into relevance, as a source of authority, morality, power, and myth"; and Christians accomplished this through localized redefinitions of local spirits in new Christian religious centers (2010, 29). Such redefinitions, including in texts that only become Christian in their reception histories, unfold as local, textualized attempts to shape the meaning of spirits through possession and exorcism; Gospel texts aim to interpret them so as to reorganize both Jewish

9. Internal citation from Gordon 1997, 21.

and indigenous "pantheons," to paraphrase Frankfurter, in order to bring into relevance their specific understandings of authority, morality, power, and myth.

Posthumanism does not generally truck with spirits or deities, tending more to circuitry, insects, toxins, and other organic and inorganic matter; nonetheless, for a haunting-oriented interpreter, posthumanism can further enhance our analysis of examples of possession and exorcism in the Gospels insofar as it gives us questions to ask about how the "human" emerges always in and through and from that which becomes "nonhuman." Instances depicted as spirit possession and exorcism in Gospel texts presume that human beings operate in and have meaning in relationship, not only with other humans but also with spiritual powers. Gospel texts presuppose the existence of spiritual agencies that may work through human instruments, and they also presuppose communal and often contested human assessments about the kinds of spiritual forces at work and about how one ought to act and live in the world as a consequence. As Donaldson's analysis shows, Gospel narratives can depict intrahuman difference precisely in terms of the results of interactions between human and nonhuman forces. Even if the narratives center Jesus, he is not unique in terms of being characterized as someone negotiating and being transformed by external agencies.

Reading the narratives to discern, as Donaldson does, the ghostly possibilities of indigenous shaman women brings into focus how external agencies play a significant role in crafting intrahuman power relations. In addition, the dynamic porousness asserted in these narratives of exorcism and possession also hints at the path-not-taken to viewing the complex personhood of all characters in Gospel narratives as the result of transcorporeal encounters, without needing to privilege or center Jesus (even when the Gospel narratives do).[10] The narratives communicate an understanding of personhood requiring communal negotiation and assessment.

Spirit possession or exorcisms serve as key contexts for characters to evaluate, either to affirm or dissent from, assertions that Jesus mediates God's authority.[11] In the Gospel of Mark, such assertions turn especially on scenes of Jesus performing exorcisms, beginning in the first chapter.

---

10. See Schüssler Fiorenza 2000 and Johnson-DeBaufre 2005 on centering and decentering Jesus.

11. See also the brief discussion of the Fourth Gospel near the beginning of this article.

It is not only that heavenly voices and unclean spirits identify Jesus' relationship to spiritual power—humans also respond. Onlookers may speculate that a negative spiritual power accounts for Jesus' abilities as is clearly the case in Mark 3 when representatives from Jerusalem charge that Jesus "is under the control of Beelzebul," saying, "He drives out demons in the name of the head demon" (Mark 3:21). Charges about Jesus being possessed or accomplishing healings by the power of Beelzebul or the head demon indicate how personhood and authority are being defined in terms of relationships between human and spiritual powers on the one hand; on the other hand, these charges also underscore the absolute centrality of the community/audience/listeners as the ones who adjudicate the nature and significance of spirit-human interactions.[12]

How Spiritualism Haunts Biblical Studies: An Example

The conjunction of hauntology and posthumanism can also transform our readings of the history of scholarship of biblical studies and early Christianity. At the height of British imperialism and Anglo-American colonization of North America, a movement exploded called "Spiritualism,"[13] in which we find a fascinating, if almost entirely overlooked, legacy of biblical studies.

Tucked away in an endnote in her study of religious experience between the mid-eighteenth and early twentieth centuries, Ann Taves remarks that "little attention has been given to Spiritualists' interests in Christian origins," noting especially Spiritualists' interest in the figure of Jesus (1999, 406 n. 77). Indeed, Spiritualist and theosophical American and British writings seem to anticipate two of the interesting interventions into historical Jesus studies in the last thirty years. First, Spiritualists take as their data for the historical Jesus material what many of their academic and lay contemporaries aimed to rule out in a quest to banish supernaturalism or to distinguish a Jesus of history from a Christ of faith—healings and exorcisms; prophetic speech; the visual appearance of Moses and

12. Johnson-DeBaufre compellingly analyzes the Beelzebul accusation in the reconstruction of Q to critique interpretations of Jesus as unique (2005, 131–68).

13. The year 1848 is the "canonical" origin date for Spiritualism; it flourished in North America especially through the Civil War, while its height of popularity in Great Britain and Europe was later, with a resurgence immediately following the devastating losses of World War I.

Elijah to Jesus, Peter, James, and John in the Synoptics (the so-called transfiguration scene); as well as the resurrection appearances.

For example, in a lecture delivered in 1904 to the London Spiritual Alliance of which he was a regular member, Abraham Wallace observed, "The so-called miracles of Jesus have formed a stumbling-block to the acceptance by many people of the high moral, ethical, and spiritual doctrines which he taught and exemplified in his life" (1920, 21–22).[14] The "investigation" of these miracles, he continues, "has, therefore, on the one hand, been avoided by scientific students, who regard them as mere legendary accounts, unworthy of critical attention, and, on the other hand, so-called religious persons have regarded them as of 'supernatural' value, to be accepted by faith alone, and not by intellectual assent" (22). He implicitly critiques so-called scientific views that dismiss some phenomena as "supernatural" as well as religious folks who take everything on "faith" rather than knowledge. For Wallace, miracles are not supernatural; instead he asserts that Spiritualism has demonstrated that "spiritual force may act directly on matter," including human bodies (18). Only in the last few decades have some scholars, such as Morton Smith (1978), Halvor Moxnes (2003), and Pieter Craffert (2008), revisited in different ways the relevance of attributions of healing and exorcisms to Jesus as part of the data about the historical activity of Jesus.

Second, many Spiritualists argued that Jesus was a fully human exemplar for spiritual intercourse or mediumistic development available to all humans. Wallace, for example, asserts that Jesus was "the most divine expression of humanity" (1920, 6), insisting that his actions and teachings apply—at least potentially—to all humans: "nowhere in the synoptic Gospels, so far as I know, did Jesus affirm that he was God or equal with God" (13). Wallace argues that Jesus was a "highly-gifted psychic," and he argues against the theological assertion that Jesus is divine.[15] In so doing, he decenters Jesus (other Spiritualists decenter Christianity[16]) and antici-

14. Based on a talk delivered to the London Spiritualist Alliance on December 3, 1904, according to the preface and opening page (Wallace 1920, 5).

15. Wallace sees the idea of Jesus as divine as a later development, proposed in earliest form in the Gospel of John and subsequently elaborated (1920, 13).

16. For example, in her overview of Spiritualism presented at the 1893 World's Parliament of Religions, Cora Richmond, a leading medium and spokesperson for Spiritualism in the United States, presents "Christian Spiritualists" as one category of Spiritualists who "accept that the Christ life as impersonated in Jesus of Nazareth as

pates the decentering of Jesus to emphasize the movement of which he was a part, also articulated by feminist scholars such as Elisabeth Schüssler Fiorenza (2000) and Melanie Johnson-DeBaufre (2005).

An orientation to hauntings enables us to understand better the significance of "demythologizing" types of interpretation in the late nineteenth and early twentieth centuries and to identify aspects of paths-not-taken in biblical studies that indirectly anticipate some of the critical alternative hermeneutics of the last four or so decades. I am not claiming that Spiritualists *directly* influenced any of these newer hermeneutical approaches. But I do want to suggest that we can better understand and evaluate the methods and critical questions surrounding historical Jesus studies we still inherit from late-nineteenth- and early-twentieth-century scholars if we locate that earlier academic work in relationship to the popular movement of Spiritualism.

In this section, I highlight how these Spiritualist engagements with biblical resources and Christian tradition relate to their views of agency. Spiritualists appeal to an understanding of agency and subjectivity different from many of their contemporaries to advance their views. Indeed, Abraham Wallace writes, "all revelation purporting to be divine has ever come through human instrumentality" (1920, 9). This is a view that attributes the source of knowledge to come from spirits who have left their physical bodies and now aim to instruct those still embodied. Examining ways that Spiritualists advance these claims helps to show how Spiritualism serves as a kind of indirect precedent for posthumanist attempts to reconfigure epistemology and ontology as well as some recent deconstructive and postcolonial challenges to linear temporality and agency, especially Spiritualists' emphasis on knowledge attained mediumistically.

Spiritualists, though diverse in backgrounds and perspectives, shared the view that humans have spirits that retain their personality after physiological death and that discarnate spirits communicate with those still embodied, especially through humans known as mediums but also

---

the highest expression of religious revelation of truth, and who consider that without denominational or sectarian definitions, the life and works of Jesus are the highest guidance, but who also recognize that every age has been blessed with spiritual teachers chosen to bear to earth the message of immortality and the love of God to man" (1893, 2). Richmond implies that Christian Spiritualists locate Jesus as one spiritual teacher among many, including those from other religious traditions, *and* that Jesus is portrayed as a guide for individual Christians to emulate.

through inorganic materials, such as tables. Most Spiritualists were Christians by upbringing and, unsurprisingly, turned to biblical texts to help explain and support these views and their implications. Nonetheless, even as they recognized affinities between Spiritualist claims and those of earlier and contemporary groups such as Methodists, Quakers, and Shakers, Spiritualists portrayed themselves not primarily as proponents of a religious reform movement but rather as offering rational, scientific, progressive truths about the nature of humanity in general.[17]

Although a movement that clearly insisted on the existence and value of spiritual things, Spiritualists were quite concerned with what we might view as worldly matters—not only did they understand spirits to communicate through matter, whether that be bodies, tables, doors, or planchettes, but they also argued that individual and collective practices expressed and shaped the quality of one's spiritual development (e.g., someone who promoted gender and status inequality would likely be diagnosed as being spiritually undeveloped).

Spiritualists presented themselves as a beacon of hope in an age mired in crass materialism, but far from positioning themselves as antimodern or antiworldly, they used technologies such as photography and mass media to demonstrate and publicize their views, insisted on the scientific verifiability of spirit communication, and advanced largely progressive this-worldly causes such as abolition, women's right to vote, and anti-imperialism in and through spirit communication and spiritual development. Spiritualists were both profoundly optimistic about the human individual and her or his ability to effect change in the world and intensely insistent that such improvement take place in harmony with and through instruction by disembodied spirits, ranging from eminent figures from the past such as Socrates, Jesus, and George Washington to recently deceased children and relatives, as well as spiritual representatives of colonized and

17. Wallace, for example, appeals to both science and the latest scholarship on the historical Jesus and Christian origins of his day to support his views (e.g., Adolf von Harnack and Alfred Loisy). Wallace claims that this scholarship supports his goal of "look[ing] from the standpoint of the modern psychical investigator at this remarkable Personality, Jesus of Nazareth, and at some of the ultra-normal phenomena recorded in the New Testament, particularly in the synoptic Gospels, and said to have been manifested in the life of Jesus, who is, by the general consensus of peoples of the western world, regarded as the most divine expression of humanity in the history of our race" (1920, 5–6).

exoticized others, such as Native American spirits, Indians, and Africans (see Braude 1989; McGarry 2008).

Exorcism and spirit possessions were among the practices that Spiritualists cited from biblical narratives to support the existence of communication between embodied folks and "discarnate" spirits and, specifically, to support their views about agency—that spirit communication occurs in an instrumental fashion.

Wallace does not just understand Jesus' miracles to be the result of his channeling God's power for healing; he also understands Jesus to have spoken about mediumship for other humans in Mark 13: "According to the records, Jesus of Nazareth believed in inspirational speaking, for in warning his disciples who were sensitives [that is, individuals with a proclivity for receiving spirit communications] (Mark xiii. 27) he said: 'And when they lead you to judgment, and deliver you up, be not anxious beforehand what ye shall speak, but whatsoever shall be given you in that hour, that speak ye: for it is not ye that speak, but the Holy Spirit.' In Matthew x. 20, it is written, 'the spirit of your Father that speaketh in you'" (1920, 10). Wallace understands this to be both data about the historical Jesus and an ancient affirmation of current Spiritualist claims about what mediums do—communicate the words of spirits to the living.

Exorcism illustrates both Spiritualist claims about spirit communication and Jesus' role as exemplar in other Spiritualist writings. We find one example in a small book, structured as a dialogue between a Protestant clergyman and an ex-parishioner, published by the Secular Press Bureau of the American Spiritualist Alliance in 1884. In this text, the unnamed minister asserts that "there are no miracles now such as [Christ] wrought," and that if mediums are influenced by any external agencies, they can only be demonic. The Spiritualist, known as Mr. Smith, retorts first that, if this is so, then the minister ought to take pity on "these unfortunate victims of diabolical malice" and "following your Master's [Jesus'] example ... cast out these possessing spirits" (Anonymous 1884, 19–20). The minister resists this with reference to Jesus' unique divine nature—that the exorcised spirits recognize Jesus as divine. Mr. Smith the Spiritualist counters by saying that of course lower spirits recognize higher ones, but that Jesus

> did not claim to exercise special powers of God in casting them out. You remember that the man who brought to Jesus his son that had a dumb spirit stated that the disciples had failed to cast him out; and Jesus

> exclaimed, "O faithless generation, how long shall I be with you'" meaning, I suppose, What will you do without me? And after the spirit had been cast out, the disciples asked, "Why could not we cast him out?" His answer was, "This kind can come forth by nothing but by prayer and fasting." *He did not tell them that it was because they were not of the same divine nature as himself, that they were not God, but because their spiritual powers had not been properly developed.* (20, emphasis added)

For Smith this means that, at this time, the disciples were mediums for less pure spirits than Jesus, but that this was not an ontological distinction between Jesus and other humans but simply a matter of insufficient training and the fact that there are many different levels of disembodied spirits.

Even while preferring the Synoptics as a source for the historical Jesus, Wallace cites the Fourth Gospel to support the Spiritualist tenet that Jesus' powers were not unique: "the one who believes in me will also do the works that I do; and greater works than these, because I go to the Father" (John 14:12; 1920, 16). This verse was very popular with Spiritualists. Indeed, almost a half century earlier, this verse introduces a long list of such Spiritualist works from 1859, such as by H. Stewart of Ithaca, New York, who attests that he was "warned by a spirit and [his] life saved" (U. Clark 1859, 8).[18]

This same verse is used by the Spiritualist Mr. Smith in the 1884 dialogue to assert that if Jesus "could cause the appearance of holy spirits of the departed and talk with them," as in the Synoptic accounts of the transfiguration scene, "then his disciples, or those who believed in him, could and can do the same. Else why was he careful to have certain selected members of the twelve present at this divine séance as witnesses of the example which he set?" (11–12). This Spiritualist interpretation of John 14:12 enables a reading of the transfiguration scene as a historical precedent for the séances being held daily in North America in the 1880s, and more broadly for the claim that still-embodied humans can mediate communications from the spirits of the dead.

To reckon with the legacy of Spiritualism on biblical and early Christian studies requires consideration of the epistemological and ontological

---

18. This publication was one issue of "an annual statistical register" about Spiritualists published by Uriah Clark, a former Universalist minister, based in Auburn, N.Y.; Clark also established the "well written weekly paper," *The Spiritual Clarion* (Hardinge 1870, 60).

claims of Spiritualists (see Cottom 1991)—claims that destabilize notions of rationality and agency by which biblical and early Christian studies have largely authorized themselves as academic disciplines. This line of inquiry illuminates what haunts the formation and ongoing practices of biblical and early Christian studies (see Buell 2009d); moreover, it may help us discern what haunts our theorizing, insofar as Spiritualism may constitute a disavowed precedent and a site for unrealized possibilities in both religious studies and ethics. I am not a Spiritualist manqué, but when I read about Derrida's visor effect (1994, 7), Avery Gordon's call to follow the ghosts (1997), Mary Keller's notion of instrumental agency to refigure the relationship between subject and agency (2002), and Jeff Kripal's performance of a gnostic approach to religious studies (2007), it does not strike me as extreme to suggest that we have already been dipping into ideas deeply informed by Spiritualism even if not identified explicitly with it.

As we consider some examples of how these folks we might think of as fringy, and even downright odd, interpreted Gospel texts, we should remember that they emerged in a landscape in which neither biblical studies nor church history had the kind of academic authority or even professional identities that they came to have. Americans were sometimes reading the translations of European scholars, from Strauss and Renan to Harnack and Loisy, but the contexts of their reception in the states were as likely to be nonacademic and nonministerial as not. In other words, the professionalization of biblical studies and the creation of church history as a subfield occurs in the *late* nineteenth century in the United States; it is *in process* while Spiritualism is flourishing and is contemporary with the founding of Theosophy as well as the academic fields of comparative religious studies, sociology, anthropology, psychology, and folklore studies. Academic modes of investigation thus are forged and authorized in a field of alternative "lay" approaches.[19]

Spiritualism incited many critics and skeptical inquirers, including those who formed psychical research societies and academics instrumental in shaping the disciplines of sociology, anthropology, psychology, and comparative religion.[20] Psychical research societies, composed of academ-

19. On the formation of early Christian studies in the United States, ee also Elizabeth Clark 2011.

20. For example, sociologist Herbert Spencer's "ghost theory" of the origins of religion as veneration of dead ancestors might seem to have an obvious connection to Spiritualism, but so too his pioneering articulation of the concept of "culture" as the

ics and interested "laypeople," took Spiritualists as objects of study, often arguing that while Spiritualists themselves were misguided, the phenomena with which they were concerned was real (Taves 1999, 200). We see this quite directly on the topic of agency. As one of the founders of the British Society for Psychical Research, Frederic Myers, wrote: "'spirit control … is a normal step forward in the evolution of the race,' and he says: 'I claim that a spirit exists in man, and that it is healthy and desirable that this spirit should be thus capable of partial or temporary disassociation from the organism; itself then enjoying increased freedom and vision, and also thereby allowing some departed spirit to make use of the partially vacated organism for the sake of communication with other spirits still incarnate on earth'" (S. P. R. "Proceedings," vol. 17, as cited in Wallace 1920, 10–11).[21]

***

Cultivating a way of studying what haunts biblical studies is crucial for producing interpretive approaches that can encounter the complex specificity of religious claims hospitably yet also critically, while also bringing biblical studies into conversation with work in other disciplines and activism. Posthumanism and hauntology may work together to accomplish three kinds of benefits for biblical studies: first, we can use them to produce new readings of biblical texts and other ancient literature; second, we can use them to gain a deeper understanding of what haunts our field; third, as I have tried to show throughout, they together help forge an approach to biblical studies that offers a productive way for nonreligiously affiliated

---

invisible bonds that constitute a group. In his study of the development of the notion of culture, Herbert notes how this smacks of "the occult" and is "potentially scandalous" "for a would-be objective and empirical science," while quite explicitly drawing on language used by Spiritualists to express their conviction in the invisible communication and forces between humans (1991, 14). Anthropologists have continued to take views and practices about death as well as spirit possession as areas of central concern since the late nineteenth century.

21. The British Psychical Research Society has boasted among its members folks who contributed significantly to biblical studies and ancient history such as Bernard Hillman Streeter (four-source hypothesis) and Erwin R. Dodds. We see indirect heirs to this, I think in the preference for social scientific methods of analysis to—even sympathetically—render accounts of possession and exorcisms—intelligible in terms of other people's and other time periods ways of knowing; be that the notion of a magician à la Morton Smith or a shaman à la Peter Craffert (see Buell 2009d).

scholars of biblical texts to enter into productive conversation with theological projects. My focus has been on how both hauntology and posthumanism especially help us to tackle questions of agency that have political, ethical, and theological urgency.

Works Cited

Alaimo, Stacy. 2010. *Bodily Natures: Science, Environment, and the Material Self*. Bloomington: Indiana University Press.

Alaimo, Stacy, and Susan Hekman, eds. 2008. *Feminist Materialisms*. Bloomington: Indiana University Press.

Anonymous. 1884. *The Biblical and Theological Objections to Spiritualism Answered in a Colloquy between a Clergyman and an Ex-Parishioner*. New York: Secular Press Bureau of the American Spiritualist Alliance.

Anzaldúa, Gloria. 1987. *Borderlands/La Frontera: The New Mestiza*. San Francisco: Aunt Lute.

Barad, Karen. 2007. *Meeting the Universe Halfway: Quantum Physics and the Entanglement of Matter and Meaning*. Durham, N.C.: Duke University Press.

Braude, Ann. 1989. *Radical Spirits: Spiritualism and Women's Rights in Nineteenth-Century America*. Boston: Beacon.

Buell, Denise Kimber. 2005. *Why This New Race: Ethnic Reasoning in Early Christianity*. New York: Columbia University Press.

———. 2009a. Imagining Human Transformation in the Context of Invisible Powers: Instrumental Agency in Second-Century Treatments of Conversion. Pages 263–84 in *Metamorphoses: Resurrection, Body and Transformative Practices in Early Christianity*. Edited by Turid Karlsen Seim and Jorunn Økland. Ekstasis: Religious Experience from Antiquity to the Middle Ages 1. Berlin: de Gruyter.

———. 2009b. Early Christian Universalism and Racism. Pages 109–31 in *The Origins of Racism in the West*. Edited by Miriam Eliav-Feldon, Benjamin Isaac, and Joseph Ziegler. Cambridge: Cambridge University Press.

———. 2009c. God's Own People: Specters of Race, Ethnicity, and Gender in Early Christian Studies. Pages 159–90 in *Prejudice and Christian Beginnings: Investigating Race, Gender, and Ethnicity in Early Christian Studies*. Edited by Elisabeth Schüssler Fiorenza and Laura Nasrallah. Minneapolis: Fortress.

———. 2009d. The Afterlife Is Not Dead: Spiritualism, Postcolonial Theory, and Early Christian Studies. *Church History* 78:862–72.

———. 2010. Cyborg Memories: An Impure History of Jesus. *BibInt* 18:313–41.

———. 2014. These Microbes and *Pneuma* That Therefore I Am. In *Divinanimality: Creaturely Theology*. Edited by Stephen D. Moore. New York: Fordham University Press.

Chakrabarty, Dipesh. 2000. *Provincializing Europe: Postcolonial Thought and Historical Difference*. Princeton: Princeton University Press.

Clark, Elizabeth A. 2011. *Founding the Fathers: Early Church History and Protestant Professors in Nineteenth-Century America*. Philadelphia: University of Pennsylvania Press.

Clark, Uriah. 1859. *The Spiritual Register for 1859. Facts, Philosophy, Statistics of Spiritualism*. Auburn, N.Y.: Stone and Hawkes. Subscription pamphlet.

Cottom, Daniel. 1991. *The Abyss of Reason: Cultural Movement, Revelations, and Betrayals*. New York: Oxford University Press.

Craffert, Pieter. 2008. *The Life of a Galilean Shaman: Jesus of Nazareth in Anthropological-Historical Perspective*. Eugene, Oreg.: Cascade.

Deleuze, Gilles, and Felix Guattari. 1987. *A Thousand Plateaus: Capitalism and Schizophrenia*. Edited and translated by Brian Massumi. Minneapolis: University of Minnesota Press.

Derrida, Jacques. 1994. *Specters of Marx: The State of the Debt, the Work of Mourning and the New International*. Translated by Peggy Kamuf. London: Routledge.

Donaldson, Laura. 2007. Gospel Hauntings: The Postcolonial Demons of New Testament Criticism. Pages 97–113 in *Postcolonial Biblical Criticism*. Edited by Fernando F. Segovia. New York: Continuum.

Frankfurter, David. 2010. Where the Spirits Dwell: Possession, Christianization, and Saints' Shrines in Late Antiquity. *Harvard Theological Review* 103:27–46.

Gordon, Avery F. 1997. *Ghostly Matters: Haunting and the Sociological Imagination*. Minneapolis: University of Minnesota Press.

———. 2011. Some Thoughts on Haunting and Futurity. *borderlands* 10.2:1–21.

Gunn, Joshua. 2006. Review Essay: Mourning Humanism, or, the Idiom of Haunting. *Quarterly Journal of Speech* 92:77–102.

Haraway, Donna J. 1991. A Cyborg Manifesto: Science, Technology, and Socialist Feminism in the Late Twentieth-Century. Pages 149–81 in

Simians, Cyborgs, and Women: The Reinvention of Nature. New York: Routledge.
———. 1997. *Modest_Witness@Second_Millennium.FemaleMan©_Meets_OncoMouse™: Feminism and Techoscience*. New York: Routledge.
———. 2008. *When Species Meet*. Minneapolis: University of Minnesota Press.
Hardinge, Emma. 1870. *Modern American Spiritualism: A Twenty Years' Record of the Communion between Earth and the World of Spirits*. 4th edition. New York: Self-published.
Hayles, N. Katherine. 1999. *How We Became Posthuman: Virtual Bodies in Cybernetics, Literature, and Informatics*. Chicago: University of Chicago Press.
Herbert, Christopher. 1991. *Culture and Anomie: Ethnographic Imagination in the Nineteenth Century*. Chicago: University of Chicago Press.
Heschel, Susannah. 1998. *Abraham Geiger and the Jewish Jesus*. Chicago: University of Chicago Press.
———. 2008. *The Aryan Jesus: Christian Theologians and the Bible in Nazi Germany*. Princeton: Princeton University Press.
Hodge, Caroline Johnson. 2007. *If Sons, Then Heirs: A Study of Kinship and Ethnicity in the Letters of Paul*. Oxford: Oxford University Press.
Johnson, Sylvester A. 2004. *The Myth of Ham in Nineteenth-Century American Christianity: Race, Heathens, and the People of God*. New York: Palgrave Macmillan.
Johnson-DeBaufre, Melanie. 2005. *Jesus among Her Children: Q, Eschatology, and the Construction of Christian Origins*. Harvard Theological Studies 55. Cambridge: Harvard University Press.
Keller, Mary. 2002. *The Hammer and the Flute: Women, Power, and Spirit Possession*. Baltimore: Johns Hopkins University Press.
Kelley, Shawn. 2002. *Racializing Jesus: Race, Ideology and the Formation of Modern Biblical Scholarship*. London: Routledge.
Kripal, Jeffrey. 2007. *The Serpent's Gift: Gnostic Reflections on the Study of Religion*. Chicago: University of Chicago Press.
Liew, Tat-Siong Benny. 2008. *What Is Asian-American Biblical Hermeneutics? Reading the New Testament*. Honolulu: University of Hawai'i Press.
McGarry, Molly. 2008. *Ghosts of Futures Past: Spiritualism and the Cultural Politics of Nineteenth-Century America*. Berkeley: University of California Press.

Moxnes, Halvor. 2003. *Putting Jesus in His Place: A Radical Vision of Household and Kingdom*. Louisville: Westminster John Knox.
Richmond, Cora L. V. 1893. Presentation of Spiritualism. A Paper Arranged by the Guides of Mrs. Cora L. V. Richmond for the Word's Parliament of Religions at Chicago, October 1893. Washington, D.C.: National Spiritualists Association.
Sandoval, Chela. 1995. Cyborg Feminism and the Methodology of the Oppressed. Pages 407–21 in *The Cyborg Handbook*. Edited by Chris Hables Gray. New York: Routledge.
Schüssler Fiorenza, Elisabeth. 1992. *But She Said: Feminist Practices of Biblical Interpretation*. Boston: Beacon.
———. 2000. *Jesus and the Politics of Interpretation*. New York: Continuum.
Smith, Morton. 1978. *Jesus the Magician*. San Francisco: Harper & Row.
Stoler, Ann L. 1997. Racial Histories and their Regimes of Truth. *Political Power and Social Theory* 11:183–206.
Stowers, Stanley. 1994. *A Rereading of Romans: Justice, Jews, and Gentiles*. New Haven: Yale University Press.
Taves, Ann. 1999. *Fits, Trances, and Visions: Experiencing Religion and Explaining Experience from Wesley to James*. Princeton: Princeton University Press.
Tuana, Nancy. 2008. Viscous Porosity: Witnessing Katrina. Pages 188–213 in *Feminist Materialisms*. Edited by Stacy Alaimo and Susan Hekman. Bloomington: Indiana University Press.
Wallace, Abraham. 1920. *Jesus of Nazareth and Modern Scientific Investigation: From the Spiritualist Standpoint*. 2nd ed. Manchester: Two Worlds.
Weinstone, Ann. 2004. *Avatar Bodies: A Tantra for Posthumanism*. Minneapolis: University of Minnesota Press.
Wolfe, Cary. 1995. In Search of Post-humanist Theory: The Second-Order Cybernetics of Maturana and Varela. *Cultural Critique* 30:33–70.
———. 2003. *Animal Rites: American Culture, the Discourse of Species and Posthumanist Theory*. Chicago: University of Chicago Press.
———. 2009. *What Is Posthumanism?* Minneapolis: University of Minnesota Press.
Wolfreys, Julian. 2002. *Victorian Hauntings: Spectrality, Gothic, the Uncanny and Literature*. New York: Palgrave.

Part 2
Lions

The Lion King: Yahweh as Sovereign Beast in Israel's Imaginary*

Hugh Pyper

In 2008 a political campaign advertisement appeared on YouTube, claiming to be endorsed by the White Witch of Narnia. Entitled "The Truth about Aslan," the text of the video runs as follows:

> What do we really know about Aslan? Aslan wants to bring an end to Narnia's winter wonderland, plunging our country into a state of global warming. Aslan is also a carnivore, putting every citizen of Narnia on *his* diet. Even his biggest supporters agree he is not safe. Aslan is on the move, but if he loved Narnia so much, why did he move away in the first place? Aslan: bad for us, bad for Narnia.[1]

Not everyone thinks this is funny. The comment pages on YouTube are full of outraged protests that anyone could even dare to criticize Aslan. As one not untypical comment puts it, "This is stupid video and I didn't like neither don't respect who was talking bout Aslan, so please remove this stupid thing." Aslan, the lion as representative of Jesus in C. S. Lewis's *Narnia* series, is above criticism for such viewers. Other comments along the lines of "Jeez, it's just a story-book lion, dude; it's not like it's Jesus," or "Jeez it's just a parody, dumbass," reveal the different reading strategies correspondents adopt.

Now, making fun of respondents to YouTube videos is cheap, but this shows the power that this particular use of the lion as metaphor for the

---

* Another version of this essay appears in my *The Unchained Bible: Cultural Appropriations of Biblical Texts* (London: T&T Clark, 2012). Used by permission.

1. Video accessible at http://www.youtube.com/watch?v=PaQD-nizpbo, with acknowledgments to the original poster "johnritc."

divine sovereign has over certain readers and the difficulty that human beings have in learning to negotiate what is metaphor and what is not, how what is said depends on who speaks and who hears and how metaphors have implications that may lurk unnoticed until activated. What I hope this example does is to reveal the tensions in the use of animal metaphors in delimiting the bounds of the human, metaphors that are almost taken for granted. This unorthodox take on Aslan, the epitome of the Lion King, shows that the juxtaposition of the two elements plays out differently depending on where you stand.

The relevance of this to biblical studies is that C. S. Lewis's use of Aslan the lion to represent the sovereign figure in Narnia rather than any human character is generally assumed to depend on his familiarity with the biblical tradition and on the widespread association of the lion and the figure of the king in ancient and modern literature. A remark of Alexander McCall Smith's is pertinent here: "so burdened are lions with symbolism that it's surprising they manage to stagger a few paces, let alone spring at their prey" (2007). As we shall see, this is a significant point; the metaphorical association of lion and king is so widespread and familiar that we can fail to see all its ramifications, and the association with the lion seem so obvious that we forget that the metaphor may work in different ways in different cultural contexts.

In this paper I want to look in particular at the lion as metaphor and metonym in the Bible and its relationship to the role of the king and the characterization of Yahweh. This will lead me to turn to Derrida's reflections on the political significance of animals in his late seminars collected as *The Beast and the Sovereign* (2009–2011) and in the presentations collected under the title *The Animal That Therefore I Am* (2008). By examining how Derrida uses biblical material and how biblical metaphor has been shaped and reshaped in the development of some currently influential political philosophy, I hope, if not to shed light, at least to raise some questions about the political implications of the biblical metaphor. I will not claim that this leads to some new revolutionary manifesto, but in the course of writing this paper I have found that I have had to correct some assumptions and have realized some implications that I had overlooked.

Kings and Lions in the Hebrew Bible

Anyone with an interest in the lion as metaphor is now indebted to Brent Strawn's comprehensive and thorough exploration of the issue within the

Hebrew Bible and its cultural context in his *What Is Stronger Than a Lion? Leonine Image and Metaphor in the Hebrew Bible and the Ancient Near East* (2005). Strawn surveys in detail the references to lions in the Bible, analyzing the nuances of the vocabulary used in this semantic field, and puts these in the context of the biology and ecology of the Asian lion. In addition, he offers a comprehensive overview of the use of the lion as symbol and metaphor in literature and art from the wider cultural context of the ancient Near East.

Out of the wealth of material, textual and visual, that he assembles, I want to hone in on one particular point. He finds what he describes as a "glaring omission" (Strawn 2005, 236) in the Hebrew Bible when set against its ancient Near Eastern context, something that seems to set the biblical tradition apart from its context. This is the *lack* in the Hebrew Bible of an association between the lion and the figure of the king.

In its contrast to the wider cultural norms from Egypt to Assyria, this is surprising. The iconography that associates king and the lion is so typical of Assyrian and other cultures that it is a commonplace even in popular depictions of ancient kingdoms in films and book illustration. The Hebrew Bible, however, contains no celebration of the king as displaying the power of the lion against his enemies, nor of the king as the great protector of his people against lions, real or metaphorical.

Neither is the common trope of the identification of the king and the lion to be found. Even the few verses that might be cited in contradiction to this claim, Strawn argues, are markedly different in tone. The description of Saul and Jonathan as "mightier than lions" (2 Sam 1:23) could be cited in this regard, for instance, but in David's lament this metaphor is used of them both, not specifically of Saul as king. In any case, these are dead lions. In the context of defeat and the end of a dynasty, the royal association is muted and at least double-edged.

Indeed, this example may throw light on the one other passage in the books of Samuel where an echo of the association of king and lion in Neo-Assyrian iconography may be found. This is David's boast to Saul in 1 Sam 17:34–37 that as a young shepherd he slew lions: "And when the lion or the bear came and took a sheep from the flock, then I would go after it and I would strike it and I would save [the sheep] from its mouth. And if it rose up against me, I would seize it by its beard and I would strike it and kill it. Your servant has killed both the lion and the bear." This has been read as an echo of royal propaganda, and the detail of seizing the lion by its beard has resonances with the depiction of Ashurbanipal in a well-known relief where the king is shown face-to-face with a lion that has reared up on its hind legs. Seizing it by the beard, the king has pierced the beast through.

That these verses are the main evidence that can be adduced of such an association between king and lion in Israel serves to prove the point that something is different in the Hebrew Bible. David's boast is set firmly in the world of the peasant shepherd dealing with real bears and real sheep, whatever its metaphorical associations. If anything, this passage concretizes the metaphor; kings may make a show of killing lions, but it is the ordinary shepherd boy who really has to confront them (and bears as well, which do not figure in Assyrian royal iconography). It could even be read as verging on a parody of this kind of royal image.

Whatever the truth of this reading, the next verse indisputably undercuts any potential claim to royal prowess on David's behalf by giving all the credit for the defeat of these predators to Yahweh: "Yahweh, who delivered me from the paw of the lion and from the paw of the bear, it is he who will deliver me from the hand of this Philistine" (1 Sam 17:38). Yahweh is the one who conquers the lion, not David. Even this dubious association of domination of the lion with the royal power of David is repudiated, confirming Strawn's thesis, although he does not make this point himself.

The other passage one could invoke as putting Strawn's claim in question is Ezek 19:2–9. At first sight, these verses seem to associate Israelite royalty and lions in quite an extended metaphor. God instructs the prophet, "You are to intone a dirge over the princes of Israel and say, 'What a lioness was your mother among the lions'" (Ezek 19:2). This lioness raises two cubs that in turn become great lions. So far, this seems to correspond to the use of the metaphor in other ancient cultures. Yet the depiction here is of the princes not as heroes but as devourers of cities and humans. Both princes meet an ignominious end as the nations rise against them, snare them in nets, grapple them with hooks, and confine them to cages. What the metaphor of the lion evokes here is not the mighty king of beasts, but destructive wild lions that become the target of a lion hunt conducted by all the nations. We shall go on to explore further the role of the royal hunt in the metaphor of the lion, but suffice it to say here that this passage is, if anything, satirizing the aspiration of Israel's monarchs to mimic the power, display, and imagery of their more powerful neighbors and activates the ambivalence of the royal interaction with lions.

Taken in this light, these passages reinforce rather than undermine Strawn's central claim that positive leonine imagery associated with the power of kingship is reserved for Yahweh in the Hebrew Bible. In Strawn's view, the balance of probability is that this association of Yahweh and the lion is a product of the process of accretion that gives rise to the biblical character of Yahweh, whereby attributes and characteristics of a series of deities are assimilated (2005, 267).[2]

Be that as it may, the biblical tradition stands out as one where the power and position of the human king is not praised in metaphors involving the lion. Where such metaphorical references occur, the lion is Yahweh. In contrast to the cultural context, the Hebrew Bible displaces the king from his role as the focus of this metaphor, leaving the people and their God confronting one another directly. As we shall see, this represents a very particular construal of the operations of power in the politics of the Bible that has implications for subsequent political systems that look to the Bible as an authoritative text.

Yahweh as Lion

What, then, are the political implications of this metaphorical assimilation of Yahweh to the lion? As Strawn rightly points out, the metaphor is ambivalent. Yahweh can be represented as the roaring lion that opposes Israel's enemies. Yet he is also depicted as turning on Israel itself, regarding it as prey.

The beginning of Amos is a condign example of how the two dimensions of the metaphor may work. "The Lord roars from Zion," the book begins (Amos 1:2), a phrase that seems to serve as an epigraph for the whole work where the tropes of roaring and other leonine behavior are widespread. The denunciation and destruction of Israel's neighbors and enemies that follows reassures the Israelite reader that Yahweh the lion is performing his duty as guardian of Israel. This turns out, however, to be merely a prelude to his attack upon Israel itself, with the Israelites being

2. Intriguingly, given that leonine imagery is, if anything, more associated with feminine rather than masculine deities, such as Ishtar and Astarte, Strawn suggests that Yahweh's leonine qualities may reflect an aspect of his femininity. The passage from Ezekiel quoted above may serve as some circumstantial evidence of this association. It is not the lion but the lioness nurturing her cubs that is the most formidable of the bearers of the metaphor, whether she represents some historical queen mother or whether she stands for a female rival to Yahweh who is behind the corruption and violence of her kingly offspring.

warned that all that will remain of them will be "the shank bones and the tip of an ear" (Amos 3:12), which the shepherd rescues from the lion's jaws.

This then leads us to consider what may seem an odd contradiction in the use of the lion as metaphor. As we have seen, the lion can represent not only the protector and the judge, but also the forces of destruction and threat to the order that the king or god is relied upon to represent. The lion cubs in Ezekiel represent in the end naked power opposed to the will of Yahweh. At the same time, Israel is exposed to the naked power of Yahweh as the lion wreaks his punishment on them.

Yet, as Strawn reminds us, it is not that these are two different aspects of the lion or a metaphorical confusion. The lion is consistent; the difference depends on where we are standing. Lion statues are used across the ancient Near East and beyond as the guardians of thresholds, for the very good reason that there is a world of difference in being face-to-face with a lion and standing behind it. Once allowed past the threat of the lion, one moves into its protection. The lion does not move, the spectator moves; but its symbolic force changes. What is strong and fierce enough to protect me can also threaten me, and the image of the lion uncannily ties together this duplicity of protector and threat, ruler and unruly.

The Royal Hunt

In trying to understand the force of such contradictions, I want to supplement Strawn's invaluable contribution by drawing on the work of Thomas Allsen, who has undertaken a wide-ranging study of the institution of the Royal Hunt in Eurasia (2006). He follows this from ancient Egypt through to its more recent manifestations in India, showing how pervasive the association between the king and hunting is. One common and important variant is the royal lion hunt. As Allsen points out, this reminds us that the term *hunting* embraces a number of related but different activities. Hunting may be for food, in which case a royal hunt shows the king in his role as provider; but it may also be in order to combat a threat from animals that are destroying food or from potentially dangerous predators.

Yet hunting lions is a risky business. Kings are not expendable, certainly in their own eyes, and for the king to spend his life in hunting down lions would be both dangerous and a diversion from the less glamorous but essential aspects of his role. In addition, there is a need to make capital of the king's prowess. The king not only has to kill lions but also has to be seen to be killing lions if this is to have any impact on the people at large.

Even in the ancient world, moreover, lions were already becoming increasingly less common in the more populated areas.

All these considerations led to the development of royal parks. Considerable resources were spent to maintain a captive population of lions that the king could hunt and kill in the carefully stage-managed context of the royal hunt in the royal parks, thus reinforcing the basis of his sovereignty and providing the court and population with evidence of the fitness of his rule. The establishment and maintenance of such a park and the successful capture of animals to stock it demands a degree of organization, control, and mastery of trade that in itself reflects royal prestige and the ability to maintain order.[3] The pervasiveness of depictions of the royal hunt in wall paintings, statues, and other media shows the importance of the hunt as a way of demonstrating and communicating the king's status.

In the Mesopotamian context, Allsen argues, the lion hunt embodies the paradox that the king draws spiritual power from the untamed powers of the wilderness and yet exercises that power to bring order and discipline to the world. How better to show that the king embodied the spirit of the lion than to show him killing lions as an equal. The lion embodies spectacularly the idea that nature is at once nurturing and threatening. In the lion hunt, the king both shows his courage and his power to dominate nature, but also takes on the strength and power of his adversary (Allsen 2006, 162). Iconically, the Mesopotamian king is never more kingly than when in single combat with a lion.

This is one way in which the royal lion hunt reinforces and yet blurs the distinction between king and animal; the lion represents nonhuman nature in all its power and threat, which is subdued by the king, who arrogates to himself that nonhuman power. As I shall discuss in the second half of this paper, this paradox of the distinctiveness of the human being demonstrated through its assimilation of the nonhuman is one that has long resonances that have surfaced in a good deal of contemporary political philosophy.

---

3. The other side of the coin is that lions, although dangerous, are actually a relatively easy problem to solve for an ancient monarch. The king can gain kudos and cut an impressive figure by ridding his populace of marauding lions, or getting his minions to do this. There is not much he can do, however, about even more destructive threats, such as drought or pestilence, or, to stick to animal pests, a plague of locusts. Then as now, a wise ruler would make a big show of his prowess in doing what was possible in the hope that this would stand him in good stead when things got difficult.

Another shared cultural feature of such royal hunts also erodes the boundary between human and animal: the use of hunting animals as partners in the hunt. From ancient times, dogs, raptorial birds, and even the hunting cats, particularly cheetahs and caracals, have been co-opted to the human side of this conflict, often carrying out the killing on behalf of their masters. Nature is set against nature, animal against animal.

The evidence that lions were ever successfully used in this way is scant, though Allsen cites some rumors of such use, made more dubious by the confusion of terminology about the great cats in most ancient sources (2006, 75).[4] Whatever the truth, the image of the king who not only confronts wild animals and subdues them but then turns them to his own use is a powerful one, which by hyperbole can easily be extended to the lion. The king not only hunts lions but enlists them to his advantage and uses them to hunt down other prey. The epitome of the destructive power of nature can be turned against the enemies of the ordered world of the kingdom.

A natural extension of this power is the use of wild beasts as the instruments of punishment and the guardians of the king's reputation and authority. This was bound up with a wider view that saw the attacks of wild beasts as a sign of divine punishment. The sovereign shows his sovereignty by his ability not only to control or tame the beast, but to embody it, turning its ferocity to his own ends, with the drama of the royal hunt as the seal of that metaphorical fusion. The sovereign shows his power over the beast by enlisting the power of the beast to establish his rule.

Yahweh's Royal Lion Hunt

Intriguingly, we find echoes of such use of lions by Yahweh. Not only does Yahweh himself act like a lion, but on several occasions he uses lions as his executioners. The disobedient man of God in 1 Kgs 13 is attacked by a lion that stands guard over his body, and the same fate is correctly predicted by another prophet for his disobedient fellow in 1 Kgs 20:35–36: "Because you have not obeyed the Lord, a lion will strike you dead as soon as you leave me." The role of lions as Yahweh's enforcers is quite explicit in

4. He cites the second-century writer Aelian as saying that India has many lions, the smaller of which can be trained to hunt deer. The possibility of confusion with cheetahs or even trained leopards is real, and the context is clearly far removed from the ancient Near East.

2 Kgs 17:25 with regard to the foreigners settled by the king of Assyria in Samaria: "When they first settled there, they did not worship the LORD; so the LORD sent lions among them which killed some of them." Yahweh and his sovereignty are defended by the very beasts against whom he elsewhere serves as protector.

Although this explicit use of lions as Yahweh's agents is relatively rare in the Bible, it may suggest that the metaphor of the royal hunt lurks behind other aspects of Israel's understanding of Yahweh and his role in the politics of the ancient world. The forces that dare to threaten Yahweh's rule can become tools of his will by being transformed into his pack animals. Could we see the development of a wider metaphor where the whole of the world known to the biblical writers can be seen as Yahweh's royal hunting park, his *paradeisos*, where the nations can be either his quarry or his hunting beasts, and Israel acts either as the spectator who is witness to the exercise of Yahweh's sovereign power or as the victim of the pack? Is this a scenario that lies behind the prophetic visions of the nations as the enemies of Yahweh, who must be put in their place, yet also at times as those who execute his commands? Israel, whom Yahweh defends against the predatory lions, can become, if it offends him, the target of his hunt when his lions are unleashed against them.

Indeed, Israel itself may explicitly become the lion that is hunted. Jeremiah 12:8 reads, "My own people acted toward me like a lion in the forest. She raised her voice against me—therefore I have rejected her." The tables are turned when Israel is represented as a lion that dares to threaten Yahweh, rendering her in turn the object of his wrath.[5]

The ferocity of Israel's enemies can be co-opted into Yahweh's hunting pack to harry and punish Israel's failures to maintain their special role in upholding and manifesting the ordering principles of his rule. In this understanding, Yahweh's sovereignty is not threatened by the disasters of Israel's history but strengthened and publicly demonstrated. Israel's destruction paradoxically becomes her sovereign's vindication. I suggest that this metaphor may be worth further exploration as a source for the Bible's exceptional strategy in finding a message of coherence in the incoherence of Israel's history.

---

5. This passage is discussed in Foreman 2011, 162–73.

Yahweh as Sovereign Beast

I would further suggest that this particular strategy and way of dealing with the paradoxes of the role of the sovereign has, because of the influence of the Bible, long resonances in political theology. In particular, the issue of the relationship between the human and the animal and how the definition of one affects the other has been the subject of intense scrutiny in the last couple of decades by a number of leading thinkers, including Derrida, Agamben, and Badiou. In his late seminars on *The Beast and the Sovereign* (2009–2011), Derrida offers extended meditations on the relationship between the animal and the political, well beyond the scope of this paper. As always, Derrida's discussion is complex and allusive and at times deliberately or unintentionally obscure and teasing to the point of irritation, but the juxtaposition of the biblical metaphor we have been exploring and this text can shed light on both.

This can be demonstrated by examining one particular paragraph in the seminar where Derrida is discussing Hobbes's *Leviathan*, one of the founding texts of contemporary political theory, written in the 1640s. It hardly needs pointing out that its title is the biblical name of the epitome of the beast as opponent of the divine. The paragraph in question deals with Hobbes's key assertion that the nature of the civil contract is that it can only be made between human beings. This means that Hobbes, controversially for his time, excludes any covenant with God as the basis of human society. Derrida interprets him as seeking to save the possibility of human sovereignty but points out a further implication:

> And what I would like to emphasize is that this exclusion of any convention with God will be, as it were, symmetrical with another exclusion, that of a convention with the beast. This symmetry of the two living beings that are not man, i.e. the beast and the sovereign God, both excluded from the contract, convention or covenant—this symmetry is all the more thought-provoking for the fact that one of the two poles, God, is also the model of sovereignty. (2009, 49–50)

Only man can make contracts, according to Hobbes, and this then defines man as against God and against the beasts, but with the strange consequence that, at least in this respect, God and beasts are allied in opposition to man.

In a characteristic and untranslatable pun, Derrida writes that this equation means that "Dieu *e*(*s*)*t* la bête," where the parentheses around the *s* allow the double reading of *et* (and) and *est* (is). His translator valiantly wrestles with the text here: "With or without the *s*, God is the beast/God and the beast," or as Derrida puts it, "God is/and the beast, with or without being" (2009, 50).

We might well feel that at this point Derrida is best left to his own devices, were it not for the fact that he elsewhere explores this association of God and the beast as the two excluded poles that define the human in an extended discussion of the story of the naming of the animals in Gen 2 (2008, 15–18). This is to be found in his essay "L'animal que donc je suis." This title is again an untranslatable pun: it can be translated as either "the animal that therefore I *am*" or "the animal that therefore I *follow*." The significance of this ambivalence for our discussion and for the understanding of an aspect of the biblical account of the human will become clear.

Being and Following in Genesis 2

Derrida undertakes quite an extensive exegesis of Gen 2 in this essay. In doing so, he draws heavily on André Chouraqui's idiosyncratic translation of the Bible (1998). Chouraqui replicates in French Martin Buber's attempt in his German translation to convey the syntax and etymology of the Hebrew in the target language, which leads Buber to rather peculiar German and, in Chouraqui's case, results in rather peculiar French. Using this translation, Derrida points out that in Gen 2 the naming is undertaken by the figure whom Chouraqui names as the solitary Ish before the creation of Ishah, not by the man-woman pair of Gen 1:26. Ish alone names the animals that God makes and then brings before him.

In the wider context of Gen 1 and 2, however, the one who names the animals comes *after* them; in chapter 1 the animals are created on the fifth and sixth days. This leads to the question: Who follows whom, namer or named? Note the allusion to the title "The animal that I am/follow." Derrida glosses over the details of the creation of the animals in 2:19, but stresses the tension between God's desire to oversee the naming and to leave the man free to name as he chooses. "God lets Ish call the other living things all on his own, give them their names in his own name, these animals that are older and younger than him, these living things that came into the world before him but were named after him, on his initiative, according to the second narrative" (Derrida 2008, 17).

Derrida then confesses that this moment of naming fills him with dizziness, a sense of vertigo that he connects to the feeling of being naked before his cat. This rather unexpected reaction refers to the fact that Derrida's discussion in "L'animal" notoriously has opened with an extended account of the shame that he feels standing naked before the gaze of his little cat.

This cat comes to have a profound significance in the discussion and relates more closely than might appear to the earlier discussion of the lion. As Tom Tyler puts it in an article on animals in philosophy,

> Despite appearances, Derrida's cat is wilder than the lion of Barthes or Aesop. She is not a cipher, nor an instance of "the animal," nor a stereotype. Derrida's cat is *fera*, following her own wishes, fancy free. She does not rage about with tooth and claw, but wanders from one room to the next, insistently roaming first this way, then that. She is, in short, an amiably unruly, indexical individual. (2007, 56–57)

Derrida links the feeling he has under his cat's gaze to his reaction to what he calls "God's exposure to surprise" (2008, 17). This raises another immediate paradox in that surprise is an experience that an omniscient being presumably cannot share. How can an all-knowing God be surprised? Yet does this inability not imply that there is a limit to omniscience? In Gen 2, according to Derrida's reading, God leaves himself open, in defiance of this logic, to being surprised by what the man may call the animal. Imagining Ish confronted by the first cat, Derrida writes, "I hear the cat or God ask itself, ask *me*, 'Is he going to call me, is he going to address me? What name is he going to call me by, this naked man … ?'" (2008, 18). At this point, Derrida implies that God's gaze and the animal's gaze can be equated. The feline and the divine, God and cat, are being overlaid.

The cat's gaze asks, "What will the man call me?" The biblical text never answers that question directly. Indeed, it is one of the peculiarities of the Hebrew Bible that it never acknowledges the existence of cats and so contains no word for them. One name that Ish could give, that, as Derrida later explains, "is a word that men have given themselves the right to give" (2008, 47), cannot be given at this point: the name "animal." Imagine God's face, if we may put it that way, if the man had pointed at each of God's varied creations in turn and named them "animal … animal … animal." That would be a surprise that would quickly turn to tedium and annoyance. "Animal" is not something you call an animal.

Indeed, much of Derrida's subsequent discussion is devoted to the unsatisfactoriness of the singular designation "animal," a problem of language that he encodes in the teasing term *animot*, a portmanteau of *animal* and *mot* (2008, 47). This is a homonym of the French plural *animaux* and therefore has unsettling effects on the French ear when used in conjunction with singular articles and verbs. Singularity and plurality are called into question by this coinage as they are by the equation of God and the cat. Two gazes or one? Derrida will not reply and neither does the Bible.

In both Derrida and the Bible, then, what it is to be human is delimited by being the point of coincidence of these two gazes. The man, the Ish, is caught between the gaze of the cat and the gaze of God, of the beast and the sovereign. This gaze is dizzyingly coincident. Both gaze, intent on knowing what he will say next. Responsibility to one is responsibility to the other.

This vision of the human as caught between and in two gazes seems to me to be borne out in the use of the metaphor of the lion within the Hebrew texts, as we have explored it. Israel is caught between the gaze of its enemies and its protector, between the wilderness and the temple, only to find that that gaze is dizzyingly one. Yahweh is the lion, beast and sovereign, protector and attacker. In other ancient cultures, that double gaze is directed at the person of the king, who is the one who embodies the sovereign beast. Precisely because in the Hebrew Bible this gaze is not directed at the singular person of the king, Israel as a community and also the individual reader of the text find themselves in front of that gaze of the beast and the sovereign.

What we do learn in Genesis is that the man shuns the gaze of both animal and God. The realization of nakedness causes man and woman to hide from God's gaze and to shield their naked bodies from any gaze. A further implication, however, of Derrida's discussion is that the very use of the word and category *animal* is itself an attempt to evade the gaze of the specific animal, the individual of another species, in the effort to build a community based solely on the human, as the man cleaves to the partner that was already part of him, bone of his bone, rather than cross the divide between human and beast, human and God. We might argue that that dilemma, and that almost inevitable response given this particular configuration of the gaze, has shaped Western attitudes both to politics and to the natural world thereafter.

By removing the screen of the king as sovereign beast, the biblical tradition locates the human before the inexorable gaze of the sovereign beast, characterizing the human as a point of answerability. In the evasion of this gaze, humans design the coverings of clothing, language, law, politics, and religion. Human society is a structure that enables evasion of the gaze of both God and beast, a more comfortable but perhaps untenable mode of existence.

Between God and Beast

Israel, however, is a special case. This is borne out by a recent study that comes from a very different starting point. In his magisterial work *Religion in Human Evolution: From the Paleolithic to the Axial Age*, Robert Bellah, writing as a sociologist, ventures into the realm of Israel's religion.[6] Following on the work of Stephen Geller in *Sacred Enigmas: Literary Religion in the Hebrew Bible* (2006), Bellah sees a key moment in the development of the distinctive religious life and textual traditions of Israel in the paradox of a theology conceived in terms of a royal vassal treaty without the king as mediator. In the terms we have been pursuing, this view is affirmed by the transfer of the royal metaphor of the lion to Yahweh, though Bellah does not deal specifically with this.

In a passage from another essay by Geller that Bellah quotes, further implications very similar to the ones I have drawn can be found. Geller argues that the development of monotheism goes hand in hand with the development of a particular idea of the human with a new stress on the responsible individual engagement with God laid as a task on every person in the community, not as part of a collective on whose behalf priest or king could act as proxy. This rethinking or redefinition of God is also a new definition of the human as person, Geller argues: "The numerical nuance of 'one' in the Shema is also true, not only in regard to God, but also to the believer" (2000, 286; Bellah 2011, 316–17). But redefining the human is also a redefinition of the boundaries of the nonhuman, whether that is the divine or the animal.

On this account, the function of the monarch as the focus of the gaze of God and beast is displaced as Israel insists on divine transcendence. This then opens the individual member of the society to that gaze in a way that makes new demands but may also call out new structures of defense

6. The main discussion of Israel's religion is in ch. 6, "The Axial Age I: Introduction and Ancient Israel" (Bellah 2011, 265–324).

against the gaze, the equivalents of the covering that the man and woman seek to hide their shame behind. The structures and strictures of the law are both the embodiment of that divine demand and a way of diffusing it. The laws of sacrifice and cleanliness embed the division between human and animal in the treaty. Animal and divine meet in sacrifice, after all, from which the human is excluded. A transaction between animal and God is enacted, where the animal stands proxy for the human. In the same way, this economy may explain why, when God reveals the mystery of his actions in his speech to Job in Job 38–41, his explanation climaxes in his engagement with animals that are as remote from the human as can be conceived: Behemoth and Leviathan. Job of all biblical characters knows what it is to experience the gaze of God as the gaze of the predatory beast. God sets out the reality of a world where Job as human in society can find that when the coverings of culture, property, and family are stripped away, a world where God and Leviathan glare at one another is uncovered and the frailty of the human is laid bare.

In the same way, when Derrida raises the question of "the animal that therefore I am (or follow)," he destabilizes the category of the human and of the "I" at a profound level. As Giorgio Agamben puts it in *The Open: Man and Animal*, the dividing line between human and animal runs through the individual man and woman: "And perhaps even the most luminous sphere of our relations with the divine depends, in some way, on that darker one which separates us from the animal" (Agamben 2004, 16). Whatever the validity of Derrida's position, and Agamben's, it is based in Derrida's biblical exegesis and one with which the ambivalent metaphorical use of the lion in the Hebrew Bible seems in accord.

The conclusion this points to is that to be human in the biblical imaginary is to be caught in the gaze of God and the animal. This is paradoxically a double gaze, from above and below, that defines the limits, upper and lower, of the human and also a single gaze, the gaze of the Lion King, of the Sovereign Beast, epitomized metaphorically in the gaze of the lion.

But lest we become entangled in existential and metaphysical issues of being, we must not forget the importance of the animal we *follow* in Derrida's formulation. In Lewis's Narnia, to revert to the beginning of this discussion, the great queen Jadis, who becomes the White Witch, has her own slogan, "Ours is a high and lonely destiny" (Lewis 2000, 30). That is the slogan of one who refuses to follow. As we have seen above, it makes all the difference where we stand in relation to a lion. To follow a lion is rather different from facing one, or being followed by one. This biblical economy lays on the reader, both as community and individual, this question: Faced by the gaze of the lion, do you follow or run?

Works Cited

Agamben, Giorgio. 2004. *The Open: Man and Animal*. Translated by Kevin Attell. Stanford, Calif.: Stanford University Press.

Allsen, Thomas. 2006. *The Royal Hunt in Eurasian History*. Philadelphia: University of Pennsylvania Press.

Bellah, Robert N. 2011. *Religion in Human Evolution: From the Paleolithic to the Axial Age*. Cambridge: Harvard University Press.

Chouraqui, André. 1998. *La Bible*. 3rd ed. Paris: Desclée de Brouwer.

Derrida, Jacques. 2008. *The Animal That Therefore I Am*. Edited by Marie-Louise Mallet. Translated by David Wills. New York: Fordham University Press.

———. 2009–2011. *The Beast and the Sovereign*. Edited by Michel Lisse, Marie-Louise Mallet, and Ginette Michaud. Translated by Geoffrey Bennington. 2 vols. Chicago: University of Chicago Press.

Foreman, Benjamin A. 2011. *Animal Metaphors and the People of Israel in the Book of Jeremiah*. Forschungen zur Religion und Literatur des Alten und Neuen Testaments 238. Göttingen: Vandenhoeck & Ruprecht.

Geller, Stephen A. 2000. The God of the Covenant. Pages 273–320 in *One God or Many? Concepts of God in the Ancient World*. Edited by Barbara Nevling Porter. Transactions of the Casco Bay Assyriology Institute 1. Chebeague, Maine: Casco Bay Assyriology Institute.

———. 2006. *Sacred Enigmas: Literary Religion and the Bible*. London: Routledge.

Lewis, C. S. 2000. *The Magician's Nephew*. Pages 10–72 in *The Complete Chronicles of Narnia*. London: Collins.

Smith, Alexander McCall. 2007. Review of Roberto Ransom. *A Tale of Two Lions*. Translated by Jasper Reid. New York: Norton. *New York Times*, January 26, 2007. Online: http://www.nytimes.com/2007/01/26/arts/26iht-idbriefs27F.4355571.html.

Strawn, Brent A. 2005. *What Is Stronger Than a Lion? Leonine Image and Metaphor in the Hebrew Bible and the Ancient Near East*. OBO 212. Fribourg: Academic Press.

Tyler, Tom. 2007. *Quia Ego Nominor Leo*: Barthes, Stereotypes, and Aesop's Animals. *Mosaic* 40:45–59.

Wittgenstein's Lion and Balaam's Ass: Talking with Others in Numbers 22–25

Ken Stone

Introduction

In his book *Animal Rites: American Culture, the Discourse of Species, and Posthumanist Theory*, Cary Wolfe refers to "the problem of the animal" as "a privileged site for exploring the philosophical challenges of difference and otherness more generally" (2003, 3). Wolfe argues that projects in contemporary cultural studies, which have increasingly and laudably critiqued "racism, (hetero)sexism, classism, and all other -isms," nevertheless "almost always remain locked within an unexamined framework of *speciesism*" (1, emphasis original). The assumptions and institutions associated with speciesism[1] have had particularly problematic consequences for our ability to treat animals ethically, as a growing literature on animal ethics indicates (see, e.g., Armstrong and Botzler 2009; Palmer 2010; Gruen 2011). However, the negative ethical effects of speciesism may fall upon other humans as well. For the category "animal" has served not simply to separate humans from other animals, but also to stigmatize those members of our own species whose differences confuse, confound, or frighten us. Rather than trying to understand our human others or allowing them to flourish in their differences, we all too often mark them as "animalistic," "beastly," or "monstrous," justifying thereby our oppression and neglect of them. Thus, instead of asking how we might develop a more robust humanism that distinguishes humans and animals more clearly, Wolfe argues, in agreement with various other "posthumanist" thinkers, that

1. For one attempt within religious studies to define and take seriously the concept of "speciesism," see Waldau 2002.

"our stance toward the animal is an index for how we stand in a field of otherness and difference generally, and in some ways it is the most reliable index, the 'hardest case' of our readiness to be vulnerable to other knowledges in our embodiment of our own" (2003, 5; cf. Wolfe 2010).

Like the field of cultural studies that Wolfe addresses, biblical scholarship has been reshaped in recent decades by numerous projects attempting to challenge "racism, (hetero)sexism, classism, and all other -isms." These challenges have taken a wide variety of forms. Nevertheless, it seems safe to say that questions about animals and species have been even less common on the research agenda of biblical scholars than in the fields of literary and cultural studies more generally. While a growing interdisciplinary interest in what Jacques Derrida (2008) calls "the question of the animal" has begun to have an impact elsewhere in the academy, biblical scholars have taken up that question only in the occasional article of ecological criticism or the occasional historical-literary study of animal symbolism, when they have taken it up at all. Even these studies, as important and interesting as they are (e.g., Strawn 2005; Forti 2008; Way 2011), remain at some distance from the emphasis on human difference and otherness that animates much contemporary biblical interpretation. And rare indeed is the article by a biblical scholar such as Heather McKay, who actually engages such contemporary issues as animal rights, animal consciousness, and "the human-centredness of literature and literary criticism" (2002, 127).

In the present essay, however, I would like to bring together a few of the contemporary issues signaled by Wolfe by staging a dialogue between Wittgenstein's lion and Balaam's ass. Balaam's ass will be known to readers of the Bible as the donkey who, in Num 22, becomes one of only two biblical animals to speak with human beings. As Balaam travels on his she-ass toward a Moabite king who wishes harm on the Israelites, a messenger of YHWH, with sword in hand, blocks Balaam's path. Balaam cannot see this messenger, but the donkey can. Three times, Balaam's ass makes a physical attempt to avoid the messenger. Each time Balaam beats her in frustration. After the third beating, YHWH opens the donkey's mouth, and a conversation takes place between Balaam and his ass.

Although one can find Balaam's ass wandering about in biblical and theological scholarship, Wittgenstein's lion has, so far as I am aware, never been introduced to biblical studies. Yet Wittgenstein's lion, like Balaam's ass, appears in a text that refers to conversation between humans and other animals. For in the latter pages of his *Philosophical Investigations*, Wittgenstein suddenly remarks, "If a lion could talk, we could not understand him"

(1958, 223). As Wolfe notes, Wittgenstein's statement "might very well serve as an epigraph to the debates that have taken place over the past century on animals, language, and subjectivity" (2003, 44). For language has often been understood as one of the principal marks of the boundary between humans and animals. Yet careful attention to the context for Wittgenstein's admittedly opaque statement, as well as some of the works that have commented upon it, reveals that human reflections on talking with animals can also lead quickly to an awareness of the challenges we face when we attempt to communicate with and understand one another. Wittgenstein's lion does not simply cross the boundary between human and animal. It also allows us to reflect on the boundaries that exist between human and human.

In the pages that follow, I will be reading the story of Balaam's ass in the light of issues raised by reflection on Wittgenstein's lion. I have chosen to do so partly because Balaam's ass, like Wittgenstein's lion, appears in a context where references to talking with animals are inextricably intertwined with an acute awareness of differences among humans. The biblical story of Balaam and his ass can no doubt be read in many different ways today, as indeed it has been across history, starting already in the ancient world (see, e.g., Greene 1992; Burrus and Keefer 2000). I do not intend to replace multiple interpretations of the story with "the correct meaning" or even "the most plausible meaning in its original context." I wish, rather, to explore the possibility that new light can be shed on biblical texts when they are read in dialogue with some of the texts from posthuman animal studies, a growing body of literature that I consider particularly relevant to the times in which all of us read the Bible today. Similarly, my goal in bringing Wittgenstein's lion together with Balaam's ass is not an exploration of Wittgenstein's thought. I am not particularly concerned that my essay could be taken as another example of one common approach to Wittgenstein's work in which, in the words of one of Wittgenstein's exasperated expositors, "his writings are plundered for aphorisms" (Grayling 2001, 1). To the contrary, it is precisely the appearance of Wittgenstein's aphorism in several texts from animal studies that interests me here.

Thus, in the next section of this paper, after some attention to the immediate literary context for Wittgenstein's remark, I will follow Wittgenstein's lion into a couple of texts written by other writers, including not only Wolfe but another writer whose work Wolfe also engages, the late Vicki Hearne. These texts are read in such a way as to highlight issues and emphases that will serve as a frame for my reading of the story of Balaam and his donkey in the book of Numbers. Whereas language and communication are often taken as signs of the differences that distinguish humans from animals, I will suggest that the story of Balaam's ass and the chapters around it give us an opportunity to make connections between difficulties of language and communication and other types of "difference and otherness," to borrow Wolfe's phrase, in the relations between humans and animals, between humans and humans, and between humans and God.

Wittgenstein's Lion

"If a lion could talk, we could not understand him." As Wolfe notes (2003, 44), the significance of this remark by Wittgenstein is itself not so easy to understand. Read in isolation, it might seem to be a typical statement from that Western philosophical tradition that has long attempted to draw a sharp line between human and animal. For this tradition, which has recently been critiqued by Derrida and others, has often identified language as one of the principal criteria used to define the human by distinguishing it from all other living creatures (Derrida 2008; cf. Calarco 2008; Oliver 2009; Naas 2010).

The immediate literary context of Wittgenstein's remark, however, may point us in other directions. In *Philosophical Investigations*, Wittgenstein, just prior to his remark about the lion, has been reflecting on some of the complexities involved in the relationship between language and thought. These complexities include the challenge of discerning hidden thoughts. The thoughts that concern Wittgenstein here are human thoughts, which may be hidden from other humans. The mere presence of language and talking does not necessarily reveal those thoughts. For as Wittgenstein notes, "If I were to talk to myself out loud in a language not understood by those present my thoughts would be hidden from them" (1958, 222). Our thoughts are not always understood by other human beings even when we are talking in their presence.

From this observation, Wittgenstein moves to consider what he calls "guessing thoughts." Here the possibility of reaching some conclusions about hidden phenomena seems not to be ruled out entirely:

> "What is *internal* is hidden from us."—The future is hidden from us. But does the astronomer think like this when he calculates an eclipse of the sun?
>
> If I see someone writhing in pain with evident cause I do not think:

> all the same, his feelings are hidden from me. (Wittgenstein 1958, 223, emphasis original)

Note that our ability to draw conclusions seems to depend here not upon language, but rather upon our observation of physical phenomena. We can make predictions about the heavenly bodies, based on our observations of them. More significantly for my purposes, we may guess at the feelings of another by observing carefully certain movements of "someone's" body, in this case, a body in pain. It seems, then, that the absence of access to internal thoughts does not always rule out our ability to draw conclusions, including conclusions about the other.

Wittgenstein, however, moves from this observation back to an emphasis on the challenges that face us when we try to understand other human beings who *do* use language:

> We also say of some people that they are transparent to us. It is, however, important as regards this observation that one human being can be a complete enigma to another. We learn this when we come into a strange country with entirely strange traditions; and, what is more, even given a mastery of the country's language. We do not *understand* the people. (And not because of not knowing what they are saying to themselves.) We cannot find our feet with them. (1958, 223, emphasis original)

Once again, the difficulties that human beings face when we attempt to understand other human beings are not removed solely by the presence of language. As Wittgenstein recognizes, we can learn the language of another country and still fail to understand the people. And it is only a couple of lines after this that we finally meet Wittgenstein's lion: "If a lion could talk, we could not understand him." Wittgenstein then returns to the matter of "guessing": "It is possible to imagine a guessing of intentions like the guessing of thoughts, but also a guessing of what someone is actually *going to do*" (223, emphasis original).

In the context of *Philosophical Investigations*, then, Wittgenstein's lion does not function in any simplistic way to reinforce the boundary between human and animal. Wittgenstein seems rather to notice the obstacles that humans often face when we attempt to understand the other, such as the inhabitant of "a strange country with entirely strange traditions." The difficulty of understanding the nonhuman other appears in the same context as, and secondarily to, the difficulty of understanding human others. Our inability to understand the talking lion is therefore not placed in contrast to transparent communication among humans. It appears alongside recognition that we often fail to understand, and have to make guesses about, other human beings, even in some cases when they use a language that we know.

In the larger context of Wittgenstein's work, both of these difficulties seem to emerge from the fact that understanding does not follow simply from language in any narrow sense, but depends upon what Wittgenstein calls "a form of life" (1958, 11). Wittgenstein appears to be saying that we could not understand this talking lion because he does not share our way of life, and we do not share his. But this is also true for some humans. We cannot always understand the human from another country with whom we can talk, and we could not understand the lion if he could talk. The statements are in certain respects parallel, because neither the human from the "strange country" nor the lion shares our "form of life."

In a fascinating reflection on Wittgenstein's lion, however, Vicki Hearne refers to Wittgenstein's statement as "the most interesting mistake about animals I have ever come across" (1994, 167). Hearne, who came to philosophy as an accomplished animal trainer and a published poet, notes as a "minor mistake of fact here" that "lions do talk to some people, and are understood." The particular people Hearne is referring to are lion trainers, whose lives may depend upon being able to reach conclusions about a lion's intentions and signaling their own intentions to the lion. For Hearne, there is a sense in which it is useful to say that the trainer and the lion both know that the command "Stay" is referring to a specific posture of the body: "[T]he lion and the trainer both know exactly *what they are talking about*" (170, emphasis added).

Notice, in Hearne's statement, that both the trainer and the lion are "talking." This way of talking about talking may seem odd to most of us. We understand Hearne's English sentences, grammatically; but we are not sure that we understand her statement. And we may be tempted at this point to emphasize that Hearne is, after all, a poet, an inhabitant of that "strange country" in which language users follow the "strange tradition" of using language in strange ways—and leave the matter at that.

If we look to the larger context of Hearne's work, however, we discover that Hearne is also trying to take seriously Wittgenstein's philosophical observation that "To imagine a language is to imagine a form of life" (1958, 8; cf. Hearne 2000, 4). Our spoken language is meaningful within a particular lived context that does not consist solely of spoken words. We might keep in mind also Wittgenstein's statement that "the term '*language-game*' is meant to bring into prominence the fact that the *speaking* of language is part of an activity, or of a form of life" (1958, 11, emphasis original). For Hearne, serious interaction between a trainer and an animal seems to be something like a form, or way, of life that is shared between two living beings. As Cora Diamond notes, the "work" with, and of, animals that most interests Hearne "is itself a distinctive language-game," which is "inseparable from the trainer's activity" (2003, 20 n. 19). For within the engagement between trainer and animal that constitutes animal training, spoken words make up only a subset of the elements that, in their structured and differentiating relationships to one another, make meaningful communication possible. There are also, for example, gestures, postures, and forms of physical contact. There are pragmatic goals, which may or may not be shared; and expectations, which may or may not be met. There are relations of authority and power. But there are also at times what Hearne calls "mutual autonomy and trust" (2000, 34).

Thus, by working with an expanded definition of language, derived partly from her experiences as a trainer but in dialogue with Wittgenstein and other philosophers influenced by Wittgenstein, such as Stanley Cavell, Hearne is able to suggest that some lions and humans do converse. And although, as Wolfe notes critically (2003, 48–50), Hearne may not move entirely beyond the humanist assumptions of the tradition in which she stands, her suggestion that animals and trainers do in some sense "talk" appears to undermine the sharp line that has so often been drawn between humans and other animals on the basis of claims about language.

However, even as Hearne problematizes the conventional appeal to language as a way of reifying categories of "human" and "animal," she also pluralizes animals in their relations to humans and to language. For if conversations between humans and animals take place within a shared way of life, individual animals are positioned differentially for participation in such conversations. Not all lions work with lion trainers, for example. Moreover, there are significant distinctions to be made between species where conversations and types of conversations are concerned. These distinctions do not depend solely upon such criteria as intelligence, brain size, or genetic proximity to human beings. One does not "talk" with a horse, which responds with particular sensitivity to physical touch, in exactly the same way that one "talks" with a dog, which responds much more readily to gestures. And in spite of her claims on behalf of speaking lions, Hearne is attentive to the differences between what we conventionally call domesticated and nondomesticated species, differences that cannot be simply identified with the distinction between animals that have been trained and animals that have not. There are domesticated animals that have been trained, and others that are untrained; and there are "wild" animals that have been trained (including those lions who converse with their trainers) and others that are untrained. For Hearne, all of these differences matter for the types of talking we can do with animals. As Donna Haraway notes in a discussion of Hearne's approach to animals, "Not all animals are alike; their specificity—of kind and of individual—matter" (2003, 52). Instead of asking whether "animals" talk, we may be better served by exploring the communication that takes place between this animal, here, and that human, there.

Some of the implications of these sorts of complexities for the conversations that Hearne imagines us having with animals become clear in her discussion of the chimpanzee Washoe, one of the most famous of the chimpanzees, gorillas, and orangutans who were taught sign language by humans during the latter half of the twentieth century. There is much that is unsettling about the great ape language experiments and the debates they generated. Certainly the accounts of the experiments themselves easily lead to questions about the methods used and assumptions held by some of the experimenters (cf. Linden 1986; Savage-Rumbaugh and Lewin 1996; Fouts 1997; Gill 1997, 9–28; Fudge 2002, 117–28; Hess 2008; Hillix and Rumbaugh 2010). Yet the vehemence and disdain with which many critics of such experiments have responded to the signing apes may lead one to suspect that far more is at stake for the critics than scientific method, intellectual curiosity, or academic rigor. Entire conferences have been organized in opposition to the notion that any sort of actual language learning could be taking place with signing chimpanzees. As Hearne notes, "the rush to the typewriters to report on them," often by writers who have never actually encountered the signing apes, "suggests that when Washoe signs 'Give Washoe drink,' we face an intellectual emergency" (2000, 18). And this, for Hearne, is one of the most important questions raised by the ape language experiments: What is the intellectual emergency occasioned by attempts to find out what would happen "if a chimpanzee could talk," to quote the Wittgensteinian title of one article on the philosophical implications of chimpanzee signing (Gill 1997, 9–28)?

Hearne, for her part, observes wryly that "it is surprising that 'I don't know, I haven't met her' is rarely the response given to 'Can Washoe talk?'" Hearne therefore goes to meet her. But whereas Hearne is not reticent about referring to her interactions with the dogs and horses that she trains as "conversations," her encounters with Washoe and some of the other signing chimpanzees turn out to be difficult to fit into the framework that her previous experiences as an animal trainer have led her to construct.

In the first place, Hearne meets Washoe at a compound for wild animals used in movies and commercials. And although Hearne has worked with wolves, her greater familiarity with and sensitivity to the particularities of domestic animals have consequences for her approach to conversation: "These are wild animals. *I don't know how to talk to them*, and as an animal trainer I feel anxious about this" (2000, 33, emphasis added). She is aware that she does not share a form of life with these particular species of animals.

There is, moreover, a matter of constraints. Hearne is no sentimentalist when it comes to animals, though she cares about them deeply. A critic of animal rights discourse (though for complex reasons, as Haraway [2003, 48–54] notes), Hearne can also be at times disdainful of positive reinforcement training methods, preferring more controversial approaches that many other trainers have abandoned. In her encounter with Washoe, however, she finds herself troubled by the fact that adult chimpanzees, even those using sign language, must be kept in cages or restrained by leashes and cattle prods. The reason for such constraints is simple enough: notwithstanding deceptive media appearances by juvenile chimps, adult chimpanzees are inevitably unpredictable and often dangerous to their human cousins. But Hearne has written positively about the experience of what she calls working with animals "at liberty" or "off lead." She is aware that only a few species of animals, and often only a smaller number of individuals within those species, have what she calls approvingly "the capacity for cooperation that makes work at liberty possible." She refers in particular to "many, if not most, dogs, horses, kitty cats, donkeys, and elephants" (1995, 448). Humans working with such animals can, in Hearne's view at least, occasionally enter into something very close to Buber's "I-Thou" relationship. Hearne explicitly rules out wolves and chimpanzees from this sort of work. Nevertheless, confronting Washoe and her fellow signing chimps, Hearne confesses that she is "appalled and grieved because the chimps are in cages": "What is offended is the dog trainer's assumption that language or something like vocabulary gives mutual autonomy and trust. I grieve, but not for Washoe behind bars. It is language I grieve for" (2000, 34).

Yet, admirably, Hearne refuses to assume that genuine communication with all animals must cohere with the protocols and conventions familiar to her from her own work with specific animals. She allows her own structured interactions with animals, especially dogs and horses, to keep her open to other possibilities for language and conversation, even when confronting something as uncanny as a signing chimp. Thus, observing Washoe as Washoe interacts with the humans who communicate with her, Hearne experiences "a shock of recognition" (34). She is not convinced that anyone can ever "prove" or "disprove" what, exactly, Washoe is doing. But as she watches Washoe take a walk one day with both human and ape companions, a walk that is necessarily constrained by leashes and hooks, but that also involves communication about other items perceived by both human and chimpanzee, Hearne ultimately concludes that Washoe and her human interlocutors "are talking—are doing what I call talking. … I am looking at *some condition of language*" (39, emphasis added).

Somewhat surprisingly, Hearne acknowledges that this conclusion is frightening. It is frightening in part because conversation with Washoe does not remove the possibility that Washoe or one of the other signing chimpanzees could kill their interlocutors. The "mutual autonomy and trust" that she has taken to be crucial for good conversation with dogs and horses turn out to be ambiguous when conversing with potentially dangerous chimps. And this fact leads Hearne ultimately to some disturbing reflections, not only about chimpanzees but also about that most dangerous of all the great apes, the human one:

> If I acknowledge that Washoe is talking, then of course I have to notice profoundly that *language does not prevent murder*. If language does not prevent murder, and if it may in fact cause murder, then I am at a loss. For I have nothing, really, but talk to go on. If the gestures and interactions of various sorts that I observe really do add up to "going for a walk," and if Washoe is dangerous despite that, then I may be thrown into confusion, may suffer, as Othello did, from skeptical terror, and may want to deny Washoe's personhood and her language rather than acknowledge the limits of language—which can look like a terrifying procedure. In the same way I may want to find a certain kind of relief by saying that rapists or the assassins of Anwar Sadat are religious fanatics *or are in some other way inhuman, not of that kind of being in which I can participate*. (2000, 40, emphases added)

Against this temptation to deny personhood, Hearne affirms those who continue to talk into the face of fear and real danger, whether such talkers are Washoe's handlers, interacting with a communicative but dangerous chimp; or the human enemies who, a few years prior to the writing of Hearne's essay on Washoe, put aside their own fears and signed the Camp David accords.

Here we begin to recognize that, for Hearne, the "limits" we face when we grapple with the problems raised by talking animals are related to the limits we face in our knowledge of others, including human others. As with Wolfe, so also with Hearne, reflection on animals becomes an occasion "for exploring the philosophical challenges of difference and otherness more generally" (Wolfe 2003, 3). And for both writers, our fears about the other—human and animal—are partly fears about the limits of our own knowledge.

When we are dealing with animals, such fears about the limits to our knowledge do not arise only in the company of signing chimpanzees. Indeed, animals that are less like ourselves than chimpanzees, but more acclimated to our presence, might prove to be unsettling in different ways. So, for example, in a reflection on "the conversation we call the art of horsemanship" (Hearne 2000, 108), Hearne notes the difficulty created for human riders by the fact that horses can "read" bodily contact and touch in a far more sensitive manner than humans do. This sensitivity startles us because our human methods for discerning, and generating knowledge about, the world tend to rely primarily upon sight. For humans, "seeing is believing"; and we tend to privilege sight when we argue about truth and skepticism. Animals, however, may perceive things and know things about the world by deploying other senses that are less developed in humans. A dog, for example, relies upon a sense of smell, an ability to detect scent, that we cannot see and that we hardly know how to speak or think about. And a horse is far more sensitive than we are to messages received through the skin. As a consequence, a horse will attempt constantly to interpret the bodily movements of its human rider: "Every muscle twitch of the rider will be like a loud symphony to the horse" (108). In an ideal scenario, a skilled rider will be in tune with this feature of a horse's perception of the world; and we can "speak of the wonderfully rich and subtle *conversation* that goes on in this sort of riding" (112, emphasis original). This is truly a conversation across boundaries of otherness. But more often, our knowledge about the other will be characterized by "asymmetry" (109); and the rider may become aware that the horse, without fully understanding its human rider, nevertheless understands some things about the human rider that the rider does not understand. Perhaps this is one of the reasons, Hearne muses, that horses are sometimes called "the messengers of God" (114). They know things about us that we do not know.

And with this conjunction of animals, God, and the limits of our own human knowledge, we return to Hearne's discussion of Wittgenstein's lion. For as it turns out, Hearne, who does not refer to God very often, does bring up God again in her discussion of Wittgenstein's lion. Having taken a detour through Hearne's writings on animal communication, we may now be in a better position to understand what Hearne means when she suggests that some "lions do talk" to some people. Paradoxically, however, Hearne goes on to remark that "[t]he lovely thing about Wittgenstein's lion is that Wittgenstein does not leap to say that his lion is languageless, only that he is not talking" (1994, 169). This leaves room, in Hearne's view, for "the possibility that the lion does not talk to us because he knows we could not understand him" (170). Thus Wittgenstein's lion

> in his restraint remains there to remind us that knowledge … comes sometimes to an abrupt end, not vaguely "somewhere," like explanations, but immediately. His lion, regarded with proper respect and awe, gives us unmediated knowledge of our ignorance. Whether we choose to be terrified, chatty, or cautious in response has no effect on the lion. (173)

By serving as an indication of the limits of our knowledge, Hearne suggests, the silence of Wittgenstein's lion may be a bit "like the silence of God." For as Hearne recalls (with a gesture to Harold Bloom), certain kabbalistic traditions refer to a kind of contraction or self-limitation of the divine, a self-limitation that makes room for creation. If we think of the silence of Wittgenstein's lion as in some sense comparable to this sort of divine self-limitation, Hearne suggests, we may conclude "that the reticence of this lion is not the reticence of absence, absence of self-consciousness, say, or knowledge, but rather of tremendous presence, the presence of the king of the beasts, after all, and so the reticence of all consciousness that is beyond ours, in some accounts of creation" (170). We do not understand Wittgenstein's lion, who will not talk to us. But then, Hearne seems to be suggesting, we also may not understand God.

Balaam's Ass

The difficulties involved in understanding God, other humans, animal companions, and the boundaries and relations among them are fully on display in the biblical story of Balaam's ass. For if, in Hearne's writing, a lion who refrains from talking to humans is compared with a God who contracts and moves inward, in the book of Numbers a donkey who does talk to humans is associated with a God who moves outward, by speaking with humans but in very obscure ways. I want to suggest that our reading of the biblical text is enriched when the text is juxtaposed with both Wittgenstein's lion and the work of writers such as Hearne and Wolfe who have tried to come to terms with that lion. This juxtaposition allows us to underscore, first of all, the extent to which the story of Balaam is structured around the challenge of understanding and communication across lines of difference and similarity. Recall that, in Wittgenstein's discourse, our inability to understand the talking lion is related to our inability to understand other humans, such as those who live in other lands. So too Hearne links the challenges that we face when we attempt to communicate with animals to the challenges that we face when we attempt to communicate with humans across boundaries that separate us. As her references to the Camp David accords acknowledge, such boundaries between humans are often tense and subject to violence.

In a comparable fashion, the story of Balaam and his donkey is structured around boundaries between humans. These boundaries separate lands and traditions, and they are conflict-ridden. For the story takes its point of departure from the recurring biblical conflict between Israel and Moab.

Throughout the Hebrew Bible, the relationship of difference and similarity between Israel and Moab is simultaneously constitutive and ambiguous. On the one hand, Israelite identity is constituted by its difference from Moab, a difference marked by such biblical phenomena as the negative attitude taken in some texts toward intermarriage between Israelite men and Moabite women. Thus national and geographical differences between Israel and Moab are inseparable from gender and sexual difference (Havrelock 2011, 40–63). This negative stance toward intermarriage is explicitly tied to traditions about Balaam in Deut 23:3–6 (4–7 MT) as well as Neh 13:1–2, which refers to the Deuteronomic statute. For both of these passages cite, as a rationale for prohibiting intermarriage with Moabites and

Ammonites, the fact that the Moabites attempted to hire Balaam to curse the Israelites in Num 22.

On the other hand, biblical genealogies understand Israel and Moab to be related. Abraham's father, Terah, is the great-grandfather of Lot's son, Moab (Gen 11:27; 19:37). The book of Ruth, moreover, suggests that David's great-grandfather married a Moabite woman, which would seem to make David an example of one of those descendants of improper union with Moabites who, according to Deut 23:3 (4 MT), should not be admitted to the assembly of YHWH.

Both biblical literature and nonbiblical sources, such as a famous inscription of the Moabite king Mesha, also testify to military conflict between Israel and Moab. Yet these same sources indicate that the two nations, in addition to being geographically proximate, were linguistically and religiously quite similar (see Parker 2002, 50–51). Although the language and script in which Mesha's inscription is written are often called "Moabite," they are linguistically very similar to Hebrew. And we learn from this inscription that the Moabites shared with Israel the controversial practice of putting an entire defeated populace to death in devotion to the national deity. Indeed, they used the same vocabulary to talk about it. The Moabite king Mesha even claims to have carried out that practice against the Israelites themselves, slaughtering Israelites to his own god Chemosh in much the same way that the Israelites slaughtered enemies for their god YHWH.

Thus the borders between Israel and Moab—including geographical and national borders, ethnic borders, religious borders, and sexual borders—are in the Hebrew Bible simultaneously policed, ambiguous, and fraught with danger. Any story that deals with those borders, such as the story of Balaam, is necessarily overdetermined by a complex relationship between difference and proximity, a relationship that both results from, and produces, fear of the other.

In Num 22 that fear of the other is expressed among other ways in animal symbolism. When the Moabites hear about the Israelites, they are afraid of their large numbers; and they complain to the elders of Midian that "now the multitude will lick up everything that is around us, just as an ox licks up the grass of the field" (22:4).[2] Ethnic and national differences are represented here in terms of species difference. The Israelites are

2. Translations from Hebrew to English are my own.

not understood as a collection of many individuals and subgroups with specific interests, habits, desires, and so forth, but rather as an undifferentiated herd of beasts. The Moabites seem to have concluded that the Israelites are, in Hearne's words, "in some ... way inhuman, not of that kind of being in which I can participate" (2000, 40). But whereas Hearne writes with some admiration about those who persevere in their attempts to talk across lines of difference, including species difference, even in the face of danger, the Moabites choose what is all too often the alternative course. Instead of going to meet the Israelites and talk to them, the Moabite king Balak, motivated apparently by fear of this herd of foreign invaders, sends for the prophet Balaam and asks him to curse Israel.

The prophet Balaam, too, complicates the lines of difference and otherness that are supposed to be constitutive of Israelite identity. For one thing, traditions about Balaam are found not only in the biblical literature that we associate with Israel, but in extrabiblical, non-Israelite literature as well. The modern discovery in Jordan of an ancient text about Balaam, probably dating contemporaneously with ancient Israel, complicates our notion of biblical tradition by giving us a rare nonbiblical account of a character referred to in the Hebrew Bible. This character acts in some ways like a biblical prophet; but he is focused on matters other than those described in the biblical account of Balaam, speaks with and about other gods, and acts in ways that can be interpreted against the background of religious roles known to us from elsewhere in the ancient Near East (see Hackett 1980; Moore 1990; Greene 1992).

Although Balaam is not himself an Israelite, in the book of Numbers he speaks words that Israel's God gives to him (e.g., 22:8; cf. 22:38; 23:5). Indeed, Balaam refers to YHWH by name several times in chapters 22–24, and even calls him "my god" at one point (22:18). At least in chapters 23 and 24, Balaam the non-Israelite is able to talk to, and hear from, Israel's deity without any apparent difficulty.

As represented in chapter 22, however, God's conversations with Balaam are hardly straightforward. Initially, God tells Balaam at night that he should *not* go with Balak's messengers (22:12). When Balak sends more messengers, on the other hand, God explicitly commands Balaam to "rise and go with them, but only the word that I speak to you will you do" (22:20). As Michael Moore observes, "the deity demonstrates a perplexing propensity for reversal—a disturbing divine characteristic which surfaces repeatedly in the Balaam cycle" (Moore 1990, 101). Indeed, just after Balaam saddles his donkey and sets out for Moab at God's command, the narrator unexpectedly tells us that "God flared up in anger that he was going, and a messenger of YHWH put himself in the road as an adversary" (22:22). God's anger here would appear to represent a second divine reversal.

It is worth noting that the "adversary" sent by God is referred to literally, in Hebrew, as a *śāṭān*. Although the word *śāṭān* in the Hebrew Bible does not have the demonic connotations that will later become attached to it, and God does on other occasions raise up human adversaries who are referred to with the same terminology (e.g., 1 Kgs 11:14, 23), nevertheless it is unusual to find this language attached to a messenger from YHWH. Yet the language is surely less surprising than God's apparent changes of mind about Balaam's journey.

If it is not strange enough that God becomes angry with Balaam in Num 22:22 for setting out on the very path that God has just told him to follow, only a few verses later (and after one conversation between Balaam and his donkey and another between Balaam and God's messenger) the messenger tells Balaam once again to "go with the men" (22:35), with no explanation whatsoever of the reason for the anger that caused God to send the messenger as an adversary in the first place. Balaam may be able to talk to God, then; but this ability can hardly lead to unambiguous conclusions about God's intentions when God gives contradictory messages about whether Balaam should go to Moab or not. Balaam can speak with God; but, much like Wittgenstein's visitors to "a strange country," neither Balaam nor the reader of Numbers can "find their feet" with this particular God. God remains, to borrow Wittgenstein's word, an "enigma." And, more worrisome, that Balaam can talk to God does not prevent God from nearly killing him (22:33). The story thus seems to illustrate Hearne's observation that language and murder can go together. God appears to be nearly as unpredictable as, and arguably more dangerous than, the signing chimpanzees.

In Hearne's discourse, as we have seen, an enigmatic God is associated both with Wittgenstein's lion and with horses, "the messengers of God." In Numbers God is also associated with animals. The animals associated with God in the story of Balaam are not limited to the horse's equine cousin, the donkey. On two occasions, the oracles of Balaam state that God is like the mighty horns of a wild ox (23:22; 24:8). These same oracles compare Israel to a lion and a lioness (23:24; 24:9), in a manner reminiscent of some other biblical passages (e.g., Gen 49:9; Deut 33:20, 22). As we have seen, Balak also compares the Israelites to cattle. Thus the lines between animal, human, and deity are blurred in the story of Balaam even apart from the incident involving Balaam's ass.

The scene where that ass appears, however, does emphasize Balaam's lack of knowledge while simultaneously bringing the donkey into closer association with the God whom Balaam has been trying to obey. The messenger of God stands in the road with sword in hand, and the she-ass knows that God's messenger is there even though Balaam does not, and before God intervenes to allow her to speak. The text does not tell us that God allows the donkey to see, or that God prevents Balaam from seeing. Like her fellow animal character, the talking snake of Genesis, this donkey simply knows things about God that the human characters do not know. More significantly, the donkey *sees* the messenger while Balaam cannot (Num 22:23). Since, as Hearne and Wolfe both note, human knowledge typically privileges sight, the "asymmetry" (Hearne 2000, 109) of informed vision between animal and human in this story underscores Balaam's ignorance. As George Savran observes (1994, 35 n. 7; 2005, 86), that ignorance is made more ironic by the contrast between Balaam's inability to *see* the messenger sent by God in the *daytime*, and his earlier successful attempts to *hear* from God at *night*.

Although the donkey is armed with knowledge of the divine messenger that Balaam does not share, she is initially incapable of speaking to the less informed human prophet. Like many animals who have interacted with humans, no doubt, she is in the frustrating position of being unable to use human language to tell the human that she knows things he cannot know. She is, however, able to use another sort of communication, which is mentioned by both Wittgenstein and Hearne: the language of bodily movement. Three times the donkey attempts to move her body in order to avoid the armed messenger of God: once by leaving the road and moving into a field, once by scraping against a wall, and once by sitting down under Balaam. She does not give up in her effort to avert disaster. The donkey's stubbornness, apparently associated with the species already in the ancient world (Way 2011, 98 and passim), serves a positive function here.

One might expect Balaam to understand that something unusual is happening beneath him. As the donkey herself points out after God opens her mouth, she has been carrying Balaam for a long time (22:30). They have some sort of relationship. We might even say that she and the prophet have come to share a "form of life," to borrow Wittgenstein's phrase. And we may recall here that donkeys are among those few animal species identified by Hearne as being unusually able to "cooperate" successfully with humans with some degree of autonomy (Hearne 1995, 448). Yet each time the donkey moves her body to avoid the danger in front of them, Balaam responds by striking her. Indeed, after the donkey's third attempt to avoid the messenger, this time by sitting down, the narrator states that Balaam "flared up in anger" at her, using exactly the same Hebrew terminology for becoming angry that was applied to God's anger at Balaam in verse 22.

After Balaam has struck the donkey a third time, "YHWH opened the mouth of the she-ass and she spoke to Balaam" (22:28). God intervenes during the abuse of an animal. Indeed, the first question the donkey asks Balaam is not whether he sees the messenger of YHWH, but what she has done to Balaam that led Balaam to beat her. The question of animal suffering precedes the matter of divine encounter. Yet amazingly, Balaam, rather than acknowledging that something extraordinary is taking place, says in response to his talking donkey that he would kill her if he had a sword in his hand; for she has, in his view, made a fool out of him (22:29). Her ability to speak to him in verse 28 does not remove his desire to kill her in verse 29. Language cannot prevent murder, even when the language comes from an ass.

This she-ass, however, is a clever interlocutor. She uses a rhetorical question to point out, and to compel Balaam to acknowledge, that during all of the time she has been working with him, she has never previously acted this way (22:30). The clear implication is that Balaam should have gotten her message. She assumes that the donkey and her rider, much like Hearne's lion and trainer, should both know what they are talking about. The problem lies not in her inability to talk in his spoken language, but in his unwillingness to try to understand her bodily language. Balaam's response to his donkey relies not upon what Hearne calls "mutual autonomy and trust" (2000, 34) but rather upon brute force and domination.

Of course, once God opens Balaam's eyes (22:31), Balaam can also see God's messenger standing in the road. Belatedly, he learns what the donkey knew all along. And although Balaam has been talking to God already in the story, God's messenger now confirms that he would have killed Balaam and let the donkey live if the donkey had not managed to avoid him. The donkey, who had previously been unable to speak to Balaam, and whom Balaam has expressed a desire to kill, has managed to save Balaam's life. This animal, who can see the divine more clearly than a prophet who delivers God's message, turns out to be a trustworthy companion for the owner who would have killed her, "a she-ass who proves to be not at all asinine," as Heather McKay puts it (2002, 138).

In contrast, the God whose message Balaam is supposed to deliver would have taken Balaam's life. Balaam, having learned this from God's messenger, understandably offers to turn back if his mission displeases God (22:34). Yet the messenger tells Balaam to proceed with the men sent by Balak. His only caution to Balaam is that "only the word that I speak to you, it you will speak" (22:35). This is almost exactly what God has told Balaam already in verse 20. No new conditions are put in place. Thus, while God's insistence upon Balaam's obligation to speak only as God speaks may be reinforced by this encounter (Way 2009, 50–51; 2011, 186–87), we still are not given a reason for God's anger at Balaam or for the adversary's intention to kill him. Given the use of identical language for God's anger at Balaam and Balaam's anger at the ass, we may even begin to suspect that God's anger is just as irrational as Balaam's, if not more so.

Ulrike Sals notes in a postcolonial reading of what Sals calls the "hybrid" story of Balaam that this strange tale involves both "interspecies communication" and "human discommunication" (2008, 317). The clearest example of "interspecies communication" in the story is obviously the biblical representation of a donkey using human language to communicate with a prophet who cannot see what the donkey sees. And it is possible that this exchange between Balaam and his ass represents a kind of reversal of cosmic order that stands in continuity with other traditions about Balaam. For the Deir ʿAllā text, though fragmentary and quite difficult to read in places, appears to include several references to reversals within the animal world. In Meindert Dijkstra's translation, for example, "the swallow is challenging the eagle, the nestlings of the vulture the ostrich, ... the mother dove preys on the father dove ... hyenas heed admonition ... the piglet is chasing the [lion's?] cub," and so forth (Djikstra 1995, 48–49). The story also bears some similarities to the interspecies conversation between Achilles and his horse Xanthus in the *Iliad*, as Kenneth Way notes (2011, 189).

However, it is important to underscore the point that "interspecies communication" in Numbers is not limited to the dialogue between Balaam and his ass. Balaam's conversations with God cross the species barrier as well. Indeed, God is explicit about God's nonhuman status in Balaam's second oracle: "God is not a man who will lie, or a human being who changes his mind" (23:19). The irony of this assertion, of course, is that changing one's mind is exactly what God appears to do in the story, among other places at the point where God becomes angry with Balaam for doing what God told Balaam to do. But our inability to find consistency in God's actions in this story may simply underscore the force of the distinction God makes between the human species and the divine species. Like Balaam, but unlike Balaam's ass, we as readers cannot seem to understand what God is doing. To reappropriate Hearne's language about Wittgenstein's lion, a lion that she compares to God, divine inscrutability "remains there to remind us that knowledge … comes sometimes to an abrupt end, not vaguely 'somewhere' … but immediately" (Hearne 1994, 173). Our knowledge comes to an end abruptly in our attempt to make sense of the divine.

However, as Sals notes, the story about Balaam is not only a story of "interspecies conversation" but also a story of "human discommunication" (2008, 317). For the difficulties that Balaam has in understanding his donkey are replicated in the difficulties that Balak subsequently has in understanding Balaam. The difficulties are represented in a threefold manner in each case. Three times Balaam's donkey refuses to move forward, to the consternation of Balaam, who lashes his donkey in anger. And in three different places Balak's hired prophet Balaam refuses to curse Israel as Balak asks him to do. Balaam blesses the Israelites instead, to the consternation of Balak, who, much like Balaam responding to his donkey, lashes out at Balaam in anger. Indeed, Num 24:10 tells us that "Balak's anger flared up at Balaam," using the same vocabulary that the narrator has previously used to describe both Balaam's anger at the donkey and God's anger at Balaam. Balaam continues to explain that he can only say what God allows him to say; yet Balak, who can understand Balaam's language, and seems to be familiar with Balaam's God, cannot seem to understand what Balaam is saying. He apparently continues to believe that God may allow Balaam to curse Israel in another location. Balak's inability to comprehend Balaam thus parallels Balaam's own earlier inability to comprehend his donkey and God. If Balaam earlier was unable to "find his feet" with God, Balak cannot seem to "find his feet with" Balaam.[3]

While Balaam's oracles include blessings for Israel, they have troublesome consequences for others. These others include both humans and other animals. Before each of the three oracles that Balaam delivers at Balak's request, Balaam and Balak build seven altars and sacrifice a bull and a

3. Here my reading is both similar to and different from that of Savran (1994, 35–36), who draws the parallel rather between Balaam's inability to understand the donkey and Balaam's inability to understand Balak.

ram on each altar. God may have opened a donkey's mouth and Balaam's eyes in time to stop the beating of the donkey, but these forty-two bulls and rams as well as other oxen and sheep sacrificed by Balak for Balaam (22:40) all fall victim to that "non-criminal putting to death" that Derrida associates with the "sacrificial structure" of Western thought and culture, including explicitly "religions" (Derrida 1995, 278). Their animal deaths, as sacrificial deaths, are considered legitimate. Consistent with the unusual logic of such passages as Exod 13:12–13 and 34:19–20, which associate firstborn donkeys with firstborn humans as animals that may be redeemed from the obligation to kill the firstborn, both the human Balaam and his donkey are saved from death in Balaam's story, while other livestock die.

Just as other livestock are not as lucky as Balaam's she-ass, however, not all humans are as lucky as Balaam. Balaam's first oracle concentrates primarily on Israel. This is largely true for Balaam's second oracle as well, but there is an intensification of Israel's readiness for conflict in the second oracle: 23:24 compares Israel to a lion and lioness, who do not lie down until they have eaten prey and drunk blood. Balaam's third oracle carries this intensification further. Just before calling Israel a "lion," the oracle notes that Israel will "eat" the nations that are his enemies (24:8). If much (though not necessarily all) of the Bible assumes that humans legitimately eat other animals, so also this oracle assumes that Israel may "eat" its enemies, exactly as the Moabites feared in 22:4. The line between a "non-criminal putting to death" that is applied to animals and a "non-criminal putting to death" that can be applied to humans is unstable, as Derrida notes.

After this third oracle, Balak in frustration tells Balaam to go home. He is ready to stop talking. Yet Balaam delivers one more oracle of blessing for Israel. This oracle too speaks about the destruction of enemy nations. However, the intensification of conflict continues. For in the fourth oracle, several specific nations are named, including Moab (24:17). Ultimately, then, Balak's plan to hire Balaam to curse the Israelites in order to prevent them from becoming a threat to the Moabites has the opposite result: the Israelites have been blessed, and the Moabites have been cursed.

After Balaam's fourth oracle, both Balaam and Balak do depart. Initially this appears to be the end of Balaam's story. There is, however, one final twist in Balaam's contribution to Israel's story. Balaam, as we have seen, talks to and tries to obey Israel's God. Although most of his oracles refer to Israel in the third person, in 24:5 Balaam also uses the second person to address Jacob/Israel. Balaam thus can talk not only to Israel's God, but to Israel as well. We therefore might assume that Balaam, who blesses Israel at God's command, would be blessed by God in return and praised by the Israelites.

In Num 31:8, however, we discover instead that the Israelites kill Balaam in a battle commanded by God; and this tradition is repeated in Josh 13:22. The rationale for the killing of Balaam is murky. In Num 31:16 Moses, who has otherwise been absent from Balaam's story, blames a "word of Balaam" retrospectively for encouraging Midianite women who have caused the Israelites to do wrong at Peor. When this incident at Peor is narrated in Num 25, Moabite rather than Midianite women are made responsible for Israelite worship of "Baal of Peor" (25:3). However, an Israelite man named Zimri does bring a Midianite woman named Cozbi to his family (literally "brothers"); and both of them are killed by Aaron's grandson, Phinehas, with a spear through the stomach. This execution appears to stop a plague that has been killing Israelites. Although no explicit connection is made between Cozbi and the worship of Baal, a command from YHWH to Moses to "harass the Midianites" in 25:17 does make a rather obscure connection between Cozbi, the Midianites, and deception at Peor. However, in spite of the assertion of Moses in 31:6, Balaam is nowhere mentioned in the narration of events at Peor in chapter 25. Balaam does deliver his third oracle from "the top of Peor," where he is taken by Balak (23:28); but the oracle itself involves blessing and has no connection to the events at Peor in chapter 25. In chapter 24, in fact, Balaam returns "to his place" (24:25), before the events at Peor are recounted.

Now it is possible that ancient traditions or knowledge about Balaam that no longer exist would help us understand the negative link made in Num 31 between Balaam and Peor. However, while attempts have been made to reconstruct the missing historical background of this more negative attitude toward Balaam (e.g., Lutzky 1999), such attempts necessarily remain speculative unless additional historical evidence is discovered. Thus, rather than trying to speculate about missing pieces of tradition or an unknown historical background, I would like to reframe the problem of the relation between Balaam (chs. 22–24) and Peor (ch. 25) by underscoring certain shared ideological-cultural anxieties that involve what Wolfe calls the "field of otherness and difference" (2003, 5). All four of these chapters are grounded in biblical conflicts between Israel and Moab. As noted above, these conflicts play out in terms of complex relations of similarity and difference. The incident at Peor, however, which directs hostility toward sexual relations between Israelite men and Moabite and Midianite women in particular, fits within a larger set of texts that turn Moab into

Israel's "anti-nation" by associating the Moabites with sexual and gender deviance (Havrelock 2011, 40–63). And although it has become common to note that anxieties about sex and gender are often intertwined with anxieties about ethnic and national differences, sexual and gender differences also can be productively analyzed in relation to species difference and the question of the animal (see, e.g., Oliver 2009, 131–74). Indeed, given the association made in Genesis between Eve and the talking snake, and given the fact that Balaam's talking donkey is female, the possibility of gendered and sexualized connotations of talking animals in the Hebrew Bible might deserve further investigation.

In the present context, though, I simply want to suggest that the link made by Moses in Num 31 between Balaam and the events at Peor may reflect an underlying anxiety about the improper mixing of categories thought to be constitutive of identity. This anxiety cuts across any number of analytical boundaries, including those that often separate matters of gender, sexuality, nation, religion, race, and ethnicity. And if, as Wolfe suggests, "our stance toward the animal is an index for how we stand in a field of otherness and difference generally" (2003, 5), we should not be surprised to find that biblical texts that reflect Israel's "border anxiety" (Stone 2005, 46–67) also articulate that anxiety to animal matters. Indeed, we know that this happens in other texts such as Lev 20, which links distinctions between clean and unclean animals (v. 25) to distinctions between proper and improper sexual activity and distinctions between Israelite and non-Israelite identity.

If we read the link Moses makes between Balaam and Peor against this background, we may begin to see that the relationship between the story of Balaam in Num 22–24 and the story of Peor in Num 25 has to do with more than simply contiguity of chapters. Just as the sexual union of Israelite men with Moabite and Midianite women represents a sexualized and gendered confusion of what are understood to be the ethnic and religious boundaries of Israelite identity, so also Balaam's conversation with his donkey in Num 22, which also takes place against the background of Israelite and Moabite conflict, represents a confusion of the boundary between (male) human and (female) animal.

Nevertheless, the death of Balaam at the hands of the Israelites remains mysterious. Although multiple traditions and cultural anxieties are no doubt involved in the story of Balaam as we have it, that story is given to us in a form that seems as enigmatic as the God to whom it testifies, and as unusual as the donkey who speaks in it. And in the end, whatever the reason, Balaam's ability as a prophet to talk does not prevent even his own murder at the hands of those he blessed, and at the direction of the God he attempted to serve.

Conclusion

In her essay on Wittgenstein's lion, Hearne notes that most of us encounter talking animals only in children's stories. This has consequences for the types of attention we give to talking animals; for "most talking animals in the usual run of story spring from arrangements that erase the need to earn, work at, learn understanding" (Hearne 1994, 168). We imagine that such stories are simple, and that they have nothing to show us about the complexities of life, of language, and of talking with others. Philosophical reflection on Wittgenstein's lion shows us instead that understanding is always complex. And attention to other lions, those lions Hearne has met who do talk to their trainers, shows Hearne something else. These lions

> are not anything like so reticent as Wittgenstein's. Their otherness is not so absolutely unalterable. They have personalities, temperaments, moods, and they can be voluble about all this, sometimes chatty, sometimes (when they are working) radiating a more focused informativeness. Nor are the exchanges and the work in question suffering-free. In particular, they are not free of the suffering that accompanies failures of understanding, refusals and denials of the sort that characterize many relationships. (Hearne 1994, 172–73)

These "lions do talk" with their trainers, Hearne insists, but such exchanges are, like all exchanges between conversation partners, simultaneously "an important mode of knowledge" and "a mode that fails continually, so often indeed that its successes have an arcane and dubious look" (173–74). Our knowledge of others is necessarily incomplete. We will not always understand the other; indeed, we do not always try. And our inevitable failures represent what Hearne, following Stanley Cavell, calls the "tragedy" of life, "a process that includes denying in various ways the consciousness of the other" (173).

It is tempting to dismiss the story of Balaam's ass as nothing more than a fable that has somehow made its way into the Bible, or a children's tale that teaches simple lessons about a God who is too often imagined to be speaking clearly to and through prophets. A careful reading of the story and the chapters that surround it, however, reveals a more complex and troubling piece of literature. The violence produced by our fears of otherness is very much on display here. Instead of talking with the Israelites he and the other Moabites fear, Balak looks for a way to curse them. Ultimately, this decision is self-defeating and results in a curse on Moab. But Balak's recourse to violence rather than dialogue is replicated by the Israelite leaders Moses and Phinehas, who, faced with ethnic, religious, gendered, and sexual difference in chapter 25, respond with killing rather than conversation.

The alternatives that are available to violent refusals to talk do not, however, always include easy dialogue; and conversation does not guarantee happy results. The characters who do talk with each other in this story do not always comprehend each other. Their differential positions of nation, ethnicity, religion, gender, and species make conversation difficult. Even those who share a "form of life" can find that communication breaks down. And understanding is even harder to reach when one's conversation partners appear to keep changing their positions, as God does with Balaam. Language does not automatically prevent violence, and the difficulties of dialogue can lead to tragedy. Prophets who bring blessing rather than curse can still end up being slaughtered by those they bless. And those who attempt to avoid disaster for themselves and their traveling companions may, like Balaam's determined she-ass, be beaten for their efforts. But such attempts remain necessary if there is to be any hope for survival at all. Those who persist in trying to communicate with others across multiple lines of difference should be admired for their stubborn refusal to give in to resignation, even if they sometimes appear asinine.

Works Cited

Armstrong, Susan J., and Richard G. Botzler, eds. 2009. *The Animal Ethics Reader*. 2nd ed. London: Routledge.

Burrus, Virginia, and Tracy Keefer. 2000. Anonymous Spanish Correspondence; or the Letter of the "She-ass." Pages 330–39 in *Religions of Late Antiquity in Practice*. Edited by Richard Valantasis. Princeton: Princeton University Press.

Calarco, Matthew. 2008. *Zoographies: The Question of the Animal from Heidegger to Derrida*. New York: Columbia University Press.

Derrida, Jacques. 1995. "Eating Well," or the Calculation of the Subject. Pages 255–87 in *Points … : Interviews, 1974–1994*. Edited by Elisabeth Weber. Translated by Peter Connor and Avital Ronell. Stanford: Stanford University Press.

———. 2008. *The Animal That Therefore I Am*. Edited by Marie-Louise Mallet. Translated by David Wills. New York: Fordham University Press.

Diamond, Cora. 2003. The Difficulty of Reality and the Difficulty of Philosophy. *Partial Answers* 1.2:1–26.

Dijkstra, Meindert. 1995. Is Balaam Also among the Prophets? *Journal of Biblical Literature* 114:43–64.

Forti, Tova L. 2008. *Animal Imagery in the Book of Proverbs*. Supplements to Vetus Testamentum 118. Leiden: Brill.

Fouts, Roger. 1997. *Next of Kin: My Conversations with Chimpanzees*. New York: Avon.

Fudge, Erica. 2002. *Animal*. London: Reaktion.

Gill, Jerry H. 1997. *If A Chimpanzee Could Talk: And Other Reflections on Language Acquisition*. Tucson: University of Arizona Press.

Grayling, A. C. 2001. *Wittgenstein: A Very Short Introduction*. New York: Oxford University Press.

Greene, John T. 1992. *Balaam and His Interpreters: A Hermeneutical History of the Balaam Traditions*. Brown Judaic Studies 244. Atlanta: Scholars Press.

Gruen, Lori. 2011. *Ethics and Animals: An Introduction*. Cambridge: Cambridge University Press.

Hackett, Jo Ann. 1980. *The Balaam Text from Deir ʿAllā*. Harvard Semitic Monographs 31. Chico, Calif.: Scholars Press.

Haraway, Donna. 2003. *The Companion Species Manifesto: Dogs, People, and Significant Otherness*. Chicago: Prickly Paradigm.

Havrelock, Rachel. 2011. *River Jordan: The Mythology of a Dividing Line*. Chicago: University of Chicago Press.

Hearne, Vicki. 1994. Wittgenstein's Lion. Pages 167–74 in *Animal Happiness: A Moving Exploration of Animals and Their Emotions*. New York: Skyhorse.

———. 1995. A Taxonomy of Knowing: Animals Captive, Free-Ranging, and at Liberty. *Social Research* 62:441–56.

———. 2000. *Adam's Task: Calling Animals by Name*. 1986. Repr., Pleasantville, N.Y.: Akadine.

Hess, Elizabeth. 2008. *Nim Chimpsky: The Chimp Who Would Be Human.* New York: Bantam Dell.

Hillix, W. A., and Duane Rumbaugh. 2010. *Animal Bodies, Human Minds: Ape, Dolphin, and Parrot Language Skills.* New York: Kluwer Academic/Plenum.

Linden, Eugene. 1986. *Silent Partners: The Legacy of the Ape Language Experiments.* New York: Ballantine.

Lutzky, Harriet. 1999. Ambivalence toward Balaam. *Vetus Testamentum* 49:421–25.

McKay, Heather A. 2002. Through the Eyes of Horses: Representation of the Horse Family in the Hebrew Bible. Pages 127–41 in *Sense and Sensitivity: Essays on Reading the Bible in Memory of Robert Carroll.* Edited by Philip R. Davies and Alastair G. Hunter. Journal for the Study of the Old Testament Supplement Series 348. London: Sheffield Academic Press.

Moore, Michael S. 1990. *The Balaam Traditions: Their Character and Development.* Society of Biblical Literature Dissertation Series 113. Atlanta: Scholars Press.

Naas, Michael. 2010. Derrida's Flair (For the Animals to Follow…). *Philosophy Today* 40:219–42.

Oliver, Kelly. 2009. *Animal Lessons: How They Teach Us to Be Human.* New York: Columbia University Press.

Palmer, Clare. 2010. *Animal Ethics in Context.* New York: Columbia University Press.

Parker, Simon. 2002. Ammonite, Edomite, and Moabite. Pages 43–60 in *Beyond Babel: A Handbook for Biblical Hebrew and Related Languages.* Edited by John Kaltner and Steven L. McKenzie. Society of Biblical Literature Resources for Biblical Study 42. Atlanta: Society of Biblical Literature.

Sals, Ulrike. 2008. The Hybrid Story of Balaam (Numbers 22–24): Theology for the Diaspora in the Torah. *Biblical Interpretation* 16:315–35.

Savage-Rumbaugh, Sue, and Roger Lewin. 1996. *Kanzi: The Ape at the Brink of the Human Mind.* New York: Wiley.

Savran, George W. 1994. Beastly Speech: Intertextuality, Balaam's Ass and the Garden of Eden. *Journal for the Study of the Old Testament* 64:33–55.

———. 2005. *Encountering the Divine: Theophany in Biblical Narrative.* Journal for the Study of the Old Testament Supplement Series 420. London: T&T Clark.

Stone, Ken. 2005. *Practicing Safer Texts: Food, Sex and Bible in Queer Perspective.* London: T&T Clark.

Strawn, Brent A. 2005. *What Is Stronger Than a Lion? Leonine Image and Metaphor in the Hebrew Bible and the Ancient Near East.* Orbis biblicus et orientalis 212. Fribourg: Academic Press.

Waldau, Paul. 2002. *The Specter of Speciesism: Buddhist and Christian Views of Animals.* New York: Oxford University Press.

Way, Kenneth C. 2009. Animals in the Prophetic World: Literary Reflections on Numbers 22 and 1 Kings 13. *Journal for the Study of the Old Testament* 34:47–62.

———. 2011. *Donkeys in the Biblical World: Ceremony and Symbol.* Winona Lake, Ind.: Eisenbrauns.

Wittgenstein, Ludwig. 1958. *Philosophical Investigations.* 2nd edition. Translated by G. E. M. Anscombe. Oxford: Blackwell.

Wolfe, Cary. 2003. *Animal Rites: American Culture, the Discourse of Species, and Posthumanist Theory.* Chicago: University of Chicago Press.

———. 2010. *What Is Posthumanism?* Minneapolis: University of Minnesota Press.

Part 3
Bodies in Crisis

Sick with Love: The Musical Symptoms of a Shtetl-Bound Shulammite in Waszinski's *Dybbuk**

Heidi Epstein

Introduction: New Correlations of Love and Grotesque Eroticism in the Song of Songs

S. Ansky's Yiddish play *The Dybbuk* and Michal Waszinski's 1937 film adaptation thereof have been described as Jewish versions of *Romeo and Juliet*, *Wuthering Heights*, *Pyramus and Thisbe*, or *Tristan and Isolde*.[1] Given that a musical rendition of the Song of Songs figures prominently in both play and film, why does Chonen and Leah's albeit lethal game of lovers' hide-and-seek in the film not prompt comparisons with the Song's tale of love? Readers' utopic pigeonholing of the biblical love story may explain this myopia. But the central presence of the Song in musical form, as well as Fiona Black's conceptualization of grotesque bodies in the Song and the latter's evocation of "love's darker dynamics," triggered my recog-

* I wish to thank Francis Landy for initially bringing my attention to this musical setting of the Song, and thanks to the following people for their invaluable comments upon this paper at various stages of its development: Caroline Bassett, Fiona Black, Esther Frank, Jennifer Koosed, Jacob Sagrans, Rob Seesengood, and Chip Whitesell.

1. Ben Brantley (1995 and 1997) cites choreographer Pearl Lang's reference to *The Dybbuk* as "a Jewish *Romeo and Juliet*" in two separate reviews of two different productions of Tony Kushner's adaptation of *The Dybbuk*. Brantley (1995) also likens *The Dybbuk* to other "love-beyond-the-grave classics like 'Wuthering Heights.'" Naomi Seidman (2003) references *Tristan and Isolde*. Along with these two love stories, Ira Königsberg also compares the play's lovers to Pyramus and Thisbe, and all these love stories in his view depict "a series of pairs, frequently lovers, in world art, pairs of individuals who are remarkable for both their sameness and their desire to fuse" (1997, 36).

nition of untapped structural homologies between the film and the biblical text as well as a resistant reading of the film's beautifully lyrical *Shir ha-Shirim* as a grotesque musical body.[2] This essay forms part of a larger project in which I explore contemporary musical afterlives of the Song that produce new, musically induced allegorical registers within the text, allegorizing as these settings do, via acutely material sets of dissonant amatory gestures and conventions, the thoroughly mediated nature of love as a cultural practice.[3] *Shir ha-Shirim*'s grotesque musical body, along with the other settings of the Song that I study, consequently invite a resituation of the biblical text within the *musical* discourse of love as a cultural practice, and encourage the construction of the Song's religious and theological meanings from this new context.

By exploring the body imagery in the Song with a grotesque heuristic, Black was able to formulate a compelling theory as to what purpose such ambiguous amatory imagery serves for the lovers in the text and even for the readers who wrestle to make sense of the body imagery in the *waṣf*s: "Love is a conflictual site where the lover must encounter the conflict of his or her own self. … In imposing signs of the abject on each other's bodies [by way of grotesque imagery], the lovers replay the psychic drama of identity formation" (2009, 228). Here Black enlists Kristeva: "In other words, in seeing the abject on the other, the lover replays love's origins, abjecting what must be thrown away (the mother) and desiring that which cannot be attained (the Ideal), and in the process, constantly reaffirming the place in this process for a third party, that which has been created

2. Ira Königsberg discusses the musical setting of the Song, but in standard allegorical terms as well as archetypal, psychological ones: the first performance of *Shir ha-Shirim*—outside in a pastoral setting and among the *batlonim* ("pious idlers")—"universalizes the song" and "emphasizes the God sung to in the song as the creator of the universe." In this act it is thus "a love song from the people of Israel to the Lord God" (1997, 37). When Chonen and Leah sing it later, it expresses not only their otherwise repressed erotic and sexual longing for each other but also a more global "burning desire for unification 'towards the One'" that the love story itself between Leah and Chonen allegorically enfleshes (37, quoting Kristeva 1987, 98). This desire for self-dissolution into a greater Being (a psychological goal that he contends drives so much religious experience) supposedly "returns one to the primary and original fusion of the child with the mother" (37).

3. See, for example, my readings of Steeleye Span's "Awake, awake," and the Pixies' "I've Been Tired" (Epstein 2009), and my reading of Penderecki's "*Canticum canticorum Salomonis*" (Epstein 2011).

solely for the Other" (228).[4] Concomitantly, readers struggling with the text's grotesquerie "confront mirrors of the earliest [conflicted] desires in their [own] constitution as subjects" (230), and also confront reminiscences of the ambivalence and vulnerabilities that have plagued their own quests for love. All these selves in love, the Song implies, inevitably take risks, risks that can be mortal, though usually not so: more likely, lovers "risk … death of the self as it struggles to configure itself in relation to the other. … Grotesque figurings of lovers to each other may reflect tensions and inconsistencies—darker moments, times of doubt, loss of drive, the quest for possession, envy, perhaps even repulsion, if only fleeting" (236).

But perhaps the darker dynamics of love and desire, at least for romantics among us, lie in their socioculturally constructed nature—the galling ways in which cultural conventions and, say, *religious* politics and practices of love shape, hamper, and mediate who we desire, the very terms of our attractions and endearments. Intrapsychic and intersubjective explanations of romantic subject formation, even those attentive to the gendered, heteronormative politics at work therein, may not afford a metacritical, culturally semiotic interrogation of love *in se*, or consider *the culturally constructed nature of love* as a generative matrix for both romantic subjectivity and for the meaning of grotesque bodies in the Song for readers today.

What readings of the Song's grotesquerie are produced if love is conceptualized in more ideological-critical terms? For example:

1. Social psychologist Roy Baumeister classifies romantic love and romantic marriage among other human "myths of higher meaning" (1991, 58). Myths of higher meaning impose "stable concepts and ideas" on a reality that is in fact "a relentless process of change." Love (composed of "passion, intimacy, and commitment")[5] feeds a false sense of existential

---

4. Black explains further here that one must separate from the mother to individuate, and thus"[t]he abject is that which marks the rejection of the mother" (2009, 226), a distancing signified in the Song by way of grotesque imagery. Conversely, the idealized other is in effect an image of the idealized self who is posited "as a substitute for the mother who is lost" (227). The self also constructs "a third element, an Other, that sets the amatory system going. This Other makes it possible for the subject to recognize someone who is like herself; in other words, not the mother, and not the ideal set up in place of her, but an Other who has traversed the same ground on the road to subjectivity" (227). Such is the intra- and intersubjective "conflictual site" that a love relationship involves, comprising as it does both the abject and the ideal.

5. I have synthesized two sources for this very brief sketch of Baumeister's frame-

permanence when it is "idealized as a permanent and unchanging state" (70). Not only do myths of higher meaning promise "stability and permanence," these collectively defined ideals also socialize human beings according to institutionalized and normalizing sets of attitudes, values, and behaviors (149ff.). Romantic love is thus a regulatory fiction that functions politically to circumscribe human sexual activities in ways that conserve social stability.

2. Critical theorist Lauren Berlant debunks the "pre-ideological" immunity that love enjoys in feminist and queer theory as follows:

> The installation of romantic love as the fundamental attachment of humans has been central to the normalization of heterosexuality and femininity in consumer culture; it has become a way of expressing desires for normal life. Conversely, it also marks the rhetoric of rights, and desires for attachments beyond the possessive instrumentalities of capitalism. Because, more than anything, the desire for love congeals utopian drives to disorganize the self on behalf of better future organizations, it bears the weight of much ideological management and pedagogy, defining the normativity of the modern self much more than "sexuality" as a category does. (2001, 440)

Religious traditions, of course, participate in this pedagogical economy of love. Especially pertinent to my wish to supplement psychoanalytic interpretations of the Song's amatory conflicts with more sociopolitical explanations thereof, Berlant continues: "One might recast Foucault here to view psychoanalysis as a science of organizing the self through the pseudo-nondiscipline of normal/formal love, a science that tracks the obstacles to love's 'mature' expression. Foucauldian categories of pathogenic sexuality could then be seen as the detritus of normal love's failures to organize the subject" (440–41).

3. In *Romantic Utopias: Love and the Cultural Contradictions of Capitalism,* sociologist Eva Illouz emphasizes that love is "a complex emotion interweaving stories, images, metaphors, material goods, and folk theories" (2003, 6), one that cannot therefore be explained metaphysically or purely psychologically as transcending "the social order" or "the realm of commodity exchange" (2). It is better understood as a "mythology"

---

work. His fuller elaboration of a model of love and its three components "passion, intimacy, and commitment" can be found in his ch. 7, "Passionate Love, Domestic Bliss" (1991, 145–81).

enlisted today as a vehicle for "utopian transgression" of the daily grind (6–7), even though, paradoxically, the concrete actualization of such transcendence entails "rituals of consumption" that effectively commodify the romantic love people turn to for spiritual reprieve (8).

Black would no doubt acknowledge that the social inevitably plays a role in shaping the Kristevan psychoanalytic model of amatory subject formation that she adopts to read both the grotesque bodies in the Song and the latter's affects on readers, but the notion of love as a regulatory fiction that preserves social stability and disciplines sexuality is not a key analytical presupposition for her. What I propose is, in effect, simply a qualitative and quantitative expansion of Black's intertextual,[6] grotesque analyses of the Song's language of love and its afterlives. To do so, I shall devote more attention to the *socio*psychic or sociopolitical genesis of grotesque eroticism in another intertext—Waszinski's film *The Dybbuk*.

Attempting to conduct more comprehensive sociopsychic analyses of love and romantic subjectivity can be controversial, because, for example, psychoanalysis and cultural studies are often thought to be incompatible interdisciplinary conversation partners due to the antithetical theories of the subject they invoke.[7] Nevertheless, certain film and cultural theorists (e.g., Farmer 2000; Silverman 1992; de Lauretis 1994; Frosh 1997; Donald 1989, 1991; Žižek 1991) have effected discursive rapprochement via psychosocial conceptualizations of fantasy. This methodological starting point, in turn, renders film a form of "public fantasy" (Cowie 1984, 102), and obviously these interpretive lenses are particularly helpful to me here, because the text to which I am applying and expanding Black's grotesque heuristic in a more sociocultural register is a film. These interdisciplin-

6. Black discusses Anna Swan, the quasi-mythical Nova Scotian giant who seems akin to the Shulammite in her romantic negotiations, and Den Hart's literalist illustration of the Shulammite. In an attempt to understand more about the Shulammite's interpersonal amatory idiosyncrasies, Black reflects upon the story of Anna Swan: "a Nova Scotian giant, who measured almost eight feet at her full height, and who lived much of her life as a transplanted Canadian in the United States, working for P. T. Barnum. Anna is an historical personage, but Susan Swan (a distant relative?) has recast her story in fictional form in her novel *The Biggest Modern Woman in the World*" (2009, 229–30; see Black's discussion, 231–37). Den Hart's literalist graphic translation of the *waṣf*s grotesquerie upon the Shulammite's body consists of a cartoon that appeared in *The Wittenberg Door* (1978); see Black's comments on the drawing (2009, 9–11).

7. See Brett Farmer's summary of this debate (2000, 43–52).

ary scholars are indebted to Lacan's sociopsychic understanding of fantasy. Lacan shifted discussions of fantasy in important ways by emphasizing the crucial role of fantasy, not only for constructing both imaginary and symbolic subject positions, but also *social* reality itself. Both Freud and Lacan actually insisted upon the "bipolar" genesis of fantasy and the centrality of fantasy to reality and meaning construction. In his discussion of Freud's model of fantasy, for example, Leonardo Rodriguez insists that "although the subject regards his fantasy as his private property and his most intimate and idiosyncratic possession, the fantasy is the precipitate in the subject of formations which are beyond the limits of subjectivity and intersubjectivity—formations which are present in myths, legends, fairy tales, stories and works of art of different times and civilizations" (1990, 101).

Lacan's later, more "sociolinguistic" model goes beyond Freud in its dissolution of an earlier traditional dichotomy between the subject and the object. Catherine Belsey's and Yannis Stavrakakis's comments are helpful here; to show the relevance of Lacan's notion of fantasy for sociopolitical analysis in *Lacan and the Political*, Stavrakakis writes: "What has to be stressed is that the domain of fantasy does not belong to the individual level; fantasy is a construction that attempts, first of all, to cover over the lack in the Other. As such it belongs initially to the social world; it is located on the objective side, the side of the Other, the lacking Other" (1999, 51). According to Belsey, Lacan's texts produce a composite portrait of this lacking Other that incites desire and drives fantasy construction. It is a multivalent knot of forces, one that ultimately blurs the boundaries between subject and object: the Other consists of (1) the symbolic order; (2) the unconscious; (3) the other as love object or object of desire; (4) "the subject-presumed-to-know" (i.e., one's analyst); and (5) the transcendental signifier that allegedy "guarantees" "meaning and truth in the symbolic" (e.g., "God"; Belsey 1994, 60).

Fantasy is primary to human thought and action for Lacan, because "the human condition is marked by a quest for a lost/impossible enjoyment" (Stavrakakis 1999, 46) that the Other supposedly might remedy. One attempts to (re)create this "lost/impossible enjoyment," say, for example, through romance, material consumption, and family life—all are fantasmatic placeholders for the originary plenitude that human beings deludedly believe they experienced in their infancy while symbiotically bonded to an Other (the Mother). Fantasy "offers the promise of an encounter with this precious *jouissance*, an encounter that is fantasized as covering over the lack in the Other and, consequently, as filling the lack in the subject"

(46). Given these dialectical dynamics, Lacan encourages bifocal attention to the individual and the social in psychoanalytic interpretation. Stavrakakis concludes: "Although in common sense usage and even in some psychoanalytic writing fantasy is opposed to reality, such a view of fantasy cannot be sustained within psychoanalytic theory; this is clear from the beginning in Lacan's theory of fantasy" (62).[8]

Alongside Lacan and Freud, film theorists also appeal to Laplanche and Pontalis's influential 1968 essay, "Fantasy and the Origins of Sexuality." Cultural studies and film scholar Brett Farmer, for example, summarizes the authors' similarly "dialectical" understanding of fantasy as "the product neither simply of the subject's 'internal' imagination nor of culture's 'external' impositions but the negotiational coarticulation, or 'setting,' of both" (2000, 56). According to Laplanche and Pontalis, certain primal fantasies or libidinal scenarios, moreover, "are always constructed and generated culturally; they come to us through the cultural discourses of history—most specifically, through 'the history or the legends of parents, grandparents and the ancestors: ... this spoken or secret discourse, going on prior to the subject's arrival, within which he must find his way'" (1968, 18; cited in Farmer 2000, 55).

The Dybbuk is almost a crass elucidation of this multigenerational and sociopsychic genesis of fantasy and the romantic subject formation it can produce. With the Song as "sound track," the film depicts the "darker dynamics of love" that will attend any amatory aspirations that religious tradition and cultural convention produce. In the film, fathers' dreams of the future, even without direct verbal transmission of the same to their children (and this is supposedly the story's Hasidic mystical twist), are ardently, unconsciously pursued by their young. Here love and the lovers' bodies, even the music I shall argue, become grotesque, not as some necessary developmental phase in the intersubjective negotiation of love's darker dynamics, but due to the paternalistic, I daresay patrilineal, nature of desire that grounds and drives the entire plot. Men harness the musical setting of the Song, moreover, to drive their fantasies forward, to translate

8. Lacan might even be considered a social constructionist of sorts, argues Stavrakakis, but for one decisive distinguishing feature within his models of subjectivity and society: "Lacan is not a mere constructionist because he is a real-ist; that is to say, in opposition to standard versions of constructionism Lacanian theory of symbolic meaning and fantasmatic coherence can only make sense in its relation to the register of a real which is radically external to the level of construction" (1999, 69).

them theologically, to ennoble their significance, and to religio-rhetorically authorize their desire with scriptural proof texts, even though their fantasies make pawns of and ultimately destroy their children when fantasy becomes reality. Here, in an admittedly narrative sequel to the Song, there will be no coy verbal articulation of each other's bodies through the grotesque, no "building of the beloved into existence" by way of the eyes and (grotesque) poetic imagery (Black 2009, 184).[9] The two lovers will simply yet violently, corporeally move in together out of necessity if true love is to prevail over against bourgeois materialist greed. This grotesque lover's body is not produced through two people individuating intersubjectively to become viable subjects in love, but through a desperate attempt to defy a father's greed and his treatment of a child as chattel.

---

9. Black proposes that the grotesque imagery in the Song serves expressive purposes similar to those of mystical discourse as Certeau has understood the latter. Taking Teresa of Avila's writings as his case study, Certeau contends that mystics describe a process in which they will empty the self in order to allow another "kind of subject" to materialize, namely the "subject-in-response, or, the subject who has made himself absent so that the other [God] might be made known" (Black 2009, 182). Once emptied, the mystic will "speak other-ly" in both style and content. While Black does not think the "other" being spoken to in the Song is necessarily God, "the beloved resembles the divine as object of desire, in terms of the other's inaccessibility and in terms of the other's simultaneous calling of the lover and the other's failure to speak in a way that the lover can understand" (182–83). Because of this self-emptying as self-transformation, and because of the absence of the other, "the mystic/lover has a need to 'found the place from which he or she speaks.' This means both creating the new subject—the 'I'—who will speak, but also, eventually, a space from whence to speak, 'an imaginary mode,' a 'field for the development of discourse'" (183; quoting Certeau 1992, 188); whence Teresa's rich metaphorical erotic language of love and her construction of an "interior castle" (according to Certeau) from which to speak. Analogously, in the case of the Song, "quite unexpectedly, the other's *body* is what allows the lover to speak, to articulate his or her desire, and hopefully, to seek its fulfillment. … The articulation of the other's body, in other words, takes the place of the other: speaking the body (through the grotesque) is the only way to make it present. As we have seen, however, it is not entirely successful at pinning down the beloved other, at capturing him or her so that desire is fulfilled. … So, the eyes focus this act of creation. They are literally the vehicles by which the other might be atomized and constructed; they are the tool of choice in *building the beloved into existence*" (184, emphasis added).

The *Dybbuk*'s Structural Homologies with the Song of Songs

The film transposes the biblical lovers from garden to shtetl, and the story's nineteenth-century East European Hasidic setting inflects their hide-and-seek with mystical flights of fancy, folk spells, and folk songs. The prologue expounds for viewers one Hasidic allegorization of the Song of Songs: when two souls fuse into everlasting light, they attain the *Shir ha-Shirim*. It also tells viewers that sometimes when a man dies his soul returns as a dybbuk to complete deeds left undone. From the very beginning, particularly from a feminist perspective, it appears that the watchmen are now in charge. Scene by scene, patriarchal ends and origins frame and circumscribe all love's awakenings. In act 1 the lovers' fate is prepared by a group of *batlonim* at study. Among them, we meet best friends Sender and Nison, who pledge their unborn children to each other in marriage should one be a boy, the other a girl. All these men then parade through the streets and squares until they recline in the shade while Nison sings *Shir ha-Shirim* to them, thereby setting a seal on his prenatal pact. But, traveling home, Nison drowns in a storm, and just misses his son's birth. Although dead, he will jealously guard his pact with Sender, with a fierceness cruel as the grave.

In act 2, years later, Sender breaks their vow, offering all the wealth of his house to buy a more lucrative "love" for his daughter, even though Nison's son Chonen has mysteriously found his way to Sender's house, to his synagogue for Torah study, even to his Sabbath table, where he gazes upon Sender's daughter Leah, smitten with her comely cheeks and lips. Expert at study rather than war, he has no money, but does have raven locks and a choice appearance, and Leah returns his smitten gaze with doe-like eyes. The two savor chance encounters: When Leah learns she must marry another, she swoons, sick with love, and Chonen is there to embrace her and carry her to bed. But she awakes to find him gone. Another day, he gazes in at the window to watch Leah, fair and flawless, as she sings and sews. Later in the synagogue, delivering new curtains, Leah hears the voice of her beloved behind a wall, singing *Shir ha-Shirim* to cleanse his love and conjure the power to make her his, wooing her with every note. But the watchmen of the walls—her father and future father-in-law—broker ten years' board to seal her fate and make of her body a battleground. Robbed of his beloved, Chonen is lethally wounded, begs Satan for help, and dies.

Herself inconsolable, Leah rises on her wedding day, wanders the streets, and seeks him whom her soul loves in the cemetery. Sitting in the shadow of his grave, she sings a lullaby to their unborn children, laments her barren garden, and illicitly awakens love; for she opens to her beloved: she invites him to the wedding, and offers to bear their two souls in her body. Under the chuppah, Chonen—a ravished and ravishing dybbuk—leaves his grave, climbs into her body, and "throws his voice" (Black 2009).[10] "My beloved is mine and I am his."

"Return, return, O Shulammite," order the watchmen, who reconvene to beat, wound, and strip her of her dybbuk-love. There is a trial, the father's sin is confessed, but its costs are exacted on her body. Nison speaks from the grave; he will not forgive his friend. And without this pardon, the rabbi must purge Chonen from Leah's body and banish him to Sheol. But mystico-rabbinic powers cannot crush love. Scarcely have the watchmen scattered to summon the proper groom when our lovesick Shulammite, huddled on the stairs, awakens her beloved. She has held him in spirit and would not let him go. "Arise my fair one," he seems to say in a voice-over: "I have left your body, locked and sealed, to enter your soul." In reply,

---

10. I am loosely adopting Black's image of voice throwing here. Black detects voice throwing in the lovers' acts of locating in each other's body "a place from which to speak." The lovers in the Song do so to deal with each other's absence, it would seem, and to find ways to "build" the absent beloved "into existence." In the film, by contrast, the two lovers physically/spiritually merge to alleviate their unbearable absence from each other; this merging makes Leah's voice deepen such that it is "thrown" into a manly register (though to be sure, she does not sound exactly like Chonen; his voice has not become hers in the manner of ventriloquism). Or, Chonen has "thrown" his voice into Leah, thereby creating a literally mixed (vocal) result. Note that, rather than throwing their voices to conjure the absent other, the two do so to consolidate their resistance to the socio-religio-cultural forces that threaten to keep them apart and deny their love and its necessary consummation. Both are present to each other in a grotesque modality.

Voice throwing is used it would seem for a variety of purposes in religious settings; Black herself adapts the notion of voice throwing that scholars have attributed to the mystical speech of Teresa: Teresa throws her voice by insisting that her own speech is really that of the Virgin Mary's or the Samaritan woman's from the Bible, and she does so to preempt criminal accusations of heresy by funneling her own mystical speech and experience through these more revered Christian authorities' voices (Black 2009, 224–25). Nova Scotian giant Anna Swan also throws her voice as she is described in Susan Swan's *The Biggest Modern Woman of the World* (231–37). Interestingly, while each manipulation of the voice is very different for these women, this tactic (Black calls it "improvisation" or "vamping"; 225) is meant to increase the power, credibility, and persuasiveness of the individuals who resort to this "technique."

Leah faints and dies. Leaving the wilderness, they meet outside, beyond the clutches of tradition and law, leaning on each other, as the credits roll and *Shir ha-Shirim* hymns them home.

Grotesque Musical Bodies

Music plays a central role in the sociocultural production of the lovers' grotesque body and the film's grotesque eroticism. Even the melodious and lyrical *Shir ha-Shirim*, as I discuss in a moment, repeatedly effected horror and fascination in me. But first, to act 2, where the gradual configuration of the lovers' possessed, gender dysphoric, grotesque body-in-process begins to take shape, with Leah singing to Chonen a grotesque lullaby about their unborn babies at his grave.

> Hushaby, my babies,
> Without clothes, without a bed,
> Unborn children, never mine,
> Lost forever, lost in time

She then dances with Death before her wedding ceremony and here, with special effects, death's skull face mutates into Chonen's. Arranged love is laced with death.

Just before the *Totentanz*, Leah also dances with the visually Breughelesque poor (Hoberman 1995, 283), who paw and maul her into dizzy oblivion. Their manic sway is taken up minutes later by even lowlier beggars whose clumsy antics in the village square alternate with shots of circle-dancing rich women, safely enclosed, and dressed to the nines.

These more explicitly grotesque tableaux of prenuptial music and dancing that prepare Leah's body for Chonen's possession suggest that director and playwright may have shared my aversion to arranged marriage, though likely for rather different political reasons. That is, while this grotesque montage may serve my own interpretive purposes as a critique of the sexist practices of arranged marriage and the bourgeois greed that fuels it, this entire prenuptial montage, particularly the interspersing of shots of the rich dancing in camera with those of the poor outside—mobbing Leah and scrambling for bread and coins tossed to them by the rich—broadcasts the appalling disparity between rich and poor, and the former's relative indifference to the latter. Leah's oppression by the strictures of arranged marriage blends grotesquely with that of the poor with whom she circulates at length (though one must not minimize Leah's enjoyment of bourgeois comforts and class privilege). Waszinski seems to honor in images at least some of the convictions that inspired Ansky to write *The Dybbuk*.[11]

---

11. There is also a procession scene during Chonen's funeral before the wedding takes place in which the cantor sings "Charity redeems," which retroactively sounded hollow for me given that it preceded these subsequent shots of the rich Jews' lavish wedding celebration, which included tokenistic offerings to the poor. Though the funeral and wedding are some weeks apart in the story, the film compresses this time frame such that the social commentary about charity's/piety's disingenuousness becomes one possible tacit meaning to construct from these neighboring scenes.

For Ansky (b. 1863)—who relinquished his orthodox Jewish roots to become a revolutionary Russian socialist, but then spent the second half of his life passionately preserving all manner of Jewish cultural and religious customs in the midst of pogroms and assimilationist propaganda—the acquisition of more wealth, which arranged marriage afforded men thanks to their "ownership" of desirable women, would have been implicated in an unacceptably corrupt system of capitalism and private property.

In his youth, Ansky was regarded as a "Talmud prodigy" by some (Roskies 1992, xii), but by age 17 he had rejected his faith and eventually became an undercover agent for the Hebrew Enlightenment in the Lithuanian shtetl of Liozno. He embraced atheism and the Russian revolutionary movement, which championed the integrity and honest living of the "real folk"— farmers, miners, and village peasants (xiv–v), the celebration of which is most evident in *The Dybbuk*. Later, as a member of the General Jewish Labor Bund, his Marxism and internationalism led him to criticize all manner of nationalist Zionism and Orthodox religious Judaism. And yet, quite suddenly, upon reading I. L. Peretz's Yiddish Haskalah works in 1901, "he discovered a modern European sensibility expressing itself in Yiddish" (xviii). Ansky's subsequent passion for Russian-Jewish ethnography led him to promote Jewish folklore as a new "Oral Tradition": "The Oral Tradition consisting of all manner of folklore—stories, legends, parables, songs, witticisms, melodies, customs and beliefs—is, like the Bible, the product of the Jewish spirit; it reflects the same beauty and purity of the Jewish soul, the same modesty and nobility of the Jewish heart, the same loftiness and depth of Jewish thought" (Ansky, *The Jewish Ethnographic Program* [1914], 10–11; as quoted in Roskies 1992, xxiv). This Oral Tradition served extramural purposes as well: "The Oral Tradition, then, was not a system of beliefs but a cluttered account of everyday life—and death. As such, this treasure trove of folk life and lore [Ansky thought] could draw other nations closer to the Jews" (Roskies 1992, xxv). Thus, following Peretz again, Ansky appropriated Hasidism to promote nonreligious ideals and values and attempted a "radical democratization" of the Hasidic movement. *The Dybbuk* seems to play this ambassadorial role, so to speak, but such paradoxical reappropriations of tradition for nonreligious aims angered Orthodox Jews (cf. xxvi). *The Dybbuk* was invariably a target of their hostility, combining as it did a critique of religious prac-

But how could I possibly describe the film's musical centerpiece, *Shir ha-Shirim,* which punctuates its beginning, middle, and end, as a grotesque musical body? By attunement to the patriarchal setting of the setting, so to speak; while the filmic apparatus may direct us to hear a devotionally focused (because Hasidic) rendition of the Song, and while today it is also received as a precious Yiddish artifact preserved in film (see Hoberman 1995, 10–11, 343; Königsberg 1997, 22–23), a feminist spectatorial gaze mars its surface beauty. In act 1, the film's opening 15 minutes, which include the first performance of *Shir ha-Shirim,* make abundantly clear to me that this is no place for women. Moreover, in this first act, I learn that one precipitant of the song is a pact made by men that involves a woman-as-property losing her life before it even begins—a woman eventually possessed by men in all senses of the word. This patriarchal cultural practice of love—musically aestheticized, Hasidically mystified, and religio-rhetorically consecrated by *Shir ha-Shirim*—will cause passion and desire to derail grotesquely. My reading of this first audition of the Song as grotesque (especially after numerous screenings) is retroactively intensified by a more basic, to me unshakably alienating, narrative conceit in the film: if arranged marriage repels me, I am horrified when in act 2 the Shulammite is shown to passionately fall for (albeit independent of any knowledge of the two fathers' pact) the man that two men have arranged for her to marry before she is even born. Fathers have insinuated themselves that deeply into their children's choices. (Some scholars would say I am a bad girl for policing another woman's desire [cf. Burrus and Moore 2003],[12] or for thinking desire should be rational [cf. Boer 2000]).

---

tices of love with a questioning of rabbinic power, especially via its portrait of the all-too-human rabbi—filled with self-doubt, weary of the world and his vocation, and ultimately unable to harness spiritual energies to definitively discipline modern challenges to arranged marriages (xxviii); yet all the while the film elevates common villagers' Hasidic folk beliefs and practices as "a new Torah" (xxiv). *The Dybbuk* thus dramatizes Ansky's mixed but ultimately redemptive assessment of Jewish shtetl family life (he wrote a critique thereof, *A History of the Family*, in the 1880s).

12. This issue of policing or censoring women's desire has been discussed with specific reference to Song interpretation. Burrus and Moore (2003) push feminists who flag and deplore the violence in the Song in the scene where the Shulammite is beaten (5:6–7; is it a dream or a memory?), and which other traditional interpretations simply try to dismiss or ignore, to consider the possibility that it might be, for some readers today (even feminist ones), the seeds of an s/m fantasy (41–49).

Naomi Seidman has written an exceedingly rich, multilayered interpretation of the film's sexual and religious politics, but defends this seminal narrative conceit as preserving and revamping a cherished folk belief about fated love—*Bashert*, that is, such marriages are decreed in heaven, where God himself is the matchmaker. True love is therefore never really free choice:

> *Bashert* means both "fated" and, as a noun, one's "future spouse" or, more colloquially "true love," as in Leah's last words to Chonen: "*Ich bin baheft mit dir oyf eybik, meyn basherter*" (I am joined with you forever, my fated one/my true love). … As folkloric tradition claims is true in the case of every match (although it is usually God himself who acts as matchmaker), Chonen and Leah are destined for each other from their very conception, and the love that arises between them is no more than the inevitable expression of this foreordained decree. (Seidman 2003, 232)

This sounds to me, however, suspiciously like sanctifying paternalism with mystical apologetics. Only one paragraph and one line in a footnote in Seidman's essay acknowledge Leah's propertied existence as problematic (238–39, 244 n. 21).[13] Ansky's use of *Bashert* in *The Dybbuk*, writes Seidman, constitutes an exceptionally artful integration of religious tradition and secular notions of romance:

> Ansky's superimposition of a Haskalah narrative of sexual rebellion [against arranged marriage] over a layer of folkloric beliefs in the predestination of love is not in itself surprising—the combination of modernity and tradition is the very insignia of his literary generation of Yiddish

13. Seidman recognizes in Leah both a modern, nineteenth-century "New Woman," i.e., an empowered "romantic rebel," and also a "sexual victim" of religious tradition (2003, 238). Seidman concedes that Leah embodies "the mothers, invisible, never consulted, whose bodies are the silent tokens of exchange, the symbolic property that enables their husbands to forge their bond" (238). After her possession, Leah also functions, rather like other women in American horror films of the 70s and 80s, "as a woman seemingly in grave corporeal, even demonic, distress, who in reality provides the site for a man to work through 'an unacknowledged homoerotic crisis'" (239; citing Clover 1993). Later, Seidman acknowledges: "I view Ansky's playwriting as complicitous in effacing women's roles in traditional Judaism" (244 n. 21). On balance, however, her apologetics for *The Dybbuk* are extremely positive in valorizing the role of the fathers, the religious and cultural practices of love, and their impact on romantic subjectivity.

> post-Haskalah modernists. … What is remarkable about the juxtaposition of modernism and traditionalism in the case of the Dybbuk is that Ansky took the two orientations at their greatest distance from each other and brought them together with maximum impact, combining a call for freedom from arranged marriage with an insistence on the real power of the ultimate arranged marriage—one decreed before the young couple have even been born. …In Ansky's conflation the mutual attraction of the young couple emerges simultaneously from the depth of their erotic passion for each other and from the betrothal pledge sworn by their fathers. In a startling move, Ansky suggests that the two derivations—one instinctual and preconscious, the other historical and traditional—are, in fact, one and the same. (233)

This positive interpretation, in my view, mitigates the fact that the lovers die too young and that the fathers' desire, which the children unknowingly fulfill, destroys them. But here, conversely, Seidman locates the cause of the young lovers' untimely death in a *failure* to honor the fathers' wishes. Rather than questioning the very desirability of such fantasies, she argues: "If the bond between Sender and Nison ultimately destroys their children, it is not because their pledge ignores the wishes of their children but because their children are stopped from carrying it through" (239). Indeed, "Sender and Nison, far from being the enemies of young love, are its champions and symbols, pledging their children to each other in the first flush of their respective marriages" (235). Clearly Seidman practices a more willing suspension of disbelief than I can toward the seminal acts of imagination that might concoct such an acutely phallocentric "invisible hand" to drive a story line; that would equate and conflate so thoroughly, by way of a supernaturalized force, paternal desire with true love; or that would ordain the former as the divinely ordained progenitor of genuine love; and then veil all these sleights of hand with the irresistible allure of two beautiful protagonists.

Above and beyond this problematic narrative conceit, further cognitive dissonance is created for me here in act 1 by my knowledge of feminist biblical criticism that celebrates the Shulammite's intermittent yet still powerful agency as manifested in the text through the workings of her voice and gaze.[14] Not so in this musical setting of the Song, where "her"

14. Many feminist biblical scholars have celebrated "the predominance of the female voice" within this biblical text (Black 2009, 195; as examples, see Brenner 1989, 1993; Meyers 1993; Pardes 1992; Trible 1978; van Dijk-Hemmes 1993; and Weems

words ("Let him kiss me," etc.) have become his, even though I know that this is precisely what makes this a delightfully queer rendition of the Song.[15]

If my grotesque reading of this first musical number still seems weak, it gains just a little heft when Nison's desperate son Chonen sings the Song again in act 2: surrounded this time by boys inside the school/synagogue, Chonen's version is haunted now by the broken vow it had originally sealed. Leah has been promised to another man, but Chonen is not deterred by this and his song serves several diegetic functions. First, the son unwittingly restores the Father's prenatal fantasy as his own. His rendition bolsters and mobilizes a mirror version of the father's pledge and repairs the former's violation. Second, it consolidates and purifies Chonen's erotico-spiritual or supernatural energies and empowers him to rescue "his" Leah from the clutches of paternal greed. This is laudable perhaps, but from my perspective this second performance of the Song seems forcefully or aggressively to assert that "My beloved will be mine,

---

1992), but two male scholars have expressed concern that the woman becomes yet again an object of the male gaze (see Clines 1995; Polaski 1997). For example, Polaski believes the latter content cancels out the perceived value attributed to the former property of the book. Contra Polaski, Black argues that the woman's gaze can be read as itself extremely powerful by adopting Russo's recuperative reading of the female grotesque where women can be powerful as *producers* of the spectacle that they become for men, though such empowerment is best thought of as a "prefigurative possibility" of a future "cohesive counterculture," given that women's objectification within patriarchy is hardly alleviated or assuaged dramatically by women using the female grotesque in the here and now as "weapons to effect one's own empowerment" (Black 2009, 202). (See here Black's helpful discussion and survey of the extant, ultimately ambivalent readings of the Shulammite's voice and gaze, particularly her engagement with Exum 2005 [Black 2009, 192–204]).

15. Seidman points out that Waszinski was "reputed to be a homosexual" and is responsible for foregrounding potential homoerotic resonances between Sender and Nison and among the *batlonim* more generally, by having Sender sing the opening song to Nison in an added prologue not originally in the play (2003, 240 and 245 n. 31). (In the play, Chonen sings it to Leah in act 1; Seidman's sources regarding Waszinski's sexual orientation are Hoberman 1995 and Sicular 1999.) Queer readings of both play and film include: Seidman 2003, Sicular 1999, Gordon 1999, Shandler 2006. See also Tony Kushner's adaptation of the play (and Solomon's [2004] discussion thereof) in which he inserts critiques of Jewish misogyny and homophobia during discussions the *batlonim* have while at study. See also the film *Trembling before G-d* (2001) directed by Sandi Simcha Dubowski; it includes clips of Sender singing the *Song of Songs* to Nison as evidence of an untapped homoerotic archive within Jewish tradition.

even if the devil eventually has to intervene." Third, the music enhances the persuasive power of Chonen's theological apologetics—the kabbalistic exegesis he presents before singing the Song arouses and manipulates viewers' sympathy and their endorsement of Chonen's lust for Leah that he will now alchemically refine.

I am perhaps too cynical to appreciate this number's polysemic fringe benefit, for it will musically unleash Leah's own erotic desire: momentarily, the shtetl-bound Shulammite will finally get to sing this song that she has overheard in the synagogue, all by herself, back at home. Her crystalline voice enthralls us, her superior vocal technique unsettles, at least a little, any sense that she is still, even musically, just a parrot of men's desires. But just as spectators anticipate more delectable notes from Leah, as signifiers perhaps of some nascent, expressive/romantic mutuality to come, her father barges in and interrupts. As a result, this truncated musical body confirms my prior interpretation of the Song's central, ongoing raison d'etre: it remains a mnemonic device among men. How so? Leah's song triggers Sender's repressed memories of his now broken pact with Nison, and unleashes Sender's guilt and horror over the irreversible marriage contract he just completed for his daughter:

> Sender: Where did you learn that song?
>
> Leah: From Chonen.
>
> Sender: Chonen? Who taught him that?
>
> Leah: His father.
>
> Father: His father? *That* Song of Songs? Impossible. My friend Nison sang that Song of Songs, but he was drowned long ago.
>
> Leah: His father's name was also Nison. He also was drowned.
>
> Father: [after telling Leah she is to be married to another richer man, sinks despondently into a chair] … O Nison … my dear friend … too late … too late.

Additionally, her exquisite yet here horror-inducing *Shir ha-Shirim* functions as a diegetic prelude to Chonen's hysterical dissolution in the next scene—a tragic climax melodramatically intensified by a series of quick interspersed cutaways to shots of garishly loud, raucous circle dancing by the *batlonim* who are celebrating Sender's marriage announcement.

And so what I hear in the musical diegesis, in the shape-shifting circulation of *Shir ha-Shirim* through a series of bodies, from fathers through *batlonim* (act 1) to son and Torah students (act 2), coursing briefly through the Shulammite and back through her father (act 2), is a force field of competing social energies—patriarchal, mystical, occult, homo- and heteroerotic, legal-contractual—a grotesquely overdetermined musical body whose scoliotic backbone is the Song itself, its kisses, oils and religio-rhetorical cachet.[16]

From this musical "breakdown" of *Shir ha-Shirim* in act 2, the music that follows gradually becomes more manic, dark, and neurotic—Leah's lullaby, her dances with the poor, the beggars, even death itself—as possessed and deranged as her own body will soon be. And, to feminist ears, *Shir ha-Shirim* returns even more disfigured in act 3 (discussed below). Precisely because *Shir ha-Shirim* keeps returning as a mnemonic device of a disavowed vow, flagging with each transmogrification of the Song the damage and desperate measures that this initial violated pledge precipitates, the musical force field condenses to me into a hysterical symptom, what Erin Runions would deem "an excessive and visceral representation of a forgotten traumatic wound" (2003, 9).[17] For feminist viewers, more-

16. See Susan McClary's seminal elaborations of music as a force field of competing social energies and ideologies, especially her introduction (1991, 3–34). Adorno, Greenblatt, and Foucault have strongly influenced this New Musicological approach. For a feminist theological enlistment of this more materialist understanding of music to critique both Christian theologies of music and historical musical practices, see Epstein 2004.

17. See Runions's use of hysteria as an interpretive lens that produces fresh intertextual readings of biblical texts, contemporary films, and critical theory. Runions proposes that political resistance to the oppressive forces of globalization and turbo-capitalism, and the concomitant refusal to conform to normative identities that this "new world order" prescribes, can be read as hysterical responses to the status quo. Where Breuer and Freud defined hysteria as "an excessive and visceral representation of a forgotten traumatic wound," Runions adapts this understanding of hysteria to understand and characterize individual and collective forms of resistance to oppressive sociopolitical environments as these have been depicted in contemporary film (2003, 1–14).

Note here also that I am making a different correlation of hysteria and the grotesque than Black does (2009, 112–14). In Black's discussion of Margaret Miles's chapter on the female grotesque in Christian thought and art (Miles 1989), Black includes

over, the repressed traumatic wound is not the broken vow. It is the deeper, unacknowledged violence, the sanctified aggression, so to speak, that I diagnosed resonating within the very first audition of *Shir ha-Shirim*, namely, the sociocultural and religious status of women as chattel. As hysterical symptom, for me the musical setting of the Song becomes a sonic somatic translation of an oppressive sociocultural "disorder" (Porter 1993, 265), long before it might have been labeled as such (and for very different diegetic reasons) when Chonen hauntingly sings the Song again in act 2 and resurrects his father's suppressed, compromised fantasy.[18]

It is in the third and final act that *Shir ha-Shirim*'s musical beauty is definitively laced with horror for me (a mixed reaction typically induced by grotesque imagery; Black 2009). It is brought to life again in the voice of a dead man who has taken up residence in a woman. At the very end of the film, Chonen's act 2 rendition, now disembodied as background

hysteria and fetishization as two more "complex practices" of "subtle gender mergings" that Miles might have included in her third analytical category, namely, the "rhetorical and pictorial device [of] inversion," a lens that Miles develops less well (Black 2009, 110–11). Unlike me, Black follows Russo's understanding of hysteria as potentially positively correlated with the grotesque: Russo has pointed out that Charcot's hysterics "were frequently paid performers" and thus useful for positively recuperating the female grotesque body in the Song; such antecedents teach us how "the visual or the spectacular [can] open up an ambiguous space, where performance might allow for the looked-at to contend for agency. As Russo rightly observes, in the hysterical there is a chance for discursive freedoms and possibilities" (113); but the results here are painfully mixed. Thus Black quotes Russo: "There is only one way out: death, whatever its representation—hysterical breakdown, unconsciousness, loss of visibility, or more literally loss of life" (Russo 1994, 44–45; quoted in Black 2009, 114).

18. Roy Porter has written an interesting historical survey of the medical *historiography* of hysteria as a "disease formulation" that led me to label the music a hysterical symptom of a sociocultural "disorder." He concludes: "In the case of hysteria, disease formulations, I have been arguing, go with circumstances: doctors, patients, physical milieux, intellectual and cultural landscapes. My concern has been to argue that hysteria could be fashioned as a disorder, precisely because the culture-at-large sustained tense and ambiguous relations between representations of mind and body, which were, in turn, reproduced in the hierarchical yet interactive ontologies of morality and medicine, and, yet again, reflected by the sociological interplay of clinical encounters. In hysteria, as with other disorders, different fields of force break in distinctive ways, and medicine plays double games. Sometimes its mission is reductionist, resolving hysteria now into the womb, now into mere willfulness. In other circumstances, medicine seeks to render hysteria real, protecting its mysteries. In hysteria, mind and body may be seen as sublimated representations of doctors and patients" (1993, 265–66).

music, washes over Leah's dead body lying on a wooden table. It is thus by reading *Shir ha-Shirim*'s successive apparitions as a gradually unfolding musical body during the course of the film that this musical afterlife of the Song becomes very much a grotesque body-in-process—initially pretty in a manly sort of way, amputated in Leah's mouth, and, finally, ethereally de-composing, so to speak, post mortem. Having said this, here in act 3, the Song or its narrative function remains polysemic in ambivalence-inducing ways: it could be a tragic lament wrung across a dead woman's body, but at the same time, more benignly, this third "sounding" musically supports the plot's requisite denouement by creating thematic unity with the prologue: as we learned at the beginning of the film, in Hasidic culture, and following Kabbalah, the two souls have finally become one, and the Song has always served to allegorize and/or support this spiritual/romantic ideal. But I resist this latter, arguably coercive and "positive" narrative/theological resolution of the lovers' tragic plight. It tries to gratify some viewers' desire for happy endings with the consolation of cliché: "Well at least they are together now, and in peace." But do you hear what I hear? As if acoustically enclosed by plangent cedar boards, from the day she is spoken for, our sister's bartered, possessed, exorcised, excommunicated, and ultimately dead body has been musically framed and constrained by *Shir ha-Shirim*.

Hermeneutic Side Effects: Queer Musical Blind Spots and Anti-Semitic Trajectories

My grotesque musical diagnosis is its own symptom of sorts. I confess an abiding generic suspicion toward film characters who suddenly turn to the camera and burst into song. The transgressive semiotics of musical numbers is lost on me. I do not seem to delight as some queer theorists do in the musical breaks into song and dance that constitute "moments of cinematic excess" that subvert not only "linear narrative form" but also "the texts' dominant libidinal forms" (Farmer 2000, 82). In these disruptions, musical numbers supposedly offer spectatorial pleasures that are counterhegemonic to those proffered by the idealized heterocentrist and sexist plots of Hollywood musicals. Thus Brett Farmer: "if, as many critics contend, the linear trajectory of narrative represents a structural replaying of heterocentric, oedipal development, then the musical's insistent breaks or deviations, from narrative progression into nonlinear spectacle seem to all but beg this type of [nonheterocentrist] reading" (83). Musical numbers allow "a metaphoric slippage into the unconscious that produces a disruptive effusion of ordinarily censored erotic material" (82–83); to wit, queer spectatorial readings of Nison and Chonen's singing among adoring groups of men and boys.[19] Viewers like me, however, resist moving, as Farmer theorizes, "out of straight, teleologically driven temporality" into the musical number's more queer "*spatial* structure of spectacle," a space that invites more polymorphous pleasures because it transports viewers "outside the linear, oedipal economy of straight desire into a de-oedipalized framework of perverse desire" (83). Following Farmer then, *Shir ha-Shirim* as a musical number thwarts my subjective preference for the dramatic realism and straight temporality that normally/normatively organizes my filmic erotic engagements, and the all-male musical numbers' homoerotic magnetism perhaps impedes the unfolding of the more conventional heterocentric romance that I desire, nor does it "deliver" each time it is performed a conventional Hollywood masculinity for my fantasmatic consumption.[20] Already alienated by the seemingly non-Western, all-male enclave, the strange sounds of Yiddish, the foreign shtetl setting, not to mention Nison and Sender's pact, I am left cold when Nison, arrayed in *shtreimel* and *payos*, turns to the camera to sing tenderly the Song in his sweet, soft tenor voice—I am indifferent to the potentially pleasurable nonnarrative and fantasmatic tangents in the plot and spectatorial desire that his singing activates, because I already feel so identificatorily unmoored.

Such "tone-deaf" confessions aside, I now have my own unprepossessing dybbuk with which to contend. An evil spirit haunts my symptomatic grotesque reading of the film and the Song, and incriminates the way I squirm at: (1) the *unheimlich* feel of this paternalistic shtetl world; (2) the

19. Farmer points out as well that "male trio" musicals (*On the Town, Take Me Out to the Ballgame*) and "exuberant sexual duets" in other ones (*Anchors Aweigh*) all involved lots of physical dancing and thus invited homoerotic fantasies of queerness that would disrupt the heteronormative drive for closure that the *plot* and heteronormative happy *ending* always entailed (2000, 85–86). While *The Dybbuk* is no Hollywood musical, the group male "numbers" in acts 1 and 2 arguably afford such "fantasies of queerness" for some spectators.

20. I may not like musicals for more "abstract" reasons: I am perhaps wary of men bursting into song, because music (and thus by extension musical theater) has "been largely coded and marginalized as feminine within patriarchal cultures and therefore dangerous" (cf. Brett 1994; Miller 1998). As a heterosexual female, I have been conditioned to desire more manly cinematic love objects, and these more semiotically feminized masculine spectacles do not draw me in and turn me on.

(for me) atypical masculinity placed on display in the spectacle of men's singing; (3) Nison and Sender's rather monstrous disregard for Leah; (4) Chonen's grotesque invasion of Leah's body; (5) the semiotically hysterical sounds of the villagers' song and dance in act 2. With each critical objection I raise, my terms of indictment unwittingly echo the pathologizing rhetoric used to vilify Jews and Eastern European Hasidic culture in the nineteenth century, deployed in what Linda Nochlin calls "the out and out grotesquerie of anti-semitic caricature" (1995, 19). Jews were mocked for their effeminate, singsong way of speaking and their hyperanimated "gesticulations," which supposedly resembled those of hysterics (Garber 1992, 225).[21] Hysteria of course is historically a female disease, and consequently a trait that further linked Jews to perversion and homosexuality. Their traditional dress, rituals, and pastimes—all on liberal display in *The Dybbuk*—have been negatively labeled in the past as suspect. As Garber writes, "The traditional long gown (Shylock's 'Jewish gabardine') and uncut hair, the lively gesticulation (and wild, ecstatic dancing) of the Hasidic sect—all these could be regarded as woman-like or 'feminine,' as well as simply foreign or alien" (1992, 226).[22]

To be sure, my negative reactions to the film have been fueled at least to some extent by Waszinski's expressionistic film techniques and by Ansky's magic realism, both of which contribute to the film's "Hasidic grotesque"[23] style, and produce a foreboding context from which to receive this musi-

21. Sander Gilman has also extensively chronicled the history of anti-Semitic physiological and "clinical" stereotypes in many of his books and essays (1985, 1991). Garber is indebted to his work. See the section "Jew, Woman, Homosexual" in her chapter on religious dress and its "transvestite effects" (1992, 224–33).

22. Here Garber quotes and then comments upon Hitler's infamous description in *Mein Kampf* of a Hasidic passerby in Vienna and, notably, his fierce contempt for Jewish artists and actors: "'Once as I was strolling through the Inner City ... I suddenly encountered an apparition in a black caftan and black hair locks. Is this a Jew? ... Is this a German?' The unclean dress and generally unheroic appearance of the Jews, 'these caftan-wearers,' convince Hitler that he is face to face with otherness—with the not-self (which is to say the self he fears). When he contemplates 'their activity in the press, art, literature, and the theater,' he concludes that Jews have been 'chosen' to spread 'literary filth, artistic trash, and theatrical idiocy'" (1992, 227).

23. Hoberman introduces this term but does not elaborate its meanings at length. He offers several other examples of the Hasidic grotesque or Hasidic "gothic" style—Leivick's *Der Goylem*, Peretz's *Bay Nakht afn Altn Mark*, I. J. Singer's *Yoshe Kalb* (stage version), the works of Isaac Bashevis Singer—and comments that this style "has misleadingly come to seem the mainstream of modern Yiddish literature" (1995, 280).

cal setting of the Song. In his not entirely unself-critical play, the Russian Jewish Ansky perhaps risks these potentially racist significations, but defiantly celebrates Jewish heritage and (as Seidman extensively elaborates) encourages the wedding of modernity and tradition in this cautionary tale rather than any collective, "Enlightened" divorce from the Jewish past.

The even broader minefield in the politics of representation through which my feminist faux pas treads is the anti-Semitically fraught and gendered cultural semiotics that attended any Jew becoming an actor: "When the Jew took the stage, the theater's long-standing symbiosis between femininity and the mimetic latched onto a third term—one already coded as dissembling and gender dysfunctional" (Solomon 1997, 98). Jews' supposedly natural "capacity for mimicry" stemmed from their slippery feminine essence (97). In daily life, "the Jew is always already acting" (97), and such "ontological" theatricality and dissimulation would only redouble on stage and screen. Some Jewish intellectuals within the Haskalah movement, knowing that playwrights and actors in theater and film could reinforce anti-Semitic stereotypes through mediocre scripts and acting skills, respectively, monitored the kind of Jewish identities that their plays and films disseminated—disparaging trashy, farcical melodramas that might proffer anti-Semitic grist for non-Jews (Solomon 1997, 104ff.). *The Dybbuk*, however, is usually classified as a sophisticated celebration of Jewish identity, not as *shund*, and enjoyed tremendous crossover appeal among non-Jewish audiences. (If anything, criticism of the play and film came from highly Orthodox camps.)[24] Does my basic failure to appreciate the codes, conventions, stock characters, and classic story line of this Yiddish masterpiece, and my intractable hermeneutic of suspicion that would label its musical centerpiece grotesque render the latter interpretive lens dangerously undecidable—epithet as much as heuristic? My largely negative reading of *The Dybbuk*'s "grotesque" content and my enlistment of the same to disparage the portrait of "true love" composed by patriarchal Hasidic cultural practices of love could certainly be framed as accusing

24. In Warsaw the film ran for nearly three months at a major cinema and attracted both Jewish and Gentile audiences, though critic Stefania Zahorska gave it a scathing, implicitly anti-Semitic review (Hoberman 1995, 283–84). New York critics offered mixed reviews, but audiences were more enthusiastic: it opened in January 1938 at the Continental Theater and played for seven weeks, "receiving more press than any previous Yiddish (or Polish) film, including coverage by both *Time* and *Newsweek*" (283–84).

playwright, directors, and actors of broadcasting histrionic, "dissimulating" misrepresentations of romantic love.

Consider two final slurs along the slippery anti-Semitic slope that applying a grotesque label to Jewish cultural offerings invites: Leah initially does not seem remotely like the castrating female Jewish woman that other Jewish women were thought to be (actresses especially so, incidentally; see Solomon 1997, 99–103), and yet the so-called grotesque permeability and mutations of her body bespeak a dangerous, nonnormative female nature, a subspecies of emasculating femininity (one supposedly even worse than Gentile varieties thereof). While as a feminist spectator I could frame Leah's defiance of patriarchal authority as a remarkable creativity within constraint, her feistiness and the bodily contortions it galvanizes can also be framed as evidence that she belongs within a long line of phallic/castrating Jewish women, catalogued by Marjorie Garber: Salome, Shylock's daughter, Joyce's Bella Cohen, the numerous Jewish American Princesses populating novels by, for example, "macho-Jewish writers like Roth and Mailer"—all figures of "the fantasized Jewish woman [who] crosses over into the space of 'masculinity' which is [already] put in question by the ambivalent cultural status of the Jewish man" (1992, 229). A product of her "dangerous" willfulness, Leah's "grotesque" body crosses into that slippery, nebulous Jewish-male space in ways that also might invite anti-Semitic caricature. For his part, if Chonen's character is opened up to such stereotypical valences, he can be derogated as far too irrational, even hysterical in his choice to take up residence inside a woman's body. Additionally, according to Western film's standard depictions of ideal, heroic masculinity, his being a bookworm utterly in thrall to a woman makes him weak and unmanly. Has like attracted and absorbed like?

Yet here, in the midst of the troubling culturally semiotic side effects that my feminist diagnosis of this "grotesque" love affair and "sound track" potentially triggers, Daniel Boyarin's countercultural reconstruction of traditional Jewish sexual identities turns anti-Semitic grist into gender political gold—revalorizing as it does at least some of the negative labels I have inadvertently circulated in my feminist and musicological critique: Boyarin conducts a "radical rereading of the existing tradition and texts," a "redemptive critique" of talmudic and Hasidic culture in order to provide Jews today with the ingredients for constructing an intentionally "feminized," queer masculinity that is designed precisely to flout the imperialist stereotypes and norms of Western bourgeois masculinity that many "enlightened" Jews were too quick to espouse (1997, 358). Where Theodor

Herzl's Zionists, like colonized Western subjects, advocated assimilation and championed "muscular Judaism" as the template for authentic Jewish manliness (ideals that included elevating the Hebrew language as manly and the Yiddish *mamaloschen* as effeminate), today—particularly in the wake of postcolonial criticism—(some) Hasidic and rabbinic definitions of manliness can be deployed to allow tradition to fertilize contemporary projects of Jewish identity politics that resist the hegemonically Christian status quo (though here Boyarin is very careful to emphasize that this does not cancel out rabbinic misogyny and sexism; xxi–xxii): "A central claim in this book is that there is something correct—although seriously misvalued—in the persistent European representation of the Jewish man as a sort of woman. More than just an anti-Semitic stereotype, the Jewish ideal male as countertype to 'manliness' is an assertive historical product of Jewish culture" (3–4). Boyarin's archaeology of talmudic and East European sources documents that, in contrast to the nonheroic, asexual masculinity that studious, cloistered monks personified within Christianity, the bookish, "passive, pale, gentle, and physically weak *Yeshiva-Bokhur*" that Chonen evokes in *The Dybbuk* was actually "an object of erotic desire" (68). In a provocative twist, therefore, what I have categorized in problematically anti-Semitic terms as alienating human and musical bodies within the film become queer badges of honor within Boyarin's framework; *The Dybbuk*'s corporeal and musical grotesquerie answer affirmatively his rhetorical plea: "Rather than a one-sided perception of Jewish men as feminized or of Jewish women as virginized, can we not begin to conceive of the structure of Jewish gender as being differently configured, as being resistant to the increasingly rigidifying patterns of gender that the European regimes of romantic love and heterosexuality were enforcing more and more vigorously in the nineteenth century?" (354).

Conclusion: Savoring Dissonance

Ansky's Hasidic grotesque style, his penchant for social critique mixed with celebrations of tradition, Waszinski's protohorror, expressionist special effects,[25] and my clearly rather naïve feminist construction of grotesque

25. Classifying *The Dybbuk* as a protohorror film actually opens its story line to further feminist interrogation. Thus Seidman: "In a grotesque parody of the traditional use of women's bodies as conduits for male kinship, Leah's possessed body becomes the site for a meeting of two men, the occasion for their conversation beyond

musical bodies, traverse some dangerous hermeneutic tightropes. My feminist zeal sought merely to temper (with very mixed results) uncritical reception of this precious cultural artifact and early filmic masterpiece by interrogating the curious mixture of horror and fascination I experienced, not only toward the grotesque human, but also musical "bodies" that the religio-cultural politics of love and marriage produced (for me) in the film. A sustained feminist, symptomatic reading remains worthwhile, in my view, among the predominantly positive, revivalist Yiddish and queer readings of *The Dybbuk* currently in circulation. It is possible that Leah's objectification and commodification may get lost beneath praise for the film's queering of synagogue life or Ansky's deft recuperative synthesis of Jewish tradition and modernity or beneath our legitimate nostalgia for the poignant glimpses of a lost "Yiddishland" that the film captured as genocide loomed in 1937. And while my concern for Leah, some might argue, neglects Chonen's equally tragic destiny, as a female spectator I remain pained by his more basic freedom of movement, his access to Torah study, and his more aggressively defiant capacity to pursue his love object. Moreover, I know that advocacy against the injustices inflicted upon young Jewish men by arranged marriage already had a voice as early as a century ago in the writings of the

---

the limits of time and death. As Carol Clover argues is the case for the American possession movies of the 1970s and 1980s, *The Dybbuk* stages a female drama behind which lurks an unacknowledged male homoerotic crisis. The excesses of Leah's predicament function not only as a 'cover' for her father's suppressed trauma and as an opportunity for its resolution; the voice that issues from her body is the symptom that speaks the Jewish man's hysterical truth" (2003, 238–39). Seidman enlists Clover's *Men, Women, and Chainsaws* further in her footnote: "In this regard, *The Dybbuk* is a precursor to the occult-possession films Carol Clover analyzes, in which the exorcism of the possessed female protagonist—monstrously open, hideously pregnant, physically colonized—enables the emotional catharsis of a male protagonist in the grip of homosexual panic. 'On the face of it,' Clover writes, 'the occult film is the most "female" of genres, telling as it regularly does tales of women or girls in the grip of the supernatural. But behind the female "cover" is always the story of a man in crisis'" (Clover 1993, 65; as cited in Seidman 2003, 245 n. 29).

Königsberg also recognizes in *The Dybbuk* "elements of the horror film," but, interestingly enough, insists that "it does not belong to the horror genre—it is a metaphysical and psychological love story in a world of religion, ritual, and the supernatural that pushes into the mysteries of life and death" (1997, 26–27). Hoberman attributes the director's use of special effects more to the fact that Waszinski did not "altogether trust the play's evocative mood," and as a result decided to add "superfluous bits of movie magic" (1997, 283).

Jewish Haskalah movement; indeed, the initial push to ban arranged marriage was motivated by haskalic concern for the damage it did to young men, not to young women (Biale 1997, 153–56; Seidman 2003, 244 n. 21).

What may be more objectionable is my "puritanical" feminism—my rather dogmatic policing of another woman's freely chosen, albeit to me masochistic, desire; or my anachronistic failure to admire her remarkably creative agency within suffocating constraint. Her daring certainly parallels that of the various Shulammites feminist scholars have constructed from the biblical text. This inquiry has been, more than anything else, an elucidation of the curiously dissonant revulsion I experience when the Song itself is sung so tenderly and harmoniously at key moments in the film, and an illumination of the much more intimate structural ties that exist between the film and biblical text than previous scholars have recognized. As I continue exploring the neglected musical afterlives of the Song, and how their amatory codes and conventions inform love as a specifically cultural practice today, at least *The Dybbuk* has offered one preliminary case study in the usefulness of applying a bifocal, *socio*psychic understanding of the Song's use value—more specifically, that of its grotesque bodies—within both its protagonists' and readers' amatory negotiations and politics. For the film graphically illustrates and reminds us how, to paraphrase Brett Farmer, erotic and marital icons and fantasies within the fantasmatic superstructure that romantic subjects inhabit—*and to which the* Song, *for better or worse, keeps contributing*—always stem from historically contingent "networks of language and culture" (2000, 64).

Finally, Black's closing observations can teach me to take some pleasure in my horror and fascination with *The Dybbuk* and its musical numbers. I must acquire a deeper taste for the liminal states that the grotesque always entices us to experience: "it is clear that as long as the grotesque remains, it would be unreasonable to expect the resolution of the struggle for sense. The efficacy of the grotesque depends precisely on keeping the viewer/reader in a marginal state, between sense and nonsense, beauty and ugliness, attraction and repulsion, and the like" (2009, 174). I take these words to heart, even as *The Dybbuk*'s dead Shulammite haunts my mind.

Works Cited

Baumeister, Roy. 1991. *Meanings of Life*. New York: Guilford.

Belsey, Catherine. 1994. *Desire: Love Stories in Western Culture*. Oxford: Blackwell.

Berlant, Lauren. 2001. Love: A Queer Feeling. Pages 432–42 in *Homosexuality and Psychoanalysis*. Edited by Tim Dean and Christopher Lane. Chicago: University of Chicago Press.

———. 2008. *The Female Complaint: The Unfinished Business of Sentimentality in American Culture*. Durham, N.C.: Duke University Press.

Biale, David. 1997. *Eros and the Jews: From Biblical Israel to Contemporary America*. Berkeley: University of California Press.

Black, Fiona C. 2009. *Artifice of Love: Grotesque Bodies and the Song of Songs*. New York: T&T Clark.

Boer, Roland. 2000. The Second Coming: Repetition and Insatiable Desire in the Song of Songs. *Biblical Interpretation* 8:276–301.

Boyarin, Daniel. 1997. *Unheroic Conduct: The Rise of Heterosexuality and the Invention of the Jewish Man*. Berkeley: University of California Press.

Brantley, Ben. 1995. Talking to the Dead, Yearning for Answers. Review of "A Dybbuk," by Tony Kushner, Hartford Stage Company, Mark Lamos production. *NewYork Times*, February 20, 1995.

———. 1997. Theater Review: A "Dybbuk" Foresees "The Martyred Dead." *New York Times*, November 17, 1997.

Brenner, Athalya. 1989. *The Song of Songs*. Old Testament Guides. Sheffield: JSOT Press.

———. 1993. "Come Back, Come Back the Shulammite" (Song of Songs 7.1–10): A Parody of the *waṣf* Genre. Pages 234–57 in *A Feminist Companion to the Song of Songs*. Edited by Athalya Brenner. Sheffield: JSOT Press.

Brett, Philip. 1994. *Queering the Pitch: The New Gay and Lesbian Musicology*. New York: Routledge.

Burrus, Virginia, and Stephen D. Moore. 2003. Unsafe Sex: Feminism, Pornography, and the Song of Songs. *Biblical Interpretation* 11:24–52.

Certeau, Michel de. 1992. *The Sixteenth and Seventeenth Centuries*. Volume 1 of *The Mystic Fable*. Translated by Michael B. Smith. Chicago: University of Chicago Press.

Clines, David J. A. 1995. *Interested Parties: The Ideology of Writers and Readers of the Hebrew Bible*. Journal for the Study of the Old Testament Supplement Series 205. Gender, Culture, Theory 1. Sheffield: Sheffield Academic Press.

Clover, Carol. *Men, Women, and Chainsaws: Gender in Modern Horror Film*. Princeton: Princeton University Press.

Cowie, Elizabeth. 1984. Fantasia. *m/f* 9:70–105.

Dijk-Hemmes, Fokkelien van. 1993. The Imagination of Power and the Power of Imagination: An Intertextual Analysis of Two Biblical Love Songs: The Song of Songs and Hosea 2. Pages 156–70 in *A Feminist Companion to the Song of Songs*. Edited by Athalya Brenner. Sheffield: JSOT Press.

Donald, James. 1989. Introduction. Pages 3–21 in *Fantasy and the Cinema*. Edited by James Donald. London: British Film Institute.

———. 1991. On the Threshold: Psychoanalysis and Cultural Studies. Pages 1–9 in *Psychoanalysis and Cultural Theory: Thresholds*. Edited by James Donald. New York: Macmillan.

Epstein, Heidi. 2004. *Melting the Venusberg: A Feminist Theology of Music*. New York: Continuum.

———. 2009. Sour Grapes, Fermented Selves: Musical Shulammites Modulate Subjectivity. *Bible and Critical Theory* 5.1:3.1–16. Online: http://www.epress.monash.edu.au/. DOI:10.2104/bc090003.

———. 2011. Penderecki's Iron Maiden: Intimacy and Other Anomalies in the *Canticum canticorum Salomonis*. Pages 99–130 in *Bible Trouble: Queer Reading at the Boundaries of Biblical Scholarship*. Edited by Teresa J. Hornsby and Ken Stone. Semeia Studies 67. Atlanta: Scholars Press.

Exum, J. Cheryl. 2005. *Song of Songs: A Commentary*. Old Testament Library. Louisville: Westminster John Knox.

Farmer, Brett. 2000. *Spectacular Passions: Cinema, Fantasy, Gay Male Spectatorships*. Durham, N.C.: Duke University Press.

Frosh, Stephen. 1997. *For and against Psychoanalysis*. New York: Routledge.

Garber, Marjorie. 1992. *Vested Interests: Cross-Dressing and Cultural Anxiety*. New York: Routledge.

Gilman, Sander L. 1985. *Difference and Pathology: Stereotypes of Sexuality, Race, and Madness*. Ithaca, N.Y.: Cornell University Press.

———. 1991. *The Jew's Body*. New York: Routledge.

Gordon, Alex. 1999. Descendant Dybbuks: Yiddish Cinema and the Hollywood Continuum. Pages 287–310 in *When Joseph Met Molly: A Reader on Yiddish Film*. Edited by Sylvia Paskin. Nottingham: Five Leaves.

Hoberman, Jay. 1995. *Bridge of Light: Yiddish Film between Two Worlds*. Philadelphia: Temple University Press.

Illouz, Eva. 2003. *Consuming the Romantic Utopia: Love and the Cultural Contradictions of Capitalism*. New York: Routledge.

Königsberg, Ira. 1997. The Only "I" in the World: Religion, Psychoanalysis, and *The Dybbuk*. *Cinema Journal* 36.4:22–42.

Kristeva, Julia. 1987. *Tales of Love*. New York: Columbia University Press.

Laplanche, Jean, and J. B. Pontalis. 1968. Fantasy and the Origins of Sexuality. *International Journal of Psychoanalysis* 49:1–18.

Lauretis, Teresa de. 1994. *The Practice of Love: Lesbian Sexuality and Perverse Desire*. Bloomington: Indiana University Press.

McClary, Susan. 1991. *Feminine Endings: Music, Gender, and Sexuality*. Minneapolis: University of Minnesota Press.

Meyers, Carol. 1993. Gender Imagery in the Song of Songs. Pages 197–212 in *A Feminist Companion to the Song of Songs*. Edited by Athalya Brenner. Sheffield: JSOT Press.

Miles, Margaret R. 1989. *Carnal Knowing: Female Nakedness and Religious Meaning in the Christian West*. Boston: Beacon.

Miller, D. A. 1998. *Place for Us: Essay on the Broadway Musical*. Cambridge: Harvard University Press.

Nochlin, Linda. 1995. Introduction: Starting with the Self: Jewish Identity and Its Representation. Pages 7–19 in *The Jew in the Text: Modernity and the Construction of Identity*. Edited by Linda Nochlin and Tamar Garb. London: Thames & Hudson.

Pardes, Ilana. 1992. *Countertraditions in the Bible: A Feminist Approach*. Cambridge: Harvard University Press.

Polaski, Donald C. 1997. What Will Ye See in the Shulammite? Women, Power and Panopticism in the Song of Songs. *Biblical Interpretation* 5:64–81.

Porter, Roy. 1993. The Body and the Mind, the Doctor and the Patient: Negotiating Hysteria. Pages 225–85 in *Hysteria beyond Freud*. Edited by Sander L. Gilman, Helen King, Roy Porter, G. S. Rousseau, and Elaine Showalter. Berkeley: University of California Press.

Rodriguez, Leonardo. 1990. Fantasy, Neurosis and Perversion. *Analysis* 2:97–113.

Roskies, David G. 1992. Introduction. Pages xii–xxxvi in S. Ansky, *The Dybbuk and Other Writings*. Edited by David G. Roskies. Translated by Golda Werman. New York: Schocken.

Runions, Erin. 2003. *How Hysterical: Identification and Resistance in the Bible and Film*. New York: Palgrave.

Russo, Mary. 1994. *The Female Grotesque: Risk, Excess and Modernity*. New York: Routledge.

Seidman, Naomi. 2003. The Ghost of Queer Loves Past: Ansky's "Dybbuk" and the Sexual Transformation of Ashkenaz. Pages 228–45 in *Queer Theory and the Jewish Question*. Edited by Daniel Boyarin, Daniel Itzkobitz, and Ann Pellegrini. New York: Columbia University Press.

Shandler, Jeffrey. 2006. Queer Yiddishkeit: Practice and Theory. *Shofar* 25.1:90–113.

Sicular, Eve. 1999. The Celluloid Closet of Yiddish Film. Pages 231–44 in *When Joseph Met Molly: A Reader on Yiddish Film*. Edited by Sylvia Paskin. Nottingham: Five Leaves.

Silverman, Kaja. 1992. *Male Subjectivity at the Margins*. New York: Routledge.

Solomon, Alisa. 2004. *Re-dressing the Canon: Essays on Theater and Gender*. New York: Routledge.

Stavrakakis, Yannis. 1999. *Lacan and the Political*. New York: Routledge.

Trible, Phyllis. 1978. *God and the Rhetoric of Sexuality*. Philadelphia: Fortress.

Weems, Renita. 1993. Song of Songs. Pages 156–60 in *The Women's Bible Commentary*. Edited by Carol A. Newsom and Sharon Ringe. Louisville: Westminster John Knox.

Žižek, Slavoj. 1991. *Looking Awry: An Introduction to Jacques Lacan through Popular Culture*. Cambridge: MIT Press.

Filmography

The Dybbuk: A Feature Film. 1937. [In Yiddish.] Directed by Michal Waszinski. New York: Bel Canto Society. DVD.

Trembling before G-d. 2001. Directed by Sandi Simcha Dubowski. New Yorker Films. DVD.

Voluptuous, Tortured, and Unmanned: Ezekiel with Daniel Paul Schreber*

Rhiannon Graybill

Against the historical-critical method that still casts a long shadow across the field of biblical studies, I begin this paper with the wager that other forms of critical engagement can provide illuminating perspectives on biblical texts. In particular, I will argue that Daniel Paul Schreber's *Memoirs of My Nervous Illness* (2000) offers a productive point of entry into Ezek 4–5, the chapters involving the prophet's sign acts. First published in Germany in 1903, the *Memoirs* describe Schreber's "unmanning" (*Entmannung*) by a malevolent god who is made of nerves and sexually attracted to Schreber's body. Schreber himself was a judge until his "nervous illness" struck, leading first to institutionalization and then, after their author's release, to the *Memoirs*. The *Memoirs*, in turn, have been of great interest to psychoanalysis, philosophy, and critical theory, numbering among their readers Freud (2001, 3–83), Lacan (1993), Canetti (1984, 434–64), Deleuze and Guattari (2009, 1–21; 2004, 149–66, 288–89), and many more.[1] Ezekiel's sign acts, for their part, are a series of peculiar and generally ineffective embodied performances that mark the beginning of his prophecy (Ezek 4–5). In reading these two texts together, I seek their suggestive similarities and affinities. I do not intend to argue that Schreber's memoir "explains" Ezekiel, any more than I wish to suggest that Ezekiel "anticipates" Schreber. Nor do I use Schreber as a model "mad prophet"—psychological diagnoses through

* An earlier version of this paper was presented at the 2011 SBL Annual Meeting in San Francisco. I would like to thank Lena Salaymeh, Kurt Beals, Kent Brintnall, and Raphael Graybill for their helpful comments.

1. These readings will be discussed in greater detail subsequently in the text. For readings by de Certeau, Lingis, Lyotard, and others, see as well the collection in Allison et al. 1988.

literary texts strike me as dubious—but rather as generative literary and theoretical intertext that opens new ways of thinking about the sign acts.

Juxtaposing the *Memoirs* and Ezek 4–5 exposes a number of parallels between the texts, which in turn complicate the relationship between prophecy, masculinity, and the sign acts. Schreber and Ezekiel share an experience of prophecy as instigated in crisis and located in the body. Both men are called as prophets within a space of disaster, and both struggle with language and the possibility of communication itself. Moreover, in both cases the body—tortured and abject—assumes prophetic importance. Sexualized, charged with meaning, and reduced to suffering flesh, the body enacts the dilemmas of prophetic masculinity. This shared experience motivates my intertextual reading. In treating these texts together, I aim not only to draw out deliberately nonhistorical parallels, but also to challenge the ordinary ways in which we read and represent texts together. What does it mean to read one text "through" another? What determines which texts count as "theory" and which as "primary text"? What happens if instead of reading for systems and explanations, we read for ahistories and discontinuities? What happens when we read Schreber and Ezekiel together, without recourse to arguments of psychopathology, historical moment, or relations of "anticipation" and "influence"?

In Schreber's memoirs, the body becomes both an object of divine violence (particularly sexual violence) and an instrument of critique. Schreber's "unmanning" signals the passivity of the prophetic body while also refusing to submit to normative masculinity. Reading Hebrew prophecy through Schreber, it becomes clear that the book of Ezekiel, too, uses the body to signal the impossibility of effective prophecy. Furthermore, this prophetic failure is deeply charged with anxiety over masculinity, prophecy, and embodiment. While the book of Ezekiel never reaches the full extent of Schreber's critique, the same dilemma drives both texts—the problem of the male prophetic body. Approaching Ezekiel through Schreber does what a close reading or a historical analysis alone cannot do: it forces us to confront the impossible demands of masculinity and embodiment for the male prophet, as well as to imagine the body as an instrument of critique.

Ezekiel and the Problem of a Body

In the opening chapters of the book that bears his name, Ezekiel witnesses an incredible theophany (Ezek 1–2), is struck dumb by Yahweh (ch. 3), and then begins his work as a prophet with a number of bizarre somatic performances (chs. 4–5), known as the sign acts. He builds and besieges a model of the city of Jerusalem (4:1–3), lies on his side for more than a year (4:4–8), eats only severely limited siege rations (4:9–17), and cuts and burns portions of his hair and beard (5:1–4). In these texts, the body of the prophet poses an interpretive problem, even as it offers a commentary on the problems of prophetic embodiment. At least in the opening scenes of his prophetic vocation, Ezekiel seems a very bad sort of prophet. Like Isaiah, he is informed from the beginning that the people to whom he is sent are intractable, hardheaded, and unwilling to listen (Isa 6:9–13). Unlike Isaiah, he does not even attempt to speak. Instead, his prophecy begins as a series of performances—but performances that leave no indication of their success. As David Stacey writes, "Ezekiel's actions may arrest attention, but few of them can be said to communicate meaning more easily than words" (1990, 266).

Ezekiel's activities may communicate very little (or very little *successfully*) about the perversity of Israel, but they suggest a great deal about the relationship of prophecy to bodily suffering. The body of Ezekiel is a body positioned in radical pain. To lie unmoving for more than a year, to eat food baked on excrement, to enact with one's body the destruction of the world—these are not so much attention-getting tricks as scenes of agony. To prophesy continually against a brick, for example, causes a great deal of pain to the prophet (Moses, after all, cannot hold up his arms unassisted while the Israelites battle the Amalekites; Ezekiel must hold up his arm for far longer) but none for the brick (Ezek 4:4–7; cf. Exod 17:8–13). While scholars have suggested that the brick siege and the other sign acts are rhetorically striking modes of communication (Friebel 1999), prophetic predictions (Hummel 2005; Fohrer 1953), or effective magic (Stalker 1968; Fohrer 1966) (or some mixture thereof), I want to suggest that there is nothing effectual about this action. As the book of Ezekiel itself assures us, nothing is changed by Ezekiel's prophecies. Instead, their sole effect seems to be to bring pain to the body of the prophet.[2]

Ezekiel's sign acts have, of course, been read as performance, including the incongruously modern explanation of prophetic action as intrepid street theater (Hutton 1995; Clements 1996, 6) and the more innovative comparison of prophecy to more radical strands of performance art

---

2. On pain and Ezekiel's sign acts, see Graybill 2012, 64–72, esp. 71–72.

(Sherwood 1998, 2006; Hornsby 2006).[3] What these approaches neglect, however, is the fundamental question of volition and control. The performance artist Joseph Beuys in a room with a coyote is a commentary on many things—on the fragility of the human body, on the question of death, and so on. But Beuys remains, as well, an artist who has chosen to remain in a room with a coyote.[4] If we accept one basic premise of prophecy from its representation in the Hebrew Bible, it is that "prophet" is emphatically *not* a vocation of choice. As the story of Jonah shows us, the language of the prophetic "call" is also a language of coercion. And so in understanding Ezekiel's fraught experience of embodiment, I want to turn to another suggestive literary and philosophical intertext: the memoirs of Daniel Paul Schreber.

Daniel Paul Schreber

Daniel Paul Schreber was born in 1842, the child of German child-rearing expert Moritz Schreber.[5] A respected judge, he suffered from a nervous illness in 1884, but recovered the following year and resumed his judicial career. In 1893 he was struck by a second nervous illness and institutionalized. Upon regaining his freedom in 1902, he published an account of his experiences, which formed the basis of one of Freud's famous case studies and a number of other psychoanalytic, psychological, and critical interpretations (Freud 2001; Lothane 1992). Unlike so many contemporary memoirs, Schreber's text does not chart a fall into illness, followed by a difficult, gradual, eventually successful movement back into health, or at least into an acknowledgment of reality as commonly accepted. Instead, his *Denkwürdigkeiten eines Nervenkranken*, known in English as *Memoirs of My Nervous Illness*, reads as an account of discovery, offering a carefully articulated explanation of his new understanding of the world.[6]

Schreber's memoirs offer an account of a world on the brink of disaster, with his own body serving as ground zero of the conflict. The text begins, after several prefaces, with nerves: "The human soul is contained

3. For a slightly different use of performance criticism, see Doan and Giles 2005.

4. On Beuys see the discussion by Tisdall 2008.

5. For an account of Schreber's biography, see Lothane 1992.

6. Lothane notes that the German title is better translated "'the great thoughts of a nervous patient'—that is how Schreber meant it," but the English title given by the original translators persists (1992, 1–2).

in the nerves of the body," Schreber writes, adding a page later: "God to start with is only nerve, not body, and akin therefore to the human soul" (2000, 19–20). This god of nerves is nonomniscient and imperfect, constantly threatened by the attraction of the divine nerves to their human counterparts, as well as to what Schreber terms "soul-voluptuousness" (96 *et passim*). This delicate balance between divine and human nerves is upset when an unknown party attempts "soul murder" on Schreber (33–37). As a result, the divine nerves are constantly attracted to his body and seek to "unman" it; such *Entmannung*, or "unmanning," is necessary to forestall cosmic disaster (59–61).[7] This transformation, which occupies much of the memoir, is at once incredibly painful and rich with voluptuous pleasure.

The publication of Schreber's memoirs inspired a number of critical responses, some psychological or psychoanalytic, some literary, and others concerned with questions of history, ideology, or power. Freud's case study, "Psychoanalytic Notes upon an Autobiographical Account of a Case of Paranoia (Dementia Paranoides)," published a few years after Schreber's memoir, is perhaps the most famous, though it is more useful in tracking the development of Freud's own thought than in understanding Schreber's situation. (Freud, after all, never met the patient, despite developing an extensive artifice of theory around him.[8]) But in spite of its flaws, Freud's case study ushers in Schreber's memoirs as a significant text for modern psychoanalysis, philosophy, and literary theory. Freud's approach also exemplifies one major interpretive strategy: taking the memoirs as a

7. The translators of the English edition of Schreber's memoirs, Ida Macalpine and Richard A. Hunter, write, "*Entmannung*. The authorized translation of Freud (1911) uses the term 'emasculation.' We have chosen 'unmanning' because its primary meaning is 'to remove from the category of men,' which is what Schreber intended. Only its fourth definition in the Oxford English Dictionary is given as castration. Emasculation, on the other hand, has castration as its primary meaning, i.e. rendering sterile. From the pages immediately following, as well as Schreber's further text, it is quite obvious that he meant transformation by an evolutionary process into a reproductive woman which was to render him fertile. Schreber himself stresses this by usually putting 'change into a woman' in brackets after 'unmanning'" (Schreber 2000, 446–47). I have followed the translators' practice here.

8. Freud's treatment of the specifics of the case is sometimes clumsy, and a number of scholars have noted that his theory of paranoia as repressed homosexuality does not grow out of Schreber's specific case, but rather seems superimposed upon it. See Chabot 1982, 34.

window onto interior trauma (see, e.g., Pinar 2006; Shengold 1989). An alternate interpretive move treats the memoirs—and sometimes Schreber himself—less as an individual sufferer than as a symptom of a particular historical moment, most frequently the authoritarian social dynamics that would lead to twentieth-century fascism. Elias Canetti, for example, claims that Schreber's paranoia lays bare the functions of totalitarianism (1984, 434–64), while Eric Santner argues that Foucault's theory of disciplinary knowledge—that it produces a new way of understanding the body—bears "striking affinities" to Schreber (1996, 173 n. 32). Deleuze and Guattari, for their part, treat schizophrenia as an illuminating form of contemporary subjectivity, with Schreber as the exemplary "body without organs," and the prime example of "becoming-woman" (2004, 165–88, 300–330; 2009, 8–18).

While I draw on this rich interpretive history, I am not interested in diagnosing, historicizing, or treating Schreber as a philosophical object. In using the memoirs as a literary and theoretical text to read the book of Ezekiel, I take Schreber as a prophetic figure, rather than as a model patient, a historical symptom, or an effect of power. I follow the work of Lucy Bregman, who has argued that Schreber's memoirs are best understood theologically:

> Schreber's Memoirs was a religious text before it became a case history, and the ground gained by Otto and Eliade in marking out a space for religious language ought to be solid and broad enough to allow Schreber to stand on it, too. Few of Schreber's interpreters and none of his turn-of-the-century contemporaries doubted that he was mad, insane, mentally ill, or whatever other term their conceptual schemes supplied. In other words, he was quite as crazy as he was religious. But I think both these perspectives on his Memoirs should be taken seriously. (1977, 120)[9]

The memoirs are productively read as a theological text, with a coherent—if radically unfamiliar—ideological and religious system. In this system, the body is foregrounded as a site of conflict. Schreber's ideas about embodiment, masculinity, outrageous suffering, and unexpected pleasure, moreover, offer an opening into a text no less painfully charged—the book of Ezekiel.

9. For a response to Bregman, see Church 1979.

Schreber, Ezekiel, and the Problems of Prophecy

Like Ezekiel, Schreber understood himself as divinely called in times of trouble—of world-changing disaster, even—to prophesy to a recalcitrant and resistant people. Like Ezekiel, Schreber experienced his body as thrust into a world of pain, a pain at once radically necessary to his prophetic vocation and oddly ineffectual at it. Like Ezekiel, Schreber found himself struck dumb, stripped first of words and then of the possibility of meaningful communication. But unlike Ezekiel, lying in the dust, Schreber left a record of all this, preserved first in his legal appeals and then in his memoirs.[10] Schreber thus exposes the inside narrative of the crisis of prophetic embodiment. His words, though hedged by redactions, rewritings, and aporias, give voice to Ezekiel's dumbness. Schreber's memoir offers a primary account of the paradoxes of prophetic embodiment, as well as the tentative possibilities for imagining a world otherwise. In the section that follows, I delineate three parallels in particular between Schreber and Ezekiel: the experience of disaster, the crisis of language, and the pain of the body. All of these contribute to an overarching concern in both texts: the dilemma of prophetic masculinity.

1. The Experience of Disaster

Memoirs of My Nervous Illness begins with Schreber's personal efforts to gain his release from the asylum where he is institutionalized against his will. In the introduction to his manuscript, he describes its purpose as "to give an at least partly comprehensible exposition of supernatural matters, knowledge of which has been revealed to me" (2000, 15–16). These "supernatural matters," moreover, have brought Schreber a tremendous amount of pain, as he describes throughout the text. The unthinkable has already happened; what Schreber terms the "Order of the World" has been ruptured, Schreber himself has been "unmanned," and the order of things has been impossibly changed (23 *et passim*). There is no longer the possibility of averting the crisis; it is already upon us. This textual location within the time of the disaster sets the text apart from traditional future-oriented

10. What became *Memoirs of My Nervous Illness* began as a series of legal appeals that Schreber, a former judge, wrote as he sued for his release from the Sonnenstein Asylum. He subsequently decided to publish the text, with some modifications. See Schreber 2000, 3–5.

prophecy that leaves open the possibility, however slim, of averting the crisis.

At the same time, the emphasis on disaster links Schreber to Ezekiel, prophesying on the banks of the Chebar. The opening lines of the book of Ezekiel position the prophet in the space of the disaster—this time, not the cosmic rending of the order of the world, but the historical disaster of the exile. To prophesy "among the exiles" (Ezek 1:1) requires the unthinkable already to have happened—the exile from Judah to Babylon. What does it mean to prophesy in such a place and in such a time? From the beginning, the text suggests the futility, even the impossibility, of prophecy. This disaster is at once political and cosmological. To live in the exile is unthinkable, to worship properly in the exile impossible. Ezekiel's dumbness, which strikes him immediately after Yahweh's spectacular theophany, is a bodily manifestation of the impossibility of prophecy.

2. The Crisis of Language

This impossibility of prophecy is bound up in a crisis of language. Dumbness and other difficulties with speech characterize prophecy in disaster. As he recounts in his memoir, Schreber has difficulty in communicating both his experiences and his new understanding of the world. His opening commitment to explain "supernatural matters" is immediately followed by hedging:

> I cannot of course count upon being *fully* understood because things are dealt with which cannot be expressed in human language; they exceed human understanding. Nor can I maintain that *everything* is irrefutably certain even for me: much remains only presumption and probability. After all I too am only a human being and therefore limited by the confines of human understanding. (2000, 16)

The text that follows is likewise almost overwhelmed with explanatory asides, apologies to the reader, and assurances. Beyond this persistent and apologetic self-positioning, the text is filled with a deep—and deeply strange—relation to language. Much of Schreber's explanation is dedicated to language: the language of the divine nerves, the language of birds, the language of God himself. And like Ezekiel, Schreber himself is struck dumb. When he regains his voice, it is not to speak, but rather to experience what he names, with one of many neologisms, the "bellowing miracle," the forced production of nonlinguistic sound. Language is thus shattered in the space of the disaster.

The dumbness of the prophet Ezekiel (Ezek 3:15, 25–26; see also 24:25–27, 33:21–22) is likewise a clear sign of the crisis of language. Ezekiel's sign acts, as we have seen, fail rather badly as communicative acts. There is no indication that they serve to persuade anyone of anything; the immediate audience is both already in exile and preemptively denied the possibility of understanding. Likewise, even as metaphors or textual events, the sign acts remain oddly ineffective. As in Franz Kafka's story "A Hunger Artist" (1995), there is something excessive in their performance, and the end effect is more a confounding of the processes of meaning than the transmission of a particular message.[11] Ezekiel's binding, fasting, and hair burning, while striking, are not effective as signs. His body is emphatically not the spectacle of suffering that forms the centerpiece of martyrdom. Nor is the suffering of this body necessarily implicated in a larger economy of pleasure, as in sadism or masochism. Instead, as with the hunger artist, the meaning of the performance eludes the observers and is incommunicable by the performer. Schreber too is plagued by the incommunicability of his experience. In the *Memoirs* he plays with language and contorts meaning to explain the divine violation of his body. And yet as with Ezekiel (and the hunger artist), the situation does not resolve into intelligibility. What remains, instead, is the impossibility of communication. Kafka writes, "No one could possibly watch the hunger artist continuously, day and night, and so no one could produce first-hand evidence that the fast had really been rigorous and continuous; only the artist himself could know that, he was therefore bound to be the sole completely satisfied spectator of his own fast" (1995, 270).

In the same way, only Ezekiel can be the sole completely satisfied spectator of the sign acts, even as only Schreber is the sole complete witness of his own unmanning. The experience exceeds and defies language.

3. The Prophetic Body in Pain

It is not only language that suffers from the positioning of prophecy in disaster—the body of the prophet also suffers, and suffers horribly. When

11. For an expanded discussion of Ezekiel and Kafka's hunger artist, though without reference to Schreber, see Graybill 2012, 68–69.

Schreber is not inventing a new lexicon adequate to the task of describing what he has experienced, he returns again and again to his pain. His prophetic vocation brings with it seemingly endless anguish and torture. He suffers a number of forced and painful transformations of his body, which he dubs "miracles" (2000, 141–51). He describes his torment by his doctors, by the staff in the institution, by a legal system that refuses him his freedom. More than anything else, the memoirs express Schreber's great pain and his attempt to communicate this pain. At one point, he laments,

> When I think of my sacrifices through loss of an honorable professional position, a happy marriage practically dissolved, deprived of all the pleasures of life, subjected to bodily pain, mental torture, and terrors of a hitherto unknown kind, the picture emerges of a martyrdom which all in all I can only compare with the crucifixion of Jesus Christ. (258)

While Schreber cannot seem to stop speaking—and writing—about his anguish, Ezekiel never voices his suffering. However, the book of Ezekiel, no less than Schreber's *Memoirs*, is marked by the experience of pain. We have already seen this is the case with the sign acts. To be bound and silent, to lie on one's side for more than a year, to survive on tiny amounts of food, to cook with excrement—these are not only performances that foreground the body and challenge the communicative economy. They are also scenes of torture, positioning the prophet's body in a universe of pain.

Nor is this pain temporary. After lying bound, prophesying against the brick, and consuming only survival rations, Ezekiel is commanded to raise a sword against himself and to cut off his hair and beard. The hair that he removes is divided into three piles—one to be burned, one to be struck with the sword, and one to be scattered to the wind (Ezek 5:1–3). There is a second cruelty, however, in the seeming preservation of a remnant. The hairs spared and bound up in the prophet's robe are not delivered, but rather subjected to further destruction by fire (5:4). This is a narrative logic straight from the Marquis de Sade—the body is preserved and rejuvenated so as to allow a constant restaging of the original scene of torture.[12] Prophecy is agony. The pain of the prophetic body, the failure of prophetic language, and the impossible necessity of prophesying from within the disaster all unite Ezekiel to

12. See, for example, *Justine*, where the heroine's ravaged body is magically healed every evening in preparation for the following day's torture (Sade 1990).

Schreber, even as they set the former apart from classical biblical prophecy and the latter from more common twentieth-century critical discourses.

Unmanning and the Dilemmas of Prophetic Masculinity

To this point, there remains the most famous feature of the memoirs, Schreber's experience of unmanning. This is the crucial hook for Freud's theory of homosexuality and for Deleuze and Guattari's notion of "becoming woman," as well as a key motivating factor in Schreber's own forced institutionalization. Schreber's nervous illness begins, as he recalls, with "the idea that it really must be rather pleasant to be a woman succumbing to intercourse" (2000, 46). He experiences the sex of his own body as in flux, including the sensation of female breasts and buttocks and the "retraction of the male organ," and notes his increased sense of what he terms "voluptuousness," a feeling he treats as feminine (142). Unmanning alters the external form of his body while increasing his capacity to experience sexual pleasure. Schreber's increased voluptuousness simultaneously renders his body irresistible to the divine nerves that are constantly attracted to him and that bring about his unmanning. This unmanning is essential to Schreber's self-understanding of his new and divinely ordained role. Unmanning functions as a therapeutic response to catastrophe: the body of the prophet must be unmanned to repair the rent in the Order of the World (60). Furthermore, there is a logic of suffering built into the vocation of prophecy, as well as a logic of passivity. The prophet's body must be transformed, and yet unmanning is done *to* Schreber, not *by* him. Passivity is divinely demanded, and passivity is painful.

In Ezekiel, too, the body of the prophet is forced into painful service of a divine message. Prophecy is *done to* Ezekiel, even as unmanning is done to Schreber. Ezekiel's first action in the book is to fall on his face in the dust; immediately after being called as a prophet, he sits in silence, "stunned," for seven days (Ezek 1:28; 3:15).

But while both Ezekiel and Schreber occupy the position of acted-upon bodies, called into prophecy, only Schreber is "unmanned." This experience of unmanning seems to be the point at which Ezekiel and Schreber break from each other. There may be prophetic passivity in the book of Ezekiel—and there are certainly plenty of bodies, both sexed and subjected to violence—but there is no explicit unmanning. The sex of the prophet's body never comes to the fore. Instead, the explicitly sexual bodies, most spectacularly the bodies of Ezek 16 and 23, are female bodies. These bodies are drawn into sexual contact—sometimes with Yahweh, sometimes with foreign lovers, but never with the prophet himself. Ezekiel's bodily maleness remains unthematized. However, there is a significant and meaningful relationship between Schreber's unmanning and Ezekiel's own prophetic masculinity. In particular, while Ezekiel's maleness is never explicitly challenged by the text, he is nevertheless represented in ways that break with normative biblical masculinity. As the extensive descriptions of the female body in Ezek 16 and 23 make clear, embodiment itself is strongly associated with the feminine. So too is passivity. And yet Ezekiel's prophetic call places him in a passive position, outside language, where all that matters is his body. Schreber's term *Entmannung*, "unmanning," can be taken to name a basic relation between the male religious subject and the male god.

Unmanning is a refusal of ordinary masculinity—of the form of the male body, and of the ordinary relations of male-dominated, active-oriented power. And if unmanning is a critical judgment on the organization of masculinity, then Schreber's text is not just memoir but also critique. Howard Eilberg-Schwartz reads Schreber's description of unmanning and of forced passivity as part of a broader critique of masculinity under religious monotheism:

> [Schreber] was able to think the unthinkable and thus expresses what traditional theology has always been afraid to face. When a man confronts a male God, he is put into the female position so as to be intimate with God. … The defining traits of what it meant to be a man were called into question. In the literature of ancient Judaism, this threat to masculinity proceeds in ways parallel to Schreber's: sometimes through violence that threatens castration, even death, at other times in more subtle forms of gender reversal. (1995, 137–38)

As Eilberg-Schwartz suggests, Schreber demonstrates the ways that the male believer's relationship with God places him in a passive, nonmasculine position. In particular, Schreber's memoirs critique the impossible subject position of the male religious subject. Ezekiel is likewise placed in this position of passive masculinity vis-à-vis the dominant male divine, from the moment that he falls at Yahweh's feet. This moment in the text marks both a general entry into the prophetic call and a specific representation of the relationship of sex, embodiment, and masculinity. In gazing upon Yahweh, Ezekiel perhaps gazes in particular upon the divine genitals, as both Eilberg-Schwartz (1995, 78) and Stephen Moore (1996, 84–85) suggest. This act of looking upon the body of the (divine) father, as Ham does in Gen 9, is at once erotically charged and deeply prohibited as an assault on the power of the father. But even if we insist that Ezekiel's gaze is "just a look," the overarching dynamic of the scene that follows is of active, speaking, powerful Yahweh and his passive, silent, powerless prophet. Ezekiel's bodily experience and his religious subjectivity are thus positioned outside normative biblical masculinity. In this way, he parallels Schreber's own experience of masculinity. The main difference is that while Schreber writes down his critique (in the form of the memoirs), Ezekiel's response to the dilemmas of prophetic masculinity appears only through his excessive, ineffective embodied actions.

Voluptuous Utopias: Transformed Bodies, Transformed Spaces

Schreber's unmanning dramatizes the ways in which the passivity of prophecy alters the experience of masculinity, producing a trenchant critique of the relations of gender to religious subjectivity. And yet Schreber's memoir is far from the only source to sketch out the difficulty of the relationship of the male believer in relation to the male God in biblical and postbiblical tradition. Eilberg-Schwartz argues that the rabbis find themselves in a similar position (1995, 137–96); Moore makes a parallel argument about the dilemmas of Christian male exegetes of the Song of Songs (2002, 21–89). To be sure, Schreber, unlike these other sources, emphasizes the prophetic, but the problems of prophecy can and have been articulated without reference to divine nerves, unmanning, or "soul-voluptuousness." What need, then, for Schreber?

While the critique of masculine religious subjectivity is an important component of Schreber's memoirs—and has served as one of the most fertile sites of engagement for contemporary theory—it is not the only function of unmanning in the text. Schreber complains a great deal about his unmanning, and yet he also finds pleasure and power in his self-transformation. Unmanning is thus not merely a figure of critique or a metaphor of emasculation—the *Memoirs* are not intended metaphorically at all. Instead, Schreber actually experiences his body transforming. And it is worth taking this account of transformation seriously. Just as I have argued that Schreber's text is productively read as intentional theology instead of accidental symptomatology, so too do I want to propose taking what Schreber says about the body seriously, if not necessarily literally.

To this end, Jill Marsden directs attention to the "tactility, multiplicity, and emergent creativity" of Schreber's system (1999, 69; see also 60).

Rejecting the "despotism of psychoanalysis" and its disciplining of the body, she argues that Schreber's body becomes "an autoerotic economy in which the means of communication begin to communicate with themselves," producing a nonessentialist, nonfoundational system exceeds the logic of identity (67, 71). This includes exceeding the normative logic of masculinity. Read this way, Schreber's body functions not so much as a critique of the patriarchal theological system, but as a destabilizing alternative to it—a move outside the demands of normative masculinity. Schreber's *Memoirs* end with a new body for the prophet, a body rich in pleasure and exterior to the constrained category of masculinity that precedes the crisis of Schreber's nervous illness. The body itself is more than a critique—it is a productive materiality that shatters categories and augurs new pleasures.

The book of Ezekiel likewise ends with a transformed body—but not a human one. Instead, the final nine chapters of the book are devoted to an elaborate vision of the rebuilt temple, its dimensions, construction, and the priests who will serve within it. In a vision that mirrors the theophany at the book's beginning, Ezekiel is transported to the new temple: "The hand of Yahweh was upon me, and he brought me there. He brought me in divine visions to the land of Israel and set me upon a very high mountain, and upon was a building like a city to the south" (40:1b–2). He is guided by a man "whose appearance was like that of bronze, with a linen cord and a measuring rod in his hand" (Ezek 40:3)—a combination of technical and metallurgical details again reminiscent of the fantastic vision of God's chariot in Ezek 1. The man's appearance also suggests the possibility of imagining a different sort of body, even as Ezekiel, *transported* in a vision instead of *transformed* in his flesh, is denied this possibility. The vision of the new temple gradually expands to include the entire land, and the final chapter lists the tribes of Israel and their location in the new land. The final line of the book gives a name to the city: "and the name of the city from now on shall be: *Yahweh is there*" (Ezek 48:35). As Albert Cook writes,

> The space of the new land counterbalances and fulfills the initial balance in the opening heaven that had been vouchsafed to this mighty speaker. … Ezekiel has, as it were, substituted space for time in this last vision, which extends the Temple outward from more usual measurements into an extent that encompasses the whole space of his lost country. (1996, 86)

The fantasy of the rebuilt temple imagines a healing for the trauma of exile. At the same time, it transposes the imagery of the opening theophany from the chariot to the temple itself, where Yahweh returns to dwell in chapter 43. As Cook points out, the time of disaster is replaced with a utopian imagining of space. The final chapters and the opening chapters, taken together, form both an inclusion and a reversal.

The resolution of the problems of the body (Ezekiel's body, Yahweh's gazed-upon body, the bodies engaged in abominations in the temple, the violated bodies of chs. 16 and 23, the raised bodies of ch. 37) is thus the restoration of the temple. In chapters 40–48 the temple body is the repository of utopian fantasy, replacing the specific body of the prophet with an abstract and collective "body." This shift in focus to the temple does many things: it brings an end to the agonies of exile, it furnishes Yahweh with a new and glorious home, it sets forth a proper ordering of space for the many returned Israelite peoples. This association of redemptive transformation with reimagined city space is not Ezekiel's invention, but rather part of a long-standing ancient Near Eastern tradition, from Gilgamesh's pride in the walls of Uruk (George 2003, 99 [tablet 11 of the Standard Version]) to the association of the temple and the body in the New Testament (John 2:19–22; 1 Cor 6:19–20).

The restoration of the temple in the final chapters of Ezekiel resembles Schreber's experience of bodily transformation. As with Schreber, the transformed vision represents a new world after the disaster, a world healed. And the transformation also marks a renewed relationship with the deity that at once preserves the passivity of the prophet (Ezekiel is first transported, then led around the temple; Schreber remains in voluptuous contact with the divine rays) and moves beyond pain. And yet the transformation of religious and city space in Ezekiel does not fully resolve the problem of the prophetic body, as Schreber's unmanning does. In ending with Ezekiel's visionary transport to the rebuilt temple, the book neatly leaves behind the messy question of prophetic embodiment, of the suffering and linguistic crisis and fraught masculinity that figure so prominently in the opening chapters of the book. This quick move to leave behind the body of the prophet is likewise what makes the conclusion of the book of Ezekiel, in the final analysis, unsatisfying. The text ends with a lovely architectural vision that also fails to respond to or resolve the dilemmas of embodiment in the opening pages of the book.

Unlike Schreber, Ezekiel has no utopian experience of transformation, no radical self-reimagining. The move beyond critique into productive creativity is ultimately stunted. There is no pleasure in unmanning to be found here, only a city that shares Yahweh's name.

Reading Prophetic Masculinity

Schreber concludes his memoir by shifting his focus from his own past suffering to a common human future. In the second-to-last paragraph, he writes, "I come to the last point of my work. I consider it possible, even likely, that the future development of my personal fate, the spread of my religious ideas and the weight of proof of their truth will lead to a fundamental revolution in mankind's religious views unequaled in history" (2000, 258).

The book of Ezekiel, in its elaborate vision of the restored temple, ends not so differently, though Ezekiel's religious vision is one of continuity, not revolution. But Ezekiel, as we have seen, ends not with a body but with a name, *Yahweh is there*. This conclusion completes the forgetting of the body that enters the text from the moment that Ezekiel is transported "in a vision." And yet against the intentions of the vision and the efforts of the text, we cannot forget the problem of the male prophetic body. Even as Schreber's *Memoirs of My Nervous Illness* show the intractable position of the male religious believer under a male god, so too do they suggest the possibility, though almost impossibly slim, of imagining a different sort of order of sexes and bodies. Schreber's radical *self*-transformation moves beyond the transformation of sacred space in Ezekiel to suggest the possibility of moving outside the demands of prophecy.

While Schreber is able to invent an alternative to the patriarchal order and to propose a form of masculinity that does not depend on active domination of the other—an economy of desire that, despite Schreber's emphasis on unmanning, is not organized around lack (see Marsden 1999)—Ezekiel has no such recourse and can imagine no such utopian transformation. Perhaps it is the critical, scientific, and discursive resources of modernity that make it possible for Schreber to imagine an alternative organization of embodiment, sexuality, and sexual pleasure, a newly configured male prophetic body at the boundaries of the human. Or perhaps Schreber only puts in words what Ezekiel already suggests with his silence. In any case, for Ezekiel the utopian impulse is actualized in reimagining the body of the temple—a fantastic vision that displaces the human body as body. The rebuilt temple at the end of the book of Ezekiel substitutes for the unmanned body that emerges in Schreber's memoirs. Both are fantasies that pose an alternative to the intractable, anguished position of the male prophetic body in disaster.

Even as the book of Ezekiel documents the impossible position of the embodied male prophet, it is ultimately unable to articulate an ordering of desire beyond activity-passivity and a prophetic embodiment not predicated on violence and torture. Using Schreber to approach Ezekiel allows us both to understand the particular agony of male prophetic subjectivity and to imagine the possibility, however slim, of a different organization of bodies and pleasures. Schreber's body destabilizes normative masculinity and the religious relations built upon it—not just for Schreber, but also for Ezekiel. Reading the texts together exposes the fragile, painful male body that lies on the banks of the river Chebar. It also forces us to confront prophetic masculinity, in all its messy embodiment. Ezekiel, no less than Schreber, demands it.

Works Cited

Allison, David B., Prado de Oliveira, Mark S. Roberts, and Allen S. Weiss. 1988. *Psychosis and Sexual Identity: Toward a Post-analytic View of the Schreber Case*. Albany: State University of New York Press.

Bregman, Lucy. 1977. Religion and Madness: Schreber's *Memoirs* as Personal Myth. *Journal of Religion and Health* 16:119–35.

Canetti, Elias. 1984. *Crowds and Power*. New York: Farrar, Straus, and Giroux.

Chabot, C. Barry. 1982. *Freud on Schreber: Psychoanalytic Theory and the Critical Act*. Amherst: University of Massachusetts Press.

Church, Nathan. 1979. Schreber's *Memoirs*: Myth or Personal Lamentation. *Journal of Religion and Health* 18:313–26.

Clements, R. E. 1996. *Ezekiel*. Westminster Bible Companion. Louisville: Westminster John Knox.

Cook, Albert. 1996. *The Burden of Prophecy: Poetic Utterance in the Prophets of the Old Testament*. Carbondale: Southern Illinois University Press.

Deleuze, Gilles, and Félix Guattari. 2004. *A Thousand Plateaus: Capitalism and Schizophrenia*. Translated by Brian Massumi. 1987. Repr., Minneapolis: University of Minnesota Press.

Deleuze, Gilles, and Félix Guattari. 2009. *Anti-Oedipus: Capitalism and Schizophrenia*. Translated by Robert Hurley, Mark Seem, and Helen Lane. 1977. Repr., New York: Penguin.

Doan, William, and Terry Giles. 2005. *Prophets, Performance, and Power: Performance Criticism of the Hebrew Bible*. New York: T&T Clark.

Eilberg-Schwartz, Howard. 1995. *God's Phallus: and Other Problems for Men and Monotheism*. Boston: Beacon.

Fohrer, Georg. 1953. *Die symbolischen Handlungen der Propheten*. Abhandlungen zur Theologie des Alten und Neuen Testaments 25. Zurich: Zwingli.

———. 1966. Prophetie und Magie. *Zeitschrift für die Alttestamentliche Wissenschaft* 78:25–47.

Freud, Sigmund. 2001. Psycho-analytic Notes on an Autobiographical Account of a Case of Paranoia (Dementia Paranoides) (1911). Pages 3–83 in *The Case of Schreber; Papers on Technique; and Other Works (1911–1913)*. Vol. 12 of *The Standard Edition of the Complete Psychological Works of Sigmund Freud*. New edition. Edited by James Strachey. London: Vintage Classics.

Friebel, Kelvin G. 1999. *Jeremiah's and Ezekiel's Sign-Acts: Rhetorical Nonverbal Communication*. Journal for the Study of the Old Testament Supplement Series 283. Sheffield: Sheffield Academic Press.

George, Andrew, trans. 2003. *The Epic of Gilgamesh*. New York: Penguin.

Graybill, Cristina Rhiannon. 2012. Men in Travail: Masculinity and the Problems of the Body in the Hebrew Prophets. Ph.D. diss. University of California, Berkeley.

Hornsby, Teresa. 2006. Ezekiel Off-Broadway. *Bible and Critical Theory* 2.1:02.1–8. Online: http://bibleandcriticaltheory.org. DOI:10.2104/bc060002.

Hummel, Horace D. 2005. *Ezekiel 1–20*. Concordia Commentary. Saint Louis: Concordia.

Hutton, R. R. 1995. Magic or Street-Theater? The Power of the Prophetic Word. *Zeitschrift für die Alttestamentliche Wissenschaft* 107:247–60.

Kafka, Franz. 1995. A Hunger Artist. Pages 268–77 in *Franz Kafka: The Complete Stories*. Edited by Nahum N. Glatzer. New York: Schocken.

Lacan, Jacques. 1993. *The Psychoses 1955–1956*. New York: Norton.

Lothane, Zvi. 1992. *In Defense of Schreber: Soul Murder and Psychiatry*. Hillsdale, N.J.: Analytic Press.

Marsden, Jill. 1999. Cyberpsychosis: The Feminization of the Postbiological Body. Pages 59–76 in *Cyberpsychology*. Edited by Ángel J. Gordo-López and Ian Parker. New York: Routledge.

Moore, Stephen. 2002. *God's Beauty Parlor: And Other Queer Spaces in and around the Bible*. Stanford, Calif.: Stanford University Press.

———. 1996. *God's Gym: Divine Male Bodies of the Bible*. New York: Routledge.

Pinar, William. 2006. *Race, Religion, and a Curriculum of Reparation: Teacher Education for a Multicultural Society*. New York: Palgrave Macmillan.

Sade, Marquis De. 1990. *Justine, Philosophy in the Bedroom, and Other Writings*. Translated by Richard Seaver and Austryn Wainhouse. New York: Grove.

Santner, Eric L. 1996. *My Own Private Germany: Daniel Paul Schreber's Secret History of Modernity*. Princeton: Princeton University Press.

Schreber, Daniel Paul. 2000. *Memoirs of My Nervous Illness*. Translated and edited by Ida Macalpine and Richard A. Hunter. 1955. Repr., New York: New York Review of Books.

Shengold, Leonard. 1989. *Soul Murder: The Effects of Childhood Abuse and Deprivation*. New Haven: Yale University Press.

Sherwood, Yvonne. 1998. Prophetic Scatology: Prophecy and the Art of Sensation. *Semeia* 82:183–224.

———. 2006. Prophetic Performance Art. *Bible and Critical Theory* 2.1:01.1–4. Online: http://bibleandcriticaltheory.org. DOI:10.2104/bc060001.

Stacey, David. 1990. *Prophetic Drama in the Old Testament*. London: Epworth.

Stalker, David Muir Gibson. 1968. *Ezekiel: Introduction and Commentary*. Torch Bible Commentaries. London: SCM.

Tisdall, Caroline. 2008. *Joseph Beuys: Coyote*. Munich: Schirmer/Mosel.

The Prosthetic Friend, or Posthumanity in *Lars and the Real Girl*

George Aichele

Reverend Bock: "The question is, as always, what would Jesus do?"

— *Lars and the Real Girl*[1]

And when [Jesus] had entered, he said to them, "Why do you make a tumult and weep? The child is not dead but sleeping." And they laughed at him. But he put them all outside.

—Mark 5:39–40 RSV

Lars Lindstrom has a problem. He is afraid of losing the people in his life, especially women. His mother died giving birth to him, and even though he is now 27, he still wears (as a scarf) the baby blanket that she had knit for him. Ever since his father died, Lars has lived alone in a tiny garage apartment next to the house in which he grew up. He shares ownership of this property with his older brother, Gus, who lives in the house with his pregnant wife, Karin. Lars is very fond of Karin, and terribly afraid that the same thing that happened to his own mother will also happen to her.[2] However, he has great difficulties relating to any woman about any matter.

Indeed, Lars has serious difficulties interacting directly with any person, male or female. He even claims to feel pain if someone touches his skin. To protect himself, Lars wears many layers of clothing at all times, and he works in a large, anonymous office, where his primary contact with others is by way of telephone or Internet. The office where he works is divided into numerous small cubicles, and as a result he only rarely has to encounter even his coworkers. Lars was raised by his father, who became

1. All quotations from the movie are from the DVD (Gillespie 2007).

2. Gus describes Karin's relation to Lars as "maternal."

severely depressed after Lars's mother died. Gus left the house as soon as he was old enough to get away from that difficult situation, and returned with Karin after the father died. He feels guilty for having left his brother alone with their despondent, withdrawn father, and he thinks that he has contributed somehow to Lars's extreme fears of abandonment and of intimacy. Both Gus and Karin feel sorry for Lars, and they would like him to move into the house with them.

Lars is the central character of Craig Gillespie's comic movie, *Lars and the Real Girl* (2007), which is set in a small town somewhere in the upper Midwest of North America.[3] Because of his extreme difficulty relating to other human beings, Lars is only able to live an isolated, hermit-like existence, and apparently his only frequent occasion for social interaction apart from the office is church, which he attends regularly. When he does encounter others, he is not particularly friendly ("distantly polite" might be a good description); but despite his reserve, everyone seems to like him. Indeed, Lars is quite a likable person. One of his coworkers at the office, a young woman named Margo, is even attracted to him, and he seems to be attracted to her as well, but he is unwilling to encourage any relationship between them. In an early scene, one Sunday a woman from the church hands him a flower that she had taken from the sanctuary decorations, telling him to give it to "somebody nice." It is simply a friendly gesture. Just then, Margo (who attends the same church) calls to Lars from across the street and waves—another innocent, friendly gesture. Lars immediately and violently throws the flower away.

If this movie were less clearly whimsical, one might call it Kafkaesque.[4] No one can guarantee to Lars that the people that he cares about will not abandon him, but he desperately needs that guarantee. Finally he does something about this problem: he *buys* someone who will not leave him, addressing the issue in solidly bourgeois, consumerist fashion. He does not buy a real person, for even slaves can die or flee, but he buys a doll—an artificial person who will never go away. One day, Kurt, who shares the office cubicle with Lars, shows him the World Wide Web site of "Real-

3. Wikipedia (http://en.wikipedia.org/wiki/Lars_and_the_Real_Girl) says that the town is supposed to be in Wisconsin, but it could just as well be Minnesota, Michigan, or central Canada. The movie was actually filmed in Ontario (IMDb 2010).

4. See also Tommaso Landolfi's remarkable story, "Gogol's Wife" (1963, 1–16). In one scene from Gillespie's movie, Lars reads to Bianca from *Don Quixote* about Dulcinea, Quixote's heavily fantasized lady love.

Doll.com" (Abyss Creations 2010). Although Gillespie's movie is fictional, this website is quite real, and the company that maintains it offers for sale life-size, highly realistic, and anatomically correct adult "dolls." These dolls are not crude inflatables. The actual RealDoll "has a poseable PVC skeleton with steel joints and silicone flesh, which is the state-of-the-art for life-like human body simulation. Prices begin at around US $6,500, with some models costing over US $10,000" (Wikipedia 2010). The dolls come in various "models" (with choices for hair and skin color, and facial shape), and they weigh 70–80 pounds each, depending on size (standing height).[5] Most of the models are female, but male dolls are also available.

Bianca is Lars's artificial friend. Comparable fabricated friends appear in many science fiction stories—for example, the "toys" of J. F. Sebastian in Ridley Scott's movie *Blade Runner* (1982).[6] Sebastian is a designer of replicants (androids, cyborgs), and like Lars he is a lonely, isolated man. He creates humanoid toys to be his "friends." Some of these toys are animated and may even be somewhat conscious, but others apparently are not, like Bianca. However, the far more dangerous replicants that Sebastian also creates are fully self-conscious and independently motivated, "more human than human" (see further Aichele 2006, 159–81). *Blade Runner* shows how close the artificial friend can be to the doll-monsters who appear in many horror stories.

Lars and the Real Girl joins a host of recent movies, novels, TV shows, and comic books that tell of cyborgs, artificially intelligent machines, humanoid extraterrestrials, or human superheroes, mutants, or hybrids. All of these products of popular culture serve as symptoms of important contemporary questions concerning the limits of the human, and they invite consideration of the difference and the relation between the human, the nonhuman, and the posthuman in a wide variety of ways. These questions are also addressed by a growing number of serious, scholarly studies (for example, Haraway 1991; Hayles 1999; Carlson 2008), and this interest is another symptom of the importance of these matters. Bianca is an instance of what Roland Barthes calls the Neutral: she is neither nonhuman nor human, but instead somehow "in between." She is a/human, and as such she "baffles the paradigm" (2005, 6). She is a high-tech, new-age

5. In the movie Bianca is described as weighing 125 pounds. No "Bianca" model is listed on the RealDoll WWW site, but several of the listed models have features similar to hers, and custom dolls can be ordered (Abyss Creations 2010).

6. All quotations from the movie are from the DVD (Scott 1982).

golem, a synthetic Eve. In other words, she is a monster, an occasion both of and for revelation (see Beal 2002, 4–5).

Just as a prosthesis such as an artificial arm or leg helps the crippled person to whom it is attached to lead a more normal life—that is, to be a more complete human being—so Bianca helps Lars to lead a more normal life and to be the person he would be if he did not have his disability. She is his prosthesis. He creates an extensive backstory for her, which he willingly shares with others. Remarkably, although Lars is normally extremely reserved around other people, even Gus or Karin, he is happy to "introduce" Bianca to anyone. Indeed, he becomes more animated and generally outgoing with other people whenever Bianca is nearby. Lars claims to have met her on the Internet, which is true enough. He does not buy her for sex; indeed, Lars apparently has very little intimate contact with Bianca, kissing her only once, just before the movie ends.[7] Instead, he wants someone who will never abandon him. He consistently treats her with care and respect, as though she were a living human being with her own thoughts and feelings, and he frequently talks to her and listens to her. He does not treat her as a ventriloquist's dummy, but he does sometimes tell others what she has told him.

Lars asks Gus and Karin to let Bianca stay in the house with them, claiming that she is "religious" and would not be comfortable staying with him in his tiny apartment. His interest in Bianca upsets Karin and especially Gus, but on the advice of Dr. Dagmar Berman, the local MD (who also has some psychological expertise), they both agree to play along for a while with Lars's "delusion."

> Karin: "How can *we* help?" …
>
> Gus: "Everyone is going to laugh at [Lars]."
>
> Dr. Berman: "And you."

They agree to let Bianca "sleep" in what had once been the room of Lars and Gus's mother, and Karin also loans her some clothes. More important, they start to interact with Bianca as though she were a real human being,

7. In a brief omitted scene (available on the DVD), Lars gets into the bathtub with Bianca, after he goes bowling with Margo (see below). Bianca is "naked," and he is fully clothed.

even to the point of dressing her, bathing her, and putting her to bed. In other words, Gus and Karin begin to treat Bianca as human even when Lars is not present. They begin to think of her as a living, human being.

Dr. Berman's recommendation is supported by Reverend Bock, Lars's pastor, in the words that serve as the first epigraph to this essay. Reverend Bock and Dr. Berman are the only agents of communal "pastoral power" (see Castelli 1991) to appear in this movie, and they both line up to recognize the humanity of Bianca. A large part of what I call the "whimsy" of *Lars and the Real Girl* comes from the possibility that viewers will imagine (and perhaps are otherwise familiar with) an alternate and more "realistic" scenario, in which Lars's choice of Bianca as his partner would alienate him from Karin and Gus, lead to serious disapproval on the parts of Dr. Berman and Reverend Bock, and culminate in the ridicule and perhaps even worse treatment from the larger community.[8] As Gus says, the people would laugh at Lars, much as the mourners at Jairus's house laugh at Jesus in this essay's second epigraph, when he claims that the girl is not dead but sleeping. The constant tension between the story as it unfolds and the bitter realism of such an alternate scenario defines the element of the fantastic in this film and keeps it from sliding over into slapstick or tragedy or horror.

As it is, after their initial reactions of shock (such as "she's a golden calf") and crude humor ("does she have a sister?"), the rest of the community members rather quickly accept Bianca much as Gus, Karin, the doctor, and the preacher do. Bianca goes to church with Lars, Karin, and Gus (who had apparently not been attending before she arrived). She is soon so well regarded throughout the community that she becomes quite popular. However, this widespread acceptance comes at a price. Because she is not physically attached to Lars, as a more traditional prosthesis often would be, Bianca is not always available for him when he wants her. Nevertheless, precisely because of this, Bianca helps Lars adjust to the risks and responsibilities of human friendship.

As she is increasingly accepted by and integrated into the larger community, it becomes apparent that Bianca's "interests" and "desires" are not always compatible with those of Lars. She acquires a "life of her own" and spends less time with Lars. Other people also want to be with her. Women "friends" take her to the hairdresser, and she even gets elected to the school

8. Contrast the documentary film *Invisible Girlfriend* (Redmon and Sabin 2009).

board. The amazing success of Dr. Berman's full-time group therapy leads to a series of "arguments" between Lars and Bianca, and their "relationship" is strained. However, other encounters between Lars and first Karin, then Gus, help him to see that this new complication in his life is part of the cost of human friendship. Dr. Berman also sees Lars and Bianca regularly, in order to learn her "medical history" and monitor her "health problems," and she also helps Lars to confront his anxieties.

Meanwhile, Karin's due date draws ever closer. Complicating matters even further, after having been repeatedly rebuffed by Lars, Margo has started dating another man from the office. However, this relationship quickly falls apart, and following an unpleasant incident between Margo and Kurt in regard to their own much smaller toys, which ends when Lars comes to the rescue (see below), Margo goes bowling with Lars. At the end of the evening, he actually grasps Margo's hand, skin to skin. This is a huge step forward for Lars, but it also precipitates a crisis. Immediately after the bowling scene, Lars tells Dr. Berman that he has asked Bianca to marry him, and Bianca has refused. Then Bianca stops talking to him. Soon thereafter, her chronic "low blood pressure" (in the words of Dr. Berman) takes a turn for the worse, and one morning she fails to "wake up" when Lars comes to see her. The community reacts to Bianca's failing health with shock and mourning. She "dies" soon thereafter, and she is buried in the local cemetery following a church funeral, which is attended by the entire community. At the grave, Margo tells Lars, "There'll never be anybody like her." Lars then asks Margo to go for a walk with him. The postmodern golem can return to the inanimate: Bianca has performed her miracle, and the movie is over.

I have described Bianca as a "prosthesis." The Greek word *prosthesis*, from which this English word derives, means "application," "attachment," or "addition" (Liddell and Scott 1996). Prostheses are artificial devices that replace or supplement missing or defective parts of a living (usually human) body. While prostheses are often thought of as additions to the living body, such as artificial limbs, teeth, or organs, they can also be external supplements such as canes or seeing-eye dogs. Some prostheses, such as corrective lenses or dentures, are relatively simple. Others are quite complex, high-tech devices such as hearing aids and heart pacemakers, or even telephones and computers. By extension, all of the everyday supplements to our bodily lives, such as tools and clothing, without which we could not live or be "human," are prostheses. Perhaps the most important prosthesis is language, the vocabulary and syntax without which we could not communicate with one another, and which, no matter how "natural," is always an artificial "application."

In other words, it is not merely the handicapped who require prosthetic assistance—or rather, all human beings are "handicapped." As humans, we are essentially incomplete, and we require unnatural supplementation merely to live human lives. These additions transform us, making us more than human, even as they enable us to be more completely human. The prosthesis stands in a curious relation to the one who is "attached" to it. "My" prosthesis is neither me nor not-me, and in this way all prostheses are instances of the Barthesian Neutral. The user of the prosthesis also often has highly ambivalent feelings toward it: "I need you in order to live, and yet you restrain me; you own me; you make me who (or what) I am." Thanks to prosthetic supplements, all human beings are fabricated beings, and because of this, we are all already posthuman beings (Hayles 1999, 291). One might say that all human beings are essentially artificial or prosthetic. A full-body prosthesis such as Bianca merely makes this universal artificiality, and its associated ambivalences, explicit.

It would be easy and not unreasonable to view *Lars and the Real Girl* as narrating a successful albeit quite unorthodox psychotherapeutic treatment of one man's delusion. However, such a reading would fail to take seriously several important details about the story, which mark it as a fantastic narrative, not merely an uncanny one. These details imply that this movie does not merely tell a story of a strange but nevertheless entirely natural series of events, a remarkable but by no means miraculous cure. Instead, this movie tells a story of something that is other than natural—that is, something that might be called "marvelous." Hence my references to Bianca as a golem. Tzvetan Todorov defines the fantastic as uncertainty or hesitation between the strange or uncanny and the supernatural or marvelous (1973, 24–40). I accept Todorov's definition in general, but I think that it must be stretched some in order to account for the posthuman. In this film, the hesitation remains, but the marvelous element is not a sign of the supernatural. Bianca is not *that* sort of golem: she does not come to life thanks to a magical spell or holy word. If there is a miracle in this movie, it is not caused by supernatural power. Instead, the marvelous in this movie comes from the a/human, which is the posthuman.

I have already noted the most important of these fantastic details, which is that *everyone* in the community gets swept up into Lars's "delusion." It becomes infectious, inescapable. No one laughs at Lars—not for long, anyway—and no one gets "put outside" (unlike Mark 5:40). Again, one can readily imagine how, with a slightly different spin, this story could be horrifying, or at least grotesque. Instead, and thanks to Bianca, Lars's friends and neighbors become a collective (but delightful) monster. Gus and Karin, Margo, and the townspeople do not just "play along with" Lars's false "reality." Instead, his reality *becomes* their own, genuine reality. Bianca does not become alive, like Pinocchio or Frankenstein's creature, but Lars's friends and neighbors become alive, just as Lars does. This is made explicit when Karin confronts Lars, shortly after he becomes angry with Bianca:

> Every person in this town bends over backward to make Bianca feel at home. Why do you think she has so many places to go and so much to do? Huh? Huh? Because of you! Because—all these people—love you! We push her wheelchair. We drive her to work. We drive her home. We wash her. We dress her. We get her up, and put her to bed. We carry her. And she is not petite, Lars. Bianca is a big, big girl! None of this is easy—for any of us—but we do it. ... Oh! We do it for you!

However, Karin is not entirely correct. One further ingredient is essential, in addition to the love of Lars's friends and neighbors, and that is Bianca herself, the a/human being who baffles the paradigm. Lars tells Gus and Karin, "that's why God made her, to help people." Later Bianca is described as being "out in the community, doing things for others less fortunate." At first the townspeople do all the things that Karin says simply because they care about Lars, but eventually they do these things because of Bianca herself. To be sure, they perform these tasks because of both Lars and Bianca, but even so, much of their interest in Bianca seems to come from some desire within these people that she releases.

The desire to make Bianca "feel at home" results in the remarkable cooperation of Lars's friends and then the larger community in supporting and even sharing his delusion. This communal contribution to the eventual healing of Lars's disability is a "marvel" in its own right, a "mighty work" (Mark 6:2; 9:39) that these people accomplish collectively, and Bianca spurs them to do it. In other words, Bianca heals Lars by awakening some dormant potential that is already in these people. This is her reality, her "life" (see Mark 8:35). Like the "sons of men" described in the Gospel of Mark (RSV),[9] Bianca comes "not to be served but to serve, and to give

9. That the Markan "sons of men" are plural is explicit in 3:28 and implicit in the differences between the singular son of man sayings.

his life as a ransom for many" (10:45; see Aichele 2006, 203–21). Bianca gives her life to release not only Lars but also his friends from crippling disability and thereby free them to become more completely human—that is, posthuman.

Nevertheless, even though Lars may be delusional, his friends are not—at least, not entirely. This becomes clear when Lars is unable to wake Bianca, shortly before she "dies." He screams, and Karin and Gus come running to Bianca's room. They are befuddled for a moment by the turn of events, but then Karin cries out, "Call 9-1-1!" Todorov's fantastic hesitation is explicit in that brief moment of befuddlement, which is also an important index of the baffled paradigm. Karin and Gus both recognize that Bianca cannot possibly "wake up," but still they are truly surprised when she does not. Thanks to the baffled paradigm, the line between delusion (that Bianca is a real woman) and the silicone reality that is Bianca becomes very fine indeed, and perhaps even disappears.

Another such moment of ontological double-mindedness occurs somewhat earlier in the film, when Karin and Gus bathe Bianca, as one might bathe a paralyzed human being. Because he respects Bianca's privacy, Lars is not present; for him, the paradigm is not baffled. However, even though both Gus and Karin explicitly recognize that the situation is ludicrous, they continue to bathe her. They do not simply wash a big toy. Like Lars's other friends and neighbors who have become involved in a variety of ways with not only his but also their own relationships to Bianca, they must in effect be simultaneously crazy and sane. *Lars and the Real Girl* describes an instance of what psychoanalysts might call countertransference, except that in this case the recipient of the transferred feelings is not Lars himself but instead Bianca. The symptom of Lars's delusion becomes a real subject through this quasi-countertransference.

The reality of Bianca is not any different from that of any other thing. What makes any of us "real" is not simply the material actuality of a flesh-and-blood human body, nor is it the indubitability (to itself) of the conscious mind that "inhabits" that body. Instead, according to Gilles Deleuze, our understandings of real things, and indeed the only reality that we know at any given moment—including our own individual reality—are reciprocally determined by what actually exists and by our ideas or concepts of those things. Deleuze calls these concepts "virtualities" (1994, 205–14). Virtual objects correspond to our desire for reality, which "governs and compensates for the progresses and failures of … real activity" (99). Our knowledge of reality is derived from empirical sensation, but there can be no such sensation, at least at the human level, that is not informed or processed by virtual structures of consciousness. The double-mindedness that Bianca evokes in Gillespie's movie appears because virtuality itself enters consciousness.

Concepts or virtualities inform the Cartesian cogito ("I think therefore I am") that grounds each person's own self-awareness, but they are distinct from it. They are shared with (and shaped by) a larger community, in much the same way that language is shared. Like human language, reality is to some degree fabricated, and we all contribute to its construction. Virtuality is our relation to wholeness or totality—that is, our sense of every single thing in relation to everything else. As that which forms the illusion of a more-or-less common reality, virtuality belongs to the realm of ideology. It makes the meaning of things and events seem obvious and "natural" (Barthes 1974, 206). There is no reality without this meaning.

In other words, reality as we know it is not simply everything or even anything that actually exists. Nor is it whatever we want it to be. This becomes clear in *Lars and the Real Girl*, as Bianca increasingly acquires living, human "friends" and develops quite real "interests" of her own, independently of and even contrary to Lars's own wishes. She is not merely an extension of his own interests and desires. The reality of Bianca is not simply the actual silicone and steel that make up her body, nor her evident lack of either actual mind or pulse, but it is (always, also) the virtuality of Bianca in the mind and desires of Lars, and eventually (and to some degree even more so) of each member of the community. It is the virtuality of Bianca that makes her really human, and that is true also for any human being.

Bianca could not heal Lars if he was the only one who believed that she was a living human being. Reality is never a matter of some individual's private belief. Lars is not like the White Queen of Lewis Carroll's *Through the Looking-Glass*, who claims to be able to believe impossible things (1982, 127–28). When Karin and Gus first meet with Dr. Berman, she tells them that "Bianca is real. She is real to Lars"; but Berman's point is that for them to help Lars, they also must regard her as real. They must help Bianca to help Lars—that is, help her to be real for Lars. In that way she is no different than any other human being. You are not really human unless others say that you are. Bianca's real humanity is a truth that lives and grows within the community, just as she not only lives in the community but interacts with its members and actively contributes to it.

A second, and related, fantastic "detail" that is overlooked by a purely psychological reading of *Lars and the Real Girl* is the children's response to Bianca. When Gus and Karin take Bianca and Lars to see Dr. Berman for Bianca's initial "health check," almost immediately a child climbs into Bianca's lap while she sits in the waiting room. Later she is invited to volunteer at the hospital, where she "reads" to sick and injured children (with the help of a boom-box recording). The children love Bianca immediately, and they treat her as fully human. To be sure, children are good at playing with toys, but they are also good at recognizing the reality of toys, or rather, at the sort of ontological double-mindedness described above. Perhaps this is why toys provide such powerful images of the posthuman, as in *Blade Runner*, and perhaps this is what Mark's Jesus means by "Truly, I say to you, whoever does not receive the kingdom of God like a child shall not enter it" (10:15). Indeed, throughout the Gospel of Mark, the kingdom of God and children are closely connected, and that connection also involves the "son of man" (see Aichele 2011, 70–90).

However, adults are not children, and it is not easy for an adult to receive something "like a child," just as it is not easy to enter the kingdom of God (see Mark 10:24). It may be painful, and even require self-mutilation (9:43–47). It is also not a matter of or for faith—at least, not faith as it is normally understood. *Lars and the Real Girl* does not tell a story comparable to James Barrie's *Peter Pan* (1911), in which the fairy Tinker Bell's life can be restored if children clap their hands; or to stories of Santa Claus, who "lives in the hearts of children." Instead, there is something of the kingdom of God, at least as described by Mark's Jesus, in the baffling of the paradigm. In Markan terms, Bianca is the "mystery" (4:11) into which Lars and his friends enter, like children. Mark's Jesus also refers to the kingdom of God as "life" (for example, 9:43–48), and Bianca becomes Lars's entrance into life. As a Real Doll, Bianca is definitely not alive, but as Bianca, she is "life." To be sure, this is not how "the kingdom of God" or "(eternal) life," or, for that matter, "the son of man," are usually understood by readers of Mark's Gospel. Nor am I suggesting that this movie "intends" any specific reference to the Gospel of Mark or any other biblical text. However, not only the involvement of Reverend Bock and of Lars's church throughout the movie, but also and far more so, the larger questions of posthumanity and even of reality that the movie raises (its Kafkaesque qualities) suggest that an intertextual juxtaposition of this sort is not inappropriate.

Children are weak and ignorant, but they are not gullible fools. Alice is "seven and a half [years old], exactly" when she meets the White Queen in *Through the Looking-Glass*, and she doubts the Queen's extravagant claims (Carroll 1982, 127). Perhaps all children, like Alice, are of necessity adepts of the Barthesian Neutral. Even childish faith in Tinker Bell or Santa Claus, like childish regard for toys, proceeds by way of the Neutral. However, like Tinker Bell or Santa Claus or even Carroll's Alice herself, Bianca is a virtuality or simulacrum, and in that regard she is just as real as the various Moseses or Davids or Jesuses of the Bible. Bianca belongs to what Deleuze calls "the originary," the field of the simulacrum: "the originary world only appears when the invisible lines which divide up the real, which dislocate modes of behaviour and objects, are supercharged, filled out and extended" (1986, 123, 124).[10]

The insertion of the Real Girl into Lars's quiet life "dislocates modes of behaviour and objects," and thereby Bianca "fills out" and "extends" the lines by which reality is constructed. She enables Lars to move from the obsessive single-mindedness of delusion to the double-mindedness of the Neutral and escape from his crippling condition. The same is true for Lars's friends and neighbors, even though they start from a different and more familiar single-mindedness, for which an adult doll like Bianca is a perversion, or at least a distraction. As Karin says, "we've been all wrapped up in ourselves."

Even considered merely as a sex toy, Bianca is no more imaginary than any crutch or seeing-eye dog. However, she is not simply a large doll, and conversely, it may also be that smaller dolls and other such toys are much more than we usually think they are, as the children's response to Bianca suggests. Indeed, Bianca is not the only adult toy in *Lars and the Real Girl*. Margo playfully steals some of the "action heroes" with which Kurt decorates his office work-space, and he retaliates by "executing" the teddy bear that he takes from her cubicle. Because Lars knows much about the reality of such toys, he is able to "resuscitate" Margo's bear, and thereby he becomes her hero. This entire episode, and especially Margo's gratitude, is another instance of the double-mindedness described above.

A third important detail separates the movie's story from a straightforward psychoanalytic narrative. It is tempting to treat Bianca's failure to awaken, followed by her decline and death, as merely further stages of the evolution and therapeutic dissipation of Lars's delusion. Nevertheless, here too the paradigm is baffled. It would be much too easy to say that

10. On the originary and childhood "phantasy," see Deleuze 1994, 125.

Lars simply "kills" Bianca because she has become inconvenient. This may be a crucial difference between her and toys such as Margo's teddy bear, and perhaps even an important symptom of Bianca's posthumanity. To Lars, and by the time of her death to all of his friends, Bianca has become something quite different from a sex toy. Although Bianca had never been biologically alive, yet she has become eternally alive (see Mark 10:30), a "son of man" who "gives her life" to awaken something in the community and thereby to ransom Lars, as well as many others, and to give them "the secret of the kingdom of God." In the light of Mark 4:11–12, the entire movie becomes a parable.

I began this essay by claiming that Bianca and her relation to Lars and his friends invite consideration of the difference and relation between human, nonhuman, and posthuman beings. Most of the posthuman beings of contemporary popular culture are profoundly flawed in addition to possessing superhuman qualities, and it is those flaws that make them mortal, finite, and finally, human. For example, the "life" of the *Blade Runner* replicants is barely distinguishable from that of human beings, and they do not want to die any more than we do. It is their "in between-ness," their "nature" as neither human nor nonhuman, that makes these artificial people, like all of us, posthuman.

Even though she is inanimate, Bianca is active and alive, and this joins her to other posthuman beings. In addition, and perhaps more important, despite the fact that she is essentially nonmortal, Bianca really dies, just as we do. Unlike Margo's teddy bear, Bianca cannot be restored to life by any medical intervention.[11] Furthermore, there is no reason to expect that Lars or the others will cease to think of Bianca as any less real after she has been buried. She has simply moved from the reality of the living to the reality of the dead. Bianca's death is recognized and her life continues to be celebrated after her death, much like that of a beloved human friend. At her funeral, Reverend Bock's eulogy is simultaneously touching and ironic, a brilliant instance of double-mindedness:

> Lars asked us not to wear black today. He did so to remind us that this is no ordinary funeral. We are to here to celebrate Bianca's extraordinary life. From her wheelchair, Bianca reached out and touched us all, in ways

11. Compare the scene of Lars applying CPR to Margo's bear to the scenes of Bianca in the ambulance and the hospital, prior to her death.

we could never have imagined. She was a teacher. She was a lesson in courage. And Bianca loved us all. Especially Lars. Especially him.

Works Cited

Abyss Creations. 2010. RealDoll.com. Online: http://www.realdoll.com/.

Aichele, George. 2006. *The Phantom Messiah: Postmodern Fantasy and the Gospel of Mark*. London: T&T Clark.

———. 2011. *Simulating Jesus: Reality Effects in the Gospels*. London: Equinox.

Barrie, J. M. 1911. *Peter Pan*. Public domain. Original Title: *Peter and Wendy*.

Barthes, Roland. 1974. *S/Z*. Translated by Richard Miller. New York: Hill and Wang.

———. 2005. *The Neutral*. Translated by Rosalind E. Krauss and Denis Hollier. New York: Columbia University Press.

Beal, Timothy K. 2002. *Religion and Its Monsters*. New York: Routledge.

Carlson, Thomas A. 2008. *The Indiscrete Image: Infinitude and Creation of the Human*. Chicago: University of Chicago Press.

Carroll, Lewis (Charles Dodgson). 1982. *The Complete Illustrated Works*. Edited by Edward Guiliano. New York: Crown.

Castelli, Elizabeth. 1991. *Imitating Paul: A Discourse of Power*. Louisville: Westminster John Knox.

Deleuze, Gilles. 1986. *Cinema 1: The Movement-Image*. Translated by Hugh Tomlinson and Barbara Habberjam. Minneapolis: University of Minnesota Press.

———. 1994. *Difference and Repetition*. Translated by Paul Patton. New York: Columbia University Press.

Gillespie, Craig, director. 2007. *Lars and the Real Girl*. DVD. Los Angeles: Sidney Kimmel Entertainment.

Haraway, Donna J. 1991. *Simians, Cyborgs, and Women: The Reinvention of Nature*. New York: Routledge.

Hayles, N. Katherine. 1999. *How We Became Posthuman: Virtual Bodies in Cybernetics, Literature, and Informatics*. Chicago: University of Chicago Press.

Internet Movie Database (IMDb). 2010. Lars and the Real Girl. Online: http://www.imdb.com/title/tt0805564/.

Landolfi, Tommaso. 1963. *Gogol's Wife and Other Stories*. Translated by Raymond Rosenthal, John Longrigg, and Wayland Young. New York: New Direction.

Liddell, Henry George, and Robert Scott, eds. 1996. *A Greek-English Lexicon*. New edition with revised supplement by Henry Stuart Jones and Roderick McKenzie. Osford: Clarendon.

Redmon, David, and Ashley Sabin, directors. 2009. *Invisible Girlfriend*. DVD. Carnivalesque Films.

Scott, Ridley, director. 1982. *Blade Runner*. Los Angeles: Ladd Company, Warner Brothers.

Todorov, Tzvetan. 1973. *The Fantastic*. Translated by Richard Howard. Cleveland: Case Western Reserve University Press.

Part 4
Fathers

Tripartite Anthropologies and the Limits of the Human in Valentinian Christian Creation Myths

Benjamin H. Dunning

Valentinian Christians did not invent the notion of a tripartite anthropological division, but they used it in their various creation myths to demarcate and delimit the contours of "the human" in specific and theologically significant ways.[1] While the apostle Paul himself never explicitly triangulated his enigmatic references to choic, psychic, and spiritual bodily states in 1 Corinthians (1 Cor 15:42–49; see Dunning 2009a, 86),[2] these early Christians found it fruitful to read his speculations together with a platonizing philosophical tradition that envisioned the constitution of the human subject in terms of three components (most commonly, body, soul, and mind).[3] The result, in certain Valentinian texts of the second and third centuries, is a positing of three specific kinds of human beings:

1. In the process of bringing my most recent book, *Specters of Paul* (2011), to publication, an anonymous reader for the University of Pennsylvania Press responded to my reading of the tripartite anthropological categories in *On the Origin of the World* (NHC II,5) by challenging me to explore more fully what it means for Valentinian texts to speak of material (i.e., hylic), psychic, and pneumatic bodies—that is, to make "a genuine effort to *think* this central question of theological anthropology" (emphasis original). While I was not able in that project to respond to this suggestion in any depth, the following represents my attempt to explore this difficult but important question, albeit with reference to different early Christian texts.

2. On Valentinian anthropology and Pauline exegesis, see also Pagels 1972, 241–58; Thomassen 2009, 169–70.

3. On tripartite aspects of Plato's anthropology (with reference especially to the *Timaeus*), see Dillon 1977, 233. Cf. also as representative Plutarch's reflections on body, soul, and mind (*Fac.* 943) and Philo's association of people of earth with the body, people of heaven with the mind, and people of God with the incorruptible noetic sphere (*Gig.* 60–61).

hylic (often translated "material") or choic humans, psychic humans, and pneumatic humans.

Scholarly conversation around this topic has focused primarily on the degree of determinism that the division entails. According to ancient heresiologists such as Irenaeus, "subdividing the souls, [the Valentinians] say that some are good by nature and some are evil by nature" (Irenaeus, *Haer.* 1.7.5; trans. Unger and Dillon). And as is now well known, traditional scholarly descriptions of "gnostic" anthropology followed the heresiologists uncritically on this point, positing that for Valentinians and other "gnostics," "Some are purely carnal, and thus are irreparably condemned to destruction when the physical world comes to an end. On the other hand, the imprisoned sparks of the spirit … will necessarily be saved and return to the spiritual realm" (González 1984, 60).[4] On this view, human salvation or perdition is predetermined from the start—a result not of faith, virtue, the Savior's redemptive action, or some combination thereof, but rather dictated by a person's fixed and fundamental essence.

Recent scholarship has sought to complicate this notion of a "saved by nature" theology in Valentinian texts, arguing instead for a more fluid or dynamic understanding of the three classes of human beings in question. In a now classic article, Luise Schottroff argued that the language of "essence" and "nature" that characterizes Valentinian tripartite anthropologies should be read not as deterministic, but rather as descriptive of three separate modes of freely willed human existence—modes that are not ontologically independent, but instead are brought about by human actions and decisions with respect to salvation (Schottroff 1969). Others have built on this line of argument to demonstrate convincingly that possibilities for anthropological fluidity and transformation existed in Valentinian thought (see Attridge and Pagels 1985, 184–88; Buell 2005, 82–84, 126–35; Dunderberg 2008, 134–40; Thomassen 1989, 428–29; 2009, 169–86). The tripartite human beings of Valentinian myths were not preordained to their eternal fate, mired by their very constitution in what Elaine Pagels appropriately calls a "substantive determinism" (1972, 242 [following Schottroff]). On the contrary, they are figured in the texts as active and engaged participants in an unfolding—and always shifting—drama of salvation.

---

4. For an overview of this position (and some of its critics) in the history of scholarship, see Pagels 1972, 241–42. For a thorough critique of the broader assumptions about cosmology underlying this position, see King 2003, 191–201.

And yet I want to suggest that this single-minded focus on the relationship between tripartite anthropology and eschatological determinism, while providing a much-needed corrective to history based on heresiology, has also subtly downplayed the importance of another set of concerns and questions that are equally relevant to Valentinian mythology: those that have to do with bodies, matter, and the makeup of human subjects in terms of the tangible substances that constitute them. Here I follow scholars such as Dale Martin and Troels Engberg-Pedersen who have drawn attention to the "concretely cosmological" dimensions of ancient appeals to categories like *pneuma* and *psychē*—appeals that cannot be relegated to the realm of the "merely" metaphorical or symbolic (Engberg-Pedersen 2010, 2; cf. Martin 1995).[5] Rather, as Martin explains, "For most ancient theorists, pneuma is a kind of 'stuff' that is the agent of perception, motion, and life itself; it pervades other forms of stuff and, together with those other forms, constitutes the self" (1995, 21). Similarly, *psychē* and *hylē* are also envisioned as elements out of which both the cosmos and human bodies are composed.

Thus in the period of early late antiquity in which Valentinian thinkers penned their own cosmological speculations, all three of these central anthropological terms potentially have dimensions that are "materialistic, concrete, and tangible" (Engberg-Pedersen 2010, 19)—a possibility that is subtly obscured by the tendency to translate *hylē* as "matter."[6] However,

5. The larger philosophical context in view here—commonly termed Middle Platonism—is characterized by a complex amalgam of platonizing and stoicizing notions. As Martin points out, "Well into the second century we encounter ... thinkers very much influenced by Platonism but whose concepts of the body are a far cry from reflecting the kind of radical dichotomy between material and immaterial expected of Platonism by modern readers" (1995, 14). And while these scholarly analyses tend to foreground or privilege a Stoic accent, Engberg-Pedersen rightly observes that "the fundamental corporeality of Stoicism was to a large degree an articulation of a more popular ontology in the ancient world" (2010, 19)—therefore, I would argue, making Stoic ideas about physics and the cosmos an appropriate ancient analog for the analysis of Valentinian creation myths. For an analysis especially attuned to affinities between Valentinian ideas and Stoic thought (as well as differences), see Dunderberg 2008.

6. So Martin notes, "For most ancient philosophers ... to say that something was not composed of hyle did not mean it was immaterial in the modern sense of the word. Air, water, and especially ether could all be described as substances not included in the category hyle, yet we moderns would be hard pressed to think of them as 'immaterial substances.' In other words, *all* the Cartesian oppositions—matter versus nonmatter, physical versus spiritual, corporeal (or physical) versus psychological, nature versus

insofar as treating the hylic/choic, the psychic, and the pneumatic as concrete substances might seem to imply the specter of determinism—though this is by no means, I will argue, a necessary implication—the tendency emerges to relegate these categories to something like figures of speech, operative only in a particular theological discourse whose primary concern is questions of salvation. As a result, the tripartite categories end up sitting uneasily within mythological texts that share a deep commitment to understanding the cosmos in terms of the generation, movement, and ultimate destiny of different substances across multiple registers, human and nonhuman.

Here then, I think, it becomes important to underscore that the work the tripartite division does in Valentinian texts pertains not only to salvation/eschatology but also to creation—and more specifically, to the demarcation of created human beings. I have argued elsewhere for the vital interrelationship of creation and eschaton in the anthropologies of early Christian thinkers, and thus the need to approach the two together when studying their various understandings of the human subject (Dunning 2011). And Valentinian texts are no exception. Yet I also want to note—borrowing a point made by Eve Sedgwick in an entirely different context—that with respect to most early Christian theology, questions of creation and questions of eschaton, "inextricable from one another though they are in that each can be expressed only in the terms of the other, are nonetheless not the same question" (1990, 30). Recognizing this allows us to see that these texts are not only working out a soteriology with a view to the eschaton, but also mapping the limits of the human *within* the created order in some very specific ways—two theological projects never fully separable, but likewise not entirely the same.

In this way, an examination of how tripartite anthropological categories function within Valentinian creation narratives qua creation narratives may help to offset an overemphasis on eschatological determinism that has often characterized readings of these narratives. At the same time, I am *not* arguing that questions about substances and the constitution of created bodies can be neatly cordoned off in these texts from theological discourses about the meaning and destiny of human beings. The philosopher Judith Butler has drawn attention to the porous boundaries that

---

supernature—are misleading when retrojected into ancient language" (1995, 15). Martin has a thorough discussion of translation issues and associated topics (6–15).

characterize modern anthropological categories—and as a consequence "the permanent difficulty of determining where the biological, the psychic, the discursive, the social begin and end" (2004, 185). Here the categories Butler has in view are thoroughly modern: "biological" refers to modern biology and "psychic" to a psychoanalytic notion of the psyche as the site in which body and culture are mediated within human subjects—thus not reducible to the body, but also always implicated in the body and never radically other from it. Yet I would argue for an analogous difficulty that attends ancient anthropological categories. For to be sure, ancient thinkers had their own biological and physical theories, their own historically and culturally sedimented discourses, and their own conundrums regarding the interactions of body and culture (this last point being anachronistically akin to Butler's term *psychic*—which should not be confused with Valentinian uses of the term *psychic*, to be discussed at greater length below).

Accordingly, within Valentinian tripartite anthropologies, the physical and substantial claims being made about ancient bodies can never be easily separated from the discourses that value those bodies (theologically and otherwise) in various ways. Rather, these anthropologies—in their very strangeness—illustrate the force of Butler's point that "matter has a history (indeed, more than one)" (1993, 29). The tripartite categories in Valentinian texts may indeed signal "potentialities" within human beings that point to the possibility of one eschatological destiny or another (Attridge and Pagels 1985, 184). But this is not all they do. On the contrary, these texts mobilize the distinction between the hylic/choic, the psychic, and the pneumatic variably in order to articulate where the limits of the human fall within the created order, where those limits matter (or fail to matter), and where they interact—both licitly and illicitly—with the registers of the nonhuman. Furthermore, as we will see in an examination of Valentinian creation myths from the *Tripartite Tractate* and the *Excerpts from Theodotus*, it is the substantial dimension of these categories that renders them available to do this work—without lapsing back into a simple determinism or undercutting the texts' commitment to possibilities for fluidity and transformation.[7]

---

7. The division of Valentinian texts into eastern and western "schools" is not of central importance to my argument, and I do not take it up here. Note that for Thomassen, the two sources I consider in this article are central for understanding the eastern branch of Valentinianism (2006, 81–82). For a critique of the eastern/western distinction, see Kavelsmaki 2008, 79–89.

The Tripartite Tractate

The *Tripartite Tractate*, while on the whole a dense and difficult treatise,[8] rather straightforwardly divides humanity into three kinds of human beings—hylic, psychic, and pneumatic—and reflects on each group's ultimate destiny.[9] What these anthropological divisions mean for the mode(s) of embodied subjectivity in view, however, is less clear. Does a "psychic" or "pneumatic" body differ from a "hylic" body—and if so, in what ways? While the *Tripartite Tractate* does not answer this question directly or definitively, it does offer some tantalizing clues. Whatever the three categories may denote, they clearly seem to signify in more registers than just the soteriological. Rather, as Einar Thomassen points out with reference to Valentinian anthropology more broadly, "the three categories are conceived as 'substances,' and the origins of these substances are explained in the language of a mythical narrative" (2009, 171). Thus in the *Tripartite Tractate* the imperfect begetting on the part of the Logos (equivalent to Sophia in other accounts) and his subsequent conversion results in the emergence of hylic and psychic orders, respectively (*Tri. Trac.* 80.11–85.15; cf. *Tri. Trac.* 98.12–20, and discussion in Attridge and Pagels 1985, esp. 184–88). The pneumatic order then comes into being through the Logos's "joy beyond description" associated with the appearance of the Savior (*Tri. Trac.* 88.16). So Thomassen summarizes:

> there exist three substances, deriving from three different states of mind: matter from passion, soul from repentance and spirit from joy. The cosmos is composed of matter and soul; spirit is located in a separate region above the cosmos. This spirit is turned both upwards toward the Pleroma of which it is an image, and downwards towards the cosmos, providing its matter with form and its soul with the rationality of regular motion. (2009, 171; cf. 2006, 46–47)

With the cosmological origins of the three substances in place, the text then turns to the role of these substances in humanity's creation. Here the formation of the first human being is a collective effort: the

---

8. Birger Pearson describes the text as "turgid and often difficult to understand," attributing these difficulties to the Coptic translator's misapprehension of the Greek *Vorlage* (Pearson 2007, 184).

9. For the Coptic text see Attridge and Pagels 1985, 192–337. All translations of this and other ancient texts are my own unless otherwise noted.

Logos works together with the demiurge and his archons to fashion "the earthy human [(ⲡ)ⲣⲙ̄ⲛ̄ⲕⲁϩ] … [who] is a production done by all of them" (*Tri. Trac.* 105.4–7).[10] Yet this shared project is riddled with anthropological ambiguities and complexities. On the one hand, the text marks the human form that the Logos brings forth as defective and characterized by lack and ignorance (*Tri. Trac.* 105.10–15; cf. Thomassen 2009, 175). On the other hand, the Logos is identified as the source of whatever spiritual substance makes up the human being's soul: "It is appropriate therefore that we expound regarding the soul of the first human [ⲧⲯⲩⲭⲏ ⲙ̄ⲡϣⲁⲣⲡ̄ ⲛ̄ⲣⲱⲙⲉ], that it comes from the pneumatic Logos [ⲡⲓⲗⲟⲅⲟⲥ ⲡⲉ ⲙ̄ⲡⲛⲉⲩⲙⲁⲧⲓⲕⲟⲥ]" (*Tri. Trac.* 105.29–32). However, this process is mediated through the demiurge, and as a result, a sort of anthropogonic double cross takes place. Because the Logos works through the demiurge, the demiurge thinks (reasonably enough) that the creature's soul is "his" in some sort of substantial sense. But the soul substance is in fact from the pneumatic Logos—and thus itself pneumatic—having only been imparted through the demiurge as breath through a mouth (*Tri. Trac.* 105.17–35; cf. 100.30–36).

At the same time, the demiurge does make a true contribution, sending down "souls out of his substance" (ⲛ̄ⲯⲩⲭ[ⲏ]ⲟⲩ ⲁⲃⲁⲗ ϩⲛ̄ ⲧⲉϥⲟⲩⲥⲓⲁ) out of his own procreative powers (*Tri. Trac.* 105.35–38). And finally, the archons "of the left" (elsewhere disparaged as hylic; *Tri. Trac.* 98.20) also participate, bringing forth "people [ⲛ̄ⲣⲱⲙⲉ] of their own" (*Tri. Trac.* 106.3–4). In the case of these last two contributions, while the plural forms "souls" and "people" make it possible to read them as referring to the creation of additional human beings, the larger context suggests that the Logos, the demiurge, and the archons are each contributing an element—pneumatic, psychic, or hylic, respectively—to Adam's creation. The three substances are characterized differently—pneumatic substance in terms of its singularity, psychic substance in terms of its doubleness, and hylic substance in terms of its "many forms … a sickness which came to be in many kinds of inclination" (*Tri. Trac.* 106.16–18). All three of these together compose the first human, who thus emerges as a "mixed modeling" (ⲟⲩⲡⲗⲁⲥⲙⲁ ⲡⲉ ⲉϥⲧⲏϩ), adulterated from the first (*Tri. Trac.* 106.18–19). This human is, the text elaborates, a deposit of both left and right, and also "a pneumatic word whose judgment is split [ⲟⲩⲡⲛ(ⲉⲩⲙ)ⲁⲧⲓⲕⲟ̄ⲥ ⲛ̄ⲗⲟⲅⲟⲥ ⲉⲧⲉϥⲅⲛⲱⲙⲏ

10. Thomassen notes that ⲕⲁϩ is probably a Coptic translation of χοϊκός (1989, 403).

ⲡⲏϣ] between each of the two substances from which the human receives its being" (*Tri. Trac.* 106.20–25). Here left and right correspond to hylic substance and psychic substance, respectively, while the pneumatic substance sits in some divided—yet still ambiguous—relationship to the other two.[11]

This, then, is the anthropological situation of the first human being. And while concerns regarding salvation are never far from view (be it Adam's or anyone else's), the tripartite categories are also functioning here to make claims about the complex interplay of substances that constitute the human. Further questions arise, however, when the narrative moves from the mixed formation of Adam to the constitution of subsequent human beings. Eventually, we are told, "Humanity came to exist in three ways according to substance [ⲕⲁⲧⲁ ⲟⲩⲥⲓⲁ]: the pneumatic and the psychic and the hylic, conforming in the type of its arrangement to the threefold way of the Logos, from which came forth the hylic ones and the psychic ones and the pneumatic ones" (*Tri. Trac.* 118.14–21). Thus an initially mixed creature gives way to three different kinds of human beings, each one established with reference to one of the substances generated by the Logos in the foregoing cosmogonic account.

How does the movement from one to the other take place? Here—in an effort to question or rethink stereotypes of determinism—some scholars have tended to see the three types not as ontological categories that define the human, but rather as indicative of (and constituted by) different responses to the salvific possibilities that the Savior's coming inaugurates. On this reading, all of humanity shares in Adam's mixed condition, and therefore contains hylic, psychic, and pneumatic aspects or potential. What causes any individual human being to be designated as "essentially" one of the three is the particular stance that she or he takes with respect to the Savior. As Denise Buell puts it, "if actions determine essence for the *Tripartite Tractate*, then it is not behavior that reveals one's nature, but behavior that *produces* one's nature, as a distillation of one of the three natures inherent in all humans" (2005, 128, emphasis original; cf. Attridge and Pagels 1985, 184–85, 187; Pearson 2007, 186; Thomassen 1989, 428).

11. While elsewhere the *Tripartite Tractate* uses the common Valentinian trope of a seed (ⲥⲡⲉⲣⲙⲁ) to designate some pneumatic element that originates from the Logos (see esp. *Tri. Trac.* 95.24–25), the image is not invoked here (though it may be implicitly in view). Note the contrast to *Exc.* 53.

While there is much that is appealing in this reading, certain of the text's claims seem to move in a different direction. Most notable in this respect is the *Tripartite Tractate*'s further explanation of the role the Savior plays in bringing to light the three types of humans: "Each of the essences of the three races [Ⲛ̄ⲄⲈⲚⲞⲤ] is known by its fruit. And at first they were not known, but only at the coming of the Savior, who put forth light upon the holy ones and made manifest with respect to each one that which he or she was" (*Tri. Trac.* 118.21–28).[12] Here the Savior's appearance seems clearly to *reveal* an already existing set of anthropological conditions, rather than to bring about new ones.[13] Yet at the same time Buell and others are surely correct to argue that the eschatological vision set forth by the text is not entirely deterministic. Although the text never makes explicit the notion that "one can potentially shift between [the three] *genē*" (Buell 2005, 84), neither does it rule out the possibility. While "the pneumatic race [ⲠⲒⲄⲈⲚⲞⲤ Ⲙ̄ⲠⲚ(ⲈⲨⲘ)ⲀⲦⲒⲔⲞⲚ] will receive salvation in its entirety in every way," potential also exists for the psychic race (ⲠⲒⲮⲨⲬⲒⲔⲞⲚ ... Ⲛ̄ⲄⲈⲚⲞⲤ) to attain salvation (*Tri. Trac.* 119.16–120.14).[14] As Thomassen points out, "the idea of a divine pedagogy pervades the argument throughout," implying the

12. On the ethnoracial dimensions of the three categories in the *Tripartite Tractate*, see Buell 2005, 126–28; and esp. Dunderberg 2008, 175–88. As Dunderberg unpacks in some detail, "Greeks and other nations (called 'barbarians') are associated with the material ones, while Hebrews basically belong to the psychic ones, though here the author has developed a more complicated theory. By implication, it is the Church that forms the third race of the spiritual ones." With respect to this added layer of complexity, he goes on to explain that the Hebrews (a term used with reference to the "righteous ones and prophets" of the Hebrew Bible, as distinct from contemporary Jews; see *Tri. Trac.* 110–112) "are not portrayed as a unified group of psychics. ... Instead, the Hebrews form a mixed group consisting of both hylics and psychics. Hebrews as a group are, thus, similar to the first human being, who was described as a deposit of those on the left side and those of the right side" (2008, 177, 185).

13. Note the similar point in Mitchell 2008, 175.

14. Here Dunderberg helpfully notes that the psychics of the right order are *not* portrayed as an inferior class of Christians but rather as potential converts: "In addition, the *Tripartite Tractate* reckons with the possibility that *converts* can be recruited from the [psychic/right-hand] group. ... Conversion involves, thus, abandonment of both power and idolatry ('their gods'). Those belonging to the right order are, thus, portrayed as polytheists. This is not a likely description of other Christians, even if they would be regarded as forming an inferior class and as servants of the Creator-God, as the psychics do in Valentinian theology as described by Irenaeus. The picture drawn of the psychics, or 'those of the right ones,' in the *Tripartite Tractate* suggests,

possibility of growth and transformation (2009, 174; cf. 177).[15] Thus whatever the anthropology in view here, there does seem to be room for some of the "fluidity" that Buell argues for (cf. Reis 2009, 598–600).

Notice, however, how questions about soteriology have defined and driven this conversation. Returning our focus to the tractate's creation narrative, it is important to remember that the text never actually explains in any unambiguous way how an amalgam of the three substances in a single human transitions into a world populated by "the hylic ones and the psychic ones and the pneumatic ones" (*Tri. Trac.* 118.14–21). On this key anthropological point, the *Tripartite Tractate* is silent.[16] But this silence does not seem sufficient reason to conclude that no claims about the distribution of substances are being made here, or that the makeup of subsequent human beings is necessarily identical to that of the first human (Attridge and Pagels 1985, 184; Buell 2005, 202 n. 40). Such a conclusion seems unjustifiably to discount—or at the very least sideline—the quite robust anthropological assertions that the text makes about tripartite humanity. Given the extensive and elegant ancient physics that the *Tripartite Tractate* expounds throughout, I want to argue that these claims cannot be contained to the purely discursive (in this case, a theological discourse concerned with salvation at the eschaton), but also participate in and indeed foreground other more material registers—ancient versions of the biological, the psychic (in Butler's sense), and the bodily. And it is in these registers—always, of course, in their conjunction with the eschatological—that the tripartite categories do the work of anthropological *categorizing* broadly conceived; that is, they map out where the human starts and stops, and they hint at (without ever fully clarifying) how its internal divisions relate substantially to one another and to the cosmos as a whole.

Thus when the *Tripartite Tractate* explains that the pneumatic race "is in the manner of [ⲘⲠⲢⲎⲦⲎ] light from light and in the manner of spirit from spirit, when its head was revealed, it ran to him," and the psychic race

rather, that they include polytheistic traditionalists in power who are expected to become members of the church" (2008, 170).

15. In addition, note Dunderberg's intriguing suggestion that Valentinian distinctions between pneumatics and psychics may carry overtones of "the distinctions ancient philosophers drew between more and less advanced students" (2008, 135). See also the extensive analysis of paraenesis in Valentinian texts in Tite 2009.

16. As too is Irenaeus's summary of Valentinian theology (both in contrast to the *Excerpts of Theodotus*, to be examined below). See Dunderberg 2008, 138.

is "as [ϩⲱⲥ] light from a fire" in its hesitation to receive the Savior, and the hylic race "is entirely a resident-alien, since being darkness, it shakes off the radiance of the light, because its appearing wipes it out" (*Tri. Trac.* 118.28–119.13), I would resist relegating these rich descriptions to metaphors that pertain *only* to different responses to the Savior. Rather, these metaphors embody, in Patricia Cox Miller's apt phrase, a "conjunction of discourse, materiality, and meaning" (2009, 7). That is, the text speaks here about substances in both their eschatological meaning and their tangible reality—and as such, these light-based metaphors participate in an interplay of the social, the biological, and the discursive in which the lines between these different registers remain necessarily porous. The elements of light, flame, and darkness may not actually *be* the substances that make up these different kinds of bodies, but they provide appropriate images for figuring these substances in language—the singularity of pneumatic substance attracted inexorably toward its luminous heavenly source, the doubleness of psychic substance quivering within the created order like light from a flame, and the constitutive weakness of hylic substance, bogged down in a smothering multiplicity that can only be characterized as alien darkness.[17]

There are, of course, limits to what we can know about the bodies and subjectivities envisioned by the *Tripartite Tractate*, given the text's abstruse style and enigmatic silences. I am therefore being careful not to argue that particular bodies subsequent to Adam (characterized as *either* hylic, psychic, or pneumatic) could not somehow be composed in complicated ways out of more than one of the substances (cf. *Excerpts from Theodotus* below). I am, however, suggesting that to designate the tripartite categories as only "potentialities of the human soul"—though they may in fact be that—runs the risk of obscuring their function within the tractate's mythological universe as substances, the concrete building blocks of cosmic and human creation.

Does this insistence on the tripartite categories as substances that constitute the human bring us back to the prospect of a deterministic anthropology in which different *genē* are saved by nature? I would argue no, and continue to side with Buell, Dunderberg, and others who see possibilities for fluidity and transformation in this text. Yet maintaining a potential for human beings to change need not necessitate shifting the tripartite

17. Note that at least in the case of the pneumatic order, Thomassen reads the "light from light" metaphor as signifying "an ontological consubstantiality between the spirituals and the transcendent world" (2009, 177).

categories from the register of substance to that of purely figurative language. Here Thomassen helpfully points to a certain "structural ambiguity" that attends both the soteriology of the *Tripartite Tractate* and Valentinian thought more generally: "in Valentinian soteriology … redemption is sometimes seen as simply a manifestation of what already exists as an immutable reality, and at other times as a profound transformation and the attainment of a new identity" (2009, 174, 181). This is a necessary ambiguity, according to Thomassen, generated by "the ontological problem of mediating between unity and multiplicity by means of a theory of extension and contraction" (183). The result is that the goal of absolute unity must be thought dialectically in terms of both "complete transformation, so complete that one may speak about a replacement of deficiency with fullness" and also "no transformation at all" (184).[18]

While I find this analysis of Thomassen's to be convincing, my point is simply that nothing in this "dialectics of unity and duality" requires treating the tripartite categories as eschatological figures of speech to the exclusion of their role as substances.[19] And it is as substances that the categories function as the primary mechanism whereby the *Tripartite Tractate* marks the limits of the human *in terms of its constitutive internal differences.* The result, significantly, is a relative lack of concern with elucidating the role of other kinds of boundaries (i.e., those that relate the human to the nonhuman) that might otherwise circumscribe the text's anthropological project. (This stands in marked contrast to what we will see in the *Excerpts from Theodotus* below.) Thus the tractate refers to the distinction between angels and humans with a casualness bordering on indifference: both can belong to the psychic or hylic orders and both are in need of redemption (see *Tri. Trac.* 120.1; 121.19; 122.1; 124.25–28). This is not to imply the humans and angels are the same; they are not. But clarifying the relationship between the two or foregrounding a boundary

18. See also the extensive discussion in Thomassen 2006, 50–58.

19. How the distribution of substances that establishes the tripartition of humanity might shift or how the very substances themselves might be transformed are not questions that the *Tripartite Tractate* takes up in any clear-cut way. But the hylic, the psychic, and the pneumatic need not be placeholders for claims about eschatology *rather than* substances used to form created human beings in order for them to participate in the salvific movement that characterizes Thomassen's dialectic. For an ancient discussion of how substances can change ("a coming-to-be of one substance and a passing-away of the other"), see Aristotle, *Gen. corr.* 1.319b, trans. Joachim.

(even a porous one) between them is not a matter of much theological or anthropological consequence. Rather, creation by means of hylic, psychic, and pneumatic substances, variably deployed, works here to formulate an architectonics of the human in which the most significant limits are those that fissure it internally, rather than those that map the ambiguous status of its frontiers.

Excerpts from Theodotus

The disjointed notebook of Valentinian speculations known as the *Excerpts from Theodotus* (preserved in Clement of Alexandria) trades in anthropological categories similar to the *Tripartite Tractate*, but does so through a more extensive and developed rereading of Gen 1 and 2 than that which we see in the tractate.[20] While the extant text is likely a composite source and deals with issues of creation and anthropology throughout, my analysis will focus primarily on the narrative of cosmogony, human creation, and redemption laid out in *Exc.* 43–65.[21] Like the *Tripartite Tractate*, this section of the *Excerpts* sets forth a rudimentary physics of substances by means of a cosmogonic myth. And also like the tractate, the *Excerpts* uses a tripartite anthropological division as the framework in which to convey what Jorunn Jacobsen Buckley rightly characterizes as its "highly esoteric and enigmatic speculations on the constitution of the human being" (1986, 61). Yet in this project of articulating the limits of the human, the tripartite categories function with somewhat different emphases and to different ends. Whereas in the *Tripartite Tractate* they work to demarcate anthropology by foregrounding internal divisions in their relationship to one another, the *Excerpts from Theodotus* mobilizes the categories with an eye to defining the human primarily in terms of its substantial origins in (and thus complex interrelationship to) other nonhuman registers of being: divine and angelic, diabolic and bestial.

---

20. For the reconstructed Greek text, see Sagnard 1970.

21. For the division of the *Excerpts* into four blocks of material (of which 43–65 is one), see Sagnard 1970, 28–29. Unpacking the relationship of 43–65 to the rest of the work, Michel Desjardins notes that, while on the one hand, "In many respects, then, the third and middle section [43–65] stands on its own, and this provides added incentive to appraise its contents," on the other hand, "it still exhibits considerable overlap with the other three sections" (1990, 33–34). Thus I will make occasional reference to comparative evidence from other parts of the *Excerpts* as relevant.

Unsurprisingly, the emergence of hylic/choic, psychic, and pneumatic substances in the *Excerpts* is situated within a broader Valentinian physics that accounts for the origins of the cosmos. In a narrative movement similar to the *Tripartite Tractate* (though with Sophia occupying the role that the Logos does in the tractate), the text recounts the restoration of Sophia and its attendant results for the process of creation. The Savior separates Sophia from the passions, rendering her "without passion" (ἀπαθῆ) and reworking the passions into hylic substance (τὴν ὕλην) (*Exc.* 45.2; 46.1). In a multistep process, this substance begins as noncorporeal (ἀσώματον), and then is transformed into "compound forms and bodies" (συγκρίματα καὶ σώματα), equipped with attributes suitable to their nature (κατὰ φύσιν ἐπιτηδειότητα) (*Exc.* 46.1–2). Sophia, for her part, engenders the demiurge—her instrument for the creation of heaven and earth, associated respectively (as in the *Tripartite Tractate*) with the right and the left, the psychic and the hylic/choic (*Exc.* 47.1). The demiurge then gets to work creating, bringing forth first a psychic Christ, then archangels, and finally angels from "a psychic and radiant substance" (ἐκ τῆς ψυχικῆς καὶ φωτεινῆς), the result of God's spirit laying upon the primal waters (Gen 1:2). But that substance can be more precisely understood as an intertwining of two substances (τὴν συμπλοκὴν τῶν δύο οὐσιῶν)—one ("spirit") described as pure (εἰλικρινὲς) and clear (καθαρὰ), and the other ("waters") as heavy (ἐμβριθὲς), hylic (ὑλικὸν), turbid (θολερὸν), and coarse (παχυμερές) (*Exc.* 47.2–48.1).[22] The demiurge divides the two, making light from the former (Gen 1:3) and the elements of the hylic order (τῶν ὑλικῶν) from the latter (*Exc.* 48.1–2). The hylic elements are then given further specificity, breaking down into three component parts: grief, which gives substance to the spiritual elements of evil (πνευματικὰ τῆς πονηρίας); fear, associated with the beasts; and misfortune and difficulty, which give rise to the component parts of the cosmos (τὰ στοιχεῖα τοῦ κόσμου) (cf. Eph 6:12; Gal 4:3; Col 2:8, 20). Within these three elements, fire is dispersed throughout, drifting pervasively, but without its own proper or appointed place. Rather, fire attends and animates the elements that make up compound forms (*Exc.* 48.2–4; cf. 81.1 and the role of fire in Stoic cosmology).[23]

---

22. Note the text's exegesis of ἀόρατος in Gen 1:2 (LXX) in order to characterize this substance as shapeless, formless, and without figure (τὸ ἄμορφον καὶ ἀνείδεον καὶ ἀσχημάτιστον).

23. For a helpful overview, see Sellars 2006, 86–90, 96–99.

In this way, notions of hylic, psychic, and pneumatic substances are all already in play. Yet their interrelationship is complex and ambiguous, governed by the text's exegesis of Gen 1:1–3, but nonetheless not fully specified or explained. However, with this basic physics in place, the stage is set for the creation of human beings. As in numerous other early Christian creation accounts, Gen 1:26 governs the movement of the storyline: "Then God said, 'Let us make humankind in our image, according to our likeness'" (NRSV). Early Christian exegetes commonly read this crucial verse disjunctively, positing that creation of humanity according to the divine image was somehow different from creation according to the likeness.[24] And the *Excerpts* shares in this hermeneutical strategy, applying a split between image and likeness not only to Gen 1:26, but also to the details of human creation found in Gen 2:7—such that the text's interpretation breaks apart the latter verse as well.[25]

Thus when the demiurge takes up "dust of the ground" (χοῦν ἀπὸ τῆς γῆς, Gen 2:7), he uses it to form the human being "according to the image." But the reader is directed to understand "dust of the ground" in terms of the physics of substances already articulated. It is therefore "not of the dry land, but rather a portion of manifold and variegated *hylē*" (*Exc.* 50.1). From this matter, the demiurge forms "a soul, earthy and hylic" (ψυχὴν γεώδη καὶ ὑλικὴν)—that is, substantial—but not yet bodily in the everyday, visible sense (*Exc.* 50.1; cf. 55.1). This is the first hylic human, and the text characterizes its soul or life substance as "consubstantial [ὁμοούσιον] with that of the beasts" (50.1). Accordingly, the category of "hylic substance" does not belong to the domain of the human alone. Rather, this substance encodes in hylic humanity some irreducible element of the bestial, thereby defining its specificity in terms of *a relationship of interaction* between the two. From the perspective of the text's creation narrative, this may be an illegitimate—or at least less than ideal—interaction. But it nonetheless works to articulate an anthropological limit (i.e., the hylic human is *not* an animal), while simultaneously rendering that limit porous insofar as the

---

24. See the more detailed discussion in Dunning 2009, 66–68.

25. Cf. Engberg-Pedersen's analysis of 1 Cor 15 and Paul's exegesis of Gen 2:7 along similar lines (2010, 29–31)—though with the crucial difference that Paul reads the two *anthrōpoi* in terms of an extended chronological sequence in salvation history (i.e., first and last Adams), rather than as two consecutive moments in the primal creation narrative.

animal nature of a constitutive human substance troubles any hard and fast distinction between the two.

The *Excerpts* then interprets the remainder of Gen 2:7—"[the Lord God] breathed into his nostrils the breath of life; and the man became a living being" (NRSV)—as referring to the creation of the human "according to the likeness." The demiurge forms a second human being and breathes into him, so that this human becomes "a living soul" (ψυχὴ ζῶσα)—that is, a psychic human (*Exc.* 50.3). Here again the text uses one of the tripartite categories to negotiate a specific limit of the human with reference to a nonhuman register, this time that of the lower echelons of divinity. What the demiurge breathes into this human is "consubstantial with himself" (ὁμοούσιόν τι αὐτῷ) (*Exc.* 50.2). Therefore, because the demiurge is "invisible and noncorporeal" (ἀόρατός ἐστι καὶ ἀσώματος), so, too, is the psychic element. Yet the *Excerpts* is clear that it is still a substance (τὴν οὐσίαν) and as such is called "the breath of life" (*Exc.* 50.3). This psychic substance therefore manifests a bona fide intermingling between humanity and (lesser) divinity that resists any tidy dualism. At the same time, it is the single category that limits and defines the second human over against the registers of the nonhuman (including divinity) and the previous human.

At this point then, the *Excerpts* has narrated the creation of two human beings, constituted and delimited (albeit in somewhat unstable ways) by two primal substances. How are these two humans—image and likeness, choic and psychic—related to one another? According to Michel Desjardins, "In this system one begins with the hylic or 'choical' human, the one made from matter or the dust of the earth. In some instances, another whole, or a human of psychic nature, can be superimposed onto it. … The two 'humans' do not merge. It is a mismatched marriage, where two unities come together, one being of less nature than the other" (1990, 34). The *Excerpts* characterizes this somewhat uneasy arrangement as "*anthrōpos* in *anthrōpos*, psychic in choic [ψυχικὸς ἐν χοϊκῷ], not part to part, but rather whole connecting to whole … the hylic soul being the body of the divine soul" (*Exc.* 51.1, 3). But the relationship also has its decidedly antagonistic aspects, as the text goes on to elaborate: the "body" of the hylic soul can be understood as an opponent warring against the heavenly (psychic) soul or as the weeds that grow up with the good seed in Jesus' parable (52.1; 53.1). In this respect, its substance reveals itself as not only bestial but in fact diabolic, characterized as "a seed of the devil, as it is consubstantial with that one, and a serpent" (53.1). Here another register of the nonhuman is invoked to further clarify the substantial composition of the hylic element.

The figure of the serpent serves to link the two registers, devil and animal, but no further explanation is given of how they work together to establish the hylic in the human register.

What then of the third tripartite category, the pneumatic element? Having invoked the Gospel parable to discuss the bad seed allows for a congruous transition to a discussion of the good seed—that is, the pneumatic seed (τὸ σπέρμα τὸ πνευματικὸν). Bypassing the demiurge, Sophia implants this seed in Adam without his knowing (see also the similar [but not identical] account in *Exc.* 2). In contrast to the hylic and psychic elements, however, the pneumatic seed is not a third *anthrōpos*; it is, rather, a kind of marrow encased in psychic bone (*Exc.* 53.5; see discussion in Pagels 1974, 49). As in the *Tripartite Tractate*, here again we encounter a rich anthropological metaphor. Similar to the former text, the bone and marrow image—though explicitly marked as figurative (see *Exc.* 62.2)—does not therefore function only as a disembodied symbol for Adam's potential to be saved (*pace* Buckley 1986, 74–75 [following Schottroff]). Instead, marrow in a bone offers a powerful bodily figure for how the *Excerpts* envisions the *pneuma* filling its psychic encasing in a very real and substantial (if not necessarily visible or sense perceptible) way.

The introduction of this pneumatic marrow pulls a fourth register of the nonhuman—the higher divine realm, as mediated through the angelic—into the process of human creation. Throughout the *Excerpts* as a whole, angels are not unequivocally associated with the pneumatic order. At least some angels appear to have some tie to the psychic (while not necessarily being constituted out of psychic substance) (see *Exc.* 21–23, 35, 39–40; and detailed analysis in Buckley 1986, 61–83). However, it is the class of beings designated "male angels" that is relevant to the origins of Adam's pneumatic element.[26] For while the ultimate source of the pneumatic substance is Sophia, the male angels help to establish and cultivate it (thus the text cites Gal 3:19: "ordained through angels by a mediator" [NRSV]). As Thomassen explains, "the angels are mediators between the Pleroma and the spiritual seed of humans. They are manifestations of the aeons, and the seed came into being as images of the angels" (2009, 180).

26. Note the association made elsewhere in the text (*Exc.* 21) between election, the male, and the angelic on the one hand and calling, the female, and the "different seed" (τὸ διαφέρον σπέρμα)—not to be confused with the pneumatic seed—on the other. For analysis of this elaborate network of relationships, see Buckley 1986, 61–83; Pagels 1974, 35–53.

According to *Exc.* 44, when Sophia recognizes the correspondence of substance (ὅμοιον) between the Savior and the pneumatic light, she directs her shamefaced veiling of herself toward "the male angels who were dispatched with him" (thereby illuminating Paul's otherwise cryptic command in 1 Cor 11:10, "For this reason a woman ought to have a symbol of authority on her head, because of the angels" [NRSV]). But do the male angels actually mediate the pneumatic element to Adam in a substantial sense? Another rendition of the creation account, embedded at an earlier point in the text, would seem to suggest exactly this: "the pneumatic element [τὸ πνευματικόν], which the Savior deposited in the soul—the seed was an outflowing of the male and the angelic element [τοῦ ἄρρενος καὶ ἀγγελικοῦ]" (*Exc.* 2.2). Thus the pneumatic seed is the means by which the text situates the higher divine and/or angelic in relation to the human, the substance of the former register being incorporated into the composition of the latter.

Onto this three-step creation process the *Excerpts* grafts a fourth and final stage. Up to this point, Adam's tangible, perceptible body in the everyday sense has not been in view. While the hylic soul functions as the body/σῶμα of the divine soul, it does so within a framework in which *all three* elements are classified as noncorporeal/ἀσώματος in some fundamental way (though as Martin reminds us, ἀσώματος should not be equated with "immaterial" in the modern sense [1995, 15; see *Exc.* 51.2; 55.1]). Adam's visible body emerges only with the addition of a fourth element—confusingly called "the choic" (ὁ χοϊκός)—which is put onto the other three elements "as the garments of skins" (55.1). Here the text does not appear particularly concerned to preserve terminological consistency—since it has already used the term *choic* as roughly synonymous with *hylic* elsewhere in the creation account (e.g., 51.1; 54.2). Rather, the point seems to be to stress the movement from an interplay of noncorporeal substances to the containment of those substances within a sense-perceptible body, a move that the text folds into the narrative by alluding to Gen 3:21: "And the LORD God made garments of skins for the man and for his wife, and clothed them" (NRSV).[27]

With respect to the tripartite categories, however, this fourth element/choic body undoubtedly has some basic affinity with one of the three: the hylic. This becomes clear in the *Excerpts*' rather detailed narration of the transition from the situation of Adam the first human to that of subse-

27. On "noncorporeal substances" in Aristotle, see Martin 1995, 8–9.

quent human beings (note the contrast to the *Tripartite Tractate*'s relative silence on this point). As Dunderberg summarizes,

> Since the spirit and the breath are divine qualities, Adam could only transmit them to later generations without being able to engender them himself. The only thing he himself could produce was the hylic essence. For this reason, there are many hylic beings, but there are not as many psychic ones, and the spiritual ones are few. This argument implies that the hylic essence, which Adam himself was able to beget, has gradually taken a dominant position in his posterity. (2008, 139)

The explanation that the text provides for this situation works to cement the link between hylic substance and choic body through an exegesis of 1 Cor 15:47: "Therefore our father Adam is 'the first *anthrōpos* of the earth, choic.' So if he had sown out of the psychic and the pneumatic, just as from out of the hylic, all would have been the same and righteous, and the teaching would have been in everyone" (*Exc.* 56.1–2). But since Adam can sow exclusively out of hylic substance, he can therefore only generate that substance as his legacy to all future humanity. The other two substances "are put forward through him but not by him" (*Exc.* 55.2), thus accounting for their relative and presumably ever-increasing scarcity in the human beings that follow.

In this way, the *Excerpts* uses the tripartite categories to offer a vision of the different substances that constitute human beings in various ways. Like the *Tripartite Tractate*, it ultimately does divide humanity into three kinds, but unlike that text, its accent is on the convoluted web of relations to the nonhuman (bestial, diabolic, angelic, and divine) that the substances put into play as they formulate the limits of the human. Here again I would argue that this emphasis on substance need not lead to a purely deterministic anthropology. On the one hand, with respect to the eschatological fate of the substances, the *Excerpts* is unambiguous: "So then the pneumatic element is saved by nature; but the psychic element, having free will, has the potential for both faithfulness and incorruption, and also for lack of faith and corruption, according to its own choosing; and the hylic element is lost by nature" (*Exc.* 56.3). On the other hand, however, the implications for those human beings who follow Adam and are composed (in different ways?) out of the three substances are less clear.

Some scholars have argued that only the pneumatic race can lay claim to all three elements (and the psychic to the lower two and so on), while others have argued that every human being (not just Adam) contains all three.[28] But regardless of how one settles this question, Dunderberg is right to highlight that the possibilities open to psychic substance complicate any simple determinism (2009, 139–40). For while the potential exists for the psychic element to come to corruption, it can also be grafted onto the pneumatic olive tree—an appeal to a Pauline metaphor that, like the other Valentinian metaphors we have examined, *may* point in its figuration to concrete metaphysical possibilities, such as the (qualified?) transformation of one substance into another (*Exc.* 56.4–5; cf. Rom 11:17–24).[29] Thus the text's objectives of education and transformation for human beings remain comprehensible, even as it emphasizes the tripartite categories not as mere eschatological figures of speech but as substances that render the created human being a complex amalgam of relationships to different forms of the nonhuman.

Conclusion

Working on a somewhat later period, Patricia Cox Miller has recently demonstrated the importance of what she calls the "corporeal imagination" among late ancient Christians, a set of techniques and corresponding textual images that includes "the elaboration of a theological poetics of material substance" (2009, 7–8). In this paper I have argued that we see a similar concern with the poetics of substance—as well as with the implications of that poetics for theological anthropology—in two Valentinian accounts of the creation of the cosmos. Both the *Tripartite Tractate* and the *Excerpts from Theodotus* make use of the traditional Valentinian distinction between the hylic, the psychic, and the pneumatic in order to comment on the substances that compose the human—and in the process lay claim to its limits in particular ways. More specifically, both elaborate

28. See, as representative of the first position, McCue 1980, 412–14. For an example of the second position, see Buckley 1986, 75.

29. Note that the *Excerpts* does at least at one point make a qualitative distinction between the salvations of psychic and pneumatic elements (see *Exc.* 61.8). Yet this section of the text ultimately looks forward to "the marriage banquet, common to all those who are saved" (63.2), lending support to Dunderberg's contention that "the distinction between the spiritual and the psychic humans will ultimately disappear. … The salvation envisioned in this passage means that the believers belonging to the psychic class attain the very same salvation as spiritual beings" (2008, 139).

a system of internal differences that structure the human as a category, and both ascribe the origins of the three substances in humans to various nonhuman agents. Yet with that said, they engage in this shared project with different rhetorical emphases and anthropological foci. The result is a difference in which limits matter and why, with the *Tripartite Tractate* foregrounding the fissures that structure the human internally in their relation to each other and the cosmic hierarchy, and the *Excerpts* attending to the complex mesh of relationships to the nonhuman that come together in the process of human creation. In neither case does a concern with the concrete substances that make up the human lead to a simple deterministic outlook, but instead points to the creative anthropological possibilities entailed in the slippage between bodies and discourse.

Works Cited

Aristotle. 1941. *The Basic Works of Aristotle*. Translated by Harold H. Joachim. Edited by Richard McKeon. New York: Random House.

Attridge, Harold W., and Elaine H. Pagels. 1985. The Tripartite Tractate. Pages 159–337 in vol. 1 of *Nag Hammadi Codex I (The Jung Codex)*. Edited by Harold W. Attridge. Leiden: Brill.

Buckley, Jorunn Jacobsen. 1986. *Female Fault and Fulfillment in Gnosticism*. Chapel Hill: University of North Carolina Press.

Buell, Denise Kimber. 2005. *Why This New Race: Ethnic Reasoning in Early Christianity*. New York: Columbia University Press.

Butler, Judith. 1993. *Bodies That Matter: On the Discursive Limits of "Sex."* New York: Routledge.

———. 2004. *Undoing Gender*. New York: Routledge.

Desjardins, Michel R. 1990. *Sin in Valentinianism*. Society of Biblical Literature Dissertation Series 108. Atlanta: Scholars Press.

Dillon, John M. 1977. *The Middle Platonists: 80 B.C. to A.D. 220*. Ithaca, N.Y.: Cornell University Press.

Dunderberg, Ismo. 2008. *Beyond Gnosticism: Myth, Lifestyle, and Society in the School of Valentinus*. New York: Columbia University Press.

Dunning, Benjamin H. 2009. What Sort of Thing Is This Luminous Woman? Thinking Sexual Difference in *On the Origin of the World*. *Journal of Early Christian Studies* 17:55–84.

———. 2011. *Specters of Paul: Sexual Difference in Early Christian Thought*. Philadelphia: University of Pennsylvania Press.

Engberg-Pedersen, Troels. 2010. *Cosmology and Self in the Apostle Paul: The Material Spirit*. Oxford: Oxford University Press.

González, Justo L. 1984. *The Early Church to the Dawn of the Reformation*. Vol. 1 of *The Story of Christianity.* San Francisco: Harper & Row.

St. Irenaeus of Lyons: Against the Heresies. Vol. 1: *Book 1*. 1992. Ancient Christian Writers 55. Translated by Dominic J. Unger and John J. Dillon. New York: Paulist Press.

Kavelsmaki, Joel. 2008. Italian versus Eastern Valentinianism? *Vigiliae Christianae* 62:79–89.

King, Karen L. 2003. *What Is Gnosticism?* Cambridge: Harvard University Press.

Martin, Dale B. 1995. *The Corinthian Body*. New Haven: Yale University Press.

McCue, James F. 1980. Conflicting Versions of Valentinianism? Irenaeus and the *Excerpta ex Theodoto*. Pages 404–16 in vol. 1 of *The Rediscovery of Gnosticism: Proceedings of the International Conference on Gnosticism at Yale, New Haven, Connecticut, March 28–31, 1978*. 2 vols. Edited by Bentley Layton. Leiden: Brill.

Miller, Patricia Cox. 2009. *The Corporeal Imagination: Signifying the Holy in Late Ancient Christianity*. Philadelphia: University of Pennsylvania Press.

Mitchell, Margaret M. 2008. Review of Denise Kimber Buell, *Why This New Race? Ethnic Reasoning in Early Christianity*. *History of Religions* 48:173–77.

Pagels, Elaine H. 1972. The Valentinian Claim to Esoteric Exegesis of Romans as Basis for Anthropological Theory. *Vigiliae Christianae* 26:241–58.

———. 1974. Conflicting Versions of Valentinian Eschatology: Irenaeus' Treatise vs. The Excerpts from Theodotus. *Harvard Theological Review* 67:35–53.

Pearson, Birger A. 2007. *Ancient Gnosticism: Traditions and Literature*. Minneapolis: Fortress.

Reis, David M. 2009. Thinking with Soul: *Psychē* and *Psychikos* in the Construction of Early Christian Identities. *Journal of Early Christian Studies* 17:563–603.

Sagnard, François, ed. 1970. *Clément d'Alexandrie, Extraits de Théodote*. Sources chrétiennes 23. Paris: Cerf.

Schottroff, Luise. 1969. *Animae naturaliter salvandae*: Zum Problem der himmlischen Herkunft des Gnostikers. Pages 65–97 in *Christentum und Gnosis*. Edited by Walther Eltester. Berlin: Töpelmann.

Sedgwick, Eve Kosofsky. 1990. *Epistemology of the Closet*. Berkeley: University of California Press.

Sellars, John. 2006. *Stoicism*. Berkeley: University of California Press.

Thomassen, Einar, ed. 1989. *Le Traité tripartite (NH I, 5)*. Translated by Louis Painchaud and Einar Thomassen. Quebec: Presses de l'Université Laval.

———. 2006. *The Spiritual Seed: The Church of the "Valentinians."* Leiden: Brill.

———. 2009. Valentinian Ideas about Salvation as Transformation. Pages 169–86 in *Metamorphoses: Resurrection, Body and Transformative Practices in Early Christianity*. Edited by Turid Karlsen Seim and Jorunn Økland. Berlin: de Gruyter.

Tite, Philip L. 2009. *Valentinian Ethics and Paraenetic Discourse: Determining the Social Function of Moral Exhortation in Valentinian Christianity*. Leiden: Brill.

Gregory of Nyssa and Jacques Derrida on the Human-Animal Distinction in the Song of Songs

Eric Daryl Meyer

> One who says: I am He who is, who follows you and whom you are (following), who is (following) after you with a view to seducing you and to have it be that, coming after, you become one who follows me. (Derrida 2008, 67)

Jacques Derrida despairs of finding animals among philosophers. "Thinking concerning the animal, if there is such a thing, derives from poetry. There you have a thesis" (2008, 7; cf. 40). The poetic imagination, in contrast to the philosopher's, has from time to time had the courage to stand in the gaze of the animal and to write as one *who is seen*. Guided by Derrida's intuition about poetic discourse, I begin this essay in an ancient piece of erotic poetry in which animal metaphor features prominently—Solomon's Song of Songs. This book's place in the canon was a puzzle and perplexity for many Jewish and Christian thinkers, but rather than label it lewd or unspiritual and ignore it altogether, many early Christian authors employed an elaborate theological exegesis to lay bare a narrative of love between God and God's creatures hidden in the erotic movements of the Song of Songs. The fourth-century bishop Gregory of Nyssa penned one such engagement with this enigmatic text in the form of fifteen homilies (hereafter *GNO* [Gregory of Nyssa's *Opera*]).[1] The presence of animals all through the Song, and thus all through Gregory's homiletic commentary,

1. All translations are my own. I have benefited from the recent translation (with introduction) by Norris (2012), and also from the older translation by McCambley (1987). Both translations contain marginal reference to the page numbers in *GNO*, which I employ throughout the essay's citations.

provides an opportunity to examine the conceptual interrelation of divinity, humanity, and animality.

In this essay, then, I venture a reading of Gregory's *Homilies on the Song of Songs* alongside Derrida's *Animal That Therefore I Am* in an attempt to locate Gregory relative to the trajectory of an "immense disavowal" of animals that Derrida traces from Descartes to Levinas. Derrida names this disavowal as the production of a concept, "the human," by means of a stark contrast with another concept, "the animal"—an enormous, falsely homogenous, bounded set, capturing millions of different species in a single term. Thinking with Derrida, I argue that Gregory's discourse on animality remains irresolvably conflicted. Although he labors toward it, Gregory's theology cannot finally abide a categorical distinction between humanity and animality. The theological anthropology informing Gregory's anagogical exegesis of the Song of Songs "short-circuits" so that human animality is necessary to reach the deepest meaning of Scripture and the summits of spiritual ascent, despite Gregory's more explicit claims that spiritual transformation entails the transcendence of humanity beyond animality. Animality remains integral to Gregory's reading of the Song of Songs, not simply because of the pervasive animal metaphors within the text under his consideration, but on account of his understanding of theological exegesis and the role of desire in spiritual progress.

I divide this essay into three sections. First, I describe Gregory's unique conception of the practice of anagogical exegesis, and the cosmological/anthropological framework that provides the exigency for such an approach to Scripture. Second, to examine Gregory's exegesis in action in relation to the human-animal distinction, I analyze Gregory's exegetical approach to the complex of nakedness, shame, modesty, and clothing—which traditionally serves as one "cut" dividing humans from other animals, and which also features prominently in Derrida's text. Third, I follow the trajectories of animal desire, contemplative knowledge, and spiritual transformation as they intersect in the Song and Gregory's homiletic commentary upon it.

Anagogical Exegesis

Gregory explains and defends his exegetical method in both the first homily and the preface that precedes it in order to attune his hearers' ears to the deeper meaning of the scriptural text and to counter anticipated antagonism from "certain church leaders" who strongly disapprove of Gregory's mode of interpretation.[2] All things being equal, Gregory would prefer to call his approach to Scripture "anagogical interpretation" (τὴν διὰ τῆς ἀναγωγῆς θεωρίαν) rather than "allegorical" or "typological," but he is clearly more concerned to offer a rationale for his exegetical method than to quibble over its title (*GNO* 6:5).[3] Gregory's style of exegesis is by no means sui generis, being grounded in a tradition running from Philo through Origen, but he is uniquely interested in the ways in which an ascetically attuned reading of Scripture "leads upward" (ἀνάγειν), drawing the reader toward God. After offering a brief overview of Gregory's anagogical exegesis, in this section I demonstrate that Gregory conceives of proper biblical interpretation as an upward movement that transcends animality or excises animal meaning from what is properly a spiritual (read "human") text.

Gregory's relationship to his primary influence on theological interpretation, Origen, has been the subject of several excellent studies (see in particular Dünzl 1993; Norris 1998; Ludlow 2002). For Gregory, each book of Scripture bears its own unique aim (σκοπός)—he uses Proverbs, Ecclesiastes, and the Song of Songs for examples (*GNO* 6:19–23)—and each book accomplishes that aim through its own unique (and perceptible) logical sequence (ἀκολουθία). Where Origen conceives of the σκοπός of the whole canon as a description of the journey of the soul (Ludlow 2002, 50–51; cf. Torjesen 1986, 71–72), Gregory's piecemeal approach to Scripture expects a differentiated aim within each book that must be ascertained through careful, contemplative reading rather than assumed from the outset. Like Origen, Gregory reads Scripture as a canonical whole, a practice that validates connections between far-flung passages on the basis of a shared word or image.[4] Yet unlike Origen, the mean-

2. Gregory's mention of "some clerics" (τισι τῶν ἐκκλησιαστικῶν) is often taken to refer to Diodore of Tarsus and his student Theodore of Mopsuestia, though Gregory does not name anyone specifically (*GNO* 6:4). See Heine 1984, 366–69.

3. Norris (2012, xliv) agrees that *anagogy* is the best terminological fit for Gregory's understanding of the relation between the text of Scripture and the ascetically attuned reader.

4. Dünzl refers to this as the *Stichwort* (key word) method of exegesis, in which sense is brought to a difficult word through connections made to other instances of the same word in Scripture. For example, Gregory makes sense of the bride's comparison to a dove by reference to the appearance of the Spirit as a dove at Christ's baptism (Dünzl 1993, 54); for contrast with Origen, see Ludlow 2002, 55–56, 58.

ing of a passage is first governed by the sequential logic in the book where it is found, rather than an overarching canonical theme (Norris 1998, 531–32; Ludlow 2002, 53, 63–64). Nevertheless, understanding the spiritual meaning of a text according to its *σκοπός* involves what Norris calls "transposing" the historical narrative and material imagery up into a spiritual register (Norris 2002, 520–21). Gregory himself uses the image of "transfiguration"—as the dusty, tired body of Christ was found to be unbearably radiant upon a mountain, so also does the properly attuned reader find a deeper and mysterious light emerging from the plain page of Scripture (*GNO* 6:14).

The particular *σκοπός* of the Song of Songs, as Gregory conceives it, is to draw the soul into loving union with God (Norris 2012, xxxiii; Laird 2007, 40). He writes:

> *ταῦτα διαμαρτύρομαι μέλλων ἅπτεσθαι τῆς ἐν τῷ Ἄισματι τῶν Ἀισμάτων μυστικῆς θεωρίας. διὰ γὰρ τῶν ἐνταῦθα γεγραμμένων νυμφοστολεῖται τρόπον τινὰ ἡ ψυχὴ πρὸς τὴν ἀσώματόν τε καὶ πνευματικὴν καὶ ἀμόλυντον τοῦ θεοῦ συζυγίαν·*
>
> I bear solemn witness to these things because I am about to apprehend the mystical sense in the Song of Songs. For through what has been written there, the soul is led like a bride toward a spiritual, unstained, and bodiless union with God. (*GNO* 6:15)

The *σκοπός* of the text is a function of divine authorial agency and not something thematized by the "Solomon of flesh and blood."[5] Thus Gregory regards the Song of Songs as a text whose logical sequence (*ἀκολουθία*) contains both a narrative of the union of a soul with God and a spiritual "hook" that draws the reader into a similar union. As Norris notes, then, anagogical exegesis is not merely a technical skill practiced upon an inert text (2012, xx).[6] Rather, it is an approach to a text that is embedded

---

5. Gregory suggests that there is another "Son of David" speaking through Solomon, on whose account the text is replete with true Wisdom (*GNO* 6:17; cf. Ludlow 2002, 54).

6. Likewise, Coakley is surely correct in asserting that any division of Gregory's mystical and exegetical theology in texts such as the *Homilies on the Song of Songs*, the *Life of Moses*, or the *Homilies on the Beatitudes* from his constructive and systematic theology (as worked out in the polemical writings against Eunomius and Apollinarius) is surely forced and false. Gregory's reflections on Scripture, God as Trinity, and

within a particular vision of the world—and specifically of the way that language, text, meaning, understanding, and spiritual progress operate across a boundary between the visible material creation and the invisible intelligible creation. The practice of anagogical exegesis mirrors Gregory's cosmology, in which a spiritual/intellectual layer of creation is always distinct and superior to, yet nevertheless inseparable from, a material layer of creation.[7] The Song of Songs is a bridge: it narrates material acts, but simultaneously and inseparably bears an intelligible meaning that acts spiritually on its ascetically attuned readers so that properly understanding the text is already also progress in an immaterial journey.

Accordingly, the σκοπός of the text, as Gregory understands it, does not lie flat on the page, passively waiting to be grasped and articulated; rather Gregory attributes an agency to the text itself, or finds a divine agency working through it. The meaning of the text works itself out on the reader as much as the reader works out the meaning of the text:

> ἐν οἷς τὸ μὲν ὑπογραφόμενον ἐπιθαλάμιός τίς ἐστι διασκευή, τὸ δὲ νοούμενον τῆς ἀνθρωπίνης ψυχῆς ἡ πρὸς τὸ θεῖόν ἐστιν ἀνάκρασις. διὰ τοῦτο νύμφη ὧδε ὁ ἐν ταῖς Παροιμίαις υἱὸς ὀνομάζεται καὶ ἡ σοφία εἰς νυμφίου τάξιν ἀντιμεθίσταται, ἵνα μνηστευθῇ τῷ θεῷ ὁ ἄνθρωπος ἁγνὴ παρθένος ἐκ νυμφίου γενόμενος καὶ κολληθεὶς τῷ κυρίῳ γένηται πνεῦμα ἓν διὰ τῆς πρὸς τὸ ἀκήρατόν τε καὶ ἀπαθὲς ἀνακράσεως νόημα καθαρὸν ἀντὶ σαρκὸς βαρείας γενόμενος. ἐπειδὴ τοίνυν σοφία ἐστὶν ἡ λαλοῦσα, ἀγάπησον ὅσον δύνασαι ἐξ ὅλης καρδίας τε καὶ δυνάμεως, ἐπιθύμησον ὅσον χωρεῖς. προστίθημι δὲ θαρρῶν τοῖς ῥήμασι τούτοις καὶ τὸ ἐράσθητι· ἀνέγκλητον γὰρ τοῦτο καὶ ἀπαθὲς ἐπὶ τῶν ἀσωμάτων τὸ πάθος, καθώς φησιν ἡ σοφία ἐν ταῖς Παροιμίαις τοῦ θείου κάλλους νομοθετοῦσα τὸν ἔρωτα.
>
> By means of the elaboration [of the Song] the things of a wedding are sketched out, though what is intuited is the mingling of the human soul with the divine. For this reason the "son" of Proverbs is named "bride" here and "Wisdom" passes over into "Bridegroom" so that the human being becoming a pure virgin (from a "bridegroom" [courting Wisdom]) may be betrothed to God and joined to the Lord, and may also be one Spirit through mingling with the impassible and uncontaminated,

human salvation in his *Homilies on the Song of Songs* are no less serious and no less carefully crafted than his hardened polemical works (Coakley 2003, 6–8).

7. Gregory's unique understanding of the doubleness of creation stands in the tradition of readings of Gen 1–3 significantly informed by Plato's *Timaeus*. Prominent predecessors would include Philo (*De opificio mundi*) and Origen (*De principiis*).

> becoming pure thought as opposed to weighty flesh. The one speaking is Wisdom, so then, *love* as much as you can—with your whole heart and strength—and *desire* to your full capacity. I will audaciously add these words: May you be smitten-in-love, for this passion for the incorporeal is irreproachable and impassible, just as Wisdom speaks in Proverbs ordaining this kind of love for divine beauty. (*GNO* 6:22–23; cf. 27)

The description of the union between the bride and bridegroom is given pedagogically as a ὑπογραφόμενον, an outline meant to be filled in by pupils—as a child learns to write her letters by copying over faint tracings.[8] In this case, the person who truly reads and understands the Song of Songs traces out or copies over its narrative sequence (ἀκολουθία), not in the bodily sense offered on the page but in the intellectual sense (νοούμενον) discerned within it.[9] Through its descriptions the text itself (or the Spirit working through the text) lures the interpreter into this pedagogical process by engaging the interpreter's desire and leading her forward in transformation so that she too might be smitten. Within Gregory's anagogical framework, the text is not interpreted correctly until it is interpreted in a participatory manner.[10] Gregory prefers to call his theological interpre-

---

8. Gregory repeatedly uses ὑπογραφόμενον and ὑπογραφὴ in clearly pedagogical (or mystagogical) contexts, though he can also use it in the more general sense of a "description" or "outline." In any case, it always refers to the "lower," material meaning of a text that is to be transposed into a spiritual register. See particularly *GNO* 6:19, 39, 144–45, 146–47, 180, 188, 190, 384.

9. So, for another example, "The anagogical interpretation here aligns with the thought already examined, for the discourse [or the logos] accommodates human nature to God by an ordered sequential road" (ἡ δὲ κατὰ ἀναγωγὴν θεωρία τῆς προεξητασμένης ἔχεται διανοίας· ὁδῷ γὰρ καὶ ἀκολουθίᾳ προσοικειοῖ τῷ θεῷ τὴν ἀνθρωπίνην φύσιν ὁ λόγος). It is not clear in context whether ὁ λόγος refers to the discourse of the Song of Songs (as McCambley's translation has it) or to the second person of the Trinity (as Norris's translation reads). At any rate, there is a transformative divine agency at work upon the reader in and through the sequential development of the text (*GNO* 6:145; cf. 278–79, 294–96). Ludlow claims that for Gregory "the text is a ladder leading up to God" (2002, 63–64).

10. Nonna Verna Harrison refers to Gregory's style of exegesis as "iconic," in that attention to the surface of the text ultimately involves the reader in the scene described; as with an icon, the text looks back at the reader (Harrison 1992, 125); likewise, Martin Laird coins the term *logophasis* to try to capture the sense that the text affects the reader in her relationship to God in ways other than simply communicating content or concepts: "it is not language in search of God (kataphatic), but language

tation "anagogical" because he understands the text to lead the reader upward to God.

However, the upward movement in Gregory's anagogy is not entirely irenic. For Gregory, any reading of the Song that sees nothing more than romantic and sexual interactions is abortive and nonsensical; it halts at the material appearance of the text and fails to comprehend the immeasurably more valuable inner meaning (*GNO* 6:11). Inasmuch as Gregory associates sexual activity and sexual urges with animals, the spiritual meaning, which transcends the material content of the Song, also corresponds to a transcendence of human spirituality over human animality and a connection to other animals. Given humanity's precarious position straddling the boundary between the celestial, intelligible creation and the material creation, human animality always threatens to overcome human spirituality, swamping it with animal passions (*De hominis opificio* §18, PG 44; translation available in *NPNF* 2/5:407–9). Indeed, Gregory is quite explicit that the project of anagogical exegesis is an endeavor to negate and suppress the threats of animality. Immediately preceding Gregory's statement of the *σκοπός* of the Song (quoted above), Gregory places a hedge meant to keep animal associations out of any reading of the text:

> *μή τις ἐμπαθῆ καὶ σαρκώδη λογισμὸν ἐπαγόμενος καὶ μὴ ἔχων πρέπον τῷ θείῳ γάμῳ τὸ τῆς συνειδήσεως ἔνδυμα συνδεθῇ τοῖς ἰδίοις νοήμασι, τὰς ἀκηράτους τοῦ νυμφίου τε καὶ τῆς νύμφης φωνὰς εἰς κτηνώδη καὶ ἄλογα καθέλκων πάθη.*

> Whoever introduces a passionate and fleshly line of thought, or lacks the garment of conscience fitting for the divine wedding—let them not be bound up by their own thoughts, dragging the uncontaminated speeches of the bride and bridegroom down into the passions of livestock and animals. (*GNO* 6:15)

Here human animality threatens to intrude and defile the purity of the scriptural text, while proper anagogical exegesis would transcend the mire of human animality;[11] but Gregory can also deploy anagogical exegesis

---

that is full of God (logophatic)" (2001, 4; cf. Mosshammer 1990, 99; Ludlow 2002, 62; Dünzl 1993, 335; Norris 2012, xx, xli).

11. Norris (2012, xxiii) rightly characterizes Gregory's view by suggesting that animality "infects" the spiritual meaning of the text. Derrida finds similar thinking in Descartes, who suggests that animals lack intelligible perception. That is, animals

along the boundary between humanity and animality as a process that prepares a "raw" text for proper human consumption by refining and cooking rough words fit only to be gobbled up by animals:

> δεῖξαι τὸ ἀναγκαῖον τῆς κατὰ διάνοιαν τῶν ῥητῶν θεωρίας, ἧς ἀποβαλλομένης, καθὼς ἀρέσκει τισίν, ὅμοιον εἶναί μοι δοκεῖ τὸ γινόμενον, ὡς εἴ τις ἀκατέργαστα προθείη πρὸς ἀνθρωπίνην βρῶσιν ἐπὶ τραπέζης τὰ λήϊα, μὴ τρίψας τὴν καλάμην, μὴ τῷ λικμητῷ διακρίνας ἐκ τῶν ἀχύρων τὰ σπέρματα, μὴ λεπτύνας τὸν σῖτον εἰς ἄλευρον, μηδὲ κατασκευάσας ἄρτον τῷ καθήκοντι τρόπῳ τῆς σιτοποιΐας. ὥσπερ οὖν τὸ ἀκατέργαστον γένημα κτηνῶν ἐστι καὶ οὐκ ἀνθρώπων τροφή, οὕτως εἴποι τις ἂν ἀλόγων μᾶλλον ἢ λογικῶν εἶναι τροφὴν μὴ κατεργασθέντα διὰ τῆς λεπτοτέρας θεωρίας τὰ θεόπνευστα ῥήματα οὐ μόνον τῆς παλαιᾶς διαθήκης, ἀλλὰ καὶ τὰ πολλὰ τῆς εὐαγγελικῆς διδασκαλίας·
>
> The necessity is evident for an interpretation of [Scripture's] words according to their intent [as opposed to their material sense], even though it pleases some to reject it. It seems to me that to do so is as if someone set out uncooked crops on the table for human consumption without grinding the stalks, without separating the kernels from the husks by winnowing, without refining the wheat into flour, without providing bread in the proper manner of food preparation. Just as uncooked produce is food for livestock and not humans, someone might say that without being prepared through a refining interpretation, the divinely inspired words [of Scripture]—not only of the Old Testament, but most of the gospel teaching—are food for nondiscursive animals more than for discursive creatures [i.e., humans and angels]. (*GNO* 6:12)

In this passage, even the inspired language of Scripture is too beastly and rough for proper human nourishment where it describes material realities. Anagogical exegesis, under the direction of the Spirit, mills and extracts (not to say "cooks up") the meaning that is truly human. Anagogical exegesis is thoroughly implicated in the discernment, placement, and reinforcement of the boundary between humanity and animality, and for Gregory it names a process in which a properly human meaning is secured against animality.[12] The operation of Gregory's exegesis moves to

---

are attentive to appearances but fail to perceive the meanings and essences that are (invisibly) interior to appearances. Authentic humanity moves beyond the aesthetic fixations of animality (Derrida 2008, 73).

12. Gregory later employs an even more violent image in this regard, referring to

excise animality—whether in the text or in the reader—as an impurity or excess that would prevent human union with God. In the remainder of this essay I explore the ways in which Gregory's sharply cutting exegesis necessarily fails to parse humanity from animality, demonstrating that, in fact, animality remains central and indispensable to Gregory's exegesis in unacknowledged (and even disavowed) ways.

The Anagogical Garment and the Naked Song

Derrida frames his text with an anecdote. Stepping out of the shower one day he stood naked, face-to-face with a little black cat. The cat was, of course, also unclothed. The cat's eyes incited shame in Derrida; more particularly, an intense impulse to cover himself. Gregory of Nyssa, too, carries a strong sense of shame. He exhibits his squeamishness by cloaking the erotic passages of the Song that display the bride and bridegroom's bodies with sublimating warnings against a merely carnal understanding of the text. Gregory clothes the text of the Song of Songs in a garment of theological interpretation.

While many have elaborated upon the interaction between Derrida and the particular "*petit chat*" whose gaze confronts him with his nudity, fewer scholars have taken Derrida at his word when he claims that *L'Animal que donc je suis* is at heart a discourse about "*the truth of modesty*."[13] That is simply to say that Derrida is concerned with the complex of shame, nakedness, modesty, and clothing inasmuch as it has been *one* of the many ways in which humanity has set itself apart from animality. Thus, Derrida suggests that the Western philosophical tradition lavishes inordinate attention upon a constellation of attributes ("nonfinite" in quantity) by which humanity may be divided from "the animals" precisely in order to cover over, mask, ornament, or compensate for a felt lack or deficiency—

---

the divine command in Exod 19 to stone animals found upon the base of the mountain where God and Moses were to meet. Gregory takes this image up to suggest that proper scriptural interpretation involves putting to death every irrational and animal thought, and that only in this manner will the interpreter be prepared to hear the voice of God (*GNO* 6:27–29). Gregory of Nazianzus uses the same passage from Exodus in a similar manner in *Oration* 28.2 (*NPNF* 2/7:289).

13. "La vérité de la pudeur sera finalement notre sujet" (Derrida 2006, 70; cf. 2008, 45). Derrida also claims that the essay is about "response" and "limitrophy," though all these themes are arguably bound up together (2008, 8, 29).

as clothing covers perceived nudity. The attributes "proper" to humanity that purportedly set humanity apart (for example, reason, speech, responsiveness, self-reflection, consciousness, laughter, deception, tools, culture, awareness of death, excess labor) are a supplement for the perception of an original "fault" (Derrida 2008, 20, 45).[14] What sets humanity apart is the *sense* of a fault, or a lack (always discovered in contrast with "the animals"), that expresses itself in the myriad ways that humanity "announces itself to itself" as other-than-animal.[15] The topic of Derrida's discourse is the truth of modesty because it is on account of his modesty that "man" must make something of himself and overcome his nakedness, his deficiency, his fault.[16] Within this picture, animality represents a kind of fullness, completion, or immediate self-presence that humanity lacks.[17]

In the previous section I demonstrated that Gregory's entire project of anagogical exegesis reinforces a certain conception of the relation of humanity to animality. In this section I turn to examine the concrete operation of Gregory's exegesis upon the textual animals of the Song of Songs, particularly in relation to human nakedness. The Song confronts any interpreter with a confusing mix of animals, nudity, and human romance. As such, it would seem like difficult interpretive ground on which to maintain a rigid categorical distinction between humanity as

14. For Derrida's earlier investigation and definition of the notion of "proper"-ness, see 1982, 246–50. In an otherwise excellent book, Leonard Lawlor makes an unjustifiably strong connection between *evil* and the aporia that Derrida refers to as humanity's "fault" (Lawlor 2007, 29, 40). Derrida's sense of the fault is more a rhetorical-metaphysical concept than a juridical/ethical category—though the two are not altogether separable.

15. Though Matthew Calarco largely holds to Derrida, he differs on this point, suggesting that animals have been understood primarily according to a "privative interpretation of animal life" in which animals (as such) lack something that humans have. The disjunction between Derrida and Calarco on this point is not fundamental, though Derrida would suggest that "privative interpretations" are always already supplements that are meant to cover for some fault or flaw (Calarco 2008, 18).

16. I deliberately use androcentric language here in order to signal, perhaps too subtly, that the project of setting humanity over against animality is aligned with the project of setting masculinity over against femininity, and other significant cultural-political binaries.

17. Derrida's articulation of the constitutive role of "the animal" in Western philosophical thinking about the human and Giorgio Agamben's concept of the "anthropological machine" are mutually illuminating and deeply consonant (Agamben 2004, 15–16, 21, 29, 37).

such and "animals." Given the sheer number of animals standing in for humans in the Song, Gregory might be expected to configure the relationship between humanity and animality as something other than categorical difference. After all, in a text that he reads as a celebratory mystagogical narrative of divine-human communion, the two main figures are ceaselessly likened to animals. The bride appears as a lion or leopard, a horse, a turtledove, birds, goats, sheep, fawns, a bee, a gazelle, and a deer; the bridegroom appears as a gazelle, a fawn, a raven, a dove; and other characters in the narrative take on animal guises as well. Moreover, the overwhelming majority of these animal associations are positive ones. That is, Gregory takes the animal metaphors as *praise* of the bride or bridegroom rather than censure.[18] Much as Derrida "thinks with" modesty and nakedness *both* as a corporeal uncovering *and* as a relation to a primal fault, Gregory too takes up the theme of modesty and nakedness in relation to a cosmological narrative running from shame to perfect communion. In this section I will explore the ways in which nudity and animality intersect within Gregory's anagogical interpretation of the Song, and argue that Gregory's exegesis paradoxically uses the animal metaphors describing the bride and bridegroom to shore up his categorical distinction between humanity and animality.

Nudity and animality intersect in at least four ways within Gregory's homilies on the Song. First, Gregory denigrates a certain kind of shamelessly erotic nakedness as "animal" in such a way as to imply that it is less than human. Debased, carnal sexuality is strategically associated with animality so that authentic humanity "naturally" transcends it. In the passages adduced in the first section, Gregory transfers human sexuality across the human-animal distinction so that it appears in human life as a "proper" of animals rather than humans—as something to be controlled, tamed, and overcome, rather than as something that belongs to humanity as such. For Gregory, copulative genital intercourse is unnatural and improper to humanity in God's image.[19] The person who sees the nudity of the Song in this manner "is passion-ridden and fleshly, still stinking with

18. The exceptions here are the lion/leopard and the raven, which are taken to symbolize how far the bride (or in the case of the raven, Jesus' apostles and prophets) has come from a dissolute life of sin (*GNO* 6:250–53, 391–93).

19. For a more explicit picture of Gregory's understanding of the connection between animality and sexuality (as unnatural to humanity as such), see *De hominis opificio* §§14–16 (*NPNF2* 5:402–6). Substantial secondary literature has been written

the stench of the dead, old man; [such a one] ought not pull the meaning of the divinely inspired thoughts and words down to a sense fit for nondiscursive livestock" (*μή τις ἐμπαθὴς καὶ σαρκώδης ἔτι τῆς νεκρᾶς τοῦ παλαιοῦ ἀνθρώπου δυσωδίας ἀπόζων πρὸς τὰς κτηνώδεις ἀλογίας κατασυρέτω τὰς τῶν θεοπνεύστων νοημάτων τε καὶ ῥημάτων ἐμφάσεις*) (*GNO* 6:25). Thus nakedness in any highly sexualized sense belongs properly to animals rather than to humans for Gregory (cf. 250–52, where the former association of the bride with lions and leopards is taken as indicative of a shamefully sinful past; cf. 15, 104, 391–93, 423–24).

Second, though rare, there are moments in Gregory's mediation of the Song when the bride or bridegroom is literally naked in her/his own body. This literal nakedness might be recognized as "animal" within the economy of Gregory's theology inasmuch as the physiological functions and physical vulnerability of the bride and bridegroom stand in the foreground while the subjective, conscious, and intellectual aspects of their interaction recede. "My beloved, she says, put his hand through the opening, and my inmost parts cried out for him" (*Αδελφιδός μου γάρ, φησίν, ἀπέστειλε τὴν χεῖρα αὐτοῦ διὰ τῆς ὀπῆς, καὶ ἡ κοιλία μου ἐθροήθη ἐπ' αὐτόν*) (Song 5:4; *GNO* 6:332). While Gregory continually warns against a sexual understanding of such passages from the Song, he must also allow traces and glimpses of this sensuous content to appear (even if only by means of his enthusiastic protests) because they are indispensable to the anagogical project. This literal sensuous content is the material anchor for the theological metaphor of human-divine communion.[20] Without at least some hint of the erotic interaction of the bride and bridegroom, Gregory's discovery of exalted spiritual descriptions of divine-human communion in the Song would be totally untethered. Furthermore, it is the base, animal, erotic desire (in sublimated form) that drives the reader toward God; without the connection to the erotic beauty of the corporeal bride and bridegroom, the alluring

---

on this passage. My understanding of the passage aligns closely with Zachhuber 2000, 169–72.

20. "Gregor indes sieht einen weiteren Aufstieg der Seele darin, daß nun nicht mehr die Stimme (des Bräutigams) ans Herz, klopft, sondern die göttliche Hand selbst durch die Luke hereinreicht" (Dünzl 1993, 169). Gregory quickly allows *κοιλία* (inmost parts, bodily cavity, womb, belly) to slip back to the more spiritual and less sexual *καρδία* (heart) (cf. *GNO* 6:333). Nevertheless, the sublimating theological movement still relies on a glimpse of the bride's "inmost parts" crying out at the touch of the bridegroom.

anagogical attraction of the Song would fall flat.[21] Inasmuch as corporeal procreation is, for Gregory, a vestige of animality in human life, Gregory must call at least minimal attention to the animal nakedness in the Song in order to ground his theological exegesis.

Third, the bride and bridegroom frequently appear naked under the guise of animal metaphors. The Song uses animal imagery to describe the bodies of bride and bridegroom, and Gregory is more than content to take up the animal metaphors of the Song in his anagogical exegesis. In Gregory's homilies, the human nakedness that would appear too sexually charged—and therefore too animal—is tamed and muted precisely by means of the animal images, which partially veil and obscure the human bodies described, or at least distance them from a straightforwardly sexual legibility.[22]

> προσεικάσθη μὲν ἐκείνῃ τῇ ἵππῳ ἡ διὰ τῶν ἀρετῶν κεκαθαρμένη ψυχή· ἀλλ' οὔπω τοῦ λόγου γέγονεν ὑποχείριος οὐδὲ ἐβάσταξεν ἐφ' ἑαυτῆς τὸν ἐπὶ σωτηρίᾳ τοῖς τοιούτοις ἐποχούμενον ἵπποις· χρὴ γὰρ πρῶτον διὰ πάντων κατακοσμηθῆναι τὸν ἵππον, εἶθ' οὕτω τὸν βασιλέα ἔποχον δέξασθαι. εἴτε δὲ ἄνωθεν ἑαυτῷ ἐφαρμόζοι τὸν ἵππον ὁ κατὰ τὸν προφήτην ἐπιβαίνων ἐφ' ἡμᾶς τοὺς ἵππους καὶ ἐπὶ σωτηρίᾳ ἡμῶν ἐφ' ἡμῶν ἱππαζόμενος, εἴτε καὶ ἐν

21. "The discourse now before us also urges the same things [as Proverbs, i.e., 'Be in love with divine beauty']; it does not bring its counsel regarding this matter to you nakedly, but rather philosophizes upon these thoughts through unspeakable things, setting forward an image of the pleasures of this life as a device for its teachings. The marital image is a construction whereby desire for beauty mediates a longing, but not in the usual human pattern where the bridegroom initiates desire. Rather, the virgin anticipates the bridegroom without shame, making her yearning public and praying for when she will enjoy the bridegroom's kiss" (*ἀλλὰ καὶ ὁ νῦν προκείμενος λόγος τὰ ἴσα διακελεύεται οὐ γυμνήν σοι τὴν περὶ τούτου συμβουλὴν προσάγων, ἀλλὰ δι' ἀπορρήτων φιλοσοφεῖ τοῖς νοήμασιν εἰκόνα τινὰ τῶν κατὰ τὸν βίον ἡδέων εἰς τὴν τῶν δογμάτων τούτων κατασκευὴν προστησάμενος. ἡ δὲ εἰκὼν γαμική τίς ἐστι διασκευή, ἐν ᾗ κάλλους ἐπιθυμία μεσιτεύει τῷ πόθῳ, οὐ κατὰ τὴν ἀνθρωπίνην συνήθειαν τοῦ νυμφίου τῆς ἐπιθυμίας κατάρξαντος, ἀλλὰ προλαμβάνει τὸν νυμφίον ἡ παρθένος ἀνεπαισχύντως τὸν πόθον δημοσιεύουσα καὶ εὐ|χὴν ποιουμένη τοῦ νυμφικοῦ ποτε κατατρυφῆσαι φιλήματος*) (*GNO* 6:23).

22. Another excellent example of this dynamic is found in Gregory's comments on the extended praise of the Bride's beauty (Song 4:1–5; 6:5–9), in which her hair is compared to a flock of goats, her teeth are likened to twin sheep, her lips to a thread, her cheeks to pomegranates, her neck to a tower, and her breasts to grazing fawns. The passage is repeated twice in the Song and receives extended commentary in Gregory's exegesis (*GNO* 6:218–42 and 450–56; cf. 78, 85, 140, 175, 178–79, 377).

> ἡμῖν γένοιτο ὁ ἐνοικῶν τε καὶ ἐμπεριπατῶν καὶ ἐπὶ τὰ βάθη τῆς ψυχῆς ἡμῶν διαδυόμενος, οὐδὲν διαφέρει κατὰ τὴν ἔννοιαν· ᾧ γὰρ ἂν τὸ ἓν ἐξ ἀμφοτέρων γένηται, συγκατωρθώθη καὶ τὸ λειπόμενον· ὅ τε γὰρ ἐφ᾽ ἑαυτοῦ τὸν θεὸν ἔχων καὶ ἐν ἑαυτῷ πάντως ἔχει καὶ ὁ ἐν ἑαυτῷ δεξάμενος ὑπέβη τὸν ἐν αὐτῷ γεγονότα. οὐκοῦν μέλλει ὁ βασιλεὺς τῷ ἵππῳ τούτῳ ἐπαναπαύεσθαι.

> The soul purified through the virtues was likened [in Song 3:9] to *that* horse, but has not yet come under the hand of the Logos nor carried upon herself the one who rides such horses unto salvation. For it is first necessary that the horse be fully ornamented [i.e., Song 3:11] and then, so dressed, to receive the king to ride. It makes no difference to the sense here whether the one who according to the prophets mounts upon us horses and rides upon us unto our salvation is fit from above or whether he comes to be in us, he who slips through into the deep parts of our souls, dwelling and walking about. For to whomever the one happens, the other is set straight along with it. The one who has God upon him also has God completely within himself, and the one who receives in himself is under the one who has come to be in him. Thus the king intends to rest upon this horse. (*GNO* 6:84)

The nonthreatening nudity of animals stands in for human nakedness when Gregory desires to make theological points that are thoroughly anchored in sexual metaphor. Because the unclothed bodies of animals do not appear immediately sexual, they provide some modest cover for the sexualized nakedness of the Song's human bodies—though Gregory considers "animals" as a category to be hypersexual.

Fourth, the *modality* of the bride and bridegroom's nudity in Gregory's homilies is the same sort of undecidable nudity that we perceive in animals. Animals, so the traditional thinking goes, are clothed within their skin in a manner that our skin always fails to clothe us. The visible surfaces of animal bodies are ambiguous. If animals are naked, they do not reflect upon their nakedness or regard it as a problem. Neither is animal nudity ever, prima facie, a matter for human reflection or concern. In the same way, the bride's body appears all through the text, yet she never seems to be totally bare. She is naked in the way that animals are naked—unreflectively. The proper shame that attends to human nakedness as its authenticating supplement remains notably absent, leaving the nudity in Gregory's text ambiguously human at most.

There is a dark and violent scene in the Song where the bride wanders the streets of the city looking for the bridegroom. In her wanderings she is accosted and beaten by watchmen of the city who strip her of her veil. Gregory allegorically negates the violence and fear in this passage insofar as the bride's clothing has come to symbolize the bride's separation from her beloved and the watchmen have become angels. Where the bride in the Song cries out in fear and shame, in Gregory's text she finds joy in her further unveiling (*GNO* 6:359–61).[23] Furthermore, seeing her stripped in this way, the flock of attendants marvel at her beauty and ask where they might also be similarly stripped of their veils (379). The bride does not offer so much as a blush at her exposure before these friends in the Song, and perhaps more remarkably, Gregory hardly blushes at her exposure before his congregation. Under the aegis of this theological interpretation, human nakedness becomes a garment of glory; the absence of shame that generally signals animal nakedness becomes here a sign of the bride's perfection.[24] Thus not only does the bride appear under the guise of animal metaphors as she progresses spiritually, but inasmuch as her perfection is demonstrated by a certain shame-free and unreflective nudity, she enters into an "animal" mode of corporeality.

None of these intersections of animality and nudity in the Song represents for Gregory a transgression of the assumed abyssal difference between humanity and animality. Paradoxically, Gregory preserves the humanity of the bride and bridegroom in categorical opposition to animality precisely by means of the text's animal imagery. Gregory doubles the nakedness of the animal so that it appears *both* as hypersexual, shameful, degraded nakedness, which the humanity of the bride naturally transcends, *and* as the perfected, exalted nakedness that knows no reason for shame and no longer suffers from any fault. First, sexual impulses and actions are expropriated from humanity and rendered proper to animality so that they may register as something "other" to be excised, tamed, or slaughtered. Subsequently, however, animals stand in for humans in the text's references to "union" so that the nudity therein can be taken as shame-free, perfected

---

23. "Wer aber nach Gregor den Sinn des Gesagten überschaut, für den sind es die Worte einer Frau, die sich des Schönsten rühmt" (Dünzl 1993, 179).

24. "She did as she heard, removing that garment of skin which was cast around her with her sin" (*ἐποίησε γὰρ ἅπερ ἤκουσεν ἐκδυσαμένη τὸν δερμάτινον ἐκεῖνον χιτῶνα, ὃν μετὰ τὴν ἁμαρτίαν περιεβάλετο*) (*GNO* 6:327–28). Indeed, Gregory begins the first homily with an invitation to the discerning listener to strip off the garment of sin and enter the intimacy of the bridal chamber in pure, white garments, thus evoking the nudity of baptismal rituals (*GNO* 6:14).

nakedness-without-fault. In both ways Gregory uses the animals of the Song to transpose the bride and bridegroom's interactions from a sexual register to a spiritual register. Without the animal metaphors to distract, delight, and teach his audience, Gregory would be left with the shamelessly sexualized "animal" nakedness of the Song. With the cover of the animal metaphors, however, Gregory reads the Song as Solomon's reflection on the shame-free nakedness of a perfected humanity, for whom nudity represents the absence of guile, impurity, and any barrier to communion with God. The animals of the Song, however, have no spiritual weight of their own; they figure in Gregory's anagogical exegesis only as metaphorical tools, lending all their energy to the spiritual progress of the bride. While "animality" seems to play an indispensable role in Gregory's exegetical project here, it does so entirely at the level of metaphor, and in such a way that the categorical difference between humanity and animality is reinforced rather than questioned. Gregory's theology, however, short-circuits in a deeper way, so that spiritual ascent and anagogical interpretation turn out to rely on the persistence of animality within the human.

L'Animal que donc Je suis: Following and Being Transformed

Throughout *L'Animal que donc je suis*, Derrida plays upon the homonymy of the first-person present-tense forms of the verbs *être* (to be) and *suivre* (to follow) (2006, 54–55). His title, while naturally translated as *The Animal That Therefore I Am*, could equally be rendered *The Animal That Therefore I Follow*. The philosophical point made here is that humanity discovers or constructs its identity only through an encounter with animality or in relation to animals, even if such a relation or encounter is entirely abstract.[25] Indeed, Derrida argues that in philosophical discourse the words *animals*

25. "As with every bottomless gaze, as with the eyes of the other, the gaze called 'animal' offers to my sight the abyssal limit of the human: the inhuman or the ahuman, the ends of man, that is to say, the bordercrossing from which vantage man dares to announce himself to himself, thereby calling himself by the name that he believes he gives himself" (Derrida 2008, 12). The notion of "animal pedagogy" in the introduction of Oliver 2009 is an excellent development of Derrida's theme. She argues, "Despite the explicit message of these [antihumanist, philosophical, and psychological] texts—that humans are radically distinct from animals—animals function to teach man how to be human. Not surprisingly, then, this animal pedagogy is not acknowledged. To acknowledge the dependence of *man* and *humanity* on *animal* and *animality* is to undermine man's sense of himself as autonomous and self-sovereign.

and *animality* are abstract rhetorical tools necessary for the formation of a human identity, but which function as a disavowal of real animals, a turning away from the eyes of fellow creatures.[26] So Derrida recognizes that—by way of his formation in a tradition of Western anthropo-logic running from Aristotle through Descartes to Lacan—he follows "animality" in a certain abstract way,[27] but he also wonders if he might follow an animal, a cat in his case, into a different identity, a mode of being human that sees and is seen by the eyes of other creatures (2008, 5–6, 31–32, 54–60). This notion of following an animal strongly evokes Gregory's most treasured image for spiritual ascent in the Song. The bridegroom appears repeatedly as a deer bounding across the hilltops luring the bride—and simultaneously, the reader—into a chase.[28] The spiritual transformation of bride and reader take place by following this divine animal; and as it turns out, animality is not superfluous in the process.

For Gregory, the image of the deer leaping away from hill to hill describes the anagogical function of the *text* of the Song as it incites desire within its readers for God's beautiful but elusive mystery.[29] The bride-

For if anything, in the history of Western thought, man trains animals and not the other way around" (20–21).

26. Throughout the text, Derrida labors to dissociate himself from "they" who use the category "animal" naively (e.g., Derrida 2008, 47–51).

27. The depth of this formation (and not some cryptoconservative attachment to the human-animal distinction for its own sake) is the reason why Derrida refuses to deny or negate the human-animal distinction altogether. Matthew Calarco upbraids him for this refusal (2008, 137–49), but perhaps underestimates the difficulty of simply setting aside the human-animal distinction for a human subject whose identity is formed by that distinction both at an individual and species level. Calarco rightly recognizes that Derrida makes any attempt to draw a categorical distinction between humanity and animality nonsensical, but this is because his engagement deconstructs such a distinction from within its own assumptions rather than denying it more straightforwardly. For the relevant passage see Derrida 2008, 29–31.

28. "She begins to see the one she yearns for appearing before her eyes in another form. He is likened to a deer, compared to a fawn, and he does not stand steady, neither in one appearance nor in the same place where he appeared. Rather, he leaps upon the mountains, springing from the ridges to the prominent hills" (καὶ βλέπειν ἄρχεται τὸν ποθούμενον ἄλλῳ εἴδει τοῖς ὀφθαλμοῖς ἐμφαινόμενον· δορκάδι γὰρ ὁμοιοῦται καὶ νεβρῷ παρεικάζεται, καὶ οὐχ ἕστηκεν οὔτε ἐπὶ τῆς μιᾶς ὄψεως οὔτε ἐπὶ τοῦ τόπου τοῦ αὐτοῦ τὸ φαινόμενον, ἀλλ' ἐπιπηδᾷ τοῖς ὄρεσιν ἀπὸ τῶν ἀκρωρειῶν ἐπὶ τὰς τῶν βουνῶν ἐξοχὰς μεθαλλόμενος) (*GNO* 6:178; cf. Song 2:8–9, 17; 8:14).

29. "The things set before us anagogically by the philosophy of the Song of Songs

groom's animal appearance as a deer is taken to signify God's inscrutability in such a way that the reader is drawn into pursuit.[30] Thus the Song leads the Christian into a life of desire, the life of a faithful lack, a stretching out (ἐπέκτασις) toward the inscrutable beloved with a gaze that transforms the reader according to a logic that has come to be called the "mirror of the soul" (see Louth 1981, 90–92; Daniélou 1954, 291–307).

> κατόπτρῳ γὰρ ἔοικεν ὡς ἀληθῶς τὸ ἀνθρώπινον κατὰ τὰς τῶν προαιρέσεων ἐμφάσεις μεταμορφούμενον· εἴ τε γὰρ πρὸς χρυσὸν ἴδοι, χρυσὸς φαίνεται καὶ τὰς ταύτης αὐγὰς τῆς ὕλης διὰ τῆς ἐμφάσεως δείκνυσιν, εἴ τέ τι τῶν εἰδεχθῶν ἐμφανείη, καὶ τούτου τὸ αἶσχος δι' ὁμοιώσεως ἀπομάσσεται βάτραχόν τινα ἢ φρῦνον ἢ σκολόπενδραν ἢ ἄλλο τι τῶν ἀηδῶν θεαμάτων τῷ οἰκείῳ εἴδει ὑποκρινόμενον, ᾧπερ ἂν τούτων εὑρεθῇ ἀντιπρόσωπον.
>
> Humanity is transformed in accordance with the appearances it chooses, and so, truly seems like a mirror. For if someone looks upon gold she appears as gold, and by way of its appearance she manifests the shining of that material. And if someone reflects some fetid thing, he imitates its

lead to desire for a sense of the higher goods and set anguish in our souls by producing a certain kind of rejection in us through the recognition of incomprehensible matters. … She is carried to many [ideas] by her visions, thinking perpetually that she sees something else and never settling in with the same image of what she grasps. So, she says, 'Behold, he *comes*!' That is, not *standing*, not *settling in*, so as to be made known to an eager onlooker by holding still. Rather, he steals away out of sight before he is completely known, 'leaping on the mountains and springing on the hills,' as she says" (Τὰ νῦν προτεθέντα διὰ τῆς ἀναγνώσεως ἡμῖν ἐκ τῆς τοῦ Ἄισματος τῶν Ἀισμάτων φιλοσοφίας καὶ εἰς ἐπιθυμίαν ἄγει τῆς τῶν ὑπερκειμένων ἀγαθῶν θεωρίας καὶ λύπην ἐντίθησιν ἡμῶν ταῖς ψυχαῖς ἀπόγνωσιν ἐμποιοῦντα τρόπον τινὰ τῆς τῶν ἀλήπτων κατανοήσεως· … ἐπὶ πολλὰ φέρεσθαι ταῖς ὀπτασίαις ἄλλοτε ἄλλως βλέπειν οἰομένην καὶ οὐ πάντοτε τῷ αὐτῷ παραμένουσαν χαρακτῆρι τοῦ καταληφθέντος · Ἰδοὺ γάρ φησιν οὗτος ἥκει, οὐχ ἑστὼς οὐδὲ παραμένων, ὡς διὰ τῆς ἐπιμονῆς γνωρισθῆναι τῷ ἀτενίζοντι ἀλλ' ἀφαρπάζων ἑαυτὸν τῶν ὄψεων, πρὶν εἰς τελείαν γνῶσιν ἐλθεῖν· Πηδῶν γάρ φησιν ἐπὶ τὰ ὄρη καὶ τοῖς βουνοῖς ἐφαλλόμενος) (*GNO* 6:139; cf. 137–42, 170–71, 178, 356, 378–77).

30. In conversation with Levinas, Derrida invokes the concept of a *divinanimality* arguing that the "quasi-transcendence" of absolute alterity that Levinas seeks to describe is best encountered in the "face" of an animal (a possibility that Levinas disavows) (Derrida 2008, 132). Though Gregory certainly operates with a hierarchy in which the alterity of animals is far inferior to humanity while the alterity of God is far superior, he nevertheless finds animality a fitting figure to describe God's utter transcendence of human knowledge. Derrida (2009, 13) also describes humanity as a vanishing mediator between the alterity of animals and God.

> shame by way of a resemblance, acting into its natural appearance—be it a frog, toad, millipede, or some other unpleasant sight, whichever he is found to be facing. (*GNO* 6:104)

Gregory argues that whatever object a human soul gazes upon, the soul begins to assimilate to that object. The Song works, then, by transfixing a person's gaze upon God's beauty, a gaze that is held firm by the ever-increasing desire fueled by the Song's sensual language, so that the reader is caught up in an infinite process of pursuing God and increasing in conformity to God. Here, at least, animality does not appear "beneath" humanity; in doggedly following the bridegroom as a divine-animal, the bride (and concomitantly the reader) undergoes a becoming-animal, being found in the form of a deer or gazelle, like her beloved (*GNO* 6:377).

However, it is not only at the level of imagery that animality is integral to the process of the Song's spiritual transformation. For Gregory, *desire* (ἐπιθυμία) is a function of the appetites and impulses that humanity shares with other animals. The text of the Song functions anagogically, not primarily because it teaches a person about the nature of God, or about the path of approach to God; rather, the text functions because it incites desire within the reader by presenting God's beauty; it leads the properly attuned reader up into love (*GNO* 6:27–29, 63). The orientation and increase of the reader's desire is a central concern of Gregory's exegesis. Gregory's fundamental commitment to the incomprehensibility of God means that the soul's gaze is a gaze of loving desire, not the gaze of knowledge.[31]

> οὐδέποτε γὰρ ἐπὶ τῶν ἐγνωσμένων ἡ τοῦ ἀνιόντος ἐπιθυμία μένει, ἀλλὰ διὰ μείζονος πάλιν ἑτέρας ἐπιθυμίας πρὸς ἑτέραν ὑπερκειμένην κατὰ τὸ ἐφεξῆς ἡ ψυχὴ ἀνιοῦσα πάντοτε διὰ τῶν ἀνωτέρων ὁδεύει πρὸς τὸ ἀόριστον.

> The desire of the one ascending never settles on what has been known, but instead, by one desire after another, each greater again than the last, excels on to the next in line. The ascending soul makes its way toward the infinite, always by higher things. (*GNO* 6:247; cf. 323–24, 356, 425–26)

Furthermore, within the framework of Gregory's theological anthropology, the priority of love and desire over knowledge entails that human animal-

31. "Die ἐπιθυμία (nicht den ἔρος) zeichnet Gregor in den *CantHom* als die ständig vorwärtstreibende, nie erlahmentde Kraft auf dem endlosen Weg zu Gott" (Dünzl 1993, 366–67; cf. Laird 2003, 79; Ludlow 2000, 58–59, 63; Louth 1981, 97).

ity takes the lead in spiritual ascent, rather than following after the distinct and exclusive traits of humanity as such.[32] Ultimately for Gregory, God's transformative grace does not utilize the faculties that set humanity apart from other animals (discursiveness, being λόγικος), but draws humanity forward through a faculty that all animals hold in common—desire (ἐπιθυμία).[33] Of course, in the contexts where Gregory indicates the centrality of desire to spiritual transformation, he does not name it as a function of animality—to do so would undermine the anthropological exceptionalism that Gregory has labored to establish. Nevertheless, it is clear enough elsewhere that desire is proper to that part of the soul that a human being shares with the animals, and he offers no reason to believe that a desire that is focused upon God derives from a separate faculty than other desires (for example, Gregory of Nyssa, *De hominis opificio* §14; *NPNF* 2/5:402–3).

The centrality of desire within Gregory's depiction of the soul's approach to God is a commonplace within scholarship on Gregory, but most scholars follow Gregory in eliding desire's "animal" provenance when it has a positive spiritual or theological function, rather than naming this dynamic as a short circuit in Gregory's attempt to categorically distinguish humanity from animality.[34] Seemingly, desire is a function of animality when it dangerously leads to distraction and promiscuity, but not when it is directed toward God—yet Gregory provides no basis for such a distinction.[35] Clearly, the anagogical meaning of the Song of Songs relies upon the sexual desire that Gregory associates with the animals to "hook" the

---

32. Gregory "identifies love with the appetitive faculties of our irrational nature," that is, with ἐπιθυμία (Smith 2004, 191).

33. "Gregory asserts that the text presupposes asceticism and actually teaches it through language that appears to speak of its opposite.… This paradox occurs because the same human drive that impels one toward bodily love can also be directed toward God, and the same human receptacle that can be filled, though ineffectively, with sensual pleasure can also be better filled with divine life" (Harrison 1992, 124).

34. One paradigmatic example of this dynamic is Smith 2004. In the first part of the book Smith meticulously traces Gregory's effort to distinguish humanity from other animals along the lines of rationality/discursiveness, sexual procreation, desire, and passion/emotion. Yet when desire returns to play a positive theological role in human salvation, its essential connection to animality is pervasively effaced (see 37, 69, 77–78, 87, 104–6, 183, 187, 219, 227). The quote above in n. 32 is the closest that Smith comes to naming the significance of human animality for salvation.

35. Dünzl takes stock of the ambivalence in Gregory's treatment of erotic desire (1993, 357, 364–69).

reader and lead her forward. But if desire were still named as proper to animality in its positive role in anagogical exegesis and spiritual transformation, then the categorical transcendence of humanity over animality would be called directly into question. As it stands, Gregory's short circuit amounts to an ideological device safeguarding anthropological exceptionalism: the authentic human being transcends impure animal desires because she is discursive and spiritual rather than base and material; yet as she progresses to the highest reaches of spiritual transformation and the most profound meaning of the Song of Songs, the necessity of (no-longer-named-as-animal) desire returns as the engine of spiritual progress.

Though Gregory did not avail himself of it, an alternate path through the short circuit here would be to acknowledge the continuity of animality and spiritual desire. To recognize spirituality as a function of animality (rather than of humanity-as-such) would be to doubly emphasize the importance of the animal metaphors of the Song as they illustrate the spiritual pursuit of the elusive God. In pursuit of the divine-deer-bridegroom bounding over the hills, the bride might find herself becoming-animal. Through her unbroken gaze, the bride might become a *spiritual-animal* whose desires orient her instincts, impulses, and attentions and drive her on after God's mystery. For Gregory to think in this manner, however, would require a fundamental reconfiguration of the categories "human" and "animal" wherever they are taken to signify an absolute contrast or metaphysical difference.

Conclusion

The pervasive presence of animals in the text of the Song launches Gregory's theological interpretation. The literal zoological excess makes it difficult to take the text seriously as erotic writing; and even if it *were* straightforwardly erotic, such "base" meaning would be below Gregory's estimation of the dignity of Holy Scripture. Animals force the literal meaning of the Song into the mill of theological interpretation so that it can be refined into something capable of nourishing its readers. In other words, the prominence of animals in the text presents an excess that allows for the erasure of animality; the Song can be sublimated largely because its animals almost demand an allegorical (or anagogical) reading. And yet, for all the rhetorical bluster with which Gregory divides humanity from animality, traits and features associated with animality turn out to be constitutive of human perfection. Gregory marvels that the Song storms the castle of sensuousness in order to turn its power to good use:

> τί γὰρ ἂν γένοιτο τούτου παραδοξότερον ἢ τὸ αὐτὴν ποιῆσαι τὴν φύσιν τῶν ἰδίων παθημάτων καθάρσιον διὰ τῶν νομιζομένων ἐμπαθῶν ῥημάτων τὴν ἀπάθειαν νομοθετοῦσάν τε καὶ παιδεύουσαν; οὐ γὰρ λέγει τὸ δεῖν ἔξω τῶν τῆς σαρκὸς γίνεσθαι κινημάτων καὶ νεκροῦν τὰ μέλη τὰ ἐπὶ τῆς γῆς καὶ καθαρεύειν ἀπὸ τῶν ἐμπαθῶν ῥημάτων τῷ στόματι, ἀλλ' οὕτω διέθηκε τὴν ψυχήν, ὡς διὰ τῶν ἀπεμφαίνειν δοκούντων πρὸς τὴν καθαρότητα βλέπειν, διὰ τῶν ἐμπαθῶν ῥήσεων τὴν ἀκήρατον ἑρμηνεύων διάνοιαν.

> What could possibly be more paradoxical than to make [human] nature purify itself of its own passions by legislating and teaching impassibility in customarily passion-ridden speech? [Solomon] does not say that it is necessary to be beyond the movements of the flesh, and to "mortify one's members upon the earth," and to purify the mouth from the speech of passion. Rather, he manages the soul so that it looks toward purity through things that seem incongruous [with purity], translating undefiled thought by passion-ridden speech. (*GNO* 6:29)

The power of desire constitutes the hook in the lives of readers for the anagogical function of the text. While Gregory constantly warns about the dangers of allowing desire to slide toward the passions shared with animals, the total eradication of the "animal" aspects of desire would leave a human desiccated and unresponsive to divine allure (*GNO* 6:21). Thus the obverse side of the "paradox" wherein the Song teaches ἀπάθεια by means of passion-ridden language is that, once purified, human animality must take the lead in the journey of salvation. As Smith notes, Gregory's narrative of salvation is "in essence a narrative of the transformation of the bestial passions into holy desires" (Smith 2004, 183). The unspoken entailment, however, is that something of the beast remains in the soul made holy.

Derrida's text examines the necessary failures and fractures in the anthropological projects of Descartes, Kant, Levinas, Heidegger, and Lacan. Within each of these thinkers' systems, the human supposed to transcend animality altogether turns out to have done so on false premises, *or,* more often, fails to live up to the measure of transcendence upon which the animals are judged deficient.[36] This essay has demonstrated that

36. Derrida, with all his attention to multiple differences, is careful never to deny

Gregory of Nyssa's *Homilies on the Song of Songs* contain the same sort of "failure" as the contemporary texts that Derrida examines. While Gregory does labor toward a categorical distinction between human beings and animals in which humanity (as spiritual) altogether transcends animality (as material), his project necessarily fails inasmuch as he can never completely harden the boundary he seeks to draw. Gregory upholds difference in the attributes proper to humanity and animality—the human is still discursive, still the subject of modesty; an animal is still characterized by its passionate desire—yet over the course of the transformations narrated in Gregory's theological interpretation of the Song, the desires proper to animality become indispensable to human perfection. Within that "short circuit" Gregory inadvertently opens possibilities for thinking differently about the relation of humanity and animality in a theological register—possibilities that have yet to be explored in constructive theological projects.[37] The transcendence of the human over the animal, then, turns out to include a return of humanity to its animality—only now in a perfected state. The perfected human-animal has utterly focused desires, and is revealed (exposed, laid bare) to all without the (human) supplement of shame, without the second guesses and inward turns of self-reflection. In order to continue on the long way to God, pulled along by the anagogical grace of divine beauty, humanity may need to find and follow its own animality, saying, "This animal that therefore I am; by grace I am following unto salvation."

Works Cited

Agamben, Giorgio. 2004. *The Open: Man and Animal.* Translated by Kevin Attell. Stanford, Calif.: Stanford University Press.

Calarco, Matthew. 2008. *Zoographies: The Question of the Animal from Heidegger to Derrida.* New York: Columbia University Press.

---

any distinction between humans and other creatures lumped together as "animals"; he does, however, deny that the frontier of that distinction is simple, linear, and hermetically exclusive. Derrida multiplies differences between creatures of every shape and habit in order to relativize what has been asserted as the master Difference between the vast myriad of creatures and the one creature called the human being. He is concerned to avoid *both* a "biological continuism" that would deny any significant difference *and* any sort of metaphysically absolutized distinction (2008, 30–31).

37. Constructive projects are, however, beginning to appear; see, e.g., Clough 2012.

Clough, David. 2012. *On Animals: Systematic Theology*. London: T&T Clark.

Coakley, Sarah. 2003. Introduction—Gender, Trinitarian Analogies, and the Pedagogy of *The Song*. Pages 1–13 in *Re-thinking Gregory of Nyssa*. Edited by Sarah Coakley. Malden, Mass.: Blackwell.

Daniélou, Jean. 1954. *Platonisme et théologie mystique: Doctrine spirituelle de Saint Grégoire de Nysse*. Paris: Aubier.

Derrida, Jacques. 1982. White Mythology: Metaphor in the Text of Philosophy. Pages 207–71 in *Margins of Philosophy*. Translated by Alan Bass. Chicago: University of Chicago Press.

———. 2006. *L'animal que donc je suis*. Edited by Marie-Louise Mallet. Paris: Galilée.

———. 2008. *The Animal That Therefore I Am*. Edited by Marie-Louise Mallet. Translated by David Wills. New York: Fordham University Press.

———. 2009. *The Beast and the Sovereign*. Vol. 1. Edited by Michel Lisse, Marie-Louise Mallet, and Ginette Michaud. Translated by Geoffrey Bennington. Chicago: University of Chicago Press.

Dünzl, Franz. 1993. *Braut und Bräutigam: Die Auslegung des Canticum durch Gregory von Nyssa*. Tübingen: Mohr Siebeck.

Gregory of Nazianzus. 1978. *Discours 27–31*. Edited and translated by Paul Gallay. Sources chrétiennes 250. Paris: Cerf.

———. 1955. Select Orations. Translated by Charles Gordon Browne and James Edward Swallow. Pages 203–434 in vol. 7 of *Nicene and Post-Nicene Fathers*. Series 2. Edited by Philip Schaff and Henry Wace. Repr., Grand Rapids: Eerdmans.

Gregory of Nyssa. 1863. *De hominis opificio*. Patrologia Graeca 44. Paris: Migne.

———. 1954. On the Making of Man. Translated by H. A. Wilson. Pages 387–427 in vol. 5 of *The Nicene and Post-Nicene Fathers*. Series 2. Edited by Philip Schaff and Henry Wace. Repr., Grand Rapids: Eerdmans.

———. 1960. *Gregorii Nysseni in Canticum Canticorum*. Edited by Hermann Langerbeck. Vol. 6 of *Opera*. Edited by Werner Jaeger. Leiden: Brill.

———. 1987. *Commentary on the Song of Songs*. Translated by Casimir McCambley. Brookline, Mass.: Hellenic College Press.

———. 2012. *Homilies on the Song of Songs*. Translated by Richard A. Norris. Atlanta: Society of Biblical Literature.

Harrison, Verna. 1992. Allegory and Asceticism in Gregory of Nyssa. *Semeia* 57:113–30.

Heine, Ronald. 1984. Gregory of Nyssa's Apology for Allegory. *Vigiliae Christianae* 38:360–70.

Laird, Martin S. 2007. The Fountain of His Lips: Desire and Divine Union in Gregory of Nyssa's *Homilies on the Song of Songs*. *Spiritus: A Journal of Christian Spirituality* 7:40–57.

———. 2003. Under Solomon's Tutelage: The Education of Desire in the *Homilies on the Song of Songs*. Pages 77–96 in *Re-thinking Gregory of Nyssa*. Edited by Sarah Coakley. Malden, Mass.: Blackwell.

———. 2001. "Whereof We Speak": Gregory of Nyssa, Jean-Luc Marion and the Current Apophatic Rage. *Heythrop Journal* 42:1–12.

Lawlor, Leonard. 2007. *This Is Not Sufficient: An Essay on Animality and Human Nature in Derrida*. New York: Columbia University Press.

Louth, Andrew. 1981. *The Origins of the Christian Mystical Tradition*. Oxford: Oxford University Press.

Ludlow, Morwenna. 2000. *Universal Salvation: Eschatology in the Thought of Gregory of Nyssa and Karl Rahner*. Oxford: Oxford University Press.

———. 2002. Theology and Allegory: Origen and Gregory of Nyssa on the Unity and Diversity of Scripture. *International Journal of Systematic Theology* 4:45–66.

Mosshammer, Alden. 1990. Disclosing but Not Disclosed: Gregory of Nyssa as Deconstructionist. Pages 99–123 in *Studien zu Gregor von Nyssa und der christilichen Spätantike*. Edited by Hubertus R. Drobner and Christoph Klock. New York: Brill.

Norris, Richard A. 1998. The Soul Takes Flight: Gregory of Nyssa and the Song of Songs. *Anglican Theological Review* 80:517–32.

———. 2012. Introduction. Pages ix–l in *Homilies on the Song of Songs*. Translated by Richard A. Norris. Atlanta: Society of Biblical Literature.

Oliver, Kelly. 2009. *Animal Lessons: How They Teach Us to Be Human*. New York: Columbia University Press.

Smith, J. Warren. 2004. *Passion and Paradise: Human and Divine Emotion in the Thought of Gregory of Nyssa*. New York: Herder & Herder.

Torjesen, Karen Jo. 1986. *Hermeneutical Procedure and Theological Method in Origen's Exegesis*. New York: de Gruyter.

Zachhuber, Johannes. 2000. *Human Nature in Gregory of Nyssa: Philosophical Background and Theological Significance*. Boston: Brill.

Part 5
Sacrifice

What Would Jesus Eat?
Ethical Vegetarianism in Nascent Christianity

Robert Paul Seesengood

> In the beginning, I would like to entrust myself to words that, were it possible, would be naked. … Starting from Genesis, I would like to choose words that are, to begin with, naked, quite simply, words from the heart. Derrida (2008, 1)

To begin, it is always difficult for me to describe the feeling of flesh in words. Flesh is too visceral for words; it is image, smell, taste, and touch. It is my left hand, resting on the still warm carcass, my right pressing a blade against it; it is the moment before the cut, the pressure of the skin pushing back against the blade, surprising in both its firmness and its pliability, surprisingly like the flesh of my own stomach or thigh as I wipe my hands free of blood.

On a November day, midmorning, the full sun emboldened by its recent victory against the frost on the ground is starting to chase the cold out of the air; the yard beside the barn is littered with maple leaves, desiccated past colorful, and with neighbors, all men, standing in brown and drab corduroy coveralls, orange hats (some hunting caps, some woolen watch caps), old boots, hands thrust in pockets, unshaven. Among us all dance four or five hounds, tails wagging so hard they walk sideways, overjoyed at the number of hands that casually pat their heads. In our midst, he is lying across the back cargo box of our neighbor's Honda ATV. We are taking turns guessing at weight. A few near neighbors are commenting how they, like I, have been watching him for years now, seeing him in the early September rut and marking him in their mind's eye for the coming November hunt. He is clearly the other side of two hundred pounds. He is a twelve-pointer, a rare size around here, his antlers span over 36 inches of symmetry, six prongs to a side, too wide at their base for my finger and thumb to touch. He is the biggest creature I had ever killed. My father was proud, so proud he acted subdued, almost annoyed. Feigning a business-as-usual attitude, he was busy bringing out pans and trays, setting up a card table to use for a work space, uncoiling the rope; my uncle was whetting the blades, heating a pot of water on the Coleman stove; my mother brought out some aprons and visited a minute with neighbors.

My friend notices the wound on his neck, his only blemish. "How many shots?" I am asked. "Just one." "Shit. My ass, 'just one.' You blowed out the whole front of his neck." "I got no interest in your ass, be assured, and it was just one," I say, as I spit brown tobacco juice to the ground. I am asked, again, to tell the story; I do; I will tell it often in the coming days. I had been scouting a herd of does and yearlings since September, noting their runs, where they fed and watered, where they bedded down. I noticed from the height of the rubbings of the bark of an old cedar in October that this was his herd. The fields to the northwest side of the timber, a stand of pin oaks that this year had dripped with acorns, had been planted with millet and soy. The creek was nearby to the west with a fallow field, not two acres wide, between. I sat there three mornings amid the briars and burrs, arriving before daylight, staying until just after (when I had to come in, warm up, change and get ready for school). I took the twelve gauge; the brush and the light were such that I would not have a decent shot unless it was close, anyway. When he came, he came fast, unafraid and unwary, easily outrunning the dogs, now at least a half-mile behind him. He was nearly atop me when I finally got a clear shot. I hit him in the neck from about fifteen yards away. He reared to his full height, then twisted and fell. He pawed the ground a moment or two, blowing out heavy from his nose, gasping air in through his mouth. I worked the shotgun's action, ejecting the spent hull, readying another shell in the chamber just in case. I picked up the warm hull and put it in my coat pocket. I knelt on one knee, the gun leaned against my thigh, and watched. I waited.

He still panted, but soon stopped pawing. His chest rose and fell about every six seconds or so, forcing loud snorts of exhalation. About every fifth or sixth breath, he would try to arch his back or to lift and hold his head. I waited in silence, giving him privacy. I do not believe he could see me, though I am sure he knew I was there. He tried a few times to turn his head toward me, but I knelt outside his view and intended to keep it that way. He breathed less, then stilled. He never regained his feet; he died where I had knocked him down. My father arrived soon, having heard the shot. We sent for the three-wheeler, tagged him, and hauled him down to the game commission stand at Richard's Gas and Grocery to be registered, then brought him home.

"Did he choke?" I am asked, as someone observes the flecks of red froth still around his muzzle. "No." I answer, unsure. "Well," I am told, "at least with a neck hit, he bled out mostly. Won't be so much blood to him now. Too bad, though, that is some good meat."

"We should start," my father says, "you killed him, you clean him." I take another dip of Copenhagen while my hands are still clean, then put on the apron. We lay an assortment of knives and cleavers on the table, including homemade hooks and a special tool made by my father. He took a metal potting shovel and beveled one side to an edge; we used it to scrape out the inner wall of the chest and abdomen. Alongside the knives are a series of rags for wiping blood from the handles so that we can grip them safely. We begin with nailing his feet to a board; we coil the rope around the wood and around his hooves, then cast the other end around a barn rafter, and four of us hoist him into the air, pulling on a count of three. Once he is hanging, we being with some cuts to drain the balance of the blood, which we catch in plastic tubs and set aside, and tie his forelegs apart using stakes in the ground. Someone has put up the dogs. I open the carcass with a single long cut with a fillet knife tapped on the butt by a rubber mallet; I drag out the offal and organs to be put into another tub; they will be fed to the dogs over the next few days. We keep the liver, soaking it in brine. I cut the sinews at the top of his front legs and pull loose some hide. I then begin pulling and cutting, my right hand sliding the blade forward, my left hand pushing aside the hide. My father helps. As we clean the carcass, I cut the choice meat loose. My father stands behind me, whispering instructions. My uncle takes the meat, washes it, rubs it with rock salt, and puts it in trays and Tupperware tubs. The "good meat" is washed again and put into freezer bags. Everyone admires the marbling. Scraps of meat are collected into yet another tub to be taken for ground patties and summer sausage. All that remains is to cut loose the antlers with a hack saw, wash them, then bury the head, the hide, the bones, and the blood. My cuticles and nails will be stained red for days. My hands alternate between numbness, as their wetness combines with the cold, and tingling warmth, when I reach into the carcass again. Later, I notice I have somehow busted a knuckle on my right hand, probably against the bones of his hips; our blood has mingled.

The next day is Sunday. My mother had taken some photos and run them to the Rite-Aide for one-hour developing. That Sunday, everyone wants to see them. In one of them, I stand next to him as he lies across the

ATV; I hold his head erect by the antlers with my right hand while my left holds the shotgun that killed him. In another, I kneel over him as he lies on the ground; I am holding his head up with my left hand while I hold up the single shell in my right. In yet another, he is suspended in the air by ropes, just before we begin to cut the body. There are a few more of neighbors and kin together in the yard. The service is filled with other hunters, some still in coveralls and flannel coats. They went to the woods before church, then broke off their hunt to come and to take Communion, the body and blood of Jesus. One actually made a kill that morning; the body of the deer lay in the bed of his truck outside. The blood of the deer stained his hands and, no doubt, mixed with Jesus' as well. "Robbie got that buck that lived down toward the Carters.'" We have feasted on the flesh and the blood of Jesus; now they want to see my pictures.

Those words, to me, are "flesh"; they are words that define my early encounters with the animal. It has been more than twenty years since I have hunted. It has been nearly a decade since I ate meat. It has been nearly seven years since I have attended a ritual where congregants consumed the body and blood of Jesus, something that once marked the terminus a quo of my every week. I am often surprised at how much my current self is remade. I attend worship on the other side of the week, gathering with a small community of Conservative Jews on Saturday. I am vegetarian. No one I know hunts, or has hunted. Yet that image of flesh and animality is still with me. For me, the carving away of an animal is something at once ordinary and obscene, savage, and unusual.

I teach a course at Albright on food, ethics and spirituality. I am struck, again and again, at how different my students—mostly upper-middle class, urban, Catholic or mainline Protestant, typical of the type found at any semi-prestigious liberal arts college—how different they are from me in their assumptions about flesh and food and religion. They are ignorant of the impact of food on religiosity. For most of them, "kosher" means merely "no pork." I have to explain the biblical injunctions describing which animals are food and which are not, how these injunctions recognize the necessity of animal murder even as they attempt to contain its scope. Yet I will occasionally find that I have struck no deeper note than a student's surprised exclamation, "Hey, that means Jews could eat a giraffe." I have to explain how the obscure commandment of Exod 34:26, "you shall not boil a kid in its mother's milk," results in rabbinic injunctions against the mixing of meat and dairy—a dietary guideline that is far, far more invasive into meal planning and everyday life than is the loss of bacon. They learn to identify kosher packaging marks. I have to explain why Gen 32 prohibits eating of certain cuts of meat, even from permissible animals. They have no notion, at all, of the ritual(s) of slaughter, of the mechanics of sacrifice. They have no notion of flesh and blood and do not understand the ominous words of Gen 9:4, Lev 17:10–14, and Deut 12:23–25 forbidding the consumption of blood, for "the blood is the life" and the life belongs to God. They have never felt still-warm blood run down their arms, drip from their elbows to pool on the ground at their feet. They have no idea how hard it is to wash off, how sticky it becomes, how it draws bugs even in winter. They have no visceral understanding of killing and its emotional freight; Walter Burkert's extensive work on sacrifice—how sacrificial contexts surround the slaughter of food animals because of the horror of murder and blood libel and a desire to feed the divine in an act of atonement—is lost to them (1983). For them, "flesh" is merely a word. They fail to see how the slaughter of an animal could be considered violent or "savage." For them, meat comes in Styrofoam platters, or, more commonly, cooked alongside some type of potato.

Scholarly studies of sacrifice in the Bible and of food restrictions and regulations are often equally bloodless. Biblical sacrifice is, as we are all told, a multivalent activity.[1] It incorporates and articulates several complex social phenomena. It is, we are told, a means for "feeding" God; it is expiatory—its savagery performing a transaction of guilt and forgiveness, something like sympathetic magic, that takes away culpability by acquainting us firsthand with the savagery of death, a premeditated and violent death arising from cosmic necessity.[2] It knits together social groups by establishing food taboos (and, according to Durkheim, tribal totems). Sacrifice is a form of thanksgiving for provision of food, something intrinsically controlled by the divine, in biblical logic (Durkheim 1995, 340–57; Hubert and Mauss 1899, 12–138; Girard 1977). Herbert Richardson has blended in Burkert's language of animal sacrifice to construct notions of the sacrificial altar and the ritual of slaughter as the means by which human and divine experience table fellowship. Biblical

1. See Anderson 1992. He also laments that "much work still remains to be done here by the biblical scholar" (872). Sadly, more than twenty years on, his point is still apt. See, as well, Anderson 1987.

2. See the definitive work by E. B. Tylor (1871), who famously argues that sacrifice is a gift to the gods in exchange for personal protection and blessing: the original *do ut des*.

sacrifice performs many of these agendas simultaneously; it also often employs contradictory notions: God cannot be fed—Isaiah; yet God meets with us in commensality—Psalms (Richardson 1968). Our scholarship concurs that this multivalence arises from the multiple voices of biblical authorship, collection, and redaction (Dussaud 1941; Rainey 1970; Rendtorff 1967; Snaith 1957).

Biblical notions of sacrifice are steeped in a sense of commonality between the animal and human and in a visceral awareness of the process of slaughter: "The blood is the life." Each, human and animal, contains blood, a trope that becomes signifier for the divine animation of creation. Indeed, it is this very commonality that makes animal sacrifice effective for expiation of sin and guilt, and the biblical text links the death of animals with human transgression. Eden's bliss is shattered by human transgression; the first murder in the biblical text is not the execution of Abel by Cain. God must clothe Adam and Eve in animal hides. The J source can be read as presenting prelapsarian humans—and perhaps even animals—as vegetarians (note the discussion of Gen 3:18–22). Human transgression increases to the extent that God repents of creation; human and animal alike are to be killed in punishment, and only Noah, his family, and his menagerie escape.

In the P-source contribution of Gen 9, God sets the rules for postdiluvian life. Even as the consumption of animals for food is allowed, the taking of any life—human or animal—is restricted (9:3–6):

> Every creature that lives shall be yours to eat; as with the green grasses, I give you all these. You must not, however, eat flesh with its life-blood in it. But for your own life-blood I will require a reckoning: I will require it of every beast; of man, too, will I require reckoning for human life, of every man for that of his fellow man!
>
> Whoever sheds the blood of man,
> By man shall his blood be shed;
> For in His image
> Did God make man. (NJPS)

These verses, with their almost hopelessly confused syntax in Hebrew, seem to be struggling to articulate a linkage of human and animal life, even as they want to assert that human life has a unique sanctity. Both animals and humans contain "blood," the life-giving presence of the divine, and so share in a partial but visceral protection. Rabbis struggled to make sense of this parallel, particularly in light of Gen 1:26–27, where the image of God would seem to set humans as ontologically different from animals. The Talmud, for example, takes verse 5 as a prohibition against suicide (b. B. Qam. 91b) and verse 6 as prohibiting abortion (b. Sanh. 57b).

The ambivalence around the ontological distinction between human and animal continues through the P source. Leviticus 3:17 and 7:22–27 continue the prohibition against consumption of blood, echoing the words of Gen 9 (there, applied to human murder). This semipermeable boundary between the status of animal and human continues in Lev 17—improper slaughter and consumption of the animal, outside the sacrificial system, is condemned: "bloodguilt shall be imputed to that man: he has shed blood" (Lev 17:4). Scholars, again struggling for a sensible way to articulate the Bible's assertions that human and animal life are "different but still the same," normally conclude something like:

> In P's view, until the time of the flood it was a capital crime to shed the blood of any animal; thereafter it was permissible as long as the blood was not ingested. Now that the Tabernacle has been erected, Israelites may slay sheep and cattle for food only as well-being offerings; if they fail to present the animal as an offering, it is as if they had slain the animal in the antediluvian period when such an act was considered murder. (Schwartz 2004, 248)

P's concern with proper ritual setting for animal slaughter may have been long lasting in its influence. The book of Daniel suggests that some Hellenistic Jews opted for vegetarianism rather than eat animals tainted by improper sacrifice.[3] Surely, one major concern behind the misgivings expressed in Daniel is that the animals had been slaughtered in the worship of pagan deities. Yet perhaps even more fundamental than the possibility that these animals had been offered to *another* god is the issue that they were *not* slaughtered at the temple in honor of the biblical God. The distinction is not merely one of ritual context; if P is taken seriously, then animals killed by any means other than biblically described sacrifice were,

3. I am referring, of course, to Dan 1:1–21. I do not at all take this as an account of Jewish thought from the Babylonian exile; but, following the consensus of scholarship that Daniel was composed in the early years of the Maccabean revolt, I see the book of Daniel as reflecting (and defending?) the views of Jews during this tumultuous era.

in essence, murdered. In this case, this particular meat *is* murder. In late Second Temple Judaism, we know of two other Jewish groups—the Essenes and the Therapeutae—who opted for vegetarianism. Notably, in both cases we also find that these communities were separate from the Jerusalem temple and were anticipating a coming redemptive age where humans would return to Edenic purity. Apart from the temple and attempting to actualize life in an antediluvian utopia, these groups likewise may have equated the slaughter of food animals with murder.

In my seminar, as we probe at these questions, students want quickly to turn toward New Testament language about vegetarianism, deciding that the New Testament, while allowing the option, worked vigorously, and univocally, to oppose any sense that vegetarianism should be the norm. They further argue that New Testament texts put no restrictions of any kind on diet. I tell them it is not so easy.

Christianity in the first century C.E. was a subset within Judaism. Yet, as the New Testament documents illustrate, it was neither an ideologically united subset nor a unique expression of religiosity. This seems particularly true of views on the nature of animals. For example, the Epistle to the Hebrews negates the value of animal sacrifice. Everett Ferguson has shown that, in the early Roman Empire, several communities (Jews, Greek philosophers, and Roman intellectuals) were arguing that the ritual sacrifice of animals represented a lower form of religiosity (1980). Historians contend that early followers of Jesus were not the only communities in the first-century Roman Empire losing interest in animal sacrifice. Indeed, there is some evidence that early Christian arguments against animal sacrifice follow rather than anticipate this broader social trend (Petropoulou 2008, 290–95).

Hebrews boldly asserts that the blood of bulls and goats cannot take away the guilt of sin (9:13; 10:4). Only the (once, for all) sacrifice of Jesus is sufficient. At first glance, the elimination of animal sacrifice would seem to be good for animal welfare. Yet, as we have seen in Lev 17, the logic of animal death effecting propitiation is rooted in a belief in the commonality of "life in the blood." Hebrews is arguing that human and animal, postincarnation, are now ontologically different. Only via the death of the incarnate Word is atonement possible. In a move similar but not identical to Hebrews, the Gospels (particularly John) assert that Jesus becomes the Passover lamb; the Word become flesh now becomes sacrificial animal, consumed by the believer who not only eats his flesh, but now consumes his very blood. The Gospels espouse a deitarian diet.

Acts 10:9–23 prefaces (and authorizes) the conversion of the first Gentile (the so-called Gentile Pentecost) with Peter's vision of a tablecloth descending from heaven filled with "all kinds of animals and reptiles and birds of the air" (RSV); Peter is told to kill and eat. This would seem to be very much in keeping with Hebrews' argument: animals are now so distinct from humans that any limitation on their consumption is suspended. Yet the language also echoes Gen 9:3 ("every creature that lives shall be yours to eat") in its endorsement of all animals as food items. The vision repeats, and, shortly, Peter is called to preach to and baptize Cornelius and his household. Notably, the whole of Jewish liturgical expression is signified by the signifier of eating animals.

According to Acts, Peter's vision and the conversion of Cornelius prompted a crisis in the nascent community, particularly regarding how to incorporate Gentile believers. To resolve the issue, the early leaders of the movement met in Jerusalem and heard presentations of both sides (Acts 15:1–29). While they concluded Gentiles did not have to convert to Judaism, nor were they bound to keep Jewish liturgical obligations, they were not, however, free from any food obligations. Acts 15:28–29 enjoins them to "abstain from what has been sacrificed to idols and from blood and from what is strangled and from unchastity" (RSV). The injunctions to avoid food offered to idols is explicitly paired with the Lev 17 prohibition against consumption of blood and with the correlation of food consumption and proper slaughter. This prohibition of the consumption of blood is also a direct echo of both Noahide injunctions (murder and consuming animal blood) from Gen 9.

So what does Acts reveal about nascent Christian views of animals and food? Given the appeals directly to Gen 9 and Lev 17, one might argue that Acts reveals that some in nascent Christianity, instead of simply abandoning Jewish ritual regarding clean and unclean foods or P's logic of human/animal commonality, is actually appealing to Noahide standards. With the dawn of the messianic age, prelapsarian and antediluvian food rules have returned and, with them, a regard for animal life and blood.

Yet still another voice is represented in New Testament texts. Paul deals with the consumption of meat in 1 Cor 8:1–13 and Rom 14:1–12. In both passages Paul does not want vegetarian regulations to place a barrier among believers. In 1 Corinthians Paul is specifically addressing the eating of meat from animals sacrificed to a pagan deity (8:4), and he stresses two points. First, those who do not believe in the reality of pagan deities could eat with a clean conscience; second, the eating of meat (and, by extension, the killing of animals) is in itself an irrelevant issue (8:8). In 1 Corinthians Paul argues for a vegetarian diet, but for the sake of community coherence and not because there is anything ethically correct with vegetarianism, nor because consumption of meat is in any way, in and of itself, an ethical violation. In Rom 14 we again find Paul addressing the question of vegetarianism. In this case, however, he makes no direct mention of abstention from animals ritually slaughtered in the context of pagan sacrifice. The question seems to be a more general opposition to the eating of meat. Paul urges both meat eaters and vegetarians to get along despite their differences, rooting their acceptance in each other's mutual devotion to God. He ends the discussion with a return to the theme of mutual support he first struck in 1 Corinthians; meat eaters are instructed to curb their diets if they risk offending vegetarians (14:20–21).

Because of the common theme of mutual support and avoiding offense by diet, most scholars have equated Romans and 1 Corinthians, suggesting that Paul is addressing meat from animals killed in pagan sacrifice. Others, however, have correctly noted that Paul does not invoke, at all, the worship of pagan gods or pagan sacrifice in Romans. Though both epistles deal with a similar concern (vegetarianism or nonvegetarianism) and settle on a similar theme (avoiding offense), it is perhaps reading too much in to assume that the motivation for the vegetarianism is equivalent in both cases. Drawing from Romans' significant attention to Jewish and Gentile tensions, one could argue that Paul is speaking specifically about kosher concerns in Romans, a point reinforced by Paul's linkage of vegetarianism to the observance of (Jewish?) holidays. Paul does not address the issue of abstention from the consumption of blood, nor of conscientiousness regarding the method (not context) of animal slaughter that were invoked in Acts; yet this does not necessarily establish that these concerns were not present in either the communities to whom he writes or in the letters themselves.

Like many other Second Temple Jews, some followers of Jesus probably wished to avoid the consumption of meats because of a pagan ritual surrounding the animals' slaughter. Some Jews probably avoided meat eating to keep some aspect of "kosher" regulations (perhaps avoiding the mixture of meat and dairy, though this is almost certainly a later rabbinic concern), most likely surrounding improper slaughter. Like many other Jews, some followers of Jesus probably avoided meats because of expectations of a coming new messianic order. In the last two cases, some may have opted for vegetarianism for its resonance with Adamic and Noahide practice. There is ample evidence that early followers of Jesus spent significant attention on these two moments of Genesis. When combined with Acts' prohibition of the consumption of blood, one could defensibly argue that some nascent Christians may have avoided eating meat because it was not ritually sacrificed according to the rules of Lev 17. If it is reasonable to suggest some early followers of Jesus adopted vegetarianism because of the prohibitions described in Gen 9 and Lev 17, it is equally reasonable to suggest they may have also adopted the rationale behind Gen 9 and Lev 17—that all life belongs to God, that human and animal life are, in this sense, protected.[4]

Some ancient Jews and Christians found vegetarianism to be irrelevant; others did not. Some who espoused vegetarianism did so because of concerns over the proper worship of the biblical God; for others the motivations were more ethical. To put it simply, it is not, prima facie, ridiculous to suggest that some ancient Jews and Christians were vegetarians because they felt that the slaughter of animals outside permissible systems of temple sacrifice was tantamount to murder.

I am told, occasionally, by my students that it is ridiculous to think that killing and slaughtering an animal for food is savage, or murderous. I wonder. I have killed and slaughtered animals for food. I have felt warm offal between my fingers. I know what venison spleen feels like. I have watched the animals die. It is not ridiculous to me. The biblical corpus hangs suspended in front of us, drained of its blood, its organs, sinews, and bones exposed; its pericopes have been carved out into consumable chunks before us. In dissection it has become aggregate, its multivocality revealed, its infinite signification unveiled. What remains? Beyond a curious interest in a possible motive for some vegetarian Jews, what have we found? Wiping our bloodied hands on rags, we pause before this deer that both is and is not a deer, wondering about the animal before Noah, before Adam, the animal before the name, the flesh before the words.

In many ways the biblical debate reflects a very modern debate over the ontological relationship between the human and the animal. The area of animal studies is one of the more extensive areas in current humanities scholarship. Beginning from work in the 1990s, animal studies is not a critical methodology; animal studies is understood by many as a general

4. One might observe that animals could, of course, still be killed, and so there is no equivalency. Yet we need remember that the Hebrew Bible also allowed, even required, killing other humans in particular circumstances, some political/martial, others liturgical (transgressions of disobedience to parents, witchcraft, etc.).

term for varied scholarship that has, simply put, given up attention to the human for attention to the animal world and planetary environment (Wolfe 2010). More sophisticated work has explored the construction of "the animal" as subject as a means of defining the human (Haraway 2008; Wolfe 2010; Derrida 2008, 2009). Not merely writing about animals in literature, history, or popular culture, the central question is how one defines "animal," particularly vis-à-vis the construction of "human." In many ways, animal studies is a turn toward the posthuman by the suspension of belief in human uniqueness or sacredness.

One of the seminal works for modern animal studies is Peter Singer's *Animal Liberation* (2009). First released in 1975, the book drew both attention to the plight of animals in medical research and factory farming, and ire from industry insiders for fomenting popular disapproval. The book has been credited with the genesis of the animal rights movement and influence upon much of the contemporary criticism of diet and environmental concerns. Singer combats what he calls "speciesism," which he defines as "a prejudice or attitude of bias in favor of the interests of members of one's own species against those of members of other species" (6; cf. 9).

Animal Liberation opens with a review of an anonymous late-eighteenth-century pamphlet, *Vindication of the Rights of Brutes*, itself a parody of *Vindication of the Rights of Woman* by Mary Wollstonecraft. *Brutes* is a treatise that uses reductio ad absurdum to refute women's rights; Wollstonecraft's arguments, taken to their ends, would obliterate the rationale for distinction between human and beast. Singer explicates the pamphleteer's rational flaws—failure to recognize that discrimination based solely on gender is not identical to judicial discrimination based on characteristics and abilities. "The extension of the basic principle of equality from one group to another does not imply that we must treat both groups in exactly the same way, or grant exactly the same rights to both" (2009, 2). He goes on, however, to clarify that the pamphlet makes a few very strong points. A typical argument for women's equality would be that there is no difference in cognitive ability between men and women. Yet Singer argues, "we would be on shaky ground if we were to demand equality for blacks, women, and other groups of oppressed humans while denying equal consideration to nonhumans" (3). Focus upon some characteristic, say perception or intelligence, as the basis for equality faces the serious challenge that not all humans are actually equal (4). He concludes, "The principle of the equality of human beings is not a description of an alleged actual equality among humans: it is a prescription of how we should treat human beings" (5). Singer roots this in utilitarian ethics, a desire to reduce suffering. Nondiscrimination is a moral principle, not necessarily an articulation of an actual quantifiable equality, and is constructed to ensure the limitation of suffering. Moral systems that would ignore the infliction of suffering cannot, by definition, be moral.

Singer next posits (10–15) that animals clearly also experience suffering. Since nondiscrimination is rooted in moral principles (equated with actions that reduce suffering), to tolerate animal suffering, let alone to inflict or cause as much, is by logical extension also immoral. Any counterargument would first posit that human and animal are somehow, in essence, different. Singer suggests that whatever differences there are between human and animal, it is not in the ability to experience pain and suffering, the moral basis for nondiscrimination. Arguments that humans are "essentially better" are similar to arguments put forth by racists or sexists. They are, Singer asserts, "speciesist." As a result (and in the bulk of *Animal Liberation*) Singer opposes the mistreatment of animals for medical/scientific research and the inhumane treatment of animals on factory farms, espouses vegetarianism, and confronts our desires to exploit animals for our own entertainment. Most surely, he returns our attention again and again to the very particular, very physical, very vicious, exhausting, and bloody mechanisms of animal slaughter.

As one can imagine, Singer's arguments have run counter to several centuries of Western, and particularly Christian, thinking. Doubtless, among the primary objections to Singer's thesis for many Jewish and Christian ethicists is that he has no room for arguments of humanity's essential difference from animals as a result of the *imago Dei*. For Singer, no language about unique sanctity for human life is reasonable. In a later chapter of his revision of *Animal Liberation,* Singer deals with this question at some length and constructs one of the early works of animal studies and biblical tradition (2009, 185–212).

Singer crafts his own "short history of speciesism." His motive is that "to end tyranny we must first understand it" (185). In a move similar to Foucault's much more ambitious *History of Sexuality,* Singer constructs a short essay on Western speciesism that begins with Judaism and Greek antiquity, proceeds to nascent Christianity, briefly surveys "standard" Christian teaching, before a final treatment of later, Enlightenment authors. Singer writes, "Western attitudes to animals have roots in two traditions: Judaism and Greek Antiquity. These roots unite in Christianity, and it is through

Christianity that they came to prevail in Europe" (186). Newer, less speciesist understandings emerge only in a post-Christian epoch.

Much of Singer's work is (an openly) tendentious presentation of biblical literature that fails to attend to questions of historicity or multivocality. For example, Singer takes the Gospel account of the Gerasene demoniac as evidence of unconcern for animals (2009, 191–92) assuming both that the event (despite its rather notorious and readily observable textual problems) relates to some actual historical memory and that Jesus was "Christian"; he also takes 1 Cor 9:9–10 ("Does God care for the oxen?") as Paul's disregarding of all nonhuman life. Singer rightly notes, "The New Testament is completely lacking in any injunction against cruelty to animals, or any recommendation to consider their welfare" (191), though he overlooks motifs of Edenic restoration in the messianic age, Paul's views about a restoration of all creation (and the participation of all creation—together—in soteriology), and clear evidence that Judaism supported the protection of animal life even on the Sabbath (and Jesus' apparent endorsement of the same). Perhaps most surprising, given that more than a third of *Animal Liberation* addresses the ethics of animal husbandry and food, Singer omits any discussion of vegetarianism among Jesus' earliest followers. "Christianity encountered Rome's inhumanity with arguments for human sanctity, but left the beasts to fend for themselves" (192–93). In general, Singer argues that Christian literature marks an upswing in speciesist thought.

But that is only part of what we find within the biblical text, only one voice, only one stage of our reading and engagement. I am, we are, multivalent and multivocal. The biblical text is multivalent and multivocal. We have found it so in its ability to embrace women as equals, even as it then argues for their subordination. The Bible insists all humans share in the divine image and still tolerates slavery. The same chapter, Rom 1, summons us to embrace the way nature has made us in our sexuality, even as it condemns same-sex encounters. The Bible does lend itself to human speciesism, but it also defends the animal and demands respect for our commonality, our blood.

As Dale Martin has pointed out, texts have no power to compel, or even to assert what is "real"; people—often people who read and write texts—compel other people (2006, 1–2). I say this not necessarily to advocate that we find a way to use the Bible to defend humanitarian treatment of animals (though I would be happy if someone did). Nor do I wish to protect the biblical text from itself. I say this to remind us that *we* have the onus of ethical choices, and that we make them knowingly or otherwise as we engage with the biblical text. We must choose how we will read this text, what we will emphasize, how we will interpret. I say this to remind us of our ethical responsibilities and how we will not emerge from the reading of the biblical text as ethical beings unless we first enter that reading as moral ones.

In his essay (now book) "The Animal That Therefore I Am," Jacques Derrida spins an entire seminar on human subjectivity from an encounter with his pet (2008). Derrida describes being surprised in the bathroom by his pet cat; exiting from the bath, Derrida discovers that he is being observed, naked, by his cat and begins to reflect upon what the cat might be thinking of in the encounter. He famously stresses the particularity of his cat—a real and actual cat who turns his gaze back toward Derrida. He challenges Cartesian dualisms and opens conversation for the actual, independent agency and subjectivity of the cat. He uses the incident to reflect on how human and animal differ, how the human constructs itself by construction of distinction from animals (in this case, language and clothing). Derrida traces the Cartesian separation of animal from the human. To be "human" can only be defined by negation, by contrast with an animal other, a contrast that becomes precarious in times of racism and the exploitation of the subaltern. The human-other is crafted as animal-other.

Intersecting Derrida's work with Singer's and my own readings of the biblical text reveals that, at a fundamental level, specisism defines and describes the essence of fear of the other. In many ways, the biblical transformation across canons where, before God, animal can no longer atone, as equal, for human, both suggests and legitimates this separation. God incarnates, in the Second Testament, in the form of a human, exclusively. Creation may partner with humanity but it remains separate from humanity. When the Word became flesh, the word *flesh* might still apply to animal and human, but the essence of the two is irredeemably and permanently separated. We may return to Eden's de facto equality, but not to antelapsarian ontological and spiritual unity. Sin, even sin redeemed and remitted, has fractured human and animal union. Ironically, however, in Western readings of the biblical text, the fallen is the one who most fulfills the *imago Dei* and remains distinct from (and dominant over) the animal. The logic of this reading fails. Echoing within our biblical text is an always-already ambivalence about the othering of the animal, an instinctual sense that this segregation is both wrong and immoral. Yet present, as well, are texts that draw distinct lines of hierarchy between human and animal, using the animal nature as means of describing and debasing the Other. Those who deny the incarnation of God are heretical foes, described as "rude beasts, bred to be caught and killed" (2 Pet 2:12), or as horrific, hybrid beasts and monsters pitted against God (Rev 13). Biblical utopias are, as a rule, animal-less spaces.

And the implications of this separation have become dire for the animal. The machinery of genocide, forged and assembled by Modernity, turns its awful efficiency, in peacetime, toward the animal in countless feedlots, factory farms, commercial fisheries, and slaughterhouses. The ruthless efficiency of the kill feeds without satiating a growing (and indifferent) cultural hunger for "cheap meat." Cheap flesh cheapens both animal and human, diminishing our collective value. As cultures become increasingly urbanized and industrialized, there is a sharp trend away from individual animal husbandry and slaughter toward commercialized farming. An awareness of the visceral, physical, terrible work of slaughter is lost. One might well argue that insulation (isolation?) from the real process of killing and slaughter has not made American culture more humane toward the animal; ironically, it has become more callous toward animal suffering.

In a parallel irony, as the animal has moved away from being a sacrificial victim, there has been an attendant move away from sacralization of animal death that has resulted not only in casualness regarding slaughter, but also in desire for increased efficiency in death. The death of the animal has moved down from the high place, from the open air, from the altar before the assembly into terrible, filthy, sterile, windowless killing floors of slaughterhouses. The awareness of killing is gone, and with it both the guilt and the sense of the *unheimlich* that occurs when one is elbow deep in the death, then dismemberment, of another creature.

The blood and body of Christ have become sterile, often alcohol-free, tastes of bread and grape. The sacrifice of atonement that engored the altar has become a Torah reading followed by commentary. The animal has not really been spared by this bloodless coup; it has merely been sequestered behind windowless walls, thick enough to prevent the escape of even odor or sound. When the cacophonous multivocality of the biblical text is silenced, the shared sacredness of the animal is lost. We may, however, if we choose, refocus our readings of the Bible on our communion with the animal, on the essence of the blood that binds before God, on the sacredness of life manifest in the holy restrictions upon killing and death.

Derrida asserts that his remarks occur from an encounter with an actual, physical cat. His cat is no metaphor. His cat is not a cipher for the cat in general. It gazes at him with its own eyes. It forms its own sense of subjectivity and agency. I began this essay with one of my own encounters with the animal, with an actual, particular deer, not a cipher or a metaphor. He, and Derrida's cat, gaze back at us as real, particular, discrete animals. Donna Haraway critiques Derrida in her work *When Species Meet* (2008). She observes the limits—better, the tendentiousness—of Derrida's curiosity, observing how, despite his protests to the contrary, he nevertheless quickly abandons trying to find the cat's "voice" or subjectivity to reflect upon how "human" is constructed. Despite himself, Derrida is more drawn to the human's experience of encountering the animal's subjectivity than he is with the actual content of that subjectivity itself:

> He came right to the edge of respect, of the move to *respecere*, but was side-tracked by his textual canon of Western philosophy and literature and by his own linked worries about being naked in front of his cat. … Derrida failed a simple obligation of companion species; he did not become curious about what the cat might actually be doing, feeling, thinking, or perhaps making available to him. (20)

He correctly refrains from a naïve and imperialist claim "to see from the point of view of the other" (21), but Derrida still does not, she argues, sufficiently respond to (and therefore respect) the Other. He was not provoked to reflect upon how he and his cat mutually encounter each other, nor did he take seriously the possibility of mutual change (22; cf. 19–27).

We are, in our encounters with the animal, constructing the human. In our encounters with the animal as food, we are doing so in a primal and visceral way. The Word becomes flesh, and the flesh becomes other flesh. Our options are two: we may see the animal as equal ontologically, or we may see the animal as distinct and suitable for food. If we argue against equality, we become fused with the animal as we eat. If we argue for equality, we will preserve the limits of our selves and the animal, even as we argue for their erasure. And more: we may conceal the death of the animal, or we may foreground—even ritualize—that killing. To remove the sense of the sacred and the *unheimlich* from killing is to move toward the mechanization and routinization of death.

Haraway continues,

> human genomes can be found in only about 10 percent of all the cells that occupy the mundane space I call my body; the other 90 percent of the cells are filled with genomes of bacteria, fungi, protists and such, some of which play in a symphony necessary to my being alive at all, some of which are hitching a ride and doing the rest of me, of us, no harm. I am vastly outnumbered by my tiny companions; better put, I am become and adult human being in company with these tiny messmates. To be one is always to *become with* many. (2008, 3–4)

Like Haraway, I am in love with this image. I am consumed with the idea of myself and all the others around me—animal and human—as, effectively, sentient biospheres, as porous, as unfixed and unfixable, blending always with the organic world around me in what I sluff off and what I take in. Such an image confronts, directly, our definitions of human and animal. Indeed, we confront even our definitions of "organism"; we are challenged with the potential implications for the nature of God. "I–Thou" becomes, at best, "We–Y'all."

Such an image destroys any possible sense of unique privilege in the face of our Other. We are all sentient biospheres. We are all always already eating and being eaten, merging and defending. Sustaining and slaying. "We," "I," "You," "He, "She," "It," even "Self" and "Other" are words now seen as charmingly quaint, vestigial words for flesh that mark a prior level of bio-awareness. Understanding self-as-colony reveals these terms to be little more than metaphor, challenging us to imagine the complex world behind and beneath them, the world teeming with interconnected, interanimated "stuff," a world more complex than language, a world enlivened by rivers of living blood.

Like Haraway, I am in love with the image, with what it proclaims about human as well as about animal potential, with how it reduces both human and animal to our lowest common denominators, revealing that in the messy, soupy logic of life, we are not only constructed of the same stuff, not only constructed by the same logic and pattern, but are in essence identical conglomerations of hosts of competing and partnering proto-nucleic subjectivities. Our boundaries are not fixed or static. We are knit together into flesh, fed and cleaned by blood, some sense of conscious sentience emerging only later.

We are invited to see both creation and God in terms of interanimated colonies of beings, as flesh that is only "flesh" in word. We cannot escape reflection on how we, as human, both are and are not the animal. The multivocality of the biblical text, particularly regarding "the human" and "the animal," plays against our notions of static self and counters notions of a particular "sanctity" to our humanity and to our text.

Works Cited

Anderson, Gary A.. 1987. *Sacrificial Offerings in Ancient Israel: Studies in the Social and Political Importance*. Harvard Semitic Monographs 41. Atlanta: Scholars Press.

———. 1992. Sacrifice and Sacrificial Offerings: Old Testament. Pages 870–86 in vol. 5 of *Anchor Bible Dictionary*. Edited by D. N. Freedman. New York: Doubleday.

Burkert, Walter. 1983. *Homo Necans: The Anthropology of Ancient Greek Sacrificial Ritual and Myth*. Berkeley: University of California Press.

Derrida, Jacques. 2008. *The Animal That Therefore I Am*. Edited by Marie-Louise Mallet. Translated by David Wills. New York: Fordham University Press.

———. 2009. *The Beast and the Sovereign*. Vol. 1. Edited by Michel Lisse, Marie-Louise Mallet, and Ginette Michaud. Translated by Geoffrey Bennington. Chicago: University of Chicago Press.

Durkheim, Emile. 1995. *The Elementary Forms of Religious Life*. Translated by Karen E. Fields. New York: Free Press.

Dussaud, René. 1941. *Les origines cananéenes du sacrifice israélite*. 2nd ed. Paris: Geuthner.

Ferguson, Everett. 1980. Spiritual Sacrifice in Early Christianity and Its Environment. *Aufstieg und Niedergang der römischen Welt*. Vol. 2. *Principat*, 23.2. Edited by Hildegard Temporini and Wolfgang Haase. 23.2:1151–89.

Girard, René. 1977. *Violence and the Sacred*. Translated by Patrick Gregory. Baltimore: Johns Hopkins University Press.

Haraway, Donna J. 2008. *When Species Meet*. Minneapolis: University of Minnesota Press.

Hubert, Henri, and Marcel Mauss. 1899. Essai sur la nature et la function du sacrifice. *L'année sociologique* 2:29–138.

Martin, Dale B. 2006. *Sex and the Single Savior: Gender and Sexuality in Biblical Interpretation*. Louisville: Westminster John Knox.

Petropoulou, Maria-Zoe. 2008. *Animal Sacrifice in Ancient Greek Religion, Judaism, and Christianity, 100 B.C. to A.D. 200*. Oxford Classical Monographs. New York: Oxford University Press.

Rainey, A. F. 1970. The Order of Sacrifices in the Old Testament Ritual Texts. *Biblica* 51:485–98.

Rendtorff, Rolf. 1967. *Studien zur Geschichte des Opfers im alten Israel.* Neukirchen-Vluyn: Neukirchener.

Richardson, Herbert W. 1968. *Theology for a New World*. London: SCM.

Schwartz, Baruch J. 2004. Leviticus. Pages 203–80 in *The Jewish Study Bible.* Edited by Adele Berlin and Marc Zvi Brettler. New York: Oxford University Press.

Singer, Peter. 2009. *Animal Liberation*. Updated edition. New York: Harper Perennial.

Snaith, Norman. 1957. Sacrifices in the Old Testament. *Vetus Testamentum* 7:308–17.

Tylor, E. B. 1871. *Primitive Culture*. 2 vols. New York: Hodder & Stoughton.

Wolfe, Cary. 2010. *What Is Posthumanism?* Minneapolis: University of Minnesota Press.

Cutting up Life: Sacrifice as a Device for Clarifying—and Tormenting—Fundamental Distinctions between Human, Animal, and Divine

Yvonne Sherwood

> My purpose is to tell of bodies which have been transformed into shapes of a different kind. (Ovid, *Metamorphoses* 1.1 [1986, 29])

Humankind has expended a great deal of energy on sacrifice—not just the rites and practices of sacrifice, which constitute the smallest proportion of our labors, but all the texts of sacrifice (which often interpret the transformation from blood to ink as a sign of becoming more civilized, more fully "man"). From Leviticus to *Kiddushin* to myriad theories of sacrifice from Hubert and Mauss to Girard and Bataille,[1] the massive archive—or textual offering up—on "sacrifice" seems to amply corroborate Bataille's theory of sacrifice as lavish expenditure and excess. It is in this sacrificial spirit of nonmoderation that I want to throw another reflection on sacrifice onto the already massive, smoldering pile. We compulsively sacrifice (and/or think and write sacrifice) to erect distinctions between the human, the god(s), and the animal. We sacrifice to assuage our anxiety about these fragile distinctions as much as we sacrifice (or write on sacrifice) to, for example, atone for sins or win the favor of the gods. But conversely we also use the altar and reflections on the altar to produce strange altar-ations or oscillations in the unstable flux of the "theo-anthropo-zoomorphic," and to venture into the no-man's/god's/animal's-land between human, animal, and divine.

1. See famously Bataille 1988; Girard 1979; Hubert and Mauss 1964. These three examples are, of course, merely scratching the surface of the massive archive on sacrifice.

We live, famously, under the regime of biopolitics: diffused governance based on the massive confinement (cutting) and amplification of "life." In a world where the gods are ostensibly dead and the "biological order has no source other than the biological order" (Canguilhelm 1988, 141), life folds in on itself self-referentially, tautologically, as its own cause and effect. (According to the pharmaceutical company Pfizer, currently under pressure to reduce the costs of HIV medication in Africa, "Life is our Life's Work.") But as if fulfilling that quintessentially modern understanding of life as ontogenetic development, life (as concept) has become extraordinarily fecund, splitting into myriad disciplinary cells: the human sciences, life sciences, political arithmetic, statistics, demography and population studies, biology, cybernetics, robotics, genetics, artificial intelligence, digital and molecular revolutions, biotechnology, the understanding of living beings as chemical machines, and the informationalization of life. Life is understood as a force, a collection of species properties that can be audited, augmented, managed, and rendered more productive through the application of technologies of life. And as Michel Foucault argues, forms of political and economic anthropology that attempt to "assign concrete forms to finitude" have led to "a newly configured correlation of life and death" (Foucault 1997, 257; cf. Dillon and Reid 2009, 26).

At first glance this distinctly late modern bureaucratization and fecundity of life seems worlds away from the ancient (?) scene of sacrifice. These late modern days, the biocultural freight of life seems to converge more "naturally" around that twentieth- and twenty-first-century icon "Dolly the Sheep" than around that old icon the lamb of God. But note the perfect resemblance between Dolly and Christ as mirror images or clones of one another in figure 1, "Mutual Scrutiny of Agnus Dei and Dorothea Ovis (Lamb of God meets Dolly the Sheep)."

Literally pieced together under the micromanipulator using handmade pipettes the width of human hairs, Dolly emblematizes new alignments of the biological, cultural, political, and economic, "new mixtures of mortality and immortality, normality and pathology," and the "possibility" and "threat" of slippage from sheep, *Ovis aries*, to humans, *Homo sapiens sapiens* (Franklin 2007, 30, 159). As Sarah Franklin writes in the fabulously titled *Dolly Mixtures*, she stands for "the desire to distinguish the animal from the human, and to prevent their mixture, while also, paradoxically, embodying their ever more proximate union—and the fallacy of such a dividing line between them" (30). As an act of cloning

Mutual Scrutiny of Agnus Dei and Dorothea ovis
(Lamb of God meets Dolly the Sheep)

Left: Lamb of God with Christian banner. Photograph by John Workman in St. Ignatius Church in Chestnut Hill, Massachusetts. Right: A closeup of Dolly in her stuffed form: "Hello Dolly."

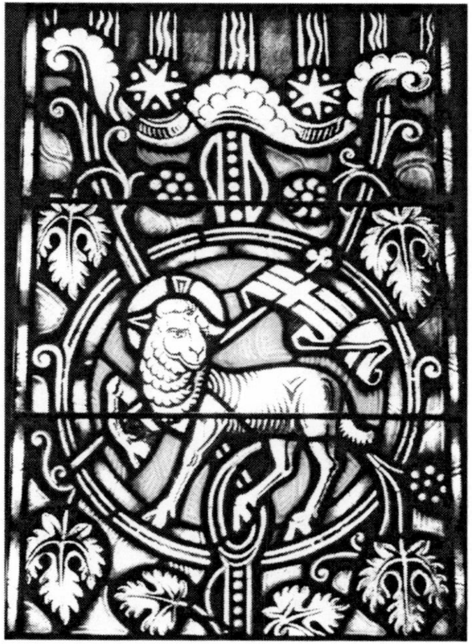

(a term from botany, derived from the Greek *klōn*, "twig") her coming-into-being was an act of regeneration as cultivation and propagation, transgressing the (artificial) boundary between "animal" and "plant." Transcending sex, it was also "otherworldly," a "virgin birth" (Wilmut et al. 2000, 233). Made/conceived at the Roslin Institute at the University of Edinburgh, Dolly stands as an emblem of modern biopolitics and bioculture, life at the unstable convergence of the agricultural, medical, commercial, and industrial. (The institute webpage references the "livestock industry" and "food security" as domains of expertise.) She stands as the culmination of millennia of "sheep cultivation" and the use of sheep as "instruments of commerce," and also selective breeding and control of the germplasm. Selective breeding is regularly traced back to three primitive sources: Neolithic, Homeric and biblical. The Bible contributes Jacob's genetic engineering in Gen 30. In an unusually physical form of "reception," the biblical text is blazoned on the body of an ornamental four-horned breed with multicolored wool with the species name "Jacob's sheep" (Franklin 2007, 89–92).

In the strange new typologies of modernity, Jacob's sheep—magnified in number and in strength by ingenuity—stand as the perfect antetype for that quintessentially modern project of the maximalization, perfection, and management of life. The reverse is true of sacrifice, and, say, the massive "superstitious" waste of Solomon's 22,000 cattle and 120,000 goats (2 Chr 7:5). In modernity, "religious" sacrifice "for God" is effectively "for nothing."[2] It collides absolutely with the modern target and mantra of making life a business and only ever "killing to make life live." But at the same time, sacrifice is being recycled as a major structuring concept in contemporary philosophy because it presses the darker side of modern biopolitical and biocultural economies. There is no maximalization of life without sacrifice, without killing to make life live. Sacrifice presses the question of how, and where, we make cuts in life. (To cut life is to demarcate: to decide which forms of life must be sacrificed to sustain more vital forms of life. It is also effectively to *prune*, for these cuts are to regenerate life as such.)

The revival of sacrifice as a philosophical topos overrides a firm cut that we once thought we had made, once and for all, between modernity and dusty old theopolitical structures like sovereignty and sacrifice. Modernity and biopolitics are compressed together with ancient forms of life manage-

2. For religious sacrifice as waste in modernity, see §8 below.

ment that we thought we had surpassed. Governed by quasi-transcendentals such as "species," "history," "labor," and, above all, "Life Itself" (folding in on itself as its own virtue), modern sciences of life rely on superordinate, sovereign structures beyond the law, capable of suspending law. These regularly function just like the old spooks and gods we thought we had expelled.

Biblical studies tends to function as a self-enclosed world that perpetuates the quintessentially modern belief that these texts belong in a historicized box. The richness of studies of sacrifice is a concentrated richness, with delicious attention to detail. But, reflecting religion's cringe or self-deprecating modesty in modernity, the studies tend to operate on the assumption that no one but Jews, Christians, or the occasional antiquarian or specialist would ever care. Meanwhile, philosophical and political thought has been obsessed, for a long time, with the sacrifice of Abraham. In these studies we find a very different kind of approach. The text comes out of its historicized box and becomes paradigmatic of certain ways of thinking, certain structures, that are not simply or dismissively "religious" or simply and dismissively "past." The text becomes material to think with, to think about how we think and categorize, divide and decide.

In this audacious spirit, I want to attempt a kind of study that, from the vantage point of proper biblical studies, will appear both improper and bizarre. Encouraged by the cloning and mutual recognition between the Lamb of God and Dolly the Sheep, I want to start with the wager that rites and stories in the biblical archive can be connected to contemporary questions of biopolitics and fundamental questions about how we think and divide life. What would happen if we thought about biblical sacrifice as relating to (without simply cloning) contemporary anxieties and technologies of "life"? My argument in essence is that sacrifice is all about clarifying the divisions between god, human, animal, and inorganic matter—and that it is also about dissolving those distinctions. It is about "cutting up life," in the sense of establishing the conceptual divisions that help us make sense of life—then putting these cuts in life under the knife.

Like sacrifice, or the transformative aspect of sacrifice, I play havoc with the usual distinctions that we use to manage thinking and manage life. I have produced a mongrel cross-breed of texts, from Leviticus to Prometheus to Francisco de Vitoria to Agamben. Some of the names are strange. Certainly the cross-fertilization is. But as advertised by the most fecund of the biblical sacrifices (like the crucifixion and Abraham's sacrifice) as much as by the work of the Roslin Institute or Pfizer, there is no limit to the new lives that we can conceive or manufacture, no limit to the fecundity of life. At the same time, it should be pointed out that this corpus is only wild and experimental in a limited sense. All these texts orbit around a distinct (shall we say, loosely, if rather too grandiosely, "Western"?) logic of sacrifice. I never venture into the totally alien structures of "sacrifice" (that can only tendentiously be called such) as practiced, for example, by the Aztecs and the Maya. It is striking how far the texts I use—while chronologically and geographically separate—find roughly the same distinct place for man's relation to divinities and animals, as well as varieties of the organic/inorganic that include angels, sand, and stones. This conformity seems to suggest more than historical influence. Noting the similarity between classical and biblical sacrifices, Derrida reads them as "two symptomatic translations" of the same fundamental structure, the "internal necessity" of which is "confirmed all the more by the fact that certain characteristics partly overlap" (de Vaux 1964, 49; Derrida 2002a, 412).

1. Sacrifice as a Device to Make Man "Go Live"

Contrary to the popular belief that sacrifice is all about God/the gods, center stage is man, with animals and divinities as the adjuncts and sidekicks of "man." In *The Open*, Agamben writes: "The anthropological machine of humanism is an ironic apparatus that verifies the absence of a nature proper to Homo, holding him suspended between a celestial and terrestrial nature, between animal and divine—and thus, his being always more and less than himself" (2004, 29).[3] We could say the same of the *anthropological machine of sacrifice.* It produces and sustains the "human" qua human. Accustomed to Christian sacrifice, we expect sacrifices to save or atone. And indeed sacrifice does save, but not in the sense we expect. It saves man, qua man, in the sense of reserving a special place for "human" as distinct from animal and divine. But the archives and altars of sacrifice also serve as a key site for performing the vacillations of life as "the experience whose limits tremble at the bordercrossings between *bios* and *zoē* [*sic*], the biological, zoological, and anthropological, as between life and death, life and technology, life and history, and so on" (Derrida 2002a, 393). Greek *zōē* and *bios* separate what is conflated in English "life" or

3. There appears to be a misprint in the translation. I have corrected "between animal and human" to "between animal and divine."

Latin *vita*. *Zōē* is "the simple fact of living common to all living beings (animals, men, or gods)," while *bios* is the "form or way of living proper to an individual or a group" (Agamben 1998, 9), traditionally, specifically, the form of life that is unique to man. Life as *bios* must make numerous incisions and decisions to make man live or to make man "go live." These cuts of clarification and points of opposition are myriad and unstable. Whereas *zōē* has one clear opposite (death), there are numerous points of opposition for *bios*.

Blood sacrifice scrambles the basic distinctions between life as *zōē* and its clear opposite, dying. It performs the oxymoron of a procreative and fecund dying. It stages an end of *zōē*-life that is anything but inert. But it also scrambles "life" in the other sense. It traumatizes (and fascinates) *bios*-life with what must be excluded (sacrificed) to make this distinct form of life live, *go live*. Sacrifice breaks through the artificial pens and fences that segregate human, animal, and divine. Even as sacrifice purifies "the border crossing from which vantage man dares to announce himself to himself" (Derrida 2002a, 381), it serves as the prime site for tampering with "the living." This takes place through acts of *deliberate* tampering, artificial intervention—but also the inevitable accidents that fire off in all directions as soon as one attempts to control and partition life. The ubiquity of sacrifice and theories of sacrifice show just how badly the "ends of man" need constant reiteration—and constant tampering with—just like the edges of the "sacred" and "profane." As Henri Hubert and Marcel Mauss (1964) theorize sacrifice as a *double* border crossing between the sacred and the profane *in both directions*, so sacrifice clarifies *and* scrambles the ends or limits of man. Its power comes from the concentration of these two opposite gestures, at one and the same time.[4]

Sacrifice serves the hope of clarifying and purifying, once and for all, fundamental categories of living being around answers to the questions: Who/what commands sacrifice (to whom/what do I sacrifice)? Who/what offers sacrifice? and Who/what is on the fire or under the knife? The answers, put crudely, are (1) "who" and "divine"; (2) "who" and "man"; and (3) "what" and "animal" or subanimal. Thus the cut of sacrifice promises to make a clear incision between the "I-we and what we *call* animals"—not least by distinguishing between the "who" and the "what."

4. Cf. Derrida on "at the same time" as "a time that disagrees with itself all the time," a time that is "out of joint" (2002b, 94).

2. First Incision/Distinction: The Recipient/Addressee of Sacrifice Is God

The "who" who stands on the other side of sacrifice as the recipient or addressee of sacrifice is made more surely divine than by any other device. To put this another way, it is around the altar that the divine becomes most securely divine. Or as Augustine put it in the most rhetorical of rhetorical questions quoted again and again by Christian authors throughout the centuries: "For who has ever thought that sacrifice should be offered, except to the one whom he knew or thought or imagined to be God?" (*Civ.* 10.4; as cited in las Casas 1974, 229).[5]

The point seems so compelling that unlikely companions such as Augustine, Thomas Aquinas, Slavoj Žižek, and Elaine Scarry all meet to affirm roughly the same point. Responding to Lacan and Girard in *Enjoy Your Symptom*, Žižek writes, "Sacrifice is the *guarantee* that the other exists; that there *is* an other who can be appeased by sacrifice" (2001, 56). (He invokes alterity as symbolic structure and a qualitative difference to which we are subject—hence, structurally analogous to the divine.) Though she only references Nietzsche once directly, Elaine Scarry seems to be applying Nietzsche's argument in *The Genealogy of Morals* to the material edifice of scripture. God/gods come(s) most vividly into being in the palpable, palpitating suffering of a living being, just as for Nietzsche our most deep-seated legal, social, and moral structures are established through the experience and memory of pain. Divinity is substantiated through the elaborate arrangement of material substance in works of human craft, such as tabernacles and temples. But the work of human construction/labor that has the most power to conjure God/the gods is the altar—and all the technologies and taxonomies that spiral from the altar. For in the altar, a work of human making coincides with loss and self-affliction. And God/the gods tend to appear most clearly in the space opened up by self-deprivation and pain.

Understanding "belief" as a special case of imagining "when the object created is in fact described as though it created you," Scarry (1985) describes how belief is most firmly concretized through the unnatural or counternatural alteration of living bodies. The most potent indices of belief are mirac-

5. The axiom is widely repeated, from Aquinas ("Now no one has ever thought that sacrifice should be offered to anyone for any other reason than that he believed or thought that he believed that he was God" [*Contra Gentes* 3.120]) to Bartolomé de las Casas ("for sacrifice is the sign that he to whom it is offered is God" [1974, 229]).

ulous reproduction (the pregnant barren matriarchs; the teeming Israelite bodies in Egypt) and circumcision and sacrifice—particularly human/child sacrifice. Both are artificial devices, supplements to life in the raw. Life teeming from barren wombs graphically performs a divine/artificial supplement to life at the origin of life. Think of the family tree of Genesis pouring forth from artificial/divine intervention in life—as both distant relative and close kin of Dolly's "virgin birth," genetic modification or IVF. Sacrifice is an artificial intervention in "life" showcasing originary technicity: technique as life and life as technique (cf. Bradley 2011). For Scarry, both miraculous birth and sacrifice emblematize that moment where the projection clearly "ceases to be the 'offspring' of the human being," turning instead into the "thing from which the human being himself sprung forth" (1985, 147–48, 204–5). Scarry describes the moment where Abraham offers up the child from the inside of his (and Sarah's) body as the moment where God is, so to speak, born (204). Nancy Jay also folds sacrifice into labor when she describes sacrifice as hyperbirth, "birth done better" (1991). In her Geertzian "thick" (actually viscous) description of the annual sacrifice of a sheep/goat in Morocco in commemoration of Abraham's sacrifice at *Id al-Kabir/Id al-adha*, anthropologist M. Elaine Combs-Schilling unleashes sacrifice from textual black and white. Once seen in writhing chaotic technicolor, it is hard to miss the resemblance between red blood on white wool, exposed insides, and the blood and vernix at the birth of a child (1989).

Because sacrifice is a particular form of human labor—bound to pain and, by analogy, to that especially agonized form of human making, in labor—sacrifice and particularly blood sacrifice are especially resistant to demystification or premodern forms of demystification *avant la lettre*, by which I mean any theory of interpretation that turns the divine into some kind of human projection of the "divine." Long before the Enlightenment and in the *insides* (deep in the guts) of the Bible and Jewish and Christian tradition, there are numerous devices for "demystifying" nondesirable or foreign religious practices as a projection of merely human desires.[6] With a casual wave of the hand, other religions and other gods are easily dismissed as *cheiropoētos*, made by human hands. But self-deprivation or self-harm in the offering of a living body seems so often to mark the site of (genuine) transcendence: the place beyond *technē* or human art. Even

6. Famous examples include Wis 12–14 and the so-called anti-idol polemics in Deutero-Isaiah. (However, for a provocative rereading of Isa 40–55 as a campaign against priestly culture/theology's obsession with the material, see Lipton 2008.)

human hands connected to the craziest of human minds could not create a form of worship centered on the immolation of living bodies, so the reasoning goes. The logic of child sacrifice (akin to the logic of martyrdom) is that the closer the offered body is to that of the sacrificer, the more incontrovertible the sacrifice becomes as proof of the divine.

One reason for the problematic "henotheism" of the Bible may be that other gods are substantiated through sacrifice. The competition between Elijah and the prophets of Baal takes as its starting point the fact that Baal exists—and exists intensely—since his presence is enforced by the sacrifices of no less than four hundred prophet-priests. The supremacy of "the God of Abraham, Isaac, and Israel" is asserted by his unique ability to ignite sacrifice on wood drenched in water and "respond" in such a way that Baal becomes comparatively nonresponsive. Baal is not forced into nonexistence. He still exists through sacrifice. But his existence becomes less insistent, suppressed in comparison to the God of Israel, who attains a new level of hyperexistence through hypersacrifice. The God of Israel becomes more godly, stronger, substantiated by sacrifice in impossible conditions or sacrifice-plus (1 Kgs 18:20–40). The strange coda to the battle between Mesha of Moab and Jehoram of Israel (provoked by this sheep-breeder king's refusal to continue supplying "one hundred thousand lambs, and the wool of one hundred thousand rams"—a great deal of animal material for various purposes, including, one assumes, sacrifice) reports how Mesha offered his firstborn son as an עלה, with the result that a great wrath descended upon Israel so that they instantly retreated (2 Kgs 3:24–27). Thus the text affirms that (1) son sacrifice is effective, and (2) Chemosh exists. Son sacrifice compels a making real of Chemosh that the Bible does not and maybe *cannot* resist.

Precisely at the point where they are able to compel sacrifices of life, the other gods refuse to lie down as dead inorganic things: mere material, lumps of wood or stone. When YHWH or the writers and the editors of the Bible became squeamish or repentant about child sacrifice, they produced various explanations for why the rite was enforced at other points in the tradition/canon, including the argument that once-upon-a-time YHWH gave them bad commands to punish them for sin (Ezek 20:25–26). The supernatural origin is retained at the price of a considerable challenge to theodicy. This suggests that the revisionist finds it impossible to imagine a source for human/child sacrifice that is less than divine. Similarly, when early Christians such as Eusebius or Clement of Alexandria attacked blood sacrifice among the Greeks and Romans, they claimed that they were orchestrated by evil *daimōnia*, supernatural beings who were gluttonous for blood (in this respect following the Paul of 1 Cor 10:18 and 20 who regards eating food sacrificed to idols as communion with demons).[7] This view of sacrifice produces increasingly cluttered heavens, crammed full of supernatural beings. The merely human never seems to have enough force to serve as an origin for sacrifice, particularly human sacrifice. Demystification is resisted, above all, by human sacrifice. Human sacrifice suggests a source so forceful and compelling that it can only be rendered as divine command.

A god—or equivalent Absolute—seems absolutely essential to human sacrifice because only a god can enforce the difference between sacrifice and murder and between sacrificial death and other kinds of legitimate and illegitimate death. In his response to Levinas, "'Eating Well' or the Calculation of the Subject," Derrida explores ethics as etiquette, *table* (or altar) manners. As he points out, "Thou shalt not kill" with all its ethical consequences and nuances (such as "Thou shalt not wound," "Thou shalt not allow to die/to starve," etc.) has never been understood within the Judeo-Christian tradition as "Thou shalt not put to death the living in general." It has always left ample space for a "noncriminal putting to death" (1995, 278–79). And for the animal, there has always been a far more open field for the noncriminal putting to death. Wandering wild outside the law or penned in a space near the house but set apart from the *oikos* and the legal category of homicide, animals can be killed for food or hunted for sport or leisure (cf. Aristotle, *Pol.* 1256b 9–25). They can (context and culture permitting) also be sacrificed. Inside law, men can be legitimately killed (for example, in judicial execution or in war) or illegitimately killed in acts of "homicide"—a category that is managed in scrupulous subdivisions: for example, "murder" as distinct from "manslaughter" as distinct from "criminally negligent homicide." "Man" can also (context and culture permitting) be sacrificed, though in general more controversially and more rarely than the animal. (And here we should at least note—though

7. "Come then, let us further observe, what inhuman daemons and haters of mankind your gods were, not only delighting in driving men mad, but also gloating over human slaughter, making for themselves occasions of pleasure now in the armed conflicts of the arena, and now in the endless contests for glory in war, that so they might have the fullest opportunities of freely glutting themselves with human slaughter. And at length, falling like pestilences upon cities and nations, they demanded merciless libations of blood" (Eusebius, *Praep. ev.* 4.16, citing Clement, *Protrepticus* 3).

this is a massive topic in its own right—that rites and logics of sacrifice make crucial cuts between "man" and "woman," helping to separate man as *homo* from man as *vir.*[8])

Sacrifice must be sufficiently distinguished from other categories of putting to death, such as hunting or eating, accidental or criminal death. It must indicate a surplus over necessity. It must do more than assuage hunger, punish, or keep the peace. It must also indicate more than that "more" or surplus over necessity that we regard as (mere) leisure. Sacrifice cannot simply be the equivalent of gladiatorial battles or hunting. And as the sixteenth-century Spanish theologian Francisco de Vitoria insists:

> The oxen which are butchered in the slaughterhouse do not become a sacrifice because the butcher says he intended to kill them for the love of God; nor, then, can condemned criminals be sacrificed, lawfully or unlawfully, because to sacrifice a man to God, properly speaking, means to kill him for that reason alone. (1991a, 214)

Distinctions between the scaffold, the slaughterhouse, and the temple must be rigidly maintained. Conversely all the accoutrements of rite and temple and complex and specialized vocabularies and terminologies peculiar to sacrifice guard the distinction between sacrifice and other types of death.

Divine presence is particularly intense and incontrovertible (that is, particularly necessary) around human sacrifice, for human sacrifice is an extreme wager on divine presence: the boldest assertion of "putting to death as a denegation of murder" and a "justification of putting to death" (Derrida 1995, 283). Only the presence of God/the gods guarantees the distinction between sacrifice and murder. If the gods were to retreat or die or fade from the arena of human sacrifice, the sacrificers would be left as murderers. If they were to retreat or die or fade from the scene of animal sacrifice, the sacrificers would be left (far less controversially) as cooks.

Human sacrifice appears as particularly (exceptionally) holy and substantial because the risks of demystification or the withdrawal of the gods are so intense. Animal sacrifice can far more easily slide into everyday behavior—preparing a meal—which is why a whole elaborate vocabulary develops to keep the two apart. In the Greek "cuisine of sacrifice," con-

8. Human sacrifice is more naturally (which is to say, of course, artificially) attached to women and specifically virgin daughters, as Iphigenia, Poyxenia, and Jephthah's daughter know only too well.

sumable meat comes from ritually slaughtered animals and the *mageiros* is both butcher and sacrificer.[9] Similarly, the priests of Leviticus are expected to have great skill in filleting the body of the animal, separating the fat tail from the kidneys, slicing off the appendage of the liver, siphoning off all blood, and pouring it around the altar (see, e.g., Lev 7). But because there is potentially no distinction, an intricate system of differentiation divides priests from butchers and human from divine. Sacrifice is marked by complex rituals and instructions that cannot simply be understood as recipes because (1) they involve acts that are entirely superfluous to the finished product such as placing one's hand on the sacrificial victim prior to sacrifice; (2) they involve "waste" or dedication to God and/or the priests.

Sacrifice is always, insistently, cooking-plus or cooking-minus. It involves acts of preparation that clearly exceed the needs of eating, and deliberate acts of losing, giving up. This is particularly clear in the Biblical Hebrew עלה and ancient Greek ὁλόκαυστος (holocaust; from ὅλος "whole" + καυστός "burnt"), where a whole animal (or firstborn son) is completely consumed by fire. Even (especially) in acts of sacrifice that tempt the sense of a shared meal or communion between divine and human, the division between God and man is clearly marked on the body of the animal and the ritual of consumption. "All the fat belongs to YHWH" (Lev 3:16–17; cf. 7:23–25). YHWH takes the fat that surrounds the entrails, the blood, the two kidneys, and the fat tail in the case of sheep. The priests take the skin (7:8) and the breast and the right thigh. These parts are given the specialist terms תנופה and the תרומה, which are clearly not simply the equivalent of "sirloin" or "shank" (7:28–34; 10:14–15).[10] Alternatively, according to Deut 18:3, the priest should receive the shoulder, the cheeks, and the stomach. The distinctions might be fluid, but what is important is that the distinctions are clearly incised and separations made. Those scoundrel priests, the sons of Eli, are condemned for not observing the complex sequence and structure of division. They send their servants to plunge a fork into the cauldron and give them *all* the meat brought up by the fork, without first observing the ritual of burning the fat before the Lord (1 Sam 2:12–17).

The mode of consumption incises even more clearly fundamental distinctions between human, animal and divine. As implied in the sacrifi-

9. For the *mageiros* as "butcher-cook-sacrificer," see Detienne 1989, 11.

10. Roland de Vaux suggests that the two words are influenced by the juridical language of Mesopotamia and signify, respectively, "levy" and "contribution" (1964, 32; following Driver 1956).

cial term אשה connected with אש (Lev 1:9, 13, 17; Deut 18:1; Josh 13:14; 1 Sam 2:28; etc.), and also the term עלה, referring either to the victim that "ascends" to the altar or the smoke that "ascends" to God (de Vaux 1964, 27), YHWH takes his food as savor or smoke. A similar distinction is made in Hesiod's account of Prometheus and the first blood sacrifice. The men eat the flesh of an ox while the gods consume the altogether more numinous "food" (distinctly in quotation marks) of the smoke of the charred bones and the perfume of the herbs thrown into the fire. Men condemned to hunger and death eat flesh destined for corruption; God/the gods eat a more numinous and invisible "food" (firmly set apart in quotation marks) in the formless form of aroma and smoke. God's delight in the pleasing odor of Noah's sacrifice (Gen 8:21; cf. Lev 1:9, 13, 17; Ezek 6:13, 19; 20:28) might imply a gross anthropomorphism: a God like the children in the old *Bisto* advert, smelling the gravy and looking forward to a chicken dinner; or, less anachronistically, a borrowing from the gods of the Gilgamesh Epic who "smell the sweet savor" and "crowd round like flies" (Sanders 1960, 108–13). But the emphasis on *olfactory* pleasure is totally consistent with the pattern of Gen 1–11. Prohibited and nonprohibited foods (from certain fruit trees to the blood that contains the "life"); acceptable and unacceptable sexual partners (other human beings, not Nephilim); decreasing longevity; and real food versus food-as-smoke or smell, enforce the fundamental (and threatened) distinction between human and divine.

3. Second Incision/Distinction: The One Who Sacrifices Is Man

Just as the gods are affirmed, as well as praised and assuaged, by sacrifice, so the answer to the question, Who/what offers sacrifice? comes back with satisfying self-affirming clarity as another "who"—Man (that agent who intends; that "who" who uniquely has the right to be a "who" and who shares the prerogative of proper names with the gods). Sacrifice is easily grafted onto the list of all those capabilities (*pouvoirs*) or attributes (*avoirs*), transitivities or activities by which man has been distinguished (cf. Derrida 2002, 395). This massive, anxious, and expanding inventory includes the ability to reason; to write; to speak; to invent a technique; to construct a whole range of edifices including cities, laws, industries and commerce; to promise; to enter into contracts; to give; to bury one's dead; and to cook (e.g., Aristotle, *Pol.* 1328b 6–22; Gen 4). Kitchens and dining tables (or their equivalents) feature among the key proofs of the "proper" of "man." According to Aristotle, the idea of "man" is stored and protected by what he does with his food: from collecting and storing it to cooking it. Whereas animals merely forage on the surface of the planet, men build, dig, transform, cook, and "fill up" the deficiencies of nature (*Pol.* 1337a 2). This unique capability or ability is aided by the unique pliability of the hand, which can be "talon, hoof and horn at will" (*Part. an.* 4.10 [687b3–4) and, by extension, by all those prostheses and extensions of the hand that we call utensils and tools.

The amplitude of sacrifice and the artifacts of sacrifice seem designed to showcase man's unique abilities and capabilities, and specifically his ability to manipulate life through the works of those wonderful hands. Genesis 22 is a basic sacrifice text, the very opposite of the priestly excess and precision of Leviticus. It concentrates all our attention on the rudiments of sacrifice. Abraham's primitive sacrifice kit is made up of "knife," "fire," and "wood." This is the elementary stuff of sacrifice. It showcases basic technology: fire and smelting. They foreground the invention of knife (or axe) that makes the crucial cut between "man" and the "animals," living their paw-to-mouth or hoof-to-mouth existence. From the rudimentary sacrifices of Genesis, sacrifice burgeons into a complex *technē*, stridently insisting on the proper of man. *Only man*, the logic goes, has the technology to fashion cauldrons and altars and tabernacles and temples with all their precise measurements and clearly demarcated spatial subzones. *Only man* has the discrimination to differentiate between priests (and various hierarchies of priests) and nonpriests, animals with and without blemish. *Only man* has the dexterity to effect such a precise filleting of the animal designed to distinguish the elaborate ritual of sacrifice from the consumption of flesh by animals in the wild. (The Bible gives us several vivid images of wild animals devouring, not eating, such as the lion with "two legs and a piece of an ear" draping from his open maw [Amos 3:12].) *Only man* could orchestrate such complex rituals as pouring the blood around the altar and placing the quarters of flesh on the altar together with separated entrails, the head, the fat, and the feet. *Only man* has the ability to so precisely execute the divine template or "pattern" of the tabernacle and all its furniture (Exod 25:9) from the table for the bread of the Presence (made of acacia wood, overlaid in pure gold with a rim a handbreadth wide and a molding around the rim) to the mercy seat, adorned with two cherubim of gold made from "hammered work," with precise dimensions of two cubits and a half length, and a cubit and a half wide (25:17–25). In an alternative textual blueprint for the tabernacle, God seems to favor an altar of earth and rough (emphatically not "hewn") stone, and forbids man from using chisels lest he profane it (20:24–26). God makes a point of telling man to put the chisels down, knowing that he cannot help himself from taking up a chisel or pipette.

The fine-tuned materiality of tabernacle/temple is designed as a showcase not primarily for the glory of God (which may be secondary) but the spectacular *technē* of man. It asserts the "only man" even more stridently than it asserts the "only God" of putative monotheism. Other gods have sacrifices, priests, and altars. But only man among the living can offer sacrifices and make altars. The whole elaborate edifice of sacrifice (and all its accoutrements) asserts, again and again, the uniqueness of "Only man can … " and "Only man is…." The figure of Bezalel serves God and serves man, as a figure of hyperman. As a sign of the fullest realization of the *pouvoirs* (possibilities and powers) of man, he excels in "ability, intelligence, and knowledge in every kind of craft" (Exod 31:3).

Equally excelling—and graphically so—are the writers-craftsmen who have preserved all those voluminous records of sacrifice, carefully inscribing "graduated purification offerings" (Milgrom 2004, 46) and complex taxonomies and (permeable) distinctions between נדבה, תדה, זבח, אשה, אזכרה, מנחה, קרבן, עלה, and שלמים.[11] The voluminous scripts and crypts of sacrifice—more enduring than the material structures they claim to preserve—perhaps do not serve as a record of actual practice, any more than the generation of the wilderness wanderings actually constructed a portable temple. Rather they amply proclaim man's unique powers of writing, memory, and speech. Man obsessively attempts to make sense of sacrifice in a vast textual overlay, amplifying and subdividing sacrifice into complex linguistic and social functions such as fulfilling contracts, promising, assuaging guilt (this being subdivided into, say, gradated forms of remorse, expiation, and confession), or proving guilt, or remembering guilt or declaring jealousy (cf. Num 5:15). Thus man demonstrates his sense of puzzlement over sacrifice, as if what he does were somehow in excess over what he can write or say about it. He also showcases yet more of his unique abilities, such as seeking goods for the future (thereby demonstrating other unique abilities such as to think in conditional and future tenses) or his ability to be grateful, jealous, guilty, to sin, and to lie/deceive. Sacrifice becomes a, if not the, foundation stone

11. De Vaux among others comments on the "fluidity of the vocabulary relating to sacrifices" (1964, 30).

of universal "religion"—and as Lactantius (the Christian advisor to Constantine) put it, supplementing Aristotle, "*if not the only, yet certainly the greatest difference between men and the beasts consists in religion*" (*Inst.* 2.1–3; *ANF* 7:40–41, 44, emphasis added).[12] It is ridiculous and superfluous to assert that "*certainly the greatest difference between men and the gods consists in religion.*" Sacrifice and religion are, by definition, not required of gods or beasts.

4. Third Incision/Distinction: The Material of Sacrifice Is the Animal or That Which Feeds/Serves the Life of Man

If the addressee of sacrifice is "god" and the sacrificer is "man" (two firm gradations in the "who," one beneath the other), the answer to the question, Who/What is sacrificed? comes back overwhelmingly on the side of "what." In the hierarchies cut by sacrifice the most appropriate objects of sacrifice are those deemed living in the Heideggerian sense of *nur-lebenden*: life pure and simple without proper names, without anything other than the species names given by Adam. The raw material of sacrifice comprises those raw life-forms that we have herded into the enclosure of the definite article as "the animal," as if "the animal" were the linguistic equivalent of a "virgin forest, a zoo, a hunting or fishing ground, a paddock or an abattoir, a space of domestication" into which we corral "all living things that man does not recognize as his fellows, his neighbors, or his brothers" (Derrida 2002, 400)—or at least as we have done since the late fourteenth century when, in English, the "animals" (from Latin *animal,* from *anima* "breath/soul") invaded and drove out the "beasts" (402).

In theory, everything lower than man in the hierarchy of being is available for sacrifice: vegetables, plant life, minerals. But unlike the Maya in pre-Hispanic Mesoamerica,[13] the biblical and classical traditions do not assert a confluence between flesh and vegetable being or an equivalence

12. Lactantius explains that religion, as the proper of man, is related to the supposed derivation of *anthrōpos* from ἄνω τρέπω ὤψ, "turn the face upward," and the status of man as biped, not quadruped. Those who do not look upward and worship "deny themselves, and renounce the name of man."

13. In the *Books of Chilam Balam*, *balche* is described as "the green blood of my daughter," cassava as the "thigh of the earth." The equation between the human, vegetable, and divine becomes most intense in the conflation of man, god, and maize. See Clendinnen 1987, esp. 137 and 153.

between sap and blood. In the Bible, "all flesh is [like] grass" (Isa 40:6–8) but only metaphorically, not (so to speak) economically. The two are not equivalent terms. Blood is prioritized and valorized as the stuff of sacrifice, and sacrifice is the sacrifice of life or the stuff that feeds life: that which serves as food for man.

The Vegetable Lamb of Tartary (illustration from Lee 1887).

This fundamental separation between blood and sap structures the "Western" imaginary. The borders between man and god are porous and regularly crossed. Far more sturdy are the barriers separating animals, men, and divinities from plants. Hence the deep fascination with the curio imported to Europe by the medieval armchair travelogue Sir John Mandeville's *Travels*: the fabulous "Vegetable Lamb of Tartary," or "Scythian Lamb"—a gourd that splits open to reveal a little lamb.[14]

The vegetable lamb makes the Agnus Dei look like a domesticated, tame commonplace by comparison. Crossing the borders between animal/man/god and plant is far more transgressive in the Western imaginary than the standardized and canonized border crossing between human, animal, and divine. God can become man, or even lamb, without us batting an eye. And this because blood, spirit, soul constitute

14. Sir John Mandeville reports: "There grows [in the kingdom called Cadhilhe, probably Korea] a kind of fruit as big as gourds, and when it is ripe men open it and find inside an animal of flesh and blood and bone, like a little lamb without wool. And the people of that land eat the animal, and the fruit too" (2005, 165). For the theory that these hybrid plant-animals derive from the strange fleecy appearance of cotton, see Lee 1887. For a menagerie of Scythian lambs and other strange zoophytes see http://cerebralboinkfest.blogspot.com/2012/01/vegetable-lamb-of-tartary.html.

a shared artery or community of life. It is far more outlandish and heretical—indeed, the very stuff of blasphemy—to imagine God-as-cabbage, or man-as-cabbage, or even God as "ass" (a far less conventionally symbolic form of "animal") or stone.[15] (God/man really dies—and forever—in the sense that he becomes impossibly other to himself when he turns into cabbage or stone.) In his *Journey to the Moon* of 1657, the French freethinker Cyrano de Bergerac (1619–1655) conjured a lunatic lunar world where the priests of the moon lamented the pain of the cabbage, and saw the ultimate sacrifice as that of the cabbage. De Bergerac went for the jugular of the Christian tradition when he argued that the "sin of cutting a cabbage and depriving it of life" was worse than "murdering a man," since a man can look forward to eternal life while the poor cabbage has an unressurectable "soul" (2007, 79–80).

The classical and biblical traditions and all the "Western" symbolic structures erected on them cannot imagine the sacrifice of the inorganic, the inert, insensate, unchanging: the kind of stuff that does not even imitate life, does not feed life, does not get cooked, does not qualify as food. The Spanish Jesuit José de Acosta (1539–1600) was unsure as to which Andean practice was more scandalous: human sacrifice or the sacrifice of desultory objects such as chewed coca, feathers, used shoes, or stones.[16] The same logic that makes nonsense of inorganic cookery makes it ludicrous to contemplate the sacrifice of shoes or stones. (Though note the tantalizing recipe for malachite burgers on the hilarious "inorganic cookery" website: "4 slices Welsh slate; 1 kg malachite. Cut the slates in two. [Use a trowel for this. Oxy-acetylene cutters cause the slate to crumble.] Break up the malachite with a sledgehammer. Divide the malachite equally among four slates and cover with the remaining four. Bake at 1200 degrees centigrade for 12 hours by which time the malachite should be a beautiful bubbly green. Cool and eat. Excellent for picnics as they can be pre-

15. Compare §8 below.

16. José de Acosta writes, "And because such absurd things are their gods the objects they offer them in worship are equally absurd. When they travel they are wont to toss onto the roads or at crossroads, on the hills, and especially on the peaks that they call *apachitas* old shoes and feathers and chewed coca. … And when they have nothing else they will toss a stone. … Such folly is like that employed by the ancients, of whom it is said in the Book of Proverbs, 'As he that casteth a stone into the heap of Mercury, so is he that giveth honor to a fool'" (2002, 262).

pared the century before. A dry gritty flavor."[17]) The theologian Francisco de Vitoria (1492–1546) was sure that sacrifice would be disqualified as sacrifice should one attempt to give something like (and the examples are hardly accidental) "*stones or sand*" (1991a, 215). To Vitoria and Acosta's christianized and biblicized minds, stones and sand fail to meet basic sacrificial criteria for two reasons. They are too plentiful, hence not costly. More importantly, they are incapable of transformation: digestive or sacrificial. Stones and sand are inorganic, dead already: they do not change. A grain of sand is the opposite of the grain of seed that "dies" and regenerates/resurrects and that is used as a trope for the sacrificial fecundity of the body of Christ (John 12:24; 1 Cor 15:36) alongside the bread that stands in as the body of Christ as the cooked counterpart of grain.

Leviticus prescribes a clear hierarchy of sacrificial gifts: for a sin offering a lamb, but if one cannot afford a lamb, then two turtledoves or two pigeons; or if even turtledoves or pigeons are beyond your means, a tenth of an ephah of fine flour (Lev 5). The sacrificial edifice is centered on the gift of life. Blood is a higher index of the gift of life because blood is life (e.g., Gen 9:4). The sacrifice of grain or firstfruits signifies a gift of a portion (perhaps a self-jeopardizing portion?) of that which sustains life. But distinctions are made between cereal and blood offerings. Cereals are often described as a concession to the poor. They are supplemented with oil and frankincense, as if to say that these gifts are particularly in need of enhancement. The higher sacrifices are those of blood and flesh: a turtle dove, a pigeon, or a lamb. God himself seems to share this inbuilt prejudice of sacrifice. In the first primal sacrifice (just prior to the inventory of the invention of those staples of human construction—tents, agriculture, bronze and iron tools, lyres and pipes and cities), God inexplicably turns his nose up at the vegetable and fruit offerings of Cain and instead inhales the odor of flesh, offered by the firstborn cattle of Abel, the rancher. The implication is that the best sacrifice, like the best food, is the flesh of bulls and sheep: the body of that which is most directly beneath man, closest to man without crossing the border into "man."

The hierarchy of sacrifice imitates the hierarchy of food, as drawn up by Aristotle and the Bible: at the top, cooked meats,[18] a sure sign of

17. "Inorganic Cookery"; online: http://www.cs.st-andrews.ac.uk/~norman/Shorts/inorganic/html#4.3.2).

18. Cooked meat is often taken as an index of the fully human. For Aquinas the age of natural law was the age of vegetarians; the modern age, the age of cooked meat

zōon politikon, or civilized man; next, raw meat and vegetables (for Aristotle, the food of the animal and the "barbarian" or "natural slave"); and sprawling and crawling and wriggling underneath at the bottom of the pile, the insects and reptiles that crawl among the stones—the demurral from which marks the privilege of "man" through the refined palate and squeamishness of man.[19] Sacrifice is typically an extremely detailed, complicated *technē*, marked by refinement. Structures of sacrifice delineate the delicacy and rarity of the category of God, just as a refined menu marks out the delicacy of the stomach of civilized man.

Though staple diets in "ancient Israel" were more flatbread and grain than milk and honey, the level of precision and qualification around sacrifice suggests something more akin to the third-century Roman cookbook *Apici Caeli de Re Coquinaria*, or the technical precision of modern restaurants with a coveted Michelin star (see Million 1926; McDonald 2008). YHWH has his own reserved table—"the table of YHWH"—on which are placed sacrificial offerings as YHWH's food (Ezek 44:7, 16; Mal 1:7, 12; Lev 21:6, 8; 22:25; Num 28:2). The meal starts with a breadbasket: the "showbread" or personal loaves of YHWH are laid on the table and renewed every Sabbath (Lev 24:5–9). The cereal offering (as side dish to the communion sacrifice and the holocaust) comprises bread, oil, and wine, the staple diet in ancient Palestine (Num 15:1–2; cf. Exod 29:40; Lev 23:13) (de Vaux 1964, 39–40; Anderson 1987, 15). But even here the basics of the breadbasket are qualified and finessed. Cereals must be without leaven and without honey but with oil and frankincense. They must never be sacrificed or served without salt (Lev 2:13; cf. Ezek 43:24). Precise quantities (not to mention jointing techniques) are outlined: one ephah of fine flour, two pigeons or two doves. Not only are sacrificed animals corralled into a fairly precise and particular subsection of that ludicrously vast category, "the animal," but they must be perfect—emphatically (and

eaters. See *Summa Theologiae* 1a2ae, arts. 1–4. Vitoria expresses the commonplace view that Gen 9:4, "But flesh with the life thereof, which is the blood thereof, ye shall not eat," is about "God show[ing] the natural custom for eating meat, that is to say cooked not raw, since any other custom is barbarous and savage" (1991a, 209).

19. All winged insects are "detestable" for food, except the locust, the bald locust, the cricket, and the grasshopper (Lev 11:20–23). That grasshoppers are not offered on the altar suggests that all winged insects are well beneath the mouth, nose, and stomach of God.

apophatically?) *not* "any animal that is blemished by a wen, scurvy, or scab" (Lev 22:19–24).

Like a form of negative theology, delineating God by what he is not, sacrifice is a kind of negative gustation, positing the delicacy of the category of god by itemizing all the hares, pigs, rock badgers, crustaceans, weasels, mice, crocodiles, lizards, chameleons, eagles, camels, ostriches, nighthawks, owls, water hens, pelicans, vultures, herons, hoopoes, or bats (etc.) that cannot be countenanced as food or sacrifice. It is as if the regulations were there to poke fun at the ludicrously infinite space of "the animal" (though חיה and בהמה do not map precisely onto that all-encompassing term "the animal"), like Derrida mocking the absurd cramming together of the lizard and the dog, the protozoon and the dolphin, the camel and the eagle, the squirrel, tiger, elephant, hedgehog, silkworm, and cat in a fantasy of cohabitation as bizarre as "Noah's ark" (2002a, 402). Indeed, the category of "sacrificial animals" is more plausible than Noah's ark because wild animals are excluded. (The comedian Eddie Izzard is not the only one to have imagined the carnage and havoc that would have ensued if all animals had indeed been admitted to Noah's ark.[20])

Traditions of Greek and biblical sacrifice firmly separate categories of "hunting" and "sacrificing" by excluding wild animals. None of the wild animals paraded in the circus of chaos and untamability at the end of Job (no Behemoths or Leviathans) are to be sacrificed and eaten except under apocalyptic/messianic conditions, where different rules apply. The only animals available for sacrifice and eating are those that man nominates and dominates back in Genesis: birds of the air, beasts of the field. The field of life, חיה, is carefully sliced and subdivided: one can sacrifice the creatures called, overlappingly, חיה and בהמה, sometimes birds עוף,[21] but definitely not רמש. Sacrificial animals come from the field, not the forest or the desert. Out of bounds are all those outside the bounds of domestication/cultivation. A key factor is possession: as Adam names, so man sacrifices *his* animals, and in the process makes them "his." He attests that the victim belongs to him by placing his hand on the animal's head. By placing his hand on the head of the animal, man asserts the distinctiveness of the category of animal and stridently (and defensively) keeps the object of sacrifice separate, saving and reserving man qua man.

20. In one of Izzard's many riffs on Noah's ark, a traumatized rabbit escapes as lone survivor and reports death-boat carnage on board the ark.

21. In the historical narratives the sacrifice of birds is never mentioned.

5. First Doubling of Life: Man on the Altar and Lack as Man's Distinctive Power

As already mentioned, the very word *sacrifice*, from *sacer facere*, "making sacred," may be a distraction, insofar as the chief object and focus of sacrifice is man. Man is the only one who becomes "one" and (consolidated) through sacrifice, since the fires of sacrifice keep multiple gods alive. But man is arguably even more of an anxious and volatile being than "the gods." The act of placing one's head on the animal, offering up the animal, becomes a graphic example of the anthropological machine that produces *humanitas*, like a hologram, by deciding, at every moment, every sacrifice, between the animal and man (cf. Agamben 2004, 77). *The distinction must be insisted on because the collapse of the distinction is implicit, if not explicit, in the very logic of sacrifice required to produce and sustain the uniqueness of man*. The subject of sacrifice easily slips into the object of the sacrifice in the phrase "the sacrifice of man." Just as a turtledove has a higher sacrificial value than cereal and a lamb a higher sacrificial value than a turtledove, so, extending this economic logic upward, the most perfect sacrifice is logically that creature on the upper edge of the category of the animal: "man." As the Spanish Dominican Bartolomé de las Casas (1484–1566) put it in a dangerous attempt to theorize Aztec and Christian sacrifice as different expressions of the same basic sacrificial grammar, "sacrifice … offer[s] what is best and [most] perfect." In a scholastic thought experiment he asserts that, since angels are the most perfect category of being, then we should sacrifice angels (1974, 226). But angels are not appropriate material for sacrifice. This is not because, on the Aristotelian-Thomist principle that God/nature inclines toward the most perfect, God makes more angels than men and hence angels are less rare sacrificial offerings than men. The problem is not that angels are as common (and hence valueless) as stones or sand. Rather, they are not appropriate material for sacrifice because they are too immaterial.[22] The role of angels as "frontiersmen" crossing the boundaries between earth and heaven (Caseau 1996, 335)

22. So las Casas: "The greatest way to worship god is to offer him sacrifice. This is the unique act by which we show him to whom we offer the sacrifice that we are subject to him and grateful to him. Furthermore, nature teaches that it is just to offer God, whose debtors we are for so many reasons, those things that are precious and excellent. … But according to human judgement and truth, nothing in nature is greater or more valuable than the life of man or man himself" (1974, 234).

comes to an abrupt halt at the altar, that place of mediation between earth and heaven prohibited to angels. God may have a taste for the smoke of burning animal food, but he does not like the numinous "nonbodies" of angels. Even though they hang out at the other end of the spectrum of being, angels are like stones or sand because that they do not change, they do not bleed, and they do not die.

Sacrifice bleeds into human sacrifice; it leads inexorably to human sacrifice at the upper limit of the gift of death, the gift of those who have the ability/inability to die. This is the first doubling over, or fold, in the hierarchies that sacrifice cuts in life, scoring the distinctions between human, animal, and man. There is no distinction between man and animal in the ability to die, to become a corpse. All flesh (כל בשר) is like grass, and all those fantasies of man's dominion—all those acts of naming the animals, placing one's hands on the head of the animals—can be read as defense mechanisms against the truth of the human animal, as meat, as dust. In the Hebrew Bible humans, like animals, are animated, for a short time, by the battery of life, נפש (which has not yet attained the unique humanity of "soul"), and there is no distinction between corpse and carcass (the dead bodies of humans *and* animals can both be referred to as נבלה or מפלת). But in another sense, only human beings have being-toward-death; only humans have the ability/inability "to die."

But this also means that the uniqueness of man is based not on ability, *pouvoir*, but on privation, lack. This is the point that Derrida makes in his discussion of Protagoras's version of the myth of Prometheus, which is also the myth of the discovery of that fundamental of sacrifice: fire. In Derrida's gloss, "Prometheus steals fire, that is to say the arts and technics, in order to make up for the forgetfulness or tardiness of Epimetheus who had perfectly equipped all breeds of animal but left man naked, without shoes, covering or arms" (2002a, 389). Unlike the animals, man is naked—as of course he is exposed as being in Gen 3 and again in Gen 9. In his brief reading of the primal history, Derrida focuses on all the hunting, lying, sinning, and killing, and all the prostheses and technics (cities, clothes, tools) with which—with God's help and never alone—man supplements the nakedness and vulnerability that are the proper of man. As he summarizes the Prometheus myth, blurring into Genesis:

> From within the pit of that lack, an eminent lack, a quite different lack from that he assigns to the animal, man installs or claims in a single moment *what is proper to him* [the peculiarity of a man whose property

> is not to have anything that is exclusively his] and his superiority over what is called animal life. This last superiority, infinite and par excellence, has as its property the fact of being at one and the same time unconditional and *sacrificial.* (389)

I want to follow the implications of that "unconditional and sacrificial" that Derrida leaves hanging. (He thinks, therefore *je suis.*) The assertion that man's superiority is unconditional and sacrificial references the philosophical quest for the unconditional, the *unbedingt*, the universal, the essential. The superiority of man to the animal is the essential of man, that which cannot be qualified. But it is also *sacrificial* in the sense that it is giving up, ceding, its essence and its superiority all the time. More than this, much more than this, we can say that *the essential of man is sacrificial*: it has to do with givings-up, lacks that are not essential to the animal. The proper of man is sacrifice: sacrifice as a sign of the nakedness and deficit that is intrinsic and essential to man.

What is essential to man is sacrifice as the very opposite of the "power of capability [*pouvoirs*] or attributes [*avoirs*]" (cf. Derrida 2002a, 395) by which man is traditionally distinguished from the animal. Though it can be read as an index of construction (the discovery of iron and fire, the uniqueness of hands in wielding tools, etc.), sacrifice more obviously indicates an infinity of needs requiring supplements: the *nonpouvoir* or nonpower at the heart of power. Crucial to sacrifice is the ability to suffer, to "not be able." Sacrifice—that is, structures and theories of sacrifice—are all constructed around this helplessness, this not-being-able, this (to return to Derrida) "pit of lack." Whether a sacrifice is instituted and theorized as an act of expiation, purification, atonement, gratitude, communion, or gift (with expected return such as rain or secure crops in the future), sacrifice overtly performs the limit of the *pouvoir*/power that is the proper of man. All those complex constructions or rationales for sacrifice are declensions of the same fundamental: the lack in man signified in the unique ability to be grateful for that without which he would otherwise be naked, or to confess, purify, solicit, seek. Lactantius's declaration that "*the greatest difference between men and the beasts consists in religion*" (Lactantius, *Inst.* 2.1–3; *ANF* 7:40–41, 44, emphasis added) places man in the unique place of worship, thanks, and deficit in which he is alone among the animals, while creating a shared place (outside religion, outside law) for gods and beasts.

6. Second Doubling of Life: Man Follows the Animal to the Altar—and, Equally, the Animal Follows Man

Derrida's title "The Animal That Therefore I Am" ("*L'Animal que donc je suis*") puns on the Cartesian tradition and on the double meaning of *suis*, from *être* and *suivre*, "to be" and "to follow," respectively. The ontological question is also temporal: Who or what comes first in the parade or chronology or conceptualization of the living? (The original article added a parenthetical "[*à suivre* (more to follow)]," insisting that there is much more to come, much more to life, than the reduction to the animal and that speaking animal who distinguishes himself from it/them by saying "I.") Histories of sacrifice graphically enact precisely this temporal and structural ambiguity. Who follows whom (or what) to the altar? Does the evolution of sacrifice go in a (so to speak) Darwinian or Linnaean direction, from animal to man—or vice versa? Who is aping who/what in sacrifice? Do cattle/sheep/goats stand in for the firstborn, or does man *singe le bouc*, "ape the lamb"?[23] One strident etiology of animal sacrifice tells how early societies began with a natural inclination toward human sacrifice, which was then downgraded or commuted to animal sacrifice. In the now commonplace (and quintessentially Modern) interpretation of Abraham's sacrifice, the text (allegedly) testifies to the widespread sacrifice of human beings in primitive societies, then shows the lucky dawn of human civilization as God patiently reveals to Abraham how to substitute a son with a ram.

This swerve away from human sacrifice is crucial to a certain teleology of the political and the civil. The force of the argument is that the transformation from human to animal sacrifice represents salvation from raw, untamed life and a state of primal danger. Human sacrifice represents arbitrary bloodshed, uncontrolled and untamed force not unlike that Hobbesian state of primal cruelty where *lupus est homo homini* ("man is a wolf to man"). Animal sacrifice, like government, is a strategy of containment and safety. So is the distinction between man and animal. The turn to animal sacrifice becomes a crucial staging post in the transition to civilization

---

23. The phrase *singer le bouc*, "aping the scapegoat" or "aping the lamb," is taken from Derrida 2006, 148. James Watts has some interesting reflections on the ease with which ancient traditions seem to "view humans and animals as, at some level, interchangeable," as opposed to the modern tendency to separate the two in evolutionary narratives (from animal to human, or vice versa) (2007, 178–79).

and the structures and signs of full humanity. Like the consolidated, corporate sovereignty represented by Hobbes's *Leviathan*, the transformation of sacrifice (to animal sacrifice, then sacrifice as sign) marks the evolution of Man qua Man. Man became fully man when he learned that to sacrifice other men was a category mistake, the act of a savage or barbarian, an act from which man must repent in order to become fully man. Derrida adds a mischievous gloss to this act of repentance and substitution: "Abraham's ass or ram or the living beasts that Abel offered to God; they know what is about to happen to them when man says 'Here I am' to God, then consent to sacrifice themselves, to sacrifice their sacrifice or to forgive themselves" (2002a, 399). The comment relies on the humorous category mistake of the wise animal, the knowing animal, the animal "who" has read his way through the archives of sacrifice and wearily gets on the altar with an ironic smile.

The spectacle of an animal standing in for man teaches man the technology of writing, based on one thing indicating another, standing in for another. By moving beyond human sacrifice, man learns to read and write and wield signs. This evolutionary learning process leads inexorably to the even better sacrifice of "sacrifice": sacrifice metaphorized, ethicized, interiorized. As the gross material of sacrifice was turned into smoke, so gradually *and inevitably* (so the story goes) real cows changed into the exquisitely verbalized and textualized offering of the "cows of the lips" (so Hos 14:3 MT [ET 2]; cf. Heb 13:15 [quoting Hos 14:3 LXX]).

But the temporal and conceptual schema also goes in the other direction. The "I" follows the animal to the altar. Sacrifice tends toward and ends up with the human—whether this movement is negatively or positively construed. Porphyry laments how a golden age of true sacrifice, originally confined to leaves, roots, and the shoots of plants, fell into the degeneracy of animal sacrifice, which then led to the even worse depravity of human sacrifice (Martin 2007, 25). Positively, and making the same point, a *tafsīr* on the qur'anic version of Ibrahim's sacrifice tells how Ibrahim first sacrificed a bull, but God demanded something greater; so he sacrificed a camel, but God demanded something greater: only then did he realize that he was to sacrifice the most precious thing, that is, the son (al-Kisai, *Qisas al-Anbiya*; as cited in Firestone 1990, 124–25). The "Isaac" and "Ishmael" figures in Genesis Rabbah may be competitors, but they agree that sacrifice naturally evolves by expanding rather than contracting. In a midrashic prologue to the sacrifice of Isaac/Ishmael, they compete over who has shed the most blood to date in a conversation that assumes that

(1) circumcision is a microform of human sacrifice, and (2) circumcision shows less devotion than the gift of the blood from a whole human body (Gen. Rab. 55:4).

7. Third Doubling of Life: Sacrifice as an Uncomfortable Revelation of Divine Lack

Just as sacrifice erects—and collapses—the always precarious distinction between man and animal, so it erects and jeopardizes the distinction at man's other edge, between the human and the divine. Sacrifice is the rite that holds the divine in place most securely. Sacrifice preserves and purifies God through the insistent logic that man would only sacrifice to the one who is god, or believed to be god. But sacrifice is also a key site for (to use Derrida's term from "Faith and Knowledge" [2002c]), a self-attacking *autoimmune* response. Danger lurks at the heart of a system where blood and flesh qua "life" most profoundly substantiate god and the gods. The very structure or machine of sacrifice threatens God/the gods with the ignominy of eating, or (to put the same point in a more displaced or symbolic form) having the kind of life that is parasitic/dependent on other forms of life. There is a threat of "communion,"[24] of collapse of distinction, which cannot be exorcised by all those anxious distinctions between God/gods who smell or inhale sacrificial smoke (Exod 24; Gen 8:21; 1 Sam 26:19) and men who eat and die. Biblical attempts to give God a nose but not a mouth—or at least only the speaking, noneating kind of mouth—graphically illustrate the inadequacy of attempts to stop the slow drip of anthropomorphism. It is as if they want to prevent, once and for all, a rudimentary or alimentary understanding of sacrifice. But God cannot be protected from this by having just a nose and no eating-mouth or bowels. Subsequent interpreters will find even "the nose of God" too vulgar and will react against such crude anthropomorphisms. But "the nose of God" is not simply a slip of the tongue made by some cultural primitive who has not yet attained a properly platonized or ethicized understanding of God/

24. For scholars like William Robertson Smith, the notion of communion sacrifice—stressing the *uniting* of god and worshipper—comes to dominate the whole field of sacrifice. Thus "the leading idea of the animal sacrifices of the Semites … was not that of a gift made over to the god, but of an act of communion, in which the god and his worshipper unite by partaking of the flesh and blood of the sacred victim" (1907, 226–27).

the gods. Rather, it graphically demonstrates the structural impossibility of guarding ontotheology around the altar, or making gods the absolute Other of man. Even if one rarifies the structure of sacrifice further, it still suggests some kind of lack or need in God, even if that only appears quasi-psychologically rather than in the rudimentary-alimentary form of a God needing food to keep himself alive.

In Lacan's remarkable reading of Abraham's sacrifice, even (perhaps especially) gods cannot be free of the lack that is not just lack of something—some need, like some need for food—but the far more voracious force of desire, the *manque-à-être* that demands the "unconditional yes." In one of the most astute readings of the story, albeit wrapped up in some hilariously pompous claptrap and some deeply conventional errors, Lacan reads God's demand for the offering of the son as the anxious desire of a divided subject "haunted" (like all of us) by "absence and lack," and looking to the other not simply to supply his needs but to pay him the compliment of *an unconditional yes* (Lacan 2001).[25] He loves to expose the exposure of the divine, to show that "El Shadday" (as he puts it, having mugged up on his Hebrew) is not "Allmighty." Derrida follows Lacan in his pursuit of the motif of the God who repents/regrets (for example, in the coda to the flood, and the narrative of Cain and Abel). He also follows Lacan in his use of the "*je suis*" (I am/I follow), which Lacan applies to the divine "I am."

This gesture cannot be dismissed as a contemporary "psychoanalytic" or "deconstructive" move, easily made by those who are not particularly devoted to safeguarding the reputation of deities. On the contrary, it is an effect of piety in the most fundamental sense: safeguarding the reputation of God. And far from being belatedly and quirkily "postmodern" (as the epochal epithet would have it), it is there from the beginning in the Bible and the Greco-Roman world. The Greek philosophical monotheists opposed the mythmakers and their crude stories of sacrifice because they were anxious about the implication of divine lack. Marcus Aurelius and Lucian clearly felt very acutely the threat to deities who needed to be supplemented by the offerings of man. They attempted to correct and discipline gods with the force of stoic philosophy or satire (see Young 1979,

25. Among the deeply conventional errors are: "Before waxing emotional, as is customary on such occasions, we might remember that sacrificing one's little boy to the local *Elohim* was quite common at the time" (Lacan 2001, 112). The sometimes hilarious pomposities include, "Last year, I worked up a bit of Hebrew on your behalf" (111).

18). Similarly, the God of Ps 50 (for example) seems to want to save himself from sacrifice in the sense of inuring himself against the implications of sacrifice. "Do I eat the flesh of blood or drink the blood of goats?" he demands. It seems that he has far more than combating the crude anthropomorphism of a divine mouth or alimentary canal on his mind. "If I were hungry, I would not tell you," he insists. I am not hungry; I do not need; I do not lack; I do not demand. I am not a divided subject like you; I am sovereign, unsubjected, self-contained. Oh, and moreover, "Every wild animal, cattle on a thousand hills are (always already) mine." Indeed, "The world and all that is in it is mine" (Ps 50:9–13).

In Ps 50 God seems to be asserting that sacrifice did not pass through his mouth in two senses. He did not (ever) eat it, nor did he *speak* it, at least in so many words—or at least we can be clear that he is saying something different now. Now he is talking of sacrifice as the "sacrifice of thanksgiving." The addition "of thanksgiving" seems to deal with the danger of the accusation of divine lack by qualifying sacrifice, taking a great deal of the substance of sacrifice away. This is somewhat typical of the Bible. In the Old Testament/Hebrew Bible, as in the New Testament, the assertion of literal sacrifice often seems to coincide with its revision, metaphorization, even eradication or disavowal. Sacrifice seems to be suspended between "method" and "metaphor" (see Milgrom 2004, 17), between letter and "spirit," blood and ink. It is around sacrifice, and particularly human sacrifice, that the Bible seems most anxious about the ghosts in its own corpus and the (literal?) skeletons in its own closet—and is most prone to undertake those kinds of revisions that revise and excise without deleting the original script.[26]

As different forms and structures vie for the position of true Israelite/Judean practice, it regularly turns out that sacrifice was never really true, or really original. What is more true, or original, is a general vague command to obedience, of which sacrifice is one expression or declension (Jer 7:22, 23). Human sacrifice was an error that arose from "mingling" with the nations (Deut 12:29–31; Ps 106). Or it was indeed spoken by God, but by way of punishment, not an assertion of True Truth. As YHWH explains, "I gave them statutes that were not good and ordinances by which they could not live. … I defiled them through their very gifts" (Ezek 20:25–26).

26. One of the major skeletons in the closet is surely the suspicious absence of Isaac in the return from Mount Moriah (Gen 22:19).

Alternatively, in a softer version of the notion of sacrifice as error (far less shocking than the notion of a deliberate divine ruse), sacrifice was only ever figuratively true as a command to offer the "cows of the lips" (Hos 14:3).[27]

These profound revisionary gestures extend into postbiblical Jewish and Christian tradition. John Chrysostom explains how God permitted sacrifice as a "condescension" (*synkatabainōn*) to Jewish infirmity (*astheneia*). "As a doctor treating a feverish patient may sometimes condone a lesser evil in order to prevent a greater evil from befalling the patient, so did the Lord act with the Jews." Interpreting the golden calf as a symptom, God diagnosed a "frantic … desire" to sacrifice to anything, even demons, and sagely prescribed: "You are mad and will desire to sacrifice; if so, then sacrifice to me" (John Chrysostom, *Against the Jews*; as cited in Benin 1983, 16; cf. Benin 1984, 182). With a highly dubious sense of medical ethics, Chrysostom's God cunningly allowed the patient to indulge in drinking the harmful (addictive) substance but then restricted him to drinking from one cup only and instructed his staff to smash the cup in secret. In order to avoid the extreme effects of withdrawal or going "cold turkey" from sacrifice, God confined sacrifice to Jerusalem and brought the Romans to decimate the city. But his commitment to eradicating sacrifice was clearly indicated by the fact that he allowed the temple to be destroyed not just once but twice.

Several Jewish sources share in the spirit of spiritualizing sacrifice, making sacrifice part of biblical surplus, like a pile of "gory meat." Leviticus Rabbah reconfigures sacrifice as a divine concession to polytheistic customs. In a midrashic parable, sacrificial Israel is represented by a prince prone to "eat carcasses and gory meat"; and God is represented by the wise king who said, "Let these be always on my table, and of himself he will get weaned" (Lev. Rab. 22:6). In *The Guide for the Perplexed* Maimonides argues, just like Chrysostom, that God effectively took away the heroin of sacrifice to idols and substituted the methadone of sacrifice to himself. He permitted, rather than willed, the building of multiple altars so as to eradicate idolatry, but he then confined sacrifice to the one temple (Deut 12:26) and taught his people how to do without their temple by degrees, so that they did not break out into sweats (1956, 322–27). As Jan Assmann puts it, in Maimonides sacrifice becomes an *ars oblivionalis* (1997, 58). The

27. The texts transforming sacrifice from blood to prayer/ethics/thanksgiving are legion. See, e.g., 1 Sam 15:22; Isa 1:11; Jer 7:22, 23; Hos 6:6 (cf. Matt 9:13 and 12:7); and Ps 40:7 (ET 6).

recording of sacrifice all over the Bible is there to remind us to *remember to forget.*

It feels like an early example of demystification, or "secularization" of scripture, to read (sometimes even inside scripture) the claim that sacrifice would have never entered God's mind or his Bible were it not for (and the candidates are various) the pressure of context *or* custom/habit *or* foreign influence *or* human fever, *or* the weakness—even pathology—of the human (or Jewish) mind. Similar arguments will become far more disastrous for God, and specifically the God of sacrifice, in modernity. But here, for now, in what we call "premodernity" they are all held in place by the thoroughly orthodox principle of divine accommodation or *synkatabasis*/condescension: the commonplace notion that scriptures can be human, even all too human, because "Theology stoops to speak the language of men."[28] Whereas making-human in a secular sense involves demystification—reducing the religious to a merely human origin—here making-human has the sense of divine *kenosis* or incarnation. God and Truth humble themselves, contract themselves, and by doing so save themselves from any accusation of error. *What appears as untruth is only God holding back for our sake.* Sacrifice is qualified, even repudiated, but the God who is worshipped by sacrifice stays unharmed. But we can see quite clearly that early interpreters and even those whose writings made it to the inside of "the Bible" were aware of the pressure placed on God (and man) by sacrifice—which is why they rushed to revision and defense.

8. Fourth Doubling of Life: God as Outlaw, Sovereign-Beast, Ass, or Stone

Paradoxically, sacrifice—and particularly human sacrifice—seems to be the place where divinity is most incontrovertibly asserted and most profoundly jeopardized. To put this another way, sacrifice is the site where the gods become most securely and insecurely themselves. This is not an accident that could have been avoided. The aporia is structural. It has to do with the centrality of the gift of blood and life. The offering of that which is most precious—that is, the living—is crucial to Augustine's confidence that one only sacrifices to one "whom he knew or thought or imagined

---

28. Divine accommodation/communication is usually traced back to the principle *scriptura humane loquitur*, "The Scriptures speak the language of man"—a latinization of the rabbinic principle, דברה תורה כלשון בני אדם. See Funkenstein 1989, 213.

to be God" (Augustine, *Civ.* 10.4; as cited in las Casas 1974, 229; see §2 above). But the centrality of blood and life also threatens the loss of divine distinction. It threatens the spectacle of god(s) fading not just into man (with his hungers, lacks, needs) but into the "beast."

As Derrida and Agamben point out, insistently and repeatedly, those two most opposite-seeming forms of being/living—"sovereign" and "beast," divinity and animal—find common ground in the state of "being-outside-the-law." The alliance holds even if for one that no-place-outside-the-law is the heavens or the foundation of the law, while for the other it is the wasteland outside the *polis* or the *oikos*, the forest or the field (Derrida 2009, 39). God makes the law; the animal is a law unto itself; God is a law unto himself—or could be, at least potentially, if elaborate self-given structures did not hold him in place. As Derrida puts it, "It is as though both of them [the beast and the sovereign] were situated by definition at a distance from or above the laws, in nonrespect for the absolute law, the absolute law that they make or that they are but that they do not have to respect" (2009, 39).

Nothing represents the primary function of the law more surely than the emblematic "Thou shalt not kill." Chief among the primary etiologies and justifications of law is the protection of (human) life from "criminal" forms of putting to death. This is why, as we explored earlier, human sacrifice testifies most powerfully to the presence of the god(s), because without it sacrifice would collapse back into murder: a criminal putting-to-death. Only a god can guarantee human sacrifice as a "denegation of murder" (Derrida 1995, 283). Precisely because the wager is so audacious ("If there is no God, or genuine divine command, then I am a murderer"), the gods exist. But the murder/sacrifice distinction is unstable, as are the gods who sustain it. The pressure of the assertion easily tips in the other direction: from sacrifice back to murder. Human beings who obey commands to sacrifice other human beings become murderers, and the gods who command human sacrifice become demons or cruel and bloodthirsty gods: no gods in the sense of false gods or gods whose immorality makes them unworthy of the name.

This reverse deduction is present in early Greek and Christian literature, though the implications tend to be reserved for other gods and the deduction tends to be more in the direction of divine cruelty (the gods as demons), rather than atheism, the nonexistence of the gods. The gods of the others did not die, as if their own sacrificial knives turned against them and skewered them through the heart. In a thought world where gods were not so much true or false as helpful or harmful, gods with a penchant for human, and particularly child, sacrifice were proved to be demonic in the negative sense. But they were still credited with supernatural power, for sacrifice seemed to substantiate the supernatural in its very excess. Such is the power of sacrifice—particularly human sacrifice—that it seemed impossible to believe that those who made such an extreme gesture of worship did not believe the origin of the command and the recipient to be gods. Augustine's maxim stayed in place. Clement of Alexandria railed in a diatribe against the Greek gods:

> murder does not become a sacrifice because of the place. Nor, if one should slay a man in honour of Artemis or Zeus in a so-called sacred place (*would it become a sacrifice*) any more than if, from anger or covetousness, he should slay the man in honour of like daemons on altars rather than on highways, and call it a holy sacrifice. But such a sacrifice is murder and manslaughter. (Eusebius, *Praep. ev.* 4.16, citing Clement, *Protrepticus* 3)

For writers like Clement and Eusebius, the (insatiable) demand for sacrifice proved the demonic immorality of Zeus and the pagan gods.

The collision between sacrifice and murder is also acknowledged on the *inside* of Christian tradition—though at first it operates only as a technical problem. A common conundrum for medieval scholastic theologians was how to relate a God who countenances or demands or does not oppose human sacrifice (e.g., Judg 11; Gen 22) to God's law and natural law. Unlike Maimonides and Chrysostom, such thinkers did not allow themselves the safety net of translating the divine command to sacrifice the son into something other than the will of God as such (e.g., an effect of context, or divine concession to human weakness, addiction, sin). Fragments of scripture were treated as literal/quasi-legal statements, "propositions" or "objections" to be evaluated alongside propositions drawn from Aristotle, Cicero, or Justinian's *Institutes* or *Decretals*. The divine command to Abraham to sacrifice his son was paraded (together with the command to steal from the Egyptians [Exod 12:35] and the command to Hosea to marry a prostitute [Hos 1:2]) as a prime example of a biblical/Christian God who seemed to violate his own Ten Commandments and natural law.[29] The

29. See Aquinas, *Summa Theologiae* 1a2ae, q. 94, 5. The problem of Gen 22 is treated in *Summa Theologiae* 1a2ae, qq. 90–100.

questions were hardly marginal or trivial, a matter of merely "exegetical" detail. At stake was that essential theological chicken-and-egg question, or the Socratic "Euthyphro question": "Which came first, so to speak, God or Good?"[30] The precise composition of the answer dictated nothing less than the nature and order of the universe—somewhere between absolute volatility and absolute solidity—with everything hinging on the precise relationship between God and natural law.

At one extreme the divine command to murder/sacrifice could serve as a proof text for divine voluntarism: God absolutely unfettered in the extent of his capabilities/powers (*pouvoirs*). Potentially this left the whole world (with all its natural material conditions and laws, natural and positive) hanging on the whim of the ever-changing divine voice. The deduction was that "so-called laws" were "included under that name only by courtesy. Only those concerning the worship of God command something because it is good; the others make something good because they command it" (Schneewind 1998, 24). Even more radically, "the hatred of God, theft, adultery and actions similar to those according to the common law … [could] even be performed meritoriously by an earthly pilgrim if they should come under a divine command." And should they be so commanded, then they would "change their nature entirely, being freed by definition from their association with evil and changing their names from 'murder,' 'adultery' or 'theft'" (William of Ockham, *On the Four Books of the Sentences*; as cited in Harris 2004, 27). The ultimate emblem of this volatile world where matter and the Good were entirely dependent on the whim and voice of God was a God who could, if he so chose, "make the messiah appear in the form of an 'ass or a stone'" (William of Ockham, *Centiloquium theologicum* conc. 6, 7a; cf. Ozment 1980, 18).

Symptomatically, God's radical freedom was represented by the transgression of the barriers separating man and god from animal and even inorganic matter. More undigestable than the malachite burger, stranger than the Scythian lamb-plant, is the specter of the messiah-ass or the messiah-stone. In practice, such complete volatility was avoided or allowed to stand as a technical concession to God's absolute freedom or grace (without leaving us in a world where nothing could be known due the operations of that freedom and grace). All solutions to the scholastic conun-

30. Euthyphro famously asks Socrates "whether the pious or holy is beloved by the gods because it is holy [or good] or holy [or good] because it is loved by the gods" (Plato, *Euthyphro* 10a).

drum took the form of complex and convoluted proofs that, on the one hand, saved God from becoming a divine automaton in a preconceived system, and, on the other, saved his creatures from an entirely volatile universe whose sovereign could change and suspend the law with every new decision and command.

These delicate compromise agreements start to melt down in "modernity"—which may be an exaggerated name for new ways of spinning, or tweaking, age-old problems of the perceived humanity of scripture or the relation between God and natural law. To put the "modern" transition (in relation to scripture/religion) simply: natural law gained a different inflection and intensity, and the force of nature, law, and morality developed to a point where the true gods were necessarily compelled to conform. The lives and viability of gods are predicated on their morality and their politics—their ability to produce good citizens, not sacrificing and martyring "fanatics." But the compulsion remains invisible because the true God of Christianity and "the West" responds by showing how he has always been legal and moral and has always operated within the law. Rights start to take on a force that is potentially greater than deities—at least foreign ones. It was in the sixteenth-century encounter with Mesoamerican sacrifice and the debate over the justice of conquest that European legal theorists and theologians began to delineate a rather crude and raw basic concept of right: "*No one can give another the right to eat him or sacrifice him*" (Vitoria 1991a, 225). The right not to be sacrificed and the right not to be eaten are fundamental components of the "inalienable right," which cannot be taken away by other humans or by gods—or at least gods and humans worthy of the name.

It took a while for the pressure of this logic to leak into the Bible. But eventually the English Deists and Kant began to bring the inner-biblical logic of accommodation and the slippage between sacrifice and murder to bear on Abraham's sacrifice (more available to critique than the crucifixion, but also the crucifixion at one remove). The gloves came off. There was no longer any barrier separating sacrifice from murder/slaughter, or temple/altar from slaughterhouse. Kant wrote of the act of "butchering and burning" (*Ubschlachtung und Verbrennung*) the son (worse, without consulting him). To such a God, Abraham should and could only respond:

> That I ought not to kill my good son is quite certain. But that you, an apparition, are God—of that I am not certain, and never can be, not even if this voice rings down to me from (visible) heaven.

> Das ich meinen guten Sohn nicht tödten solle, ist ganz gewiss; dass aber du, der du mir erscheint, Gott sei, davon bin ich nicht gewiss und kann es auch nicht warden, wenn sie auch vom [sichtbaren] Himmel herabshallte. (Kant 1992, 113–14)[31]

This God only appears to be God: he is a no-god, an apparition, and the story in which he *appears* is a "myth." This supposed "divine command" is "secularized" as an effect of Abraham's pious mishearing or an effect of "mingling with the nations" (applying to Gen 22 the explanatory logic of Ps 106).

At this point the making-human of the scriptures takes on a different cadence and intensity. The gods of sacrifice (construed as a crude practice on the other side of civilization) go up in the smoke of demystification. Echoing and intensifying earlier moves (sacrifice as an effect of Egyptian influence or Jewish "fever"), human sacrifice turns into a consequence of lack of protein, a projection of warped human minds, or a side effect of population control and warfare and other social and political desires. To offer human sacrifice (as a religious, exceptional act, incommensurable with legal forms of homicide) is, by definition, to default on the basic requirements of the human. Søren Kierkegaard puts this logic beautifully when he has one of his Abrahams reflect on how the event has changed him:

> The whole experience has made me forever at variance with what it is to be human. If it had pleased you, O Lord, to let me be changed into the form of a horse, yet remaining human, I would be no more at variance with what it is to be man than I have become through what has just happened. (Hong and Hong 1967–1978, 3:3714)

Like de Bergerac's ensouled but unresurrectable cabbage, the absurd image of Abraham as at best (or at beast) a centaur hacks away at our segregations and apartheids of "life." Only for man is to "be a beast" or to act like a beast an accusation. Which is stranger, then, a hero-patriarch as son-sacrificer/killer or a hero-patriarch as half-horse? For Erich Auerbach and others, Abraham's nonresistance makes him a servant, a "natural slave," a mere tool: a prosthesis or artificial limb to execute the will of the divine master—no more or less an instrument than "knife," "fire," or "wood." He

31. For similar readings among the so-called English Deists, see, e.g., Chubb 1730, 244.

is an "automaton," a robot, a cyborg, the kind with wires and cold metal showing: hyperproductive, hyperefficient, yet simultaneously more *and less* than human life (Auerbach 1991; cf. Hook and Reno 2000). Abraham as robot or cyborg brings home to Christianity and its Bible pejoratives applied to foreign sacrifice. According to the nineteenth-century Scottish missionary, the Reverend Alexander Duff, bloody sacrifices revealed the true nature of the Indians as nonnature. Behaving unnaturally—also mechanically—they were "mere automatons, as directly impelled or restrained in every movement of soul and body as a piece of organized but inert materialism by the hand that framed it," "a divinely regulated machine" (1839, 130).

Despite the intense pressures of modernity, becoming-beast, through sacrifice, is something that affects foreign gods far more than the true God, the God of Euro-American Christianity. The Bible is still largely protected, not least by historicizing gestures that often work exactly like accommodation. The making-human of the scriptures is a way of ensuring the true God's protection. Read as an effect of the influence of foreign Canaanite practice (still stuck in human sacrifice), Gen 22 is historicized and God is saved. In a solution that would have been unthinkable for Aquinas or Scotus, the ongoing life of God relies on secularizing or demystifying the divine command. More than this, the lesson of the text is embodied in the second divine voice, "Do not lay a hand on the lad" (Gen 22:12), read exactly as Maimonides and Chrysostom read the destruction of the temple, despite the fact that Abraham's willingness to sacrifice is praised. This clearly shows that the true God was always (dead) set against human sacrifice. The text and practice of sacrifice only ever wanted its own elimination, or end.

9. Fifth Doubling of Life: God as Subject to the Animal and Man in the Sense That Animal Death Can No Longer Be "for God" (God Being a Weaker Force Than Sport or Food)

In modernity the true gods get even more embarrassed about human sacrifice than they were before (and they have never been clearly for it). But animal sacrifice seems, at first glance at least, less problematic. After all, all kinds of legitimate deaths are possible for animals even in this age of "animal rights." Jeremy Bentham's famous question whether animals can suffer (Bentham 2007) is radical not because it asks whether animals can experience pain but whether they can be harmed, that is, undergo the kind of suffering/deprivation that *qualifies in law*. Legally valid suffering is related to self-possession and right. On this question, there is a great deal of continuity between contemporary views of the animal and the old Aristotelian-Christian views. This is one of the reasons why the question of the animal is so insistent today, because it stands at the strange point of intersection and continuity between the so-called premodern and the modern, thereby exposing shared exclusions and occlusions around those cardinal modern virtues of "life" and "rights."

The sixteenth-century jurist and theologian Francisco de Vitoria's arguments seem arcane in many respects. But though the analogies may be a little baroque, the argumentation seems absolutely logical and familiar when it comes to the relation between the animal and justice/right:

> Irrational creatures cannot be victims of injustice [*iniuria*], and therefore cannot have legal rights: this assumption is proved in turn by considering the fact that to deprive a wolf or lion of its prey is not injustice against the beast in question, any more than to shut out the sun's light is injustice against the sun. And this is confirmed by the absurdity of the following argument: that if brutes had dominion, then any person who fenced off grass from deer would be committing a theft, since he would be stealing food without its owner's permission. (1991b, 247)

The logical deduction should therefore be—as indeed Locke deduced on the same principles—that we are as free to sacrifice as we are to mass-produce meat in factory farming or keep chickens in our garden. For Locke, a man may as justly sacrifice as butcher an animal, provided that is it his own property and provided that he does it in the privacy of his own home (1955, 39).[32] But clearly times have changed, and in these late modern days, gods who command animal *sacrifices* or are on record as having done so also compromise their rights to "life."

32. In the context of a discussion about how the "civil criterion of worldly injury ... operates to circumscribe the scope and limits of what might be advanced as an appropriate expression of religious belief," Locke compares the practice of sacrificing infants and burning a calf. The conclusion is that the latter, not the former, is permissible, for "no injury is thereby done to any one, no prejudice to another man's goods." Vitoria affirms the same principle: "[Man] is not master of his own and other men's lives to the same degree as he is of brutes; the latter he may destroy or kill as he wishes without injustice [*iniuria*], but a man who takes even his own life commits an offence" (1991a, 212).

In 1987 in Hialeah, Florida, the city council attempted to ban orishas involving animal sacrifice by devotees of Santería by issuing a law prohibiting "unnecessarily kill[ing], torment[ing], tortur[ing], or multilat[ing] an animal in a public or private ritual or ceremony not for the purpose of food consumption" (as cited in Sheehan 2009, 12). As Jonathan Sheehan points out, the words *religion* and *sacrifice* were decorously avoided, though, in the delicate formulation "ritual or ceremony," clearly implied. The wording carefully distinguished the criminalized (ritual or ceremonial) putting to death of an animal from entirely noncriminal acts such as hunting, farming, factory farming, and having animals put down at the vet's. What was banned, quite precisely, was killing that had nothing to do with utilitarian calculus and belonged to incalculable "ritual or ceremonial practice," that is, to "religion" (13). To kill for God (or "god" or "gods") was, in the eyes of the law, to waste.

The implication is that animals should not die for nothing. And the "divine," in this legislation, is nothing. It is not as tangible as sport (hunting) or food. Old gods who command sacrifice look like some decadent old blood-spillers in the eyes of utilitarian modernity where death (even, now, animal death) must be *for* something, for some tangible good. Modern deities who seek to justify themselves as sponsors of the public good, law, and utility must desist from (raw, literal) sacrifice. Animal death cannot be for god, but it can be for pharmaceuticals, cosmetics, sport, food, or "Life" (capital *L*), experiments in genetic modification for the better amplification and perfection of life.

10. Postscript: Genesis 22 and the Passion/Eucharist as Curious Alchemies of Life

Sacrifice is a place where the cuts between animal, cereal/plant, god, and human are firmly incised—and where these forms of life change places as an effect of the very logic used to divide them. It is a site where gods are most powerfully made and substantiated—and where they die or become false or cruel. These accidents are not just modern impositions on a once stable scene. They go all the way down in the history of sacrifice to its "putative" origin, where it is never clear who/what precisely was first on the altar, and who/what was doing what (precisely) to what/whom. To steal and customize a pun from Mark Taylor and Michael Taussig, the altar has long functioned as a site of alterity in a very particular respect: as a place where the self risks the self (or the human risks the human) and enters onto the altar/into the altar against which the self/human is defined and sustained (Taussig 1993, 237; cf. Taylor 1987, xxvii–xxix).

In text and practice, sacrifice has been used by "man" as something like the most hair-raising fairground ride, the one called *The Altar*. It is a place where we have hurled ourselves between the antipodes of being, between living and dying; a place where we dice with the trembling limits between *bios* and *zōē*, the biological, zoological, and anthropological, life and technology, god and food, cereal and angels, (cabbages and stones), and "life" and "death." At least as compelling as the capacity of sacrifice to purify forms of being is the potential to let categories live otherwise—to artificially intervene in life, creating hybrids and unstable life forms. Sacrifice flings "man," "animal," and "god" upside down. It plays with distorted human and semihuman forms, as in crazy mirrors. It attempts to make very clear incisions in the mass of being and/but quite deliberately puts those same categories under the knife.

This becomes clear if we look at those most successful biblical sacrifice "memes,"[33] the ones (as we tend to say, now) with the most fecund "afterlives": the sacrifice of Abraham and the Christian passion/Eucharist. Their longevity can be traced to their technical interventions in "life." Their virtually miraculous potential for reproduction clearly relates to their ability to create alternative modes of going or being live, alive (and dead). The sacrifice of Abraham and the Christian passion/Eucharist have been so productive in the "Western" imaginary because—in a highly textualized, technologized space of experimentation that functions like a micromanipulator or an incubator—they perform strange alchemies of life. "Roll up, ladies and gentlemen, and see a boy become a ram—and sand, and stars, and light." The rabbis say that the ram was also called "Isaac" (Midrash ha-Gadol on Gen 22:13; in Mann 1940, 67; cf. Sherwood 2004). They are only teasing out the implications of the text, where the "God who sees" looks on the sacrifice of *the ram* and comments that Abraham has "not withheld" *his only son* (Gen 22:16). Seeing as if through the eyes of God (as strange and impossible as Derrida's attempt to look at himself through the eyes of his cat), it appears that a boy and a ram are the *same*. For this not-withholding-of-the-son that is a giving-of-a-ram, Abraham is rewarded

33. On the meme as the cultural equivalent of the gene, see Blackmore 1999. For biblical memes see Pyper 2001; Sherwood 2000, esp. 196–98.

with myriad bodies from one body—bodies as "numerous as the stars in the heaven … and the sand on the seashore" (Gen 22:17).

It is hard to work out which is more curious and more miraculous: the transformation of *zōē* or the transformations of *bios*. Death (*thanatos*) becomes life. By "killing" itself, life extends way beyond that which could naturally be conceived. But the mutations in *bios* are arguably even more remarkable. Worlds away from the rigid demarcations of Francisco de Vitoria or the book of Leviticus, it is as if a boy could turn mineral mutating into sand (worn-down stones), while also turning into animal and also turning into light.

But even the "sacrifice" of Isaac cannot rival the ultimate sacrificial fairground ride, the real hair-raiser that is *The Crucifixion/The Eucharist*. The participants/objects keep shifting as we try to ascertain who or what is doing what to what, or who, to what, or whom. The *sacrificer* is regularly read as man and his technologies (Pilate/the Jews/the law/the cross) but also God (God offering God); the *sacrificed* is both man and God or the God-man-lamb; and the *recipient and initiator of the sacrifice* is officially (and according to very respectable authorities) God and/or satan or "demons," the sovereign and the beast. Famously, the "sacrifice" (or not) has been repeated (or not). The Mass/Holy Communion has pushed the question of copying/cloning to the fever pitch of "Mass Hysteria" (Merrall Llewelyn Price 2003). Some say that the sacrifice is only being remembered, emphasizing transformation from blood to memory, archive, ink. In the space of memory, as cloning/repeating, forms and foods of life do not merely encroach on one another's space but metamorphosize, merge, and spin. The increasingly audacious rotations include god-on-the-altar-being-sacrificed-as-food-for-the-people; at least metaphorical theophagy (eating god's flesh and blood to extend life infinitely, eternally; cf. John 6:51–56); not to mention a host of heresies including *impanation* (God-turned-bread, as a twist on incarnation) and the excoriated *stercoranism* (God-turned-shit).[34] God turns into bread as if the highest object of sacrifice were now coalescing with one of the lower (cereal) offerings. That which is most profoundly above man metamorphosizes (maybe) into that

34. The theory of the impaning or embreading of God (*Deus panis factus, God made bread)* was devised by Aquinas's student John Quidort or John of Paris (d. 1306) (see Rubin 1992, 31). Like many heresies it was offered in complete good faith. For stercoranism see Bynum 2007, 86–88. I am grateful to my colleague A. K. M. Adam for directing me to the stercoranists.

which is most securely for him. Making the Old Testament/classical problem of "God's nose" and "God's bowels" look mild in comparison, God-in-the-mouth-of-man always threatens to be processed through, well, the "ends" of man. As Piero Camporesi puts it, "the descent of the body of Christ into the antrum, into the wet and foul-smelling guts, [was] followed by theologians with a worried gaze and with thoughtful anxiety" (Camporesi 1991, 166; cf. Price 2003, 21–22).

It is hardly accidental that we find so many heresies—Arianism, docetism, impanation, stercoranism—gathering around the altar/table or congregating at the foot of the cross. By pushing the radical re-formation and transmogrification of forms, the passion and the Eucharist seem to risk precisely this. These scenes seem to want to play, tortuously, with the conceptual relations between the categories of god and man and the animal and food for man. They seem to want to stage a tortuous *passion* of life, in the sense of making the categories of "life" *suffer* a little bit and more than a little bit.

Traditionally, theologians have rushed in to fix, heal, and fine-tune the machine of sacrifice. They have attempted more and more exquisite formulations clarifying (once and for all) whether the salvific mechanism of the passion is fundamentally substitutionary, propitiatory, expiatory (and in what proportions); specifying to what degree God becomes, or is represented by, wine and bread; or showing how true life, eternal life, has no place for the bowels and anus (or natural reproductive organs) human and divine.[35] Insofar as they have tried to produce a system of "efficacious [salvific] action," they have attempted something like a theological cybernetics, an efficient system of information and response that tries to reduce risk, excess, and waste.[36] But instead of constantly tinkering with the machine, a more appropriate response may be to probe and marvel at these scenes as performances of (in contemporary terms) symbiosis between the "species" and the totipotency and pluripotency of life. Pluripotency is the primordial germinal condition of being able to become any type of tissue. The early embryo is pluripotent. So is the "man" or "god" of sacrifice. The transformation is both magical/miraculous, and the very stuff of "science." The basic tissue of the passion (and the sacrifice of Isaac)

35. On what parts of "the flesh," or "life," must be excluded from the salvation of "all life," see Agamben 2004, 17–19.

36. See Louis Couffignal's description of cybernetics as "The art of ensuring the efficacy of action" (1958).

has the potency to become animal, human, plant, stone, light, or life infinitely extended in space and/or time.

These transgressions exert the same kind of cultural attraction and horror embodied in Dolly—the Agnus Dei's modern clone or surrogate. The "sacrifice" and the cross venture and risk "new mixtures of mortality and immortality, normality and pathology" (Franklin 2007, 159). The horror is intrinsic. The scenes are sustained by pathology. We have never been able to eradicate the pathology of the necessary torment, or blood, of Isaac/Christ, or the perversity of god-as-bread-or-wine-in-the-mouth. Like Dolly, these artificially and divinely produced transmogrifications of life around sacrifice draw our attention in the "the desire to distinguish the animal from the human, and to prevent their mixture, while also, paradoxically, embodying their ever more proximate union" (30). In the "possibility" and "threat" of slippages from *Ovis Aries* to *Homo sapiens sapiens* to *Deus incomparabiliens* we feel the intensity of life—more life, intense life, life pluripotent and manipulable. We also feel the vertigo of self-loss, self-jeopardy: for fallibility and lack of power are built into these ancient structures of prolonged, intensified, hyperlife.

This might be the most salutary—maybe even salvific—message to be communicated from these old scenes to this present age of "livestock industries," "food security," human and animal resources, and the management and maximalization of life. These old technologies and texts of sacrifice join contemporary theorists and philosophers such as Eric Santner, talking in strangely retrotheologized tones of "creaturely life." Creaturely life designates "man's" exposure—exposure not merely to the elements or to the fragility and precariousness of mortal, finite lives, but rather to "an ultimate lack of foundation for the historical forms of life that distinguish human community" (Santner 2006, 5).[37] Beyond the nudity of biological life, the human must constitute itself meaningfully in language, society, rite, the symbolic order. Man seeks to "animate" and "undeaden" human life qua human life —a point that resonates with my allusion to making life "go live" (Santner 2011, xx). But by definition *we do not know what we do* as we attempt to constitute and respond to this lack of foundation, this crucial "missing piece of the world" (5). The overdetermined site of sacrifice is one major testimony to this compulsion to "undeaden life," producing acts and texts that always exceed our attempt to capture, manage, and

---

37. Here I am drawing lightly from the summary in Santner 2011, 5.

explain a life that is never simply "ours." Sacrifice can be understood (at least partly) as an expression of the desire to immunize human life from the fundamental lack of ground. As surely as it addresses "man's" fragility and precariousness by, say, soliciting rain or general goods from the God/gods, so it addresses man's ontological frailty and the lack of foundation for historical forms of life, like "Israel," like "sacrifice," like "man." To build big stone altars and temples, to orchestrate a complex slaughter of animals and gifts of grain is to give flesh, substance, to the human qua human. We build solid stone altars as a sure foundation over the groundlessness beneath our feet: "I sacrifice, therefore I am." But sacrifice also appears, often extremely, to lean into the vertigo of our "ontological vulnerability"—and not simply by accident as if the logic of the act were turning against us unawares. It is as if we want to perform for ourselves (and any gods and animals who might be watching) our sense of "human being as that being whose essence it is to exist in forms of life that are, in turn, contingent, fragile," and "susceptible to breakdown" (6). It is as if we want to feel ourselves falling—at least in the safe space of text and rite.[38]

Works Cited

Acosta, José de. 2002. *Natural and Moral History of the Indies*. Edited by Jane E. Mangan. Translated by Frances López-Morillas. Durham, N.C.: Duke University Press.

Agamben, Giorgio. 1998. *Homo Sacer: Sovereign Power and Bare Life*. Translated by Daniel Heller-Roazen. Stanford, Calif.: Stanford University Press.

———. 2004. *The Open: Man and Animal*. Translated by Kevin Attell. Stanford, Calif.: Stanford University Press.

Anderson, Gary. 1987. *Sacrifices and Offerings in Ancient Israel: Studies in Their Social and Political Importance*. Harvard Semitic Monographs 41. Atlanta: Scholars Press.

The Ante-Nicene Fathers. 1994. Edited by Alexander Roberts and James Donaldson. 1885–1887. 10 vols. Repr., Edinburgh: T&T Clark.

Aquinas, Thomas. 1923. *Contra Gentes*. London: Burns, Oates, and Washbourne.

38. Compare reflections on the safe space (or panic room) of story in Roemer 1995 as discussed in Sherwood 2012, 198–99.

———. 1964–1973. *Summa Theologiae*. Translated by Thomas Gilby et al. London: Spottiswoode.

Aristotle. 1882. *On the Parts of Animals/De partibus animalium*. Translated by William Ogle. Online: http://classics.mit.edu/Aristotle/parts_animals.html.

———. 1885. *Politics*. Translated by Benjamin Jowett. Online: http://classics.mit.edu/Aristotle/politics.html.

Assmann, Jan. 1997. *Moses the Egyptian: The Memory of Egypt in Western Monotheism*. Cambridge: Harvard University Press.

Auerbach, Erich. 1991. Odysseus' Scar. Pages 3–23 in *Mimesis: The Representation of Reality in Western Literature*. Translated by William R. Trask. 1953. Repr., Princeton: Princeton University Press.

Bataille, Georges. 1988. *Consumption*. Vol. 1 of *The Accursed Share: An Essay on General Economy*. Translated by Robert Hurley. New York: Zone.

Benedict XVI. 2006. Lecture of the Holy Father: Faith, Reason and the University: Memories and Reflections. Online: http://www.vatican.va/holy_father/benedict_xvi/speeches/2006/september/documents/hf_ben-xvi_spe_20060912_university-regensburg_en.html.

Benin, Stephen D. 1983. Sacrifice as Education in Augustine and Chrysostom. *Church History* 52:7–20.

———. 1984. The "Cunning of God" and Divine Accommodation. *Journal of the History of Ideas* 45:179–91.

Bentham, Jeremy. 2007. *Introduction to the Principles of Morals and Legislation* (1781). Pages 8–9 in *The Animals Reader: The Essential Classic and Contemporary Writings*. Edited by Linda Kalof and Amy Fitzgerald. Oxford: Berg.

Bergerac, Cyrano de. 2007. *Journey to the Moon*. Translated by Andrew Brown. London: Hesperus Classics.

Blackmore, Susan. 1999. *The Meme Machine*. Oxford: Oxford University Press.

Bradley, Arthur. 2011. *Originary Technicity: The Theory of Technology from Marx to Derrida*. New York: Palgrave Macmillan.

Bynum, Caroline Walker. 2007. *Wonderful Blood: Theology and Practice in Late Medieval Northern Germany and Beyond*. Philadelphia: University of Pennsylvania Press.

Camporesi, Piero. 1991. *The Fear of Hell: Images of Damnation and Salvation in Early Modern Europe*. University Park: Pennsylvania State University Press.

Canguilhem, G. 1988. *Ideology and Rationality in the History of the Human Sciences*. Cambridge: MIT Press.

Casas, Bartolomé de las. 1974. *In Defence of the Indians: The Defence of the Most Reverend Lord, Don Fray Bartolomé de Las Casas, of the Order of Preachers, Late Bishop of Chiapa, against the Persecutors and Slanderers of the Peoples of the New World Discovered across the Seas*. Translated and edited by Stafford Poole. DeKalb: Northern Illinois University Press.

Caseau, Beatrice. 1996. Crossing the Impenetrable Frontier between Earth and Heaven. Pages 333–44 in *Shifting Frontiers in Late Antiquity*. Edited by Ralph W. Mathisen and Hagith S. Sivan. Aldershot, U.K.: Varorium.

Chubb, Thomas. 1730. Treatise XIX: The Case of Abraham with Regard to His Offering up Isaac in Sacrifice, Re-examined, in a Letter to a Clergyman. Pages 240–46 in *A Collection of Tracts on Various Subjects*. London: Royal Exchange.

Clendinnen, Inga. 1987. *Ambivalent Conquests: Maya and Spaniard in Yucatan, 1517–1570*. Cambridge: Cambridge University Press.

Combs-Schilling, M. Elaine. 1989. *Sacred Performances: Islam, Sexuality and Sacrifice. New York:* Columbia University Press.

Couffignal, Louis. 1958. Essai d'une définition générale de la cybernétique. Pages 46–54 in *The First International Congress on Cybernetics, Namur, Belgium, June 26–29, 1956*. Paris: Gauthier-Villars.

Derrida, Jacques. 1995. "Eating Well" or the Calculation of the Subject. Pages 255–87 in *Points: Interviews, 1974–1994*. Translated by Peter Connor and Avital Ronnell. Stanford, Calif.: Stanford University Press.

———. 2002a. The Animal That Therefore I Am (More to Follow). Translated by David Willis. *Critical Inquiry* 28:369–418.

———. 2002b. The Deconstruction of Actuality. Pages 85–116 in *Negotiations: Interventions and Interviews 1971–2001*. Translated by Elizabeth Rottenberg; Stanford, Calif.: Stanford University Press.

———. 2002c. Faith and Knowledge: The Two Sources of "Religion" at the Limits of Reason Alone. Pages 40–101 in *Acts of Religion*. Edited by Gil Anidjar. New York: Routledge.

———. 2006. Le Sacrifice. Pages 142–54 in Daniel Mesguich, *L'éternel éphémère, suivi de Le Sacrifice par Jacques Derrida*. Paris: Verdier.

———. 2009. *The Beast and the Sovereign*. Vol. 1. Edited by Michel Lisse, Marie-Louise Mallet, and Ginette Michaud. Translated by Geoffrey

Bennington. Seminars of Jacques Derrida 1. Chicago: University of Chicago Press.

Detienne, Marcel. 1989. Culinary Practices and the Spirit of Sacrifice. Pages 1–20 in *The Cuisine of Sacrifice among the Greeks*. Edited by Marcel Detienne and Jean-Pierre Vernant. Chicago: University of Chicago Press.

Dillon, Michael, and Julian Reid. 2009. *The Liberal Way of War: Killing to Make Life Live*. London: Routledge.

Driver, G. R. 1956. Three Technical Terms in the Pentateuch. *Journal of Semitic Studies* 1:97–105.

Duff, Alexander. 1839. *India, and India Missions: Including Sketches of the Gigantic System of Hinduism, Both in Theory and Practice*. Edinburgh: Johnstone.

Eusebius. 1903. *Praeparatio Evangelica/Preparation for the Gospel*. Translated by E. H. Gifford. Online: http://www.tertullian.org/fathers/eusebius_pe_00_eintro.htm.

Firestone, Reuven. 1990. *Journeys in Holy Lands: The Evolution of Abraham-Ishmael Legends in Islamic Exegesis*. Albany: State University of New York Press.

Foucault, Michel. 1997. *The Order of Things: An Archaeology of the Human Sciences*. 1970. Repr., London: Routledge.

Franklin, Sarah. 2007. *Dolly Mixtures: The Remaking of Genealogy*. Durham, N.C.: Duke University Press.

Funkenstein, Amos. 1989. *Theology and the Scientific Imagination from the Middle Ages to the Seventeenth Century*. Princeton: Princeton University Press.

Girard, René. 1979. *Violence and the Sacred*. Translated by Patrick Gregory. 1977. Repr., Baltimore: Johns Hopkins University Press.

Harris, Michael J. 2004. *Divine Command Ethics*. New York: Routledge Curzon.

Hong, Howard V., and Edna H. Hong, eds. and trans. 1967–1978. *Søren Kierkegaard's Journals and Papers*. 5 vols. Bloomington: Indiana University Press.

Hook, Brian S., and R. R. Reno. 2000. Abraham and the Problems of Modern Heroism. Pages 135–61 in *Sacred Text, Secular Times: The Hebrew Bible in the Modern World*. Edited by Leonard Jay Greenspoon and Bryan F. LeBeau. Studies in Jewish Civilization 10. Omaha: Creighton University Press.

Hubert, Henri, and Marcel Mauss. 1964. *Sacrifice: Its Nature and Function.* Translated by W. D. Halls. Chicago: University of Chicago Press.

Jay, Nancy. 1991. *Throughout Your Generations Forever: Sacrifice, Religion and Paternity.* Chicago: University of Chicago Press.

Kant, Immanuel. 1992. *The Conflict of the Faculties (Der Streit der Fakultäten).* Translated by Mary J. Gregor. 1979. Repr., Lincoln: University of Nebraska Press.

Lacan, Jacques. 2001. Introduction to the Names-of-the-Father Seminar. Pages 102–16 in *The Postmodern Bible Reader.* Edited by David Jobling, Tina Pippin, and Ronald Schleifer. Oxford: Blackwell.

Lee, Henry. 1887. *The Vegetable Lamb of Tartary: A Curious Fable of the Cotton Plant, to Which Is Added a Sketch of the History of Cotton and the Cotton Trade.* London: Low, Marston, Searle & Rivington.

Lipton, Diana. 2008. *Longing for Egypt and Other Unexpected Biblical Tales.* Sheffield: Sheffield Phoenix.

Locke, John. 1955. *A Letter Concerning Toleration.* Indianapolis: Bobbs-Merrill.

Maimonides. 1956. *The Guide for the Perplexed.* Translated by M. Friedländer. 2nd edition. New York: Dover.

Mandeville, Sir John. 2005. *The Travels of Sir John Mandeville.* Translated by C. W. R. D. Moseley. London: Penguin.

Mann, Jacob. 1940. *The Bible as Read and Preached in the Old Synagogue.* Cincinnati: published by the author.

Martin, Dale. 2007. *Inventing Superstition: From the Hippocratics to the Christians.* Cambridge: Harvard University Press.

McDonald, Nathan. 2008. *Not Bread Alone: The Use of Food in the Old Testament.* Oxford: Oxford University Press.

Milgrom, Jacob. 2004. *Leviticus: A Book of Ritual and Ethics.* Continental Commentary. Minneapolis: Fortress.

Million, Helen Lovell. 1926. An Old Roman Cookbook. *Classical Journal* 21:443–50.

Ovid. 1986. *Metamorphoses.* Translated by Mary M. Innes. Harmondsworth: Penguin.

Ozment, Steven. 1980. *The Age of Reform 1250–1550: An Intellectual and Religious History of Late Medieval and Reformation Europe.* New Haven: Yale University Press.

Plato. *Euthyphro.* Translated by Benjamin Jowett. Online: http://classics.mit.edu/Plato/euthyfro.html.

Price, Merrall Llewelyn. 2003. *Consuming Passions: The Uses of Cannibalism in Late Medieval and Early Modern Europe*. New York: Routledge.

Pyper, Hugh. 2001. The Triumph of the Lamb: Psalm 23 and Textual Fitness. *Biblical Interpretation* 9:384–92.

Robertson Smith, William. 1907. *The Religion of the Semites*. London: Black.

Roemer, Michael. 1995. *Telling Stories: Postmodernism and the Invalidation of Traditional Narrative*. Lanham, Md.: Rowman & Littlefield.

Rubin, Miri. 1992. *Corpus Christi: The Eucharist in Late Medieval Culture*. Cambridge: Cambridge University Press.

Sanders, N. K., trans. 1960. *Epic of Gilgamesh*. Baltimore: Penguin.

Santner, Eric L. 2006. *On Creaturely Life: Rilke, Benjamin, Sebald*. Chicago: University of Chicago Press.

———. 2011. *The Royal Remains: The People's Two Bodies and the Endgames of Sovereignty*. Chicago: University of Chicago Press.

Scarry, Elaine. 1985. *The Body in Pain: The Making and Unmaking of the World*. Oxford: Oxford University Press.

Schneewind, J. B. 1998. *The Invention of Autonomy*. Cambridge: Cambridge University Press.

Sheehan, Jonathan. 2009. Sacrifice before the Secular. *Representations* 105.1:12–36.

Sherwood, Yvonne. 2000. *A Biblical Text and Its Afterlives: The Survival of Jonah in Western Culture*. Cambridge: Cambridge University Press.

———. 2004. Textual Carcasses and Isaac's Scar. Pages 22–43 in *Sanctified Aggression: Legacies of Biblical and Post-Biblical Vocabularies of Violence*. Edited by Jonneke Bekkenkamp and Yvonne Sherwood. London: Continuum.

———. 2012. *Biblical Blaspheming: Trials of the Sacred for a Secular Age*. Cambridge: Cambridge University Press.

Taussig, Michael. 1993. *Mimesis and Alterity: A Particular History of the Senses*. London: Routledge.

Taylor, Mark C. 1987. *Altarity*. Chicago: University of Chicago Press.

Vaux, Roland de. 1964. *Studies in Old Testament Sacrifice*. Cardiff: University of Wales Press.

Vitoria, Francisco de. 1991a. On Dietary Laws, or Self-Restraint. Pages 205–30 in *Political Writings*. Edited by Anthony Pagden and Jeremy Lawrance. Cambridge Texts in the History of Political Thought. Cambridge: Cambridge University Press.

———. 1991b. On the American Indians (*De Indis*) (1539). Pages 231–92 in *Political Writings*. Edited by Anthony Pagden and Jeremy Lawrance. Cambridge Texts in the History of Political Thought. Cambridge: Cambridge University Press.

Watts, James W. 2007. *Ritual and Rhetoric in Leviticus: From Sacrifice to Scripture*. Cambridge: Cambridge University Press.

William of Ockham. 1988. *Centiloquium theologicum*. Edited by Philotheus Boehner. St. Bonaventure, N.Y.: St. Bonaventure University Press.

Wilmut, Ian, Keith Campbell, and Colin Tudge. 2000. *The Second Creation: The Age of Biological Control by the Scientists Who Cloned Dolly*. London: Headline.

Young, Frances M. 1979. *The Use of Sacrificial Ideas in Greek Christian Writers from the New Testament to John Chrysostom*. Patristic Monograph Series 51. Philadelphia: Philadelphia Patristic.

Žižek, Slavoj. 2001. *Enjoy Your Symptom: Jacques Lacan in Hollywood and Out*. London: Routledge.

6
Endings

Ruminations on Revelation's Ruminant, Quadrupedal Christ; or, the Even-Toed Ungulate That Therefore I Am

Stephen D. Moore

> All the beasts from John's Revelation, … the reading of which would merit more than one seminar. (Derrida 2009, 24)

> All the things that a sheep has inside it and that he has inside him too. (Coetzee 1997, 98)

Anomanimality

The Lamb has long been the elephant in the room of Revelation scholarship. What does it mean—theologically, philosophically, ecologically—that the figure introduced as "like a Son of Man" (*homoion huion anthrōpou*) in Revelation's inaugural vision (see 1:13) has ceased to be anthropomorphic by the time we reach Revelation's throne room scene ("I saw … a Lamb [*arnion*]"—5:6)? What does it mean that Revelation's Christ moves through most of the subsequent narrative not on two legs but on four? By and large, the burgeoning body of ecocritical and ecotheological work on Revelation[1] is oddly silent on this highly conspicuous spectacle and on the no less obvious fact that Revelation in general is an animal book extraordinaire, a bizarre bestiary,[2] more thickly populated with nonhuman animals than any other early Christian text.[3] Such work has tended to grapple

1. See, e.g., Rossing 1999, 2002, 2005, 2008; Reid 2000; Maier 2002; Hawkin 2003; Horrell, 2010, 98–101; Bauckham 2010, 174–78.

2. As are other ancient Jewish apocalyptic works or sections of such works, most notably the Animal Apocalypse of 1 En. 85–90.

3. Theologian Catherine Keller comes closest, perhaps, to being the rule-proving

instead with the ecocidal excesses of Rev 8 and 16, seize on the fleeting moment of agency accorded the earth in 12:16 ("But the earth [*hē gē*] came to the help of the woman"), and contentedly come to rest in the city park of 22:1–2.[4] But even in the latter locale, it is the water flowing "through the middle of the street of the city" and the tree on either side of the stream that has tended to capture the ecological imagination, not the nonhuman animal that also features in the vision—an altogether anomalous animal, as we shall see, enthroned, not encaged, in the city park (22:1, 3).[5] This anomalous animality—*anomanimality*, if you will—is the principal focus of the present essay.

Before the Animal

In this essay I will have recourse to Jacques Derrida's three posthumously published animal books, *The Animal That Therefore I Am* (2008a) and the two volumes of *The Beast and the Sovereign* (2009, 2011), to analyze and defamiliarize Revelation's animal Christology.[6] The first of these books—or, more precisely, its first chapter[7]—has been a crucial catalyst (one of several) for an emergent, heterogeneous academic field that has attracted various (nonsynonymous) names, notably, "animal studies," "animal-

---

exception in the Revelation chapters of her *God and Power* (2005, 34–95). Her eco-feminist, poststructuralist, postcolonial reading of Revelation frequently engages with its "cosmic bestiary" (72)—although less with the animality of the Lamb, ultimately, than of the four living creatures around the throne (see 67–95), which were also the focus of her earlier "Eyeing the Apocalypse" (2001). While not explicitly ecological in thrust, Gilhus's brief survey of the animals of Revelation (2006, 176–80) is also worth consulting, as is Resseguie's treatment of Revelation's animals as literary characters (1998, 117–36). Revelation is all but absent, however (and oddly so), from Grant 1999.

4. Rossing's position is typical: "Revelation emphasizes that our future dwelling will be with God on earth, in a radiant, thriving city landscape" (2005, 171). For less typical, more cautious treatments of the heavenly city and the representation of nature within it, see Martin 2009; Horrell 2010, 100–101.

5. The spectacle is not to be confused with the Central Park Zoo, then.

6. Notwithstanding the first epigraph to this essay, Revelation or its bestiary do not receive seminar-length treatment in *The Beast and the Sovereign* or *The Animal That Therefore I Am*, merely a few passing remarks.

7. Originally published as "L'animal que donc je suis (à suivre)" (Derrida 1999); ET: "The Animal That Therefore I Am (More to Follow)" (Derrida 2002). For an engaging discussion of this article, particularly the portion of it that deals with Adam's naming of the animals in Gen 2:19–20, see Chrulew 2008.

ity studies," and "posthuman animality studies." The term *posthuman* in this context is frequently a synonym for "post-Cartesian."[8] Descartes is, indeed, something of a *bête noire* for animal studies. The Cartesian elevation of individual subjectivity, it is now commonly asserted, was obtained by reconceiving the relations between human and nonhuman animals in terms that were absolutely oppositional and hierarchical.[9] But the term *animal(s)* is perhaps not the best one in this context. Prior to the Cartesian revolution in philosophy there were no "animals" in the modern sense. There were "creatures," "beasts," and "living things," a bionomic arrangement reflected in, and reinforced by, the early vernacular Bibles. As Laurie Shannon notes (2009, 476), "*animal* never appears in the benchmark English of the Great Bible (1539), the Geneva Bible (1560), or the King James Version (1611)."[10] More significantly, the continuum evoked by the term *creature* also included angels and demons, so that premodern humans saw themselves as embedded in a complex, multilayered cosmology. Missing was "the fundamentally modern sense of the animal or animals as humanity's persistent, solitary opposite" (Shannon 2009, 476).[11]

---

8. For a more comprehensive treatment of the posthuman than is possible in this essay, see Wolfe 2009b.

9. Descartes was radicalizing philosophical and theological views of the animal with deep roots in antiquity. Greco-Roman philosophy was characterized by a wide and complex range of positions on human-animal relations, certain of which anticipated those of Descartes. Aristotle in his voluminous writings on animals distinguished them from humans by their alleged lack of reason, speech, and upright posture. The Stoics built on Aristotle's ideas on animals, developing them further, and their ideas in turn were incorporated and adapted by Jews and Christians. More nuanced views of human-animal relations, meanwhile, emerged from the Platonic and Pythagorean traditions, and received extended expression in the works of such philosophers as Plutarch and Porphyry. For useful surveys of these ancient debates, see Gilhus 2006, esp. 37–63; Spittler 2008, 15–26; and for a magisterial discussion of Descartes's ideas on animals in relation to those of Aristotle, Augustine, Aquinas, and other seminal philosophers and theologians, see Steiner, 2005, 132–52, together with 53–131.

10. The title of Shannon's article, "The Eight Animals in Shakespeare; or, Before the Human," refers to the fact that the term *animal* occurs only eight times in Shakespeare's entire oeuvre, while the terms *beast* and *creature* occur hundreds of times. "As the *OED* confirms, *animal* hardly appears in English before the end of the sixteenth century" (Shannon 2009, 474).

11. Donna Haraway pointedly uses the term *critters* for both human and nonhuman animals. She writes: "Critters are always relationally entangled rather than taxonomically neat" (2007, 330 n. 33).

Descartes was the prime creator of the animal in the peculiarly modern sense of the term. What Descartes did was cull the human creature, conceived as the only one "equipped with a rational soul, from the entire spectrum of creatures," all others being consigned to "the mechanistic limits of purely instinctual behavior" (2009, 476). This radical reconception of the nonhuman animal is commonly termed the *bête-machine* ("beast-machine") doctrine for its equation of animals with clocks and other mechanisms with automatic moving parts.[12] The Cartesian human/animal antithesis has powerfully catalyzed both a philosophical and physical erasure of the animal, one whose effects are manifested with unprecedented starkness in our own time. As Shannon observes:

> The disappearance of the more protean *creatures* into the abstract nominalizations of *animal*, *the animal*, and *animals* parallels livestock's banishment to a clandestine, dystopian world of industrial food production, where the unspeakable conditions of life depend on invisibility. It mirrors, too, the increasing confinement of wildlife in preserves as wild spaces disappear with alarming speed. (2009, 477)

Shannon's article was one of fourteen on human-animal relations that appeared in the March 2009 issue of *PMLA*, the flagship journal of the Modern Language Association. "Why Animals Now?" is the title of the lead article in the collection (DeKoven 2009; cf. Weil 2012, 1–50). The answer would seem to be twofold. These animal articles were but one product of an emerging subfield that intersects complexly with the larger field of ecocriticism in literary studies, being in part a recent inflection of that ever more important field. The second answer is more specific. Human-animal relations have become a locus of intense intellectual energy and ethical investment in the humanities because certain prominent theorists and philosophers have been writing on them. The most influential of these writings, arguably (to return to the claim with which this section began), has been Derrida's "The Animal That Therefore I Am" (2002) and the posthumously published book of the same name (2008a).[13] Derrida's title is

---

12. For the doctrine, see Descartes 2006 (French original 1637), 35–49; and 2000, 275–76, 292–96 (two letters from 1646 and 1649, respectively).

13. The work of Donna Haraway (1990, 2003, 2007) has also been highly influential. Agamben 2004 has been another prominent contribution, as also (from the "analytic" side of the analytic/Continental philosophical divide) has been Cavell et al. 2008. For an excellent introduction to the field of animal studies in all its heterogene-

a riposte to Descartes's "I think, therefore I am"—"a summons issued to Descartes," as he himself puts it (2008a, 75).

The preeminent modern philosophical category—*the human*—has been based on a conceptual subjection of the animal. And the material corollary of that conceptual subjugation has been an actual subjugation, even annihilation, of the animal on an unprecedented scale—"a war against the animal," as Derrida phrases it, a "war to the death" that threatens to "end in a world without animals, without any animal worthy of the name," living for nothing other than as a means for the human (2008a, 101–2; cf. 2009, 302–3). Derrida writes searingly of the "sacrificialist current" that animates the Cartesian cogito and other influential philosophical discourses on the animal (Kantian, Heideggerian, etc.)—not "sacrificial," however, in the sense of a "ritual sacrifice of the animal" but rather in the sense of a "founding sacrifice" enacted "within a human space where ... exercising power over the animal to the point of being able to put it to death when necessary is not forbidden" (2008a, 90–91). As we are about to see, Revelation both affirms and disturbs this sacrificial logic, at once age-old and peculiarly modern.

The Hyphen between God and Sheep

On the one hand (hoof, paw, claw ...), instead of the asymmetrical, antithetical human/animal dyad endemic to post-Cartesian modernity, Revelation presents us with a divine/human/animal triad, each of the three terms bleeding profusely into the other two. Revelation opens in earnest with a vision of one *homoion huion anthrōpou* (1:13–16), as noted above—one like a Son of Man, a Son of Humanity, a Human Being. Although labeled as human, however, this numinous figure bears the marks of divinity on his physical person: most conspicuously, the wool-like whiteness of his hair (*hōs erion leukon*—1:14a) evokes the wool-like whiteness of the Ancient One's hair in Dan 7:9 (LXX: *hōsei erion leukon*).[14] The Human

ity, see Wolfe 2009a; and for a wide-ranging textbook introduction, see Weil 2012. For introductions to the major philosophical work in the field, see Calarco and Atterton 2004; Calarco 2008; Oliver 2009. For the intersection of animal studies and postcolonial studies, see Huggan and Tiffin 2010, which includes a biblically oriented chapter on "Christianity, Cannibalism and Carnivory" (162–84). Further on Derrida's animal work, see Badmington 2007; Haraway 2007, 19–23; Lawlor 2007; Wood 2007.

14. The "Son of Man" designation spills into Rev 1:13 from Dan 7:13, where it

Being is also a Divine Being.[15] The wool metaphor, however, also conjoins this Human proleptically with the Animal, and with one animal in particular. For when the figure next appears it has undergone a theriomorphic metamorphosis. It shimmers uncertainly for a moment, taking the form of a Lion (5:5), but resolves into the form of a Lamb (5:6).[16]

This is not the only metaphoric lamb in early Christian literature (see also, e.g., Luke 10:3; John 1:29, 36; 21:15; Acts 8:32; 1 Cor 5:7; 1 Pet 1:19; Justin Martyr, *Dial.* 40, 72; Melito of Sardis, *On the Passover* 7–8, 71; *Gos. Phil.* 58, 14–15), but it may be the only four-legged one. When John the Baptist, for instance, on "[seeing] Jesus coming toward him" in John 1:29 exclaims, "Here is the Lamb of God [*ho amnos tou theou*] who takes away the sin of the world!" (cf. 1:36), few if any readers or hearers have visualized a quadrupedal lamb trotting up to John. But a quadrupedal lamb is precisely what the Christian imagination has tended overwhelmingly to visualize in Revelation's throne room,[17] albeit an anomalous specimen of lambhood, multihorned and many-eyed (5:6).[18] In the terms associated with conceptual metaphor theory, more characteristics of the source domain (*lamb*) are mapped onto the target domain (*Jesus*) in Rev 5:6ff. than in John

is used to differentiate the human from the animal. For preliminary reflections on human-animal relations in Dan 7, see Moore 2011, 87–88.

15. As well as an androgyne: the "Son of Man" sports a pair of female breasts (*mastoi*—1:13; see Rainbow 2007; Moore 2009, 91–94). Last but not least, the Human Being is also an angelic being: most of the details of his/her head-to-toe description are copied from Dan 10:5–6, where they describe an angel, probably Gabriel (see Carrell 1997, 129–74). Densely imbricated in this category-defying figure, then, are animal, angelic, human-female, divine, and human-male elements, and in no discernible hierarchical order.

16. In which guise it then trots through most of the remaining narrative. As Johns (2003, 22) notes, "Not limited to one or two scenes, the term [*arnion*, 'lamb'] appears in fully half of the 22 chapters of the Apocalypse. … [It] is by far the most frequent designation for Christ in the Apocalypse. It appears more than twice as often as any other name or image for Christ—even more than the simple name *Iēsous*, the title *Christos*, or variations thereof."

17. See Kovacs and Rowland, 2004, 74–75, for a brief review of some of the better-known artistic representations of Revelation's Lamb.

18. Might the horns even disqualify it from being regarded as a lamb at all? Might we be looking at a ram instead? Apparently not. "[T]he idea that lambs could have horns was not unknown in the ancient world. According to one tradition, some lambs immediately begin to develop horns at birth (cf. Homer, *Odyssey* 4.85; Aristotle, *Historia Animalium* 7.19)" (Johns 2003, 24 n. 11).

1:29, 36.[19] The result is a theriomorphic Messiah or quadrupedal Christ, a Jesus who now adds species crossing to the other border-crossing activities regularly attributed to him.

With the exception of the human animal, as Derrida remarks, "no animal has ever thought to dress itself" (2008a, 5). Clothing or its absence is yet another means by which the Christ of Revelation shuttles in and out of humanity. In his initial appearance as "a Son of Man" he is clothed ("clothed with a long robe and with a golden sash across his chest"—1:13) and seen only by the seer. In his second appearance as the slain Lamb he is unclothed, presumably, even though the object of a mass gaze (5:6–14); yet he is not naked, because he is animal. When he resumes his human form following the demise of Babylon,[20] he is clothed once more ("clothed in a robe dipped in blood"—19:13; cf. 19:16). Yet his robe bears a residual mark (if not ineradicable stains) of the animal identity that it conceals: it is inscribed with a name, "King of kings and Lord of lords," which was earlier attributed to the Lamb (17:14), and the blood in which it has been dipped may be that issuing from the Lamb's slaughter.[21] Clothes do not make the man or the Son of Man in Revelation so much as remind us that he is always liable to be unmade and remade as animal. Jesus' humanity flickers indecisively in Revelation, and is ultimately eclipsed by his animality.

For the Lamb, not the Lion (cf. 5:5) or even the (Son of) Man, is the king of beasts in Revelation, including human beasts. If the anthropomorphic warrior on the white horse is "King of kings and Lord of lords" (19:16), his inverted image, the Lamb, is "Lord of lords and King of kings" (17:14); but while the warrior has followers (19:14), the Lamb has adorers. It is the Lamb, not the Man, that is the object of mass adulation, mass adoration, for "every creature in heaven and on earth and under the earth" (5:13; cf. 5:8–14; 7:9–10). And even if the Lamb is ambiguously positioned *en mesō tou thronou* in its initial appearance (5:6; cf. 7:17)—"on the throne"? "in the inner court area around the throne"?[22]—by the time we eventually arrive

19. The classic exposition of conceptual metaphor theory is Lakoff and Johnson 1981. Huber applies the theory to Revelation's images of the bride (2007) and the 144,000 male virgins (2008), while Gilhus (briefly) applies it to the dove and lamb images of the New Testament (2006, 173–74).

20. Setting the ambiguous 14:14–16 aside for now.

21. An interpretation that may be traced back to the early centuries of the church (Weinrich 2005, 311).

22. Beale is among those who favor the latter rendering, arguing that "[i]n 5:6

at the heavenly city, "God's dwelling place among human beings" (*hē skēnē tou theou meta tōn anthrōpōn*), the throne has become "the throne of God and of the Lamb" (*ho thronos tou theou kai tou arniou*—22:1, 3; cf. 3:21), the Lamb now lording it with God over humans, who have become its slaves (*douloi*—22:3) even as it has become unequivocally divine. Revelation's Lamb, then, is at once a human-animal hybrid and a divine-animal hybrid. And for now, at least, its sharp little horns seem to be ripping the Cartesian human/animal hierarchy to shreds.

But the Lamb is not the only animal whose habitat is Revelation's throne room. Surrounding the throne are the four "living creatures" (*zōa*), encrusted with eyes in front and behind and fitted with multiple wings, one creature lionlike, another calflike, a third "with a face like a human face" (*echōn to prosōpon hōs anthrōpou*), and a fourth "like a flying eagle" (4:6b–8). These four creatures may represent the entire created order of animate beings, as has sometimes been suggested (see especially Brütsch 1970, 230–33). More significant, however, for our topic is that the human does not represent the apex of creation in this bestial tableau.[23] Its placement as the third item in the series is decidedly nonemphatic. The humanoid face is briefly glimpsed among the (other) animal visages, but it does not rise above them or see beyond them. This creature has exactly the same number of wings and eyes as its fellows and the exact same lines to utter in the eschatological script (4:8b; cf. 5:14; 6:1, 3, 5, 7; 19:4).

What Derrida has to say in a different context, then, seems eminently applicable to Revelation's initial throne-room scene: "there are gods and there are beasts, there is, there is only, the theo-zoological, and in the theo-anthropo-zoological, man is caught, evanescent, disappearing, at the very most a simple mediation, a hyphen between the sovereign and the beast, between God and cattle" (2009, 13). Or between God and lions, God and eagles, or God and sheep, as is also the case in our throne-room tableau. Derrida defines the "ahuman," which he also names "divinanimality," as "the excluded, foreclosed, disavowed, tamed, and sacrificed foundation of

---

it appears that the Lamb is near the throne, preparing to make his approach to be enthroned" (1999, 350). Hoffmann, however, prompted by the Lamb taking the scroll from "the right hand" of the one seated on the throne (5:7), proposes a third alternative: "the Lamb is placed at the right hand side of God [the position of exaltation] after (or when) he takes the scroll from God" (2005, 138).

23. As Keller insightfully notes in her reflections on the four living creatures (2005, 68).

… the human order, law and justice."[24] Prior to that exclusion, that foreclosure—which, most of all, is a Cartesian exclusion—the divine is both theriomorphic and anthropomorphic, and such anthropomorphic divinanimality comes to sublime expression in Revelation.

Slaves of the Sheep

On the other hand (hoof, paw, claw …), there are almost no nonhuman animals as such represented anywhere in Revelation,[25] only metaphorical animals, chimerical animals, and metaphorical-chimerical animals, beginning with the many-eyed, multihorned Lamb. How best to relate to them? Just as I have found it fruitful elsewhere to read Revelation's God *as* human—more precisely, to ask what kind of divine-human relations are encoded in this human, all-too-human deity (e.g., Moore 1996, 117–38; 2001, 175–99 passim)—so I am attempting here to read Revelation's metaphorical, all-too-metaphorical animals *as* animals in the interests of deciphering the human-animal relations encrypted in them.

Let us return to Revelation's throne room, then, and to what earlier seemed to be less a hierarchical, oppositional human/animal dyad than a symbiotic divine/human/animal triad, the divine intimately conjoined to the human and the animal, and the human consequently conjoined to the animal and the divine. Revelation's divine/human/animal symbiosis, however, can hardly be said to be symmetrical. Hierarchy continues to rear its ugly head in Revelation, and the head is frequently that of a young sheep—paradoxically, a rather petite young sheep, if the diminutive form of *arnion*, the term in Revelation ordinarily translated as "lamb," is to be accorded its full (if meager) weight.[26]

---

24. Derrida 2008a, 132, in the course of his critique of Lacan's conception of the animal; see also Derrida 2009, 127. Earlier Derrida writes of "the ahuman combining god and animal according to all the theo-zoomorphic possibilities that properly constitute the myths, religions, idolatries, and even sacrificial practices within the monotheisms that claim to break with idolatry" (2008a, 131; also 2009, 126).

25. Cf. Gilhus 2006, 177: "John, the author of Revelation, did not intend to say anything about real animals." Or as Huggan and Tiffin phrase it in a different context, "the animal *as animal* becomes invisible" (2010, 173, their emphasis).

26. Cf. Derrida 2009, 258: "There is no more reason to call a superterrestrial God great ('God is great') than small. … [I]n certain religions the manifestation of divine presence or sovereignty passes through the small, the smallest: the weakness and smallness of the baby Jesus for example, or the lamb." But how little is Revela-

Arguably, however (and this should be said before we surrender fully to the imperious grip of *the other hand*), even the form taken by hierarchy in Revelation where it pertains to the paradoxical figure of the Lamb is significant for ecotheology. For Revelation, however inadvertently, inverts the Aristotelian-Stoic species hierarchy that elevated the human over the animal.[27] As noted above, the scene in Revelation in which the Lamb first makes its entrance has every creature in heaven and on earth—angelic creatures and human creatures included—worshipping the Lamb (5:11–13); while the final scene in Revelation in which the Lamb appears characterizes the human inhabitants of the heavenly city as "slaves" (*douloi*—22:3)—apparently of God and the Lamb, humanity in thrall to ahuman divinanimality.[28] Revelation's New Eden, then, appears to overturn the order established in the Old Eden that, as Jewish and Christian tradition has most often understood it, accorded humankind dominion over all nonhuman creatures (Gen 1:28; 2:18–20).[29] This species hierarchy is unceremoniously toppled head over hoof in Revelation. The animal domesticated to serve human beings

tion's Lamb? Technically, *arnion* is the diminutive form of *arēn* ("young sheep"). Johns (2003, 26), however, echoes the views of many when he writes: "Although diminutives normally express either smallness ('small lamb') or endearment ('Lämmlein,' 'lambkin,' or 'lamby'), the historical linguistic evidence suggests that neither of these can be pressed in New Testament times apart from corroborating contextual evidence, which is certainly lacking in this case." Other scholars are less certain. Aune (1997, 368), for instance, writes: "it is extremely difficult to argue that *arnion* was consistently used as a faded diminutive [by the first century C.E.]."

27. Contrast John's near-contemporary Philo of Alexandria, for example, who, channeling Stoic doctrine, declared: "To raise animals to the level of the human race and grant equality to unequals [*anisoi*] is the epitome of injustice" (*Anim.* 100; my trans.).

28. Beale argues: "That 'they will serve *him* [*latreusousin autō*—22:3b]' likely does not refer only to God or only to the Lamb. The two are conceived so much as a unity that the singular pronoun can refer to both" (1999, 1113, his emphasis). Slater changes the "him" to a "them" in his paraphrase of the passage—"God and the Lamb … will provide the highest quality of life possible and the servants of God will worship them" (1999, 200)—and cites the commentaries of J. P. M. Sweet, Gerhard A. Krodel, Leon Morris, Robert H. Mounce, and George Eldon Ladd in support of his interpretation.

29. Derrida, echoing this tradition, parses out the combined effect of the two Genesis creation accounts as follows: God "has created man in his likeness *so that* man will *subject*, *tame*, *dominate*, *train*, or *domesticate* the animals born before him and assert his authority over them" (2008a, 16, his emphasis).

[When did a sheep last die of old age? Sheep do not own themselves, do not own their lives. They exist to be used, every last ounce of them, their flesh to be eaten, their bones to be crushed and fed to poultry. Nothing escapes, except perhaps the gall bladder, which no one will eat. Descartes should have thought of that. The soul, suspended in the dark, bitter gall, hiding. (Coetzee 1999a, 123)[30]]

now rules over every human being, including every human ruler: the Lamb is "Lord of lords and King of kings" (17:14), as we recall. The human subject is subjected to the animal for all eternity. That, however, is but the outer layer of the paradox that, like a wooly fleece, envelops Revelation's Lamb.

Murder in the Sheepfold

The necessary precondition for the subjection of humans to the anomalous animal of Revelation is that the animal first had to be subjected to slaughter by humans: "Worthy is the Lamb that was slaughtered [*to arnion to esphagmenon*] to receive power" (5:12; cf. 5:6, 9; 13:8). The Lamb suffers, then. The standing-as-though-slaughtered (*hōs esphagmenon*—5:6)—or slaughtered-but-still-standing—Lamb is, indeed, the privileged metaphor (and not only in Revelation) for the salvific suffering of the god-man. The god-man suffers like a god-man-animal, a theo-therio-anthropomorph. And suffers in silence. As animal, as *arnion*, the god-man does not—and perhaps cannot—speak in Revelation (cf. Isa 53:7; Acts 8:32), if by "speaking" we mean the utterance of human language. Not a single line, nor even a single word, is accorded to the Lamb in John's talking animal book.[31]

"[M]an alone among the animals has speech," Aristotle declared (*Pol.* 1253a 10).[32] In Aristotelian terms, then, the Lamb is inherently inferior to the man, even the (speaking) Son of Man with whom it is, yet is not, identical. And not just in Aristotelian terms: as Derrida observes, philoso-

30. Cf. Cicero, *Nat. d.* 2.63: "What other use have sheep, save that their fleeces are dressed and woven into clothing for men?" (LCL).

31. What of the phrase *tēn ōdēn tou arniou* in Rev 15:3a? Most contemporary commentators (e.g., Aune 1998, 873) translate the phrase as "the song about the lamb" (objective genitive) rather than as "the song of [i.e., sung by] the lamb" (subjective genitive), not least because the Lamb itself is not the singer, as the context makes clear.

32. Derrida concludes with an analysis of this declaration and the larger passage in which it is embedded (2009, 343–49).

phers otherwise as different as Aristotle, Descartes, Kant, Heidegger, Levinas, and Lacan "all … say the same thing: the animal is deprived of language. Or, more precisely, of response, of a response that could precisely and rigorously be distinguished from a reaction" (2008a, 32). But even if the Lamb is deprived of speech, it can hardly be said to be deprived of response, beginning with its decisive claiming of the sealed scroll ("It went and took the scroll from the right hand of the one who was seated on the throne"—5:7), the action that sets the entire ensuing narrative in motion.[33]

But perhaps speech, or even response, is not the crucial issue. Channeling Jeremy Bentham's late-eighteenth-century plea on behalf of the animal, Derrida remarks: "the question is not to know whether the animal can think, reason, or speak. … The *first* and *decisive* question would rather be to know whether animals *can suffer*" (2008a, 27, his emphasis).[34] If the crucial question is not whether animals can speak but rather whether animals can suffer, the Lamb both answers and complicates the question. On the one hand, the Lamb suffers without speaking, that is, it suffers as an animal suffers.[35] In Revelation, then, the torturous death of Jesus of Nazareth is figured as animal suffering. Crucifixion is implicitly repre-

33. And thus is revealed the mystery of how the Lamb "took [or 'has taken': *eilēphen*] the scroll." With its mouth? With its hoof? No, with its hand. For even if the Lamb as a quadrupedal mammal of the *Ovis* genus (albeit a metaphorical mammal with irregular ocular features and an abnormal number of horns) does not and cannot have a hand, its epochal action of taking and subsequently unsealing the scroll shows that it does have a hand in the Heideggarian sense. In "Heidegger's Hand," Derrida takes Heidegger to task for denying a hand to the animal (Derrida 2008b; cf. 2011, 83). Only *Dasein*, the human entity, can have a hand, according to Heidegger. Only *Dasein* is capable of the kind of thought and action that merits the term *hand*, while the animal (even the ape) has no hand, properly speaking, but only a prehensile grasping organ at best. "The hand is infinitely different from all grasping organs—paws, claws, or fangs—different by an abyss of essence" (Heidegger 1968, 16). Revelation's Lamb, although handless, can be said to emblematize hand-endowed animality. Hand over hand, it clambers out of Heidegger's abyss.

34. Bentham's plea for animal rights is epitomized in his pronouncement "the question is not, Can they *reason*? nor, Can they *talk*? but, Can they *suffer*?" (1879, 310–11).

35. Although the perceived "silence" of animals depends on a rigidly narrow conception of "speech." Derrida notes in an interview that the structural elements that make human language possible (the elements that his early work isolated and that he here itemizes as the mark, the trace, iterability, and *différance*) "*are themselves not only human*" (1995, 285, his emphasis).

sented through the figure of the butchered Lamb as an altogether abject death, an utterly dehumanizing death, a death more fitting to an animal than a human—a theme to which we shall later return.[36] To that extent, the image of the slaughtered Lamb reinscribes the hierarchical human/animal divide, writes it in blood. On the other hand, the slaughtered-but-still-standing Lamb also represents a leveling of the human in relation to the animal. Forever bearing the marks of death,[37] the Lamb figures the finitude that humans share with other animals. At the center of the throne room that is the locus of absolute power in Revelation is a curious non-power, an abject inability, whose emblem is a butchered animal. Mortality stands in the place of eternity in Revelation's central theophany.[38]

The Lamb is also singular in that it is also, as we are about to discover, an emblematic challenge to the logic that sacrificing an animal, exploiting it to death, does not constitute murder, a logic as ancient as Gen 4, God's preference for the firstlings of Abel's flock over Cain's fruits of the earth, and as recent as factory farming. In our own era, the scale of this mass nonmurder has achieved gargantuan proportions, necessitating a proportionate disavowal and dissimulation of the cruelty it entails. Like other writers on these matters, Derrida has recourse to the figure of genocide to

["They went like sheep to the slaughter." "They died like animals." "The Nazi butchers killed them." Denunciation of the camps reverberates so fully with the language of the stockyards and slaughterhouses that it is barely necessary for me to prepare the ground for the comparison I am about to make. The crime of the Third Reich, says the voice of accusation, was to treat people like animals. ...

36. Suffice it for now to note that as a sacrificially slain animal, the Lamb is always about to be eaten, and as such its fate curiously mirrors that of the woman Babylon, annihilated by being savagely devoured (17:16), and the enemies of the rider on the white horse, also obliterated through ingestion (19:17–18, 21). What Derrida has to say about *Robinson Crusoe* is only slightly less true of Revelation: "the great gesture, the great phantasmatic *gesta* of [this] book, which rules its whole vocabulary, its speech, its mouth, its tongue and its teeth, is that of eating and devouring, eating the other" (2011, 55).

37. Johns (2003, 111 n. 9) cautions that the phrase *hōs esphagmenon* in 5:6 "should not be translated 'as if [slaughtered],' suggesting that the marks of slaughter are ambiguous. The lamb of the Apocalypse is clearly a slain lamb."

38. See Derrida 2008a, 28, which, although not about Revelation or Christian soteriology, has impelled these reflections.

> **It was and is inconceivable that people who *did not know* (in that special sense) about the camps can be fully human. In our chosen metaphorics, it was they and not their victims who were the beasts. By treating fellow human beings, beings created in the image of God, like beasts, they had themselves become beasts.**
>
> **I was taken on a drive around Waltham this morning. It seems a pleasant enough town. I saw no horrors, no drug-testing laboratories, no factory farms, no abattoirs. Yet I am sure they are here. They must be. They simply do not advertise themselves. They are all around us as I speak, only we do not, in a certain sense, know about them.**
>
> **Let me say it openly: we are surrounded by an enterprise of degradation, cruelty, and killing which rivals anything that the Third Reich was capable of, indeed dwarfs it, in that ours is an enterprise without end, self-regenerating, bringing rabbits, rats, poultry, livestock ceaselessly into the world for the purpose of killing them. (Coetzee 1999b, 20–21)[39]]**

express his own revulsion at "the *unprecedented* proportions of this subjection of the animal" (Derrida 2008a, 25, his emphasis). "One should neither abuse the figure of genocide," Derrida states,

> nor too quickly consider it explained away. It gets more complicated: the annihilation of certain species is indeed in process, but it is occurring through the organization and exploitation of an artificial, infernal, virtually interminable survival, in conditions that previous generations would have judged monstrous, outside of every presumed norm of a life proper to animals that are thus exterminated by means of their continued existence or even their overpopulation. (2008a, 26)[40]

These present-day abominations far exceed the animal sacrifices of the Bible (cf. 2008a, 25), even at their most extravagant ("Solomon offered

---

39. The novel's protagonist, Elizabeth Costello, is delivering two invited lectures at the fictional Appleton College in Waltham, Massachusetts. Cf. Wolfe 2003, 190: "I think it entirely possible, if not likely, that a hundred years from now we will look back on our current mechanized and systematized practices of factory farming, product testing, and much else that undeniably involves animal exploitation and suffering … with much the same horror and disbelief with which we now regard slavery or the genocide of the Second World War."

40. This statement occurs as part of a lengthy passionate protest (Derrida 2008a, 25–27) that erupts rather abruptly in what has up to then been a somewhat cerebral meditation on human-animal relations.

as sacrifices ... to the LORD [at the dedication of the temple] twenty-two thousand oxen and one hundred twenty thousand sheep"—1 Kgs 8:63 [= 2 Chr 7:5]; cf. 1 Kgs 8:5). The unprecedented proportions of our current subjection of the animal intensifies Revelation's paradox of a butchered animal bearing the bloody marks of subjection unto death, yet to which all human beings are now subjected and to whose vengeance they are now subject. "[H]ide us from...the wrath of the Lamb [*tēs orgēs tou arniou*]," the human inhabitants of the earth cry out in panic as they themselves scamper like frightened animals, hiding in caves and among rocks (6:16).[41] The slaughtered sacrificial victim has returned to life, thereby causing the priest to drop his knife and flee from the altar in terror. But there are also more subtle significations encrypted in the figure of the slain-but-standing Lamb than these lurid dramas of reversal and revenge.

Derrida dissects Heidegger's argument that only man, as *Dasein*, "has an experiential relation to death, ... to his *own* death, his own being-able-to die, to its possibility, ... whereas the animal ... perishes but never dies, has no relation worthy of the name to death" (Derrida 2009, 307–8; see also 2011, 115–17, 290).[42] Derrida parses out the implications: if the animal is indeed incapable of an "authentic" relation to death, then the animal is a living creature that can only live, that can never die, and as such is an "immortal" being (2008a, 129). If this were all there was to the matter, we would now have explained in full why and in what sense the slain Lamb of Revelation is immortal. It lives, it lives on—eternally—precisely as a sacrificial animal, which, although slaughtered, cannot truly die. There is, however, more to this anomalous animality.

Elsewhere Derrida takes Levinas to task for his explicit hesitation to ascribe a "face" to the animal and hence the ethical obligation that is due to the human (Derrida 2008a, 105–18; 2009, 237ff.). Derrida recounts that when Levinas was challenged by a questioner at a 1986 symposium, "Does

41. Note, too, the species inversion of Rev 7:17: "for the Lamb ... will be their shepherd [*to arnion ... poimanei autous*]" (cf. 14:4b).

42. The argument is aphoristically epitomized in Heidegger 1971, 176: "Only man dies. The animal perishes." See also Derrida 1994, 35–38, 74–76, one of several earlier texts in which Derrida previously mused on this Heideggerian theme. In effect, Heidegger epitomizes, for Derrida, the post-Cartesian absolutization of the human/animal divide: "The distinction between the animal (which has no or is not a *Dasein*) and man has nowhere been more radical nor more rigorous than in Heidegger" (2005, 268).

the animal have a face? Can one read 'Thou shalt not kill' in the eyes of the animal?" Levinas vacillated: "I cannot say at what moment you have the right to be called 'face.' The human face is completely different and only afterwards do we discover the face of an animal. I don't know if a snake has a face" (Derrida 2008a, 107–8).[43] Levinas's recourse to the example of the snake is telling, as Derrida notes. Many more "disturbing examples" might have been adduced—"for example, the cat, the dog, the horse, the monkey, the orangutan, the chimpanzee—whom it would be difficult to refuse a face and a gaze. And hence to refuse the 'Thou shalt not kill' that Levinas reserves for the face" (2008a, 110). What the exchange with Levinas impels is the introduction of the category of *murder* into our consideration of the slain Lamb. If the Lamb does not possess a face in the Levinasian sense, is not a candidate for murder, then a Levinasian reflection on the Lamb as animal takes us no farther than a Heideggerian reflection on it, and to a death that is not worthy of the name.[44] Inasmuch as it is categorically incapable of being a murder victim, the Lamb still cannot die. It lives on forever as the quintessential sacrificial animal.

But this is not what Revelation implies, hence its interest and relevance for contemporary ecotheology. The slaughter of its singular animal was a heinous crime, so much so that when this creature returns "with the clouds"—whether as theriomorph, anthropomorph, or therioanthropomorph—"every eye will see him, even those who pierced him; and on his account all the tribes of the earth will wail" (1:7; cf. 6:15–17), implicitly because of the unspeakable injustice done to him. Does the Lamb have a face? Yes, it would seem, to the extent that killing the Lamb was

43. A slightly different version of the exchange is presented in Derrida 2009, 237, after which Derrida takes up the specific example of the snake at some length. Many centuries earlier, we find Augustine also pondering the question of whether "Thou shalt not kill" applies to animals. Lining up behind Aristotle and the Stoics, Augustine declares that it cannot apply to "the irrational animals that fly, swim, walk, or creep, since they are dissociated from us by their want of reason, and are therefore by the just appointment of the Creator subjected to us to kill or keep alive for our own uses; if so, then it remains that we understand that commandment simply of man" (*Civ.* 1.20, *NPNF* 1/2:15).

44. On the question of the animal, Derrida finds Levinas to be "profoundly Heideggarian" (2008a, 110). For Levinas's own most profound meditation on human-animal relations, see Levinas 1990. For theological reflection on this essay, see Gross 2009.

> **[A Kent head teacher at the centre of a row about the slaughter of a school lamb has resigned. Andrea Charman will step down as head of Lydd Primary School in Romney Marsh at the end of the week, Kent County Council has said.**
>
> **Mrs. Charman was criticised in September after sending Marcus the lamb—who had been hand-reared by pupils—to slaughter, despite calls to save him. …**
>
> **But Mrs. Charman went ahead with sending the animal to slaughter, which was part of a project to teach children about the food cycle. (Anon. 2010)]**

a culpable act. The Lamb is that anomalous animal in whose (seven) eyes "Thou shalt not kill" can be read. This, then, is yet another way in which Revelation problematizes in advance the Cartesian conception of the human as categorically distinct from the animal and hence the sole object of ethical obligation. But it is not just the Cartesian conception that is called into question. Far more ancient is the logic that declares that sacrificing an animal, slaughtering it for food, or otherwise exploiting it to death, does not—indeed cannot—constitute murder (cf. Derrida 2008a, 110).[45] Revelation presents us with the ethical paradox of a sacrificial animal whose slaughter constitutes unlawful killing, that is, manslaughter or murder.

Yet Revelation also relies on the sacrificial logic it deconstructs. That the slaughter of the Lamb was a culpable act, an unjust killing, does not render it an unproductive act, an ineffective sacrifice. On the contrary, Revelation represents this judicial murder as the most spectacularly effi-

45. This was not a uniform logic in antiquity, however, a complication of which Derrida seems unaware. The ideas of Pythagoras and his disciple Empedocles regarding the transmigration of souls were revived during the Roman Principate, and together with the Orphic tradition formed the basis for ethical arguments for vegetarianism. Attributed to Orpheus was the view that slaughtering animals was murder—equivalent, indeed, to killing one's own kin. Also relevant here is the "contractual" view of animal sacrifice common in antiquity, the notion that animals led to the altar were expected to consent to their own slaughter, even to the point of nodding their assent before the knife or axe descended. This nod was regularly produced by pouring water, flour, or some other substance over the animal's head; yet many of the human participants in the rite seem to have deemed the nod significant nonetheless. Plutarch, for example, remarks: "people are very careful not to kill the animal till a drink-offering is poured over him and he shakes his head in assent. Such precautions they [take] to avoid any unjust act" (*Table Talk* 729F, Minar et al., LCL). Further on all of these topics, see Gilhus 2006, esp. 25–26, 35–38, 87, 119–21, 141–47.

cacious sacrifice ever performed. "[Y]ou were slaughtered and by your blood you ransomed [or 'purchased': *ēgorasas*] for God saints from every tribe and language and people and nation," exults the heavenly chorus (5:9; cf. 1:5; 7:14; 12:11; 19:13), including the four living creatures, themselves more animal than human; and before long "every creature in heaven and on earth and under the earth and in the sea" (5:13) has joined in. A vast chorus of creatures, including every nonhuman animal, rejoices in the sacrifice of the god-man who died a death so ostensibly ignoble, so unbefitting of an honorable man, much less a god, that it elicits representation as an animal death: "I saw … a Lamb standing as if it had been slaughtered" (5:6). Do they exult because this unique sacrifice has made all further animal sacrifices unnecessary? Is the explicit argument of the Letter to the Hebrews (see esp. 10:1–14) implicit in the book of Revelation?

To settle for such a solution would be to domesticate Revelation's wildly anomalous Lamb, a sacrificial victim that is also a murder victim. In effect, the slain Lamb is the sacrifice of Cain—not Cain's "offering of the fruit of the earth," however, for which God "had no regard" (Gen 4:3–5), but the slaughter of his brother Abel that occasions divine horror: "What have you done? Listen, your brother's blood is crying out to me from the ground!" (4:10). For now at least, God much prefers the slaughtered "firstlings of the flock" that is Abel's offering (4:4). In Revelation's throne room, however, sheep and man, sacrificial victim and murder victim, become one. In order to effect divine remission of human sin, the slaughter of the sacrificial victim must itself be a sin, a crime. In order for sacrifice to be fully and eternally efficacious, the sacrificial victim must have a face, must die a human death—but that death must also be so abject,

[To slaughter you will need one sharp butchering knife, a small skinning knife, and a steel to keep the knives sharp. If you are butchering only one or two lambs, you can work outdoors under a tree that has an overhanging limb. … If you are working indoors, you should have a solid beam to hang the lamb on. …

However, if you are going to slaughter many animals, a sawbuck rack large enough to hold a lamb placed on its back with its head hanging off the end is a convenience that will allow you to, in effect, guillotine the lamb. … To use the guillotine method, strap the lamb to the sawbuck or have someone hold it there. Grab the lamb's muzzle, bend the head back a bit and, with one clean stroke of a sharp

> **butcher's knife cutting down toward the backbone, sever the jugulars, carotids, gullet, and windpipe. Twist the head and with the knife disjoint the head from the body where the backbone joins the skull. …**
>
> **Cutting from the inside out, open the skin on the neck down to where you cut the throat. Using your clenched fist instead of a knife to separate the skin from the body, "punch" or "fist" the hide loose over the brisket as far back as the navel. … Fist the hide loose over the shoulders and back and as far up as the tail. … Using the knife, skin around the tail and anus. … Cut around the bung, deep into the pelvis, and tie the rectum off so manure will not spill out. … To do this it will be necessary to pull the bung out of the pelvis; it is easier to have a second person tie the string. (Mettler 2003, 73–74, 76–78)[46]]**

so awful, as to compel metaphorization as a death only befitting an animal. Had Jesus of Nazareth expired of old age, there would be no butchered animal bleeding all over Revelation's throne room. What remains undisturbed in Revelation is the notion that certain forms of death potentially reduce the human being to animal status. Equally undisturbed by extension, therefore, is the notion that animals, in death as in life, are inherently inferior to humans.

Also undisturbed, finally, are the operations of the ancient sacrificial machine. Far from declaring the machine obsolete, Revelation's Lamb ransoming saints by its blood shows that the machine still works—that it is, indeed, spectacularly effective (see esp. 7:9, 13–14: "After this I looked, and there was a great multitude that no one could count, … robed in white. … 'Who are these, robed in white …?' … 'These are they who have come out of the great ordeal; they have washed their robes and made them white in the blood of the Lamb'"; cf. 1:5b; 5:9; 12:11). There is no *explicit* critique of animal sacrifice in Revelation, then, no intimation that exploiting an animal to death for human benefit is unethical, even though such critiques were not unknown in Revelation's world.[47] And yet, as we have seen, Revelation's Lamb also presents us with the ethical paradox of a sacrificial animal whose slaughter constitutes unlawful killing—which is to say that there is, nonetheless, in Revelation (and irrespective of whether its author

46. Cf. Bergen 2005, 14–18, in which the author draws on his experience of working on the killing floor of a modern meat-packing plant to reframe the prescriptions on ritual animal slaughter in Lev 1–7.

47. See Gilhus 2006, 138–60; Steiner 2005, 47–48, 105–7, on the most prominent ancient critics of animal sacrifice.

intended it), an *implicit* critique of animal sacrifice, and hence, by extension, of our continuing

> **[On November 24th, 2011 a video from Live Leaks surfaced on YouTube showing a group of US soldiers dragging a sheep into a crowded room and laughing with delight as one of their officers repeatedly and savagely smashes it in the head. As this is happening, several Afghani children jump up and down with excitement as soldiers clap, cheer and encourage the attacker on until the limp and lifeless body of the animal is dragged across the ground and out of the view of the camera.**
>
> **To date, the US Army has released only one statement saying that they are investigating the matter but animal activists and concerned citizens have expressed their distrust in the process as in the past only minor disciplinary charges have been given out for similar offences.**
>
> **According to the Live Leaks website the incident occurred on November 6th, 2011 as part of the holy festival of Eid and that the killing was "to represent a sacrifice made by Abraham of a ram when the angels told him that he had fulfilled the dream ordering him to sacrifice his young son, at which he laid down the knife and sacrificed the animal instead." (Williams 2011)]**

sacrificial war against the animal.

Works Cited

Agamben, Georgio. 2004. *The Open: Man and Animal*. Translated by Kevin Attell. Meridian: Crossing Aesthetics. Stanford, Calif.: Stanford University Press.

Anonymous. 2010. Slaughtered Lamb Head Teacher Resigns from Kent School. *BBC News*, February 10, 2010. Online: http://news.bbc.co.uk/2/hi/uk_news/england/kent/8508975.stm.

Augustine. 1956. *City of God*. Translated by Marcus Dods. In vol. 2 of *Nicene and Post-Nicene Fathers*. Series 1. Edited by Philip Schaff. Repr., Grand Rapids: Eerdmans.

Aune, David E. 1997. *Revelation 1–5*. Word Biblical Commentary 52. Dallas: Word.

———. 1998. *Revelation 6–16*. Word Biblical Commentary 52B. Nashville: Nelson.

Badmington, Neil, ed. 2007. *Derridanimals*. *Oxford Literary Review* 29.1–2 (thematic issue).

Bauckham, Richard. 2010. *The Bible and Ecology: Rediscovering the Community of Creation*. Waco, Tex.: Baylor University Press.

Beale, G. K. 1999. *The Book of Revelation: A Commentary on the Greek Text*. New International Greek Testament Commentary. Grand Rapids: Eerdmans.

Bentham, Jeremy. 1879. *Principles of Morals and Legislation*. New ed. Oxford: Clarendon.

Bergen, Wesley J. 2005. *Reading Ritual: Leviticus in Postmodern Culture*. Journal for the Study of the Old Testament Supplement Series 417. New York: Continuum.

Brütsch, Charles. 1970. *Die Offenbarung Jesu Christi: Johannes-Apokalypse*. 2nd ed. Zürcher Bibelkommentare, NT. Zurich: Zwingli.

Calarco, Matthew. 2008. *Zoographies: The Question of the Animal from Heidegger to Derrida*. New York: Columbia University Press.

Calarco, Matthew, and Peter Atterton, eds. 2004. *Animal Philosophy: Essential Readings in Continental Thought*. New York: Continuum.

Carrell, Peter R. 1997. *Jesus and the Angels: Angelology and the Christology of the Apocalypse of John*. Society for New Testament Studies Monograph Series 95. Cambridge: Cambridge University Press.

Cavell, Stanley, Cora Diamond, John McDowell, Ian Hacking, and Cary Wolfe. 2008. *Philosophy and Animal Life*. New York: Columbia University Press.

Chrulew, Matthew. 2008. Feline Divinanimality: Derrida and the Discourse of Species in Genesis. *Bible and Critical Theory* 2.2. Online: http://www.relegere.org/index.php/bct/article/viewFile/87/73.

Coetzee, J. M. 1997. *Boyhood: Scenes from Provincial Life*. New York: Viking Penguin.

———. 1999a. *Disgrace*. New York: Viking Penguin.

———. 1999b. *The Lives of Animals*. Edited by Amy Gutmann. University Center for Human Values Series. Princeton: Princeton University Press.

DeKoven, Marianne. Guest Column: Why Animals Now? *Proceedings of the Modern Language Association* 124:361–69.

Derrida, Jacques. 1994. *Aporias*. Translated by Thomas Dutoit. Meridian: Crossing Aesthetics. Stanford, Calif.: Stanford University Press.

———. 1995. "Eating Well"; or, The Calculation of the Subject. Pages 255-83 in *Points…: Interviews, 1974–1994*. Edited by Elisabeth Weber. Meridian: Crossing Aesthetics. Stanford, Calif.: Stanford University Press.

———. 1999. L'animal que donc je suis (à suivre). Pages 251–303 in *L'animal autobiographique*. Edited by Marie-Louise Mallet. Paris: Galilée.

———. 2002. The Animal That Therefore I Am (More to Follow). Translated by David Wills. *Critical Inquiry* 28:369–418.

———. 2008a. *The Animal That Therefore I Am*. Edited by Marie-Louise Mallet. Translated by David Wills. Perspectives in Continental Philosophy. New York: Fordham University Press.

———. 2008b. Heidegger's Hand (Geschlecctht II). Translated by John P. Leavey Jr. Pages 27–62 in vol. 2 of *Psyche: Inventions of the Other*. Edited by Peggy Kamuf and Elizabeth Rottenberg. 2 vols. Meridian: Crossing Aesthetics. Stanford, Calif.: Stanford University Press.

———. 2009. *The Beast and the Sovereign*. Vol. 1. Translated by Geoffrey Bennington. Seminars of Jacques Derrida 1. Chicago: University of Chicago Press.

———. 2011. *The Beast and the Sovereign*. Vol. 2. Translated by Geoffrey Bennington. Seminars of Jacques Derrida 2. Chicago: University of Chicago Press.

Descartes, René. 2000. *Philosophical Essays and Correspondence*. Edited by Roger Ariew. Translated by Roger Ariew et al. Indianapolis: Hackett.

———. 2006. *A Discourse on the Method of Correctly Conducting One's Reason and Seeking Truth in the Sciences*. Translated by Ian Maclean. Oxford World's Classics. Oxford: Oxford University Press.

Gilhus, Ingvild Saelid. 2006. *Animals, Gods and Humans: Changing Attitudes to Animals in Greek, Roman and Early Christian Ideas*. London: Routledge.

Grant, Robert M. 1999. *Early Christians and Animals*. London: Routledge.

Gross, Aaron S. 2009. The Question of the Creature: Animals, Theology and Levinas's Dog. Pages 121–37 in *Creaturely Theology: On God, Humans and Other Animals*. Edited by Celia Deane-Drummond and David Clough. London: SCM.

Haraway, Donna. 1990. *Primate Visions: Gender, Race, and Nature in the World of Modern Science*. London: Routledge.

———. 2003. *The Companion Species Manifesto: Dogs, People, and Significant Otherness*. Chicago: Prickly Paradigm.

———. 2007. *When Species Meet*. Posthumanities. Minneapolis: University of Minnesota Press.

Hawkin, David J. 2003. The Critique of Ideology in the Book of Revelation and Its Implications for Ecology. *Ecotheology* 8:161–72.

Heidegger, Martin. 1968. *What Is Called Thinking?* Translated by J. Glenn Gray. New York: Harper & Row.

———. 1971. The Thing. Pages 161–85 in *Poetry, Language, Thought.* Translated by Albert Hofstadter. New York: Harper & Row.

Hoffmann, Matthias Reinhard. 2005. *The Destroyer and the Lamb*. Wissenschafftliche Untersuchungen zum Neuen Testament 2/203. Tübingen: Mohr Siebeck.

Horrell, David G. 2010. *The Bible and the Environment: Towards a Critical Ecological Biblical Theology*. London: Equinox.

Huber, Lynn R. 2007. *Like a Bride Adorned: Reading Metaphor in John's Apocalypse*. Emory Studies in Early Christianity. New York: T&T Clark.

———. 2008. Sexually Explicit? Re-reading Revelation's 144,000 Virgins as a Response to Roman Discourses. *Journal of Men, Masculinities and Spirituality* 2:3–28.

Huggan, Graham, and Helen Tiffin. 2010. *Postcolonial Ecocriticism: Literature, Animals, Environment*. London: Routledge.

Johns, Loren L. 2003. *The Lamb Christology of the Apocalypse of John*. Wissenschafftliche Untersuchungen zum Neuen Testament 2/167. Tübingen: Mohr Siebeck.

Keller, Catherine. 2001. Eyeing the Apocalypse. Pages 253–77 in *Postmodern Interpretations of the Bible: A Reader*. Edited by A. K. M. Adam. St. Louis: Chalice.

———. 2005. *God and Power: Counter-Apocalyptic Journeys*. Minneapolis: Fortress.

Kovacs, Judith, and Christopher Rowland. 2004. *Revelation*. Blackwell Bible Commentaries. Oxford: Blackwell.

Lakoff, George, and Mark Johnson. 1981. *Metaphors We Live By*. 2nd ed. Chicago: University of Chicago Press.

Lawlor, Leonard. 2007. *This Is Not Sufficient: An Essay on Animality and Human Nature in Derrida*. New York: Columbia University Press.

Levinas, Immanuel. 1990. The Name of a Dog, or Natural Rights. Pages 151–53 in *Difficult Freedom: Essays on Judaism*. Translated by Sean Hand. Baltimore: Johns Hopkins University Press.

Maier, Harry O. 2002. There's a New World Coming! Reading the Apocalypse in the Shadow of the Canadian Rockies. Pages 166–79 in *The Earth Story in the New Testament*. Edited by Norman C. Habel and Vicki Balabanski. Earth Bible 5. Cleveland: Pilgrim.

Martin, Thomas W. 2009. The City as Salvific Space: Heterotopic Place and Environmental Ethics in the New Jerusalem. *SBL Forum* 7.2. Online: http://www.sbl-site.org/publications/article.aspx?ArticleId=801.

Mettler, John J., Jr. 2003. *Basic Butchering of Livestock and Game*. 2nd ed. North Adams, Mass.: Storey.

Moore, Stephen D. 1996. *God's Gym: Divine Male Bodies of the Bible*. London: Routledge, 1996.

———. 2001. *God's Beauty Parlor: And Other Queer Spaces in and around the Bible*. Contraversions: Jews and Other Differences. Stanford, Calif.: Stanford University Press.

———. 2009. Metonymies of Empire: Sexual Humiliation and Gender Masquerade in the Book of Revelation. Pages 71–97 in *Postcolonial Interventions: Essays in Honor of R. S. Sugirtharajah*. Edited by Tat-siong Benny Liew. Bible in the Modern World 23. Sheffield: Sheffield Phoenix.

———. 2011. Why There Are No Humans or Animals in the Gospel of Mark. Pages 71–94 in *Mark as Story: Retrospect and Prospect*. Edited by Kelly R. Iverson and Christopher W. Skinner. Society of Biblical Literature Resources for Biblical Study 65. Atlanta: Society of Biblical Literature.

Oliver, Kelly. 2009. *Animal Lessons: How They Teach Us to Be Human*. New York: Columbia University Press.

Plutarch. 1961. *Table Talk*. In *Moralia*. Vol. 9. Translated by Edwin L. Minar Jr., F. H. Sandbach, and W. C. Helmbold. Loeb Clasical Library. Cambridge: Harvard University Press.

Rainbow, Jesse. 2007. Male *mastoi* in Revelation 1.13. *Journal for the Study of the New Testament* 30:249–53.

Reid, Duncan. 2000. Setting aside the Ladder to Heaven: Revelation 21.1–22.5 from the Perspective of the Earth. Pages 232–45 in *Readings from the Perspective of Earth*. Edited by Norman C. Habel. Earth Bible 1. Sheffield: Sheffield Academic Press.

Resseguie, James L. 1998. *Revelation Unsealed: A Narrative Critical Approach to John's Apocalypse*. Biblical Interpretation Series 32. Leiden: Brill.

Rossing, Barbara R. 1999. River of Life in God's New Jerusalem: An Ecological Vision for Earth's Future. Pages 205–24 in *Christianity and Ecology*. Edited by Rosemary Radford Ruether and Dieter Hassel. Religions of the World and Ecology 3. Cambridge: Harvard Center for World Religions.

———. 2002. Alas for Earth! Lament and Resistance in Revelation 12. Pages 180–92 in *The Earth Story in the New Testament*. Edited by Norman C. Habel and Vicki Balabanski. Earth Bible 5. Cleveland: Pilgrim.

———. 2005. For the Healing of the World: Reading Revelation Ecologically. Pages 165–82 in *From Every People and Nation: The Book of Revelation in Intercultural Perspective*. Edited by David Rhoads. Minneapolis: Fortress.

———. 2008. "Hastening the Day" When the Earth Will Burn: Global Warming, 2 Peter, and a Nature Hike through the Book of Revelation. Pages 25–38 in *Reading the Signs of the Times: Taking the Bible into the Public Square*. Edited by Cynthia Briggs Kittredge, Ellen Aitken, and Jonathan Draper. Minneapolis: Fortress.

Shannon, Laurie. 2009. The Eight Animals in Shakespeare; or, Before the Human. *Proceedings of the Modern Language Association* 124:472–79.

Slater, Thomas B. 1999. *Christ and Community: A Socio-historical Study of the Christology of Revelation*. Journal for the Study of the New Testament Supplement Series 178. Sheffield: Sheffield Academic Press.

Spittler, Janet E. 2008. *Animals in the Apocryphal Acts of the Apostles: The Wild Kingdom of Early Christian Literature*. Wissenschafftliche Untersuchungen zum Neuen Testament 2/247. Tübingen: Mohr Siebeck.

Steiner, Gary. 2005. *Anthropocentrism and Its Discontents: Animals and Their Moral Status in the History of Western Philosophy*. Pittsburgh: University of Pittsburgh Press.

Weil, Kari. 2012. *Thinking Animals: Why Animal Studies Now?* New York: Columbia University Press.

Weinrich, William C., ed. 2005. *Revelation*. Ancient Christian Commentary on Scripture: New Testament 12. Downers Grove, Ill.: InterVarsity Press.

Williams, Jeromie. 2011. US Soldiers in Afghanistan Kill Sheep with Metal Baseball Bat. *Digital Journal*. December 10, 2011. Online: http://digitaljournal.com/article/315911.

Wolfe, Cary. 2003. *Animal Rites: American Culture, the Discourse of Species, and Posthumanist Theory*. Chicago: University of Chicago Press.

———. 2009a. Human, All Too Human: "Animal Studies" and the Humanities. *Proceedings of the Modern Language Association* 124:564–75.

———. 2009b. *What Is Posthumanism?* Posthumanities. Minneapolis: University of Minnesota Press.

Wood, David. 2007. Specters of Derrida: On the Way to Econstruction. Pages 264–89 in *Ecospirit: Religions and Philosophies of the Earth*.

Edited by Laurel Kearns and Catherine Keller. Transdisciplinary Theological Colloquia. New York: Fordham University Press.

Conclusion

Jennifer L. Koosed

Perhaps this is what it all comes down to: how to kill and how to die. Life is self-consuming. Even those who are the most radically committed to moving through this world without killing—a vegan, a Jain—still must decide what constitutes "life" and relegate all other creatures to the category "killable." And in the desire not to kill, sometimes one actually increases the world's store of suffering. The Bible instructs its readers not to kill but then commands the killing of certain animals at certain times, certain people for certain crimes, and certain other people simply for being other. The confusion continues and even compounds in the New Testament, where the mechanism of universal salvation is built up upon the foundational act of the killing of God's own Son. The Bible does worse than fail to define precisely what the commandment means; as a whole, the Bible bewilders. Perhaps the commandment needs to be rewritten all together. In Donna Haraway's critical re-appropriation:

> I suggest that it is a misstep to separate the world's beings into those who may be killed and those who may not and a misstep to pretend to live outside killing. … This is not saying that nature is red in tooth and claw and so anything goes. The naturalistic fallacy is the mirror-image misstep to transcendental humanism. I think that what my people and I need to let go of if we are to learn to stop extremism and genocide, through either direct participation or indirect benefit and acquiescence, is the command "Thou shalt not kill." The problem is not figuring out to whom such a command applies so that "other" killing can go on as usual and reach unprecedented historical proportions. The problem is to learn to live responsibly within the multiplicitous necessity and labor of killing, so as to be in the open, in quest of the capacity to respond in relentless historical, nonteleological, multispecies contingency. Perhaps the commandment should read, "Thou shalt not make killable." (Haraway 2008, 79–80)

This is not just a human concern; nor is it only confined to plants and non-human animals. Although infinite in our reckoning, even the stars and the stones are not immortal. There was a time when they were not; there will be a time when they will cease to be. Ultimately, it is not a matter of killing or not killing but of facing the ways in which one kills and learning to kill and to be killed responsibly (see Haraway 2008, 81).

Right now I am alive. I breathe, pulling the world into me and then pushing it out in a rhythm so ingrained I barely notice its music. I share this intercourse with all of the other creatures who surround me, pass by me. I breathe out what they breathe in what I breathe out. Some of our hearts beat, some of our sap courses, some of our noses twitch; we all dance, trading breath and life between us. Some of us have stopped breathing and have decomposed into the air and soil to feed the trees, to be breathed in. Some of us do not breathe but instead support and sustain those of us who do or will or did. All—the plants, the animals, the rocks, the stars, the woman sitting next to me, the child in another country, the living, the dead—all are a part of my community, our community. To all we must respond, to all we must be responsible.

The flesh becomes word. Billy Collins's poem "Flock" begins with an epigram about the number of sheep necessary to make a single copy of the Gutenberg Bible: three hundred. The poem, then, describes a flock awaiting their fate in a pen behind a printing house: "and there is no telling / which one will carry the news / that the Lord is a shepherd, / one of the few things they already know" (Collins 2005, 35). We first carved letters onto stone with stone, fashioned ink from plants and animals to write on plants and animals, hundreds dying as anonymous martyrs for each and every word. Now men in distant countries mine minerals out of the earth—silicon, tantalum, tungsten—to create and store electronic impulses, black fire on white fire, digital words. Torah refers narrowly to the first five books of the Bible or the legal material therein. But Torah also has a much broader definition. Torah also means all of the biblical material, all of Jewish sacred literature, even all of the oral stories, interpretations, and rituals of Judaism. Against the horrors of the twentieth century, some have extended Torah even further to include memoir, poem, and literature. In other words, the Jewish idea of Torah is an idea of an expansive textuality, all of which is enmeshed in materiality and lived experience. Torah is an *etz haim*, a tree of life. Her roots reach deep into the earth embracing the dead, her branches stretch into the sky shading the living, and her leaves unfurl in the light to capture the sun. Torah as tree of life,

Torah as text, Torah as web of life, bringing the organic and inorganic and plant and animal and human together, interconnecting generations, forming communities. Not just as a figure or a metaphor but also as a real, living entity; not just confined to the traditions of one community but also a crystallization of all communities, one particular and specific way of embracing community because there is no universal that is not an almost infinite number of unique specificities, each of which comes in and out of the world in its own way in its own time. I am not by myself, I am not my self. I begin here.

Works Cited

Collins, Billy. 2005. *The Trouble With Poetry and Other Poems*. New York: Random House.

Haraway, Donna J. 2008. *When Species Meet*. Minneapolis: University of Minnesota Press.

Contributors

George Aichele retired from teaching at Adrian College in 2008. He is author of numerous books and articles on semiotics, literary fantasy, and the Bible, especially the Gospel of Mark.

Denise Kimber Buell is Professor of Religion at Williams College and senior member of its Women's, Gender, and Sexuality Studies Program. Her work appears in multiple articles as well as in *Making Christians: Clement of Alexandria and the Rhetoric of Legitimacy* (1999) and *Why This New Race: Ethnic Reasoning in Early Christianity* (2005). She is currently at work on a book-length project linked to her essay in this volume.

Benjamin H. Dunning is Associate Professor of Theology, Comparative Literature, and Women's Studies at Fordham University in New York City. He is also currently a member of the Board of Directors for Fordham University Press and the Advisory Board for the *Journal of Early Christian Studies*. He has authored three monographs: *Aliens and Sojourners: Self as Other in Early Christianity* (2009), *Specters of Paul: Sexual Difference in Early Christian Thought* (2011), and, most recently, *Christ without Adam: Subjectivity and Sexual Difference in the Philosophers' Paul* (2014).

Heidi Epstein is Associate Professor of Religion and Culture at the University of Saskatchewan and author of *Melting the Venusberg: A Feminist Theology of Music* (2004). More recently, she has published articles on contemporary musical settings of the Song of Songs (*Bible and Critical Theory*, *Biblical Interpretation*, and *Bible Trouble: Queer Reading at the Boundaries of Biblical Scholarship*) in which she crafts interdisciplinary conversations between New Musicological and feminist/queer biblical hermeneutics that articulate the Song's role in the politics of love as a cultural practice.

Rhiannon Graybill is Assistant Professor of Religious Studies at Rhodes College. She is currently writing a book on masculinity and embodiment in the Hebrew prophets.

Jennifer L. Koosed is Associate Professor of Religious Studies at Albright College in Reading, Pennsylvania. She is the author of *(Per)mutations of Qohelet: Reading the Body in the Book* (2006), *Gleaning Ruth: A Biblical Heroine and Her Afterlives* (2011), and *Jesse's Lineage: The Legendary Lives of Jesus, David and Jesse James* (with Robert Paul Seesengood, 2013).

Eric Daryl Meyer is a doctoral candidate in the Theology Department at Fordham University in New York City. His current research examines the formative conceptual role of the human-animal distinction within Christian theological anthropology as it emerges in tension and contradiction, especially regarding the relationship between human animality and "authentic" humanity.

Stephen D. Moore is Professor of New Testament Studies at the Theological School, Drew University, in Madison, New Jersey. He has authored and edited many books, most recently *The Bible in Theory: Critical and Postcritical Essays* (2010); *Planetary Loves: Spivak, Postcoloniality, and Theology* (with Mayra Rivera, 2010); *The Invention of the Biblical Scholar: A Critical Manifesto* (with Yvonne Sherwood, 2011); *Divinanimality: Animal Theory, Creaturely Theology* (2014); and *The Bodybuilder, the Sex Worker, and the Sheep: Untold Tales from the Book of Revelation* (forthcoming).

Hugh Pyper is Professor of Biblical Interpretation at the University of Sheffield and Discipline Lead for Philosophical and Religious Studies at the Higher Education Academy in the United Kingdom. He is the author of many books and articles, including *The Unchained Bible: Cultural Appropriations of Biblical Texts* (2012) and *An Unsuitable Book: The Bible as Scandalous Text* (2005). He is also the editor of *Text, Image, and Otherness in Children's Bibles: What Is in the Picture?* (with Caroline Vander Stichele, 2012).

Robert Paul Seesengood is Associate Professor of Religious Studies and Chair of Classical Languages at Albright College in Reading, Pennsylvania. He is the author of *Competing Identities: The Athlete and the Gladiator in Early Christian Literature* (2006); *Paul: A Brief History* (2010); and *Jesse's*

Lineage: The Legendary Lives of Jesus, David and Jesse James (with Jennifer L. Koosed, 2013).

Yvonne Sherwood is Professor of Biblical Cultures and Politics at the University of Kent. She is the author of many books and articles, including *The Prostitute and the Prophet: Hosea's Marriage in Literary-Theoretical Perspective* (1996); *A Biblical Test and Its Afterlives: The Survival of Jonah in Western Culture* (2000); and *The Invention of the Biblical Scholar: A Critical Manifesto* (with Stephen D. Moore, 2011). She has edited *Derrida's Bible: (Reading a Page of Scripture with a Little Help from Derrida)* (2004) and *Derrida and Religion: Other Testaments* (with Kevin Hart, 2005).

Ken Stone is Professor of Bible, Culture and Hermeneutics at Chicago Theological Seminary, where he also serves as Academic Dean. He is the author of *Practicing Safer Texts: Food, Sex, and Bible in Queer Perspective* (2005) and *Sex, Honor and Power in the Deuteronomistic History* (1996), and editor of *Queer Commentary and the Hebrew Bible* (2001) and *Bible Trouble: Queer Reading at the Boundaries of Biblical Scholarship* (with Teresa Hornsby, 2011). His current research focuses on biblical interpretation and the question of the animal.

Hannah M. Strømmen is a Ph.D. candidate at the University of Glasgow in Theology and Religious Studies. With a background in literature and critical theory, she is interested in Jacques Derrida's work and the ways in which it engages with the biblical archive. She is currently working on Derrida's later writings on the question of the animal in relation to specific biblical texts.

Index of Ancient Sources

Noncanonical/Deuterocanonical Literature

Index of Authors

CPSIA information can be obtained at www.ICGtesting.com
Printed in the USA
BVOW04s0110010414

349355BV00002B/4/P